POLAND !

EUROPE IN 1944

THROUGH
DARKNESS
TO
LIGHT

—Patrick Macdonald—

BADGE OF
31 SQN (S.A.A.F.)

THROUGH
DARKNESS
TO
LIGHT

Patrick Macdonald

Published in 1994 by
IMAGES PUBLISHING (MALVERN) LTD
Upton upon Severn

British Library Cataloguing in Publication Data
A catalogue record for this book is available from the British Library

ISBN 0 946270 90 2 (1st edition and reprint)

ISBN 1 897817 17 7 (new edition)

Designed and produced by Images Publishing (Malvern) Ltd, Worcestershire.
Printed and bound by Bookcraft Ltd, Midsomer Norton, Bath, Avon.

CONTENTS

LIST OF MAPS AND DRAWINGS

This book is for

— The eighty young airmen who lie in their quiet Romanian graves

— Their brothers-in-arms who came home

— Those who want to know.

'Through Darkness to Light'
is the motto of No 205 Group Royal Air Force and is used
by kind permission of the Ministry of Defence, London

AUTHOR'S PREFACE (Cuvînt Înainte Autorului)

This is an account of the RAF's night-bomber operations against targets in Romania in the Spring and Summer of 1944. The targets included the oil industry, at that time Germany's principal source, as well as the road and railway distribution networks, the Danubian ports and minelaying in the Danube itself.

These operations were not, of course, the only contribution made by No 205 Group's bombers to the strategic bombing offensive. They did, however, represent a typical cross-section of the tasks which this force carried out as they ranged across southern, central and eastern Europe and into the Balkans. Equally, the RAF was not alone in raiding these targets. The mass of the American 15th Air Force attacked by day in far greater numbers.

The story here does not need to embrace the whole offensive against these Romanian targets. The daylight raids have been well-covered by a number of American authors. Such works as *Ploieşti* by Dugan and Stewart, *Target Ploieşti* by Newby, or the more recent *Those Who Fall* by Muirhead in 1988 and *The War of the Cottontails* by Cubbins in 1989 and *Into the Guns of Ploieşti* by Newby in 1991 are absorbing reading and leave little more to be said.

Beside the main road from Bucharest to Ploieşti, some twenty five kilometres north of the capital, by Tîncăbeşti village, is a small, carefully maintained graveyard. This is the Commonwealth War Graves Commission Cemetery containing the dead of two World Wars. In this peaceful place lie the graves of 83 Commonwealth servicemen who lost their lives in Romania in World War 2. Of these 80 are aircrew of the RAF, RAF(VR), RAAF, RCAF, RNZAF and SAAF who died between May and August 1944.

It is to the memory of these men that this book is dedicated.

In November 1979 I was posted as Defence Attaché at the British Embassy at Bucharest. Over the next two and a half years I made many visits to the 'British Cemetery'. The more I visited the more interested I became in discovering how these young airmen came to be here by the road to Ploieşti. I had some knowledge of American daylight raids. What English schoolboy of the 1940s

9

did not know of the famous low-level raid? But the British part in any offensive seemed unknown. I wished to learn more – and that is how this book began. The story becomes the more poignant because in their vibrant youth, these men's achievements were largely overshadowed by the huge American daylight bombing effort. Now in death they are alone in Romania. The American dead have gone home. There is no memorial or anything to mark their sacrifice, that I could find. It is as though they had never been.

While this account concentrates on the night-bomber operations flow during those five months in 1944, the American daylight raids are included in summary in their chronological context and given in italics, to give a balanced overview of the offensive. It is significant to note here that more Medals of Honor were won by US airmen in these attacks than over any other target, before or since. Seven were won in these skies between 1 August 1943 and 9 July 1944.

Each night raid is described in the words of the Official Record Books. While these may not make exciting reading, they are nevertheless important as the contemporary reports of the actions and benefit in no way from hindsight. Wherever I can I have fleshed these out with the descriptions and recollections of those who were there. Parts of the story are exciting and gripping: other parts describe routine operations and other activities. The proportion would be, I suspect, about the same in any modern war and I make no apologies for not having crafted a collection of 'ripping yarns'.

I am not able to stand in judgement on controversial military or political matters of the day, nor would I want to. I have tried to be a reporter of what has been related to me. There was a considerable debate and some professional rivalry between the daylight and night-bomber proponents about which method of attack and whose tactics and bombing practices were the most efficient – by whatever yardstick. I have avoided adding to that.

The Postscript, Part 3 completes the historical account to a degree which should stand any future researches into these events in good stead.

This has not been an easy story to compile for a number of reasons.

1. Writing in earnest did not begin until 40 years after the events and memories dim after such a long time. Even so, 140 veterans have given their reminiscences and these are vital threads in the whole fabric.

2. This offensive ended when Romania capitulated in August 1944. Many subsequent changes, not just a radical switch in Alliances, did little for the tranquillity of Romanian life and a degree of chaos permeated officialdom. Material from Romanian sources was, therefore, understandably thin. That said, the Ministry of National Defence in Bucharest gave me valuable help and encouragement.

3. In spite of generous and industrious support from a present day Luftwaffe colleague, German sources have been arid. Enquiries received a more or less stereotyped answer – 'almost all the documents and records of those days were lost during the *Rückzug* (Retreat), destroyed as ordered by the *Führung* (High Command), or taken away by interested persons at the end of the war.'

4. Fourthly, as many of the veterans have asserted, this was a 'forgotten front'. These operations were not in the forefront of public consciousness, the limelight having moved away from the Mediterranean Theatre to more readily interesting events nearer to home that Summer. This apparent lack of awareness was not restricted to the man in the street. Official documents and published accounts, contemporary or since, dwell only briefly on the Mediterranean-based strategic bombing effort, particularly the British and Commonwealth part in it. There may, perhaps, be a temptation to conclude from all this, that the offensive was something of a sideshow beside other events nearer to the main arena of the war.

Some unique features argue against that: the unusual Anglo-American command arrangements, the only use of the Liberator as a night-bomber in European skies, the continued and successful use of the Wellington bomber, the effective Danube minelaying operations, the primitive conditions at the Foggia airfields where these airmen lived and from where they daily set forth to risk their lives and, finally, the great importance which the enemy quite obviously gave to the targets under attack.

The courage, skill and determination displayed by these young men is by no means unique. That seemed to know almost no bounds. Perhaps it is a combination of all these features which has, as much as anything else, inspired me to tell their story.

Language

Though not, perhaps, a matter to change the impact of the story, a word or two on the Romanian language may not be out of place. In this book the names of well-known places or geographical features, however mis-spelt in English usage, are left in that form. Examples are Bucharest rather than Bucureşti, Danube rather than Dunărea and Carpathians rather than Carpaţii. Otherwise names are rendered in their modern Romanian spelling. Since most of us do not know them in any other way, we might as well use their proper form.

Romanian is a language beautiful to the ear and is arguably, more loyal to its Latin heritage than most of the others with the same beginnings. Its survival in a very pure state when surrounded by such a babel of other tongues and placed as it is at the crossroads of Europe and Asia is remarkable.

The Romanian people are very proud of it.

For those who might wish to pursue this aspect a little further some very brief comments on pronunciation might be worthwhile. Most important of all is that all the letters in a word are pronounced, however fleetingly. Most letters are sounded in the same way as their English equals but with more 'freedom'. One example may be enough – 'o' is spoken as 'bob' and not as in 'phone'. The modified letters do make un-English sounds:

1. ă is the 'er' syllable in 'jerk': not as long as *fir*.

2. î has no equal: its nearest sound is the 'ir' in B*ir*mingham, in the local dialect: the most difficult for a stranger to get right. (The letter â in the country's name – Românïa – is the same and nowadays only appears in that context.)

3. ş makes the sound of 'sh' as in *sh*ed.

4. ţ is the ts in ca*ts* or in *tsetse*.

So, the village nearest to the British Cemetery, Tîncăbeşti, might be re-spelt in English as Tirnkerbesht and the famous target city, Ploieşti as Plohyesht.

A final point – the 'ti' ending of so many place names is to ensure that the 't' is sounded and not swallowed as it might be so often, in English. The ending never rhymes with Humpty-Dumpty!

Laurence Binyon's famous verse from his *Poems for the Fallen*, used at so many acts of Remembrance –

> They shall grow not old, as we that are left grow old.
> Age shall not weary them, nor the years condemn.
> At the going down of the sun and in the morning
> We will remember them.

has taken on a new significance for me. The story is one of young men and the contemporary accounts were prepared by these same young men. The dead have remained young and, as Binyon predicts, they always will. Those who survived and upon whose reminiscences this story is founded, have lived the intervening years through and are no longer young. Their enthusiastic support for the present enterprise has lost little with the passage of time.

A refreshing light was thrown on their contemporary philosophy by one airman:

In 1944, one must remember, it was only about 40 years since man had flown an aeroplane for the first time. It was all much more adventurous then, 'Biggles-like' and amateur – and above all – very much a man's world. I don't think, looking back, that we worried too much that the city which we had just bombed had beautiful sixteenth century buildings. We just wanted to 'bomb the bastards out of the war' and go home.

For many, remembering has not been easy. An RCAF ex-prisoner of war in Romania has written:

The first surprise is the mental distress that surges back to me when I force myself to recall that night . . . It would be reasonable to suppose that, after 45 years, my attitudes of mind of that night would be so deeply buried in my sub-conscious that they would never surface again. Although not so intense as they once were, those feelings of tension, sadness and regret are with me still.

Others have felt the same. I am grateful that they have allowed me to intrude and to tell the story of this part of their war.

A full list of acknowledgements is in Part 3 – The Postscript, but I wish to express my thanks here and now to all the former members of 205 Group who contributed in some way. I must especially thank Jack Bruce, who was Keeper of the RAF Museums. We first met in 1977 when an aircraft exchange between the Polish Air Force Museum at Kraków and the RAF Museum at Hendon was being arranged. Later, it was Jack who responded to my first cautious probings about the Romanian raids with a fund of knowledge, convincing me that here were tales to tell. I also wish to thank my colleague, Michael Bardell, who drew the maps, Reg Sampson, who drew the crew-layout pictures and my wife Sue, who has put every word of this work through our word-processor. Without her support the whole thing simply could not have happened.

Part 1

INTRODUCTION

CHAPTER 1 - Setting the Scene

The events described here made an important contribution to the overall air offensive in Europe, however comparatively small the forces executing them happened to be. To understand these operations in their context, a brief look at the origins and development of the strategic bombing offensive is worthwhile and helps an appreciation of the generally little-known part played by the air forces in the Mediterranean Theatre, particularly the night-bomber element.

During the time when United States air-power was being built-up and deployed into Europe, allied strategic bombing policy lacked overall cohesion and direction: objectives had to be identified and priorities assigned. The Air Ministry in London and the Mediterranean Air Command both believed that a powerful bomber force should be established to operate from Italy. The British Chiefs of Staff were not convinced. The strength of the German fighter force was increasing in spite of all that Bomber Command could do. Its reduction and, if possible, destruction were accepted pre-requisites to any cross-channel invasion of France. The supporters of an Italian-based force held that adding the weight of a sustained offensive operating from Italy against German industry and its defences would give the Allies considerable advantages. It would force the enemy to extend their elaborate ground and air defences already covering north-west Europe to face the new threat. In addition, many targets which had been invulnerable for geographical reasons would now be open to attack. The protagonists, led by the Chief of Air Staff at the Air Ministry, Sir Charles Portal, believed that the whole Allied Strategy and the success of the planned invasion (OVERLORD) would be enhanced by a strong bomber force in Italy. Sir Arthur Harris, AOC-in-C Bomber Command, strongly disagreed as did the US Chief of Air Staff, General Hap Arnold. Any dissipation of forces which would weaken the total Allied effort was to be decried. General Arnold later changed his views and he became a prime mover in the creation of a strategic air force operating from bases in the Mediterranean. A condition for that, however, was that there should be one commander for all strategic air forces in Europe.

These matters were debated and resolved at the Casablanca Conference in January 1943 and the policy which emerged for the air attack on Germany, her satellites and the occupied countries was embodied as the Combined

Bomber Offensive (CBO) and was promulgated by the Combined Chiefs of Staff within a few days. It was at Casablanca that President Roosevelt first called for Germany's 'unconditional surrender'.

The presence of strategic air forces in the Mediterranean was therefore primarily for geographical convenience, so that they could participate effectively in the CBO, rather than support theatre land operations, although they did so on very many occasions. Perhaps paradoxically, a requirement of early operations by ground forces in Italy was to seize and subsequently secure the complex of airfields and landing grounds in the Foggia Plain for the use of the Strategic Air Force: an unusual reversal of roles. The Mediterranean Allied Strategic Air Force (MASAF) was to work under the direction, not of the Supreme Allied Commander Mediterranean (SACMED), but under that of Lieutenant General Carl W. Spaatz, the overall commander of Strategic Air Forces in Europe, underlining MASAF's fundamental role – the Combined Bomber Offensive against Germany.

Air Commodore J.H.T. Simpson AOC 205 Group when operations began against Romanian targets. (Courtesy Imperial War Museum)

The offensive was to be waged by three distinct long-range bomber forces. From bases in Great Britain, the US 8th Air Force (8 AF), by day and RAF Bomber Command by night would range deep into enemy and occupied Europe fully committed to the CBO and their battles would be fierce. From their Italian airfields, MASAF bombers would carry the war to the enemy in France, Italy, Austria, Hungary, Czechoslovakia, Poland, Romania, Yugoslavia, Bulgaria and Greece, as well as into the Reich itself – by day and night.

The major component of MASAF was the US 15th Air Force (15 AF) commanded in 1944 by Major General Nathan F. Twining. No 205 Group RAF, the British night-bomber force, an integral part of 15 AF, was commanded by Air Commodore J.H.T. Simpson DSO RAF.

Allied Command

At the turn of the year, while units of MASAF were establishing themselves on their Italian bases and in the skies over southern Europe, the Allied Command which was to achieve victory in the west was being assembled in Britain and in the Mediterranean.

The first major changes took place on 1 January 1944 when General Dwight D. Eisenhower moved to England to become Supreme Commander of the Allied Expeditionary Forces then concentrating in Great Britain for the invasion of northern Europe. His place as Supreme Allied Commander Mediterranean (SACMED) was taken by General Sir Henry Maitland-Wilson.

Changes in air commands included two new appointments. The first was the post of Air Commander-in-Chief, Mediterranean Theatre of Operations (AIR CINC MTO) to coincide with the evolution of the Mediterranean Air Command (MAC) into Mediterranean Allied Air Forces (MAAF). The second was the appointment of a Commanding General of US Strategic Air Forces in Europe (USSAFE) who would coordinate the structure and tasking of 8 AF in England and 15 AF in Italy.

The span of the first incumbency was short. Air Chief Marshal (ACM) Sir Arthur W. Tedder became AIR CINC MTO with USAAF Lieutenant General Carl W. Spaatz as his Deputy. However, before the new organisation could be completed, both these officers followed Eisenhower to Britain, Tedder to become his Deputy and Spaatz to inaugurate the second new air post – Commanding General USSAFE.

Commanders bid farewell to the Mediterranean. Lieutenant General Carl Spaatz leaves to Command the Allied Strategic Air Forces and Air Chief Marshal Sir Arthur W. Tedder GCB to become Deputy Supreme Commander Allied Forces.

On 12 January 1944 their successors in the Mediterranean were appointed. The new AIR CINC MTO was to be Lieutenant General Ira C. Eaker USAAF who came from command of 8 AF in England. Air Marshal (AM) Sir John Slessor came from Coastal Command to be his Deputy and Commander-in-Chief RAF Middle East (CINC RAFME). Although procedures existed for combined operations between 8 and 15 AFs, only ten, in practice, were launched, even though 30 more which were planned were subsequently abandoned for a number of reasons. Again, while combined night operations were planned, no concentrated attacks took place.

Fifteenth Air Force and MASAF

The origins of 15 AF and MASAF are worthy of a closer look. The Allied campaign in north-west Africa had been supported by US 12th Air Force (12 AF). The British bomber contribution had been provided by 330 Wing and together they comprised the North African Strategic Air Force (NASAF).

Air Chief Marshal Sir Arthur W. Tedder GCB (right) welcoming Air Marshal Sir John Slessor who had arrived from England to succeed him as Deputy Commander MAAF. (Coutesy Imperial War Museum)

Major General Nathan F. Twining, Commander 15th Air Force and Lieutenant General Ira C. Eaker, Commander-in-Chief Mediterranean Allied Air Force. (Courtesy Imperial War Museum)

When 1st and 8th Armies combined to defeat the last Axis forces on African soil, 330 Wing joined 205 Group (231 and 236 Wings) in Tunisia at the end of May 1943. 205 Group, which had been formed at Shallufa in Egypt in November 1941, had been the bomber force supporting operations in the eastern Mediterranean as well as land operations in Libya and Tunisia.

As 1943 drew to its close, Allied forces had established a firm foothold in Italy. By the end of October the Allied advance had reached the line of the Volturno River across to Termoli on the Adriatic Coast and the conditions for the CBO to be implemented from Mediterranean bases were now almost complete.

To supplement the CBO it was decided to divide 12 AF into a tactical air force and a new strategic air force. The former would retain the 12 AF title. The new strategic air force, designated the Fifteenth Air Force (15 AF) would be expanded to concentrate on CBO and other targets across southern Europe and into the German heartland. It was hoped that better weather conditions could be expected in the Mediterranean area, allowing these strategic air forces to operate more frequently than English-based forces.

15 AF was activated on 1 November 1943, under the command of Major General James H. Doolittle with his Headquarters at Tunis. On 1 December this moved to Bari where it remained until the end of the war. Major General Nathan F. Twining succeeded to command 15 AF on 3 January 1944 when General Doolittle moved to Britain to take command of 8 AF there, succeeding Lieutenant General Ira C. Eaker who now became Air CINC MTO, as we have seen.

Although a sizeable part of MASAF's strength was established on bases hewn out of the olive groves and fields of the Foggia Plain by the end of the winter of 1943–44, it was not until the Spring that the bomber offensive was able to move into top gear and could reap the full advantage from its longer punch.

By the Spring of 1944 when attacks on Romania became a regular feature of the 15 AF's operations, the force mustered six B-17 and fifteen B-24 Bomb Groups with seven Fighter Groups. The P-47 Thunderbolts were being replaced by P-51 Mustangs by this time. In USAAF terms, a Group consisted of a number of squadrons of aircraft and equated to a British Wing. A USAAF Wing, the next senior level of command, in its turn, equated to a British Group: the two terms were completely reversed. 205 Group RAF added four Wings (US-style Groups) to the Order of Battle. Three of them operated Wellingtons. The fourth (240 Wing), operating Halifaxes and Liberators, would join the Group on 1 March 1944 from RAF ME. The Group was under the operational command of 15 AF from its inception and was the only RAF bomber force to have this status.

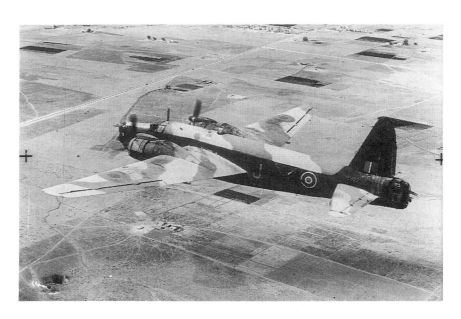

150 Squadron's Wellington Mark X HE 627 'J' caught in daylight on air test.
(Courtesy Wally Talbot)

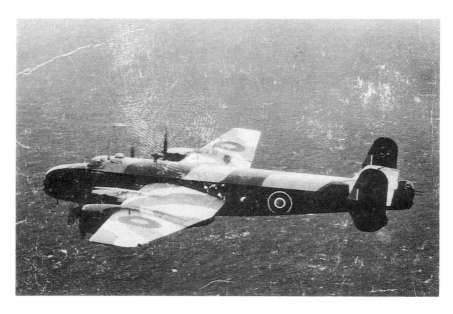

A well-thumbed photograph of a Mark II Halifax of 614 Squadron. The H_2S radome under the rear fuselage has been "brushed out" for security reasons in this contemporary photograph. (Courtesy J. Frank Cowie)

31 Squadron's Liberator 'K' airbourne over Yugoslavia. (Courtesy T.W. Timoney)

MASAF began its operations with four main objectives which would remain unchanged throughout the rest of the war, although the emphasis evolved later:

1. To destroy the Luftwaffe.

2. To participate in the CBO, which called for the destruction of the aircraft industry, ball-bearing factories, oil, rubber and munition factories and naval bases.

3. To support land operations in Italy, mainly by deep interdiction.

4. To weaken the enemy effort in south-eastern Europe and the Balkans in support of Soviet land operations.

Some USAAF and RAF units and crews had completed few or no previous operations before joining the Theatre and some of the delays which prevented

23

MASAF from reaching an early peak of operational efficiency were caused by a real need to work these up to acceptable levels. Experience had to be gained on actual operations because units could not be spared for periods dedicated to lengthy training.

It ought also to be remembered that no single item of equipment or supply for land or air forces in this Theatre was available from local sources. Every nut and bolt, boot, bomb or bomber had to be brought in from elsewhere often at considerable risk over hazardous routes.

As the severe weather in the East eased towards the Spring support for the Soviet drive westwards became a strategic bombing priority. By early April, the Germans had been driven out of the Ukraine and the Romanian frontier in the north-east had been breached to a depth of seventy miles. Axis forces attempting to contain this offensive relied heavily on the Hungarian and Romanian railway systems and MASAF was ordered to attack them as a new priority.

In pursuit of these objectives, the USAAF made its return to Romania on 4 April 1944 with its first attack since Operation TIDALWAVE, the low-level attack on Ploiesti and Cîmpina on 1 August 1943. This time the target was railway yards in Bucharest which were attacked from high-level.

The next day – 5 April – railway installations in the Ploieşti area were attacked. The inevitable spill-over of bombs into the neighbouring refineries created havoc and considerable damage, proving the vulnerability of these targets to bombing attacks. This 5 April operation therefore launched MASAF on a campaign against German oil and began the offensive to destroy the enemy's oil production capability, centred on Ploieşti. The oil industry supporting the German war effort was to become the CBO's top priority in May.

The RAF entered the lists on the night of 8 April when a force of Wellingtons and Liberators laid mines in the Danube between Baziaş and Belgrade.

From these early beginnings Romanian targets were to become a regular feature of the Strategic Air Forces operations by day and night.

By 19 August, when MASAF's day bombers made their last attack, Romanian oil targets had been attacked twenty times in daylight and eight by night resulting in production being reduced to a fifth capacity. The cost of these 1944 attacks would be 2,829 Allied aircrew killed or captured for the loss of 286 bombers.

It is also a reflection on the success of this and other elements of the CBO that, on this day, only nine defending fighters were seen, but none closed to attack the 65 bombers.

A pall of smoke rises from the storage tank farm of the Prahova Refinery in the northern suburbs of Bucharest during a 15th AF attack. The shadow of the smoke falls across the lakes of the River Colentina which form a major recreational area for the Bucharestians. Băneasa Airport's main runway shows clear and white at the lower left and Fort Otopeni lies at the bottom right centre. The highway to Ploieşti, some 60 kms away, passes out of the bottom of the picture to its right (west) as it heads northward.

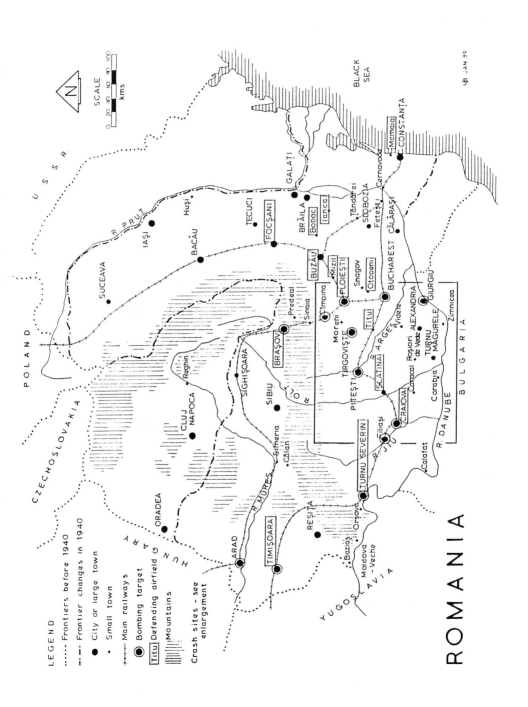

N

SCALE
kms
0 20 40 60 80 100

MB JAN 90

POLAND

U · S · S · R

CZECHOSLOVAKIA

HUNGARY

YUGOSLAVIA

BULGARIA

BLACK SEA

R PRUT

R MURES

R DANUBE

SUCEAVA

IAŞI

Huşi

BACĂU

TECUCI

GALAŢI

BRĂILA

[Bodoc]

[Iancă]

CONSTANŢA

[Mamaia]

Carnavodă

CĂLĂRAŞI

SLOBOZIA

Feteşti

Tăndărei

[FOCŞANI]

[BUZĂU]

Mizil

[PLOIEŞTI]

Snagov

Otopeni

BUCHAREST

GIURGIU

ALEXANDRIA

Vidoţe

Câmpina

Moreni

[Titu]

Roşiori de Vede

TURNU MĂGURELE

Zimnicea

ORADEA

ARAD

[TIMIŞOARA]

CLUJ NAPOCA

Reghin

SIGHIŞOARA

SIBIU

[BRAŞOV]

Predeal

Sinaia

TÎRGOVIŞTE

PITEŞTI

[SLATINA]

Corabia

Caracal

[CRAIOVA]

R ARGES

R OLT

REŞIŢA

Simeria

Călan

TURNU SEVERIN

Filiaşi

R JIU

Calafat

Orşova

Bazias

Moldova Vache

ROMANIA

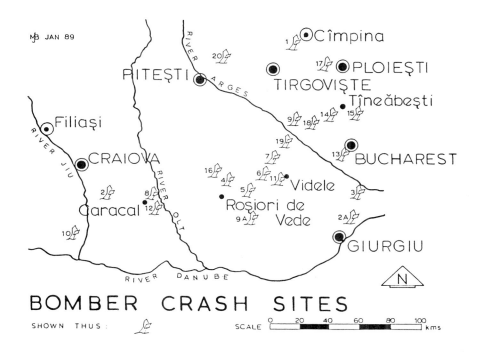

BOMBER CRASH SITES

SHOWN THUS :

SCALE 0 20 40 60 80 100 kms

205 Group's Share

The RAF's part in this offensive, admittedly much smaller in scale, is almost unknown. On twenty-eight spring and summer nights between 14 April and 18 August 1944, the wide-ranging missions of 205 Group's nine squadrons included over 1000 sorties against the Romanian oil industry, the road and rail networks on which that industry depended, as well as the Danube waterway. They delivered some 1200 tons of high-explosive and countless thousands of incendiaries and laid over 260 mines in the Danube and its navigable tributaries.

The cost to 205 Group was 46 aircraft and the lives of 154 young airmen who flew them. Another 73 became Prisoners of War (PW) while 27 more evaded capture and were able to return safely to their squadrons. Of the dead there are 27, the manner of whose deaths remains unsure and who have no known graves.

Bomber Command, based in England, was playing a greater role close to home and in the public eye, carrying the war to the enemy by night and, furthermore, it had been doing so relentlessly from the early months of the war. It was quite reasonable, perhaps, that operations taking place elsewhere, in the Mediterranean for example, would tend to be overlooked at the time and, later, almost forgotten. Nevertheless, the night-bomber offensive into southern and eastern Europe from their Italian airfields was no less vital an area of operations. Furthermore, while the defences facing Bomber Command were generally heavier, there was a greater attacking force against which to defend.

The air defences facing the MASAF attacks were also formidable and this was particularly so in the Bucharest–Ploieşti area. Indeed, USAAF Intelligence assessed this defensive zone as being third in severity only to Berlin and the Ruhr. They were defending a complex of oil-associated industries, the output of which was critical to the German war effort.

The command arrangements of this small British force are interesting. In December 1943, when 15 AF moved to Bari from Tunis to establish MASAF, it set up a Combined Headquarters with 205 Group. Overloaded communications between Group Headquarters and the wings and squadrons later caused Air Commodore Simpson to set up an Advanced Operational HQ under the command of Wing Commander D.R.P. Mills OBE at Cerignola, one of the Group airfields, 60 miles away.

This HQ was responsible for the operational control of aircraft, signals procedures and intelligence reporting. However, in spite of great goodwill on all sides, distances still caused command and control problems. The AOC decided that the only way to overcome these was to move HQ 205 Group complete into the Foggia area. General Twining approved and the move forward took place on 31 March. To maintain liaison with HQ 15 AF an Intelligence Staff Officer remained at Bari to assist Group Captain J.A. Powell DSO OBE, Senior RAF Officer at MASAF. This arrangement proved very successful in practice.

Three Wings – 231 Wing with 37 and 70 Squadrons, 236 Wing with 40 and 104 Squadrons and 330 Wing with 142 and 150 Squadrons operated the Wellington Mk 10 bomber throughout most of 1944. It had been withdrawn from Bomber Command's home-based squadrons the previous year as being no longer adequate for the task in the night skies above the Reich. Nevertheless, it was a type much loved and respected by its crews in the Mediterranean Theatre. Two more Squadrons, 178 and 31 Squadron SAAF, in 240 Wing flew American-built Liberator bombers, in this case the B Mk 6 (B-24 H or J) version: their only employment in Europe in the night-bomber role. As Autumn 1944 moved into winter the remaining Wellington squadrons converted to Liberators. The ninth squadron, 614, using the Halifax II Series 1A, had a target-marking role as Pathfinders for the Group. Unfortunately, 614 Squadron had little and hurried role-training and it took some time and some losses before it reached its later high standard. It always lacked many of the ground-based navigational aids which were available to Pathfinder Forces operating over North-west Europe.

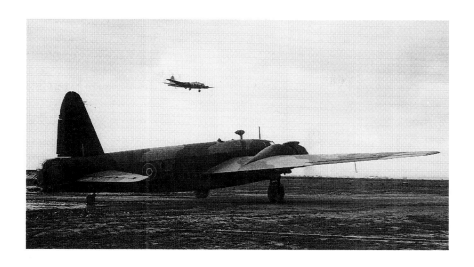

70 Squadron's A-Apple waiting to take-off at Tortorella airfield, holds while a 99th Bombardment Group B-17 Fortress comes to land. (Courtesy Imperial War Museum)

The Foggia Plain bases, which 205 Group shared with USAAF squadrons and from which they set out night after night, were overcrowded and short of facilities. The slightest rain reduced them to mud which the Italian sun could quickly convert to a fine penetrating dust. These conditions placed considerable strains on aircrews and aircraft and were a constant source of nightmares for the loyal and devoted supply staffs and ground crews who slaved endlessly to keep their squadrons on line against all odds.

(A Summer 1944 Command and Staff list is at Appendix 1.)

CHAPTER 2 - Mining the Danube

The major part that 205 Group played was the mining of the Danube. This action denied the enemy the use of this waterway for the transportation of oil for those vital months. The C-in-C RAF ME, Air Marshal Sir John Slessor said that, in his opinion, the mining of the Danube had paid greater dividends than any other single operation of the entire war in the Theatre.

Brigadier J.T. Durrant CB DFC AOC 205 Group, writing in April 1983.

Brigadier J.T. Durrant CB, DFC, SAAF Air Officer Commanding 205 Group. He succeeded Air Commodore J.H.T. Simpson on 3rd August 1944.
(Courtesy Imperial War Museum)

The Danube, the longest river in Europe, rises in the Black Forest of Germany and emerges 1,770 miles later into the Black Sea between Romania and the Moldovan Republic. It was under international control in pre-war days and the States making up the Danube Commission were Britain, France, Italy and Romania.

At that time the river was navigable for 1,500 miles, up to Regensburg by river steamers and sea-going vessels could reach Turnu Severin. The Iron Gates rapids above Turnu Severin were still a restricting factor, although a canalised way through (opened in 1896) allowed the daily passage of barge traffic to a capacity of 10,000 tons. This was considerable when put alongside the transportation difficulties created for road and rail-borne traffic through the Carpathian and Yugoslav mountains.

River ports which could handle huge tonnages of produce, from Vienna down to the sea were at Bratislava, Budapest, Novi Sad, Belgrade and below the Iron Gates at Turnu Severin, Giurgiu, Ruse and Brǎila. The principal oil products river port was Giurgiu fed by pipeline and railway, with Turnu Severin also in the field via railway connections.

The Danube was vital to the German economy in wartime for the movement of agricultural produce from Hungary and Romania, as well as a lifeline to the Romanian oilfields and a strategic route to the Balkan flank of the Russian front. Over 8 million tons of material reached Germany along the Danube waterway in 1942.

The mainstay of this river traffic was the 'Rhine-type' barge which could carry 1000 tons. The ease with which one barge could be loaded compared with the complicated handling of 100 ten-ton railway wagons, illustrates the barge's superiority for the movement of large quantities. In the handling of bulk oil products too the barge was far superior to the railway tank wagon.

At the outbreak of the war, 60% of Germany's oil came from the Romanian oilfields. Ranked number four in world oil production, Romanian oil was largely moved by pipeline to the Black Sea at Constanta or to the Danube at Giurgiu. 150,000 tons per month of oil and oil products reached Germany by barge via railheads at Bratislava and Vienna.

The loss of key railway routes in eastern Europe during their retreat forced the Germans to increase the volume of military traffic on the already overloaded Hungarian and Romanian railway systems just at a time when these became vulnerable to Allied air attack. Greater use had to be made of the Danube lifeline. A contemporary assessment of the craft available was 250–300 tugs each of which could pull between 1,200 and 1,500 tons loaded into barges. These make uneconomical bombing targets as they can be easily dispersed. For the movement of bulky and non-perishable goods, not requiring speedy movement, river transport would provide an ideal way of maintaining a steady flow of goods into Germany. By the middle of March 1944 oil traffic, in particular, was being concentrated on movement by barge rather than the railways. Allied Intelligence estimated that, between October 1943 and February 1944, river traffic had increased to exceed the railways by 28%. In the following month this had leapt to 200%. It was clear by this time that even temporary stoppages to this traffic would have far-reaching consequences for the enemy's war effort. Plans were thereupon made for MASAF to carry out strategic interdiction by mining stretches of the river by night to impede river traffic to the maximum effect.

Gardening was the code name given to air-laid mining operations and these were carried out by the Wellington and Liberator Squadrons of 205 Group under the close supervision of and in liaison with naval specialists who selected the 'beds', decided on suitable nights to operate and allocated the types of mines to be used.

The mine-laying aircraft were originally launched on their gardening missions during moon periods because success depended very largely on good visibility. Later on flares and pathfinder aircraft were used to allow mining to be carried out at any time.

Tactics and techniques varied with the aircraft being used and the stretch of the river being 'planted'. If there was a sufficient depth of water high-level release was possible but usually the summer water level was so low that the average release height could be no more than 200 feet above the river. Much lower altitudes were, however, commonplace and 40–50 feet was not unusual. The mines had small parachutes to reduce the impact on hitting the water.

Accounts of the *gardening* missions follow in their chronological sequence with raids on other targets. The results are summarised in the Postscript at Chapter 14. The German reaction to the operations is, however, worth reviewing here.

It seemed clear that they were initially taken by surprise, but they reacted with typical thoroughness to produce defensive measures, but these were not truly effective until August when the Romanian and Bulgarian length of the river was removed from the gardening scene. Countermeasures came in four categories:

1. *Information* – from border guard posts along the river, reinforced by civilian police and militia and augmented later by flak and other defensive units deployed along the river. Once reports were verified, details of the attack were telephoned promptly to the appropriate headquarters.

2. *Minesweeping* – the naval headquarters in each river sector controlled minesweeping operations. The 'Maritime Sector' covered from the river mouth up to Brăila, with its HQ at Galaţi. The 'Lower Danube Sector' was controlled from Giurgiu and stretched up river to Turnu Severin. The 'Middle Danube Sector' with its HQ at Belgrade covered the river up to Budapest.

The equipment used to sweep the mines varied. Some river tugs were adapted to sweep magnetic or acoustic mines or both and a squadron of Ju 52 transport aircraft were fitted with mine-detonating rings. A contemporary account describes a tug fitted with an impressive array of both magnetic and acoustic countermeasures, but the crew arrangements were by far the most intriguing element. The personnel allocated were a captain (minesweeping) who directed operations from the shore and seven seamen, all of whom were terrified of mines. No mine was ever countered by this vessel.

When mines were sown in the Romanian/Bulgarian length of the river, the mine-detonating Ju 52s first swept the area for shallow mines and any of high sensitivity. This was followed by Romanian vessels concentrating on the mined zone, while German and Bulgarian minesweeping vessels maintained continuous sweeps up-river from Giurgiu, until the river was assessed as safe.

Up to the end of July the assessment of safe was made after 24 sweeps. It was at this point, however, that a timing device was introduced into the magnetic mines. This refinement allowed them to remain unexploded on the river bed for an indeterminate period, rendering the 24 sweeps ineffective.

After the *gardening* of the Giurgiu area of the river on 30 July sweeping for four days afterwards failed to clear the river. In the end this degree of uncertainty caused mine-sweeping operations to be conducted incessantly. At the same time the risk of losing vessels was accepted and the passage of shipping was no longer held up. As matters deteriorated the final measure was to allow old vessels to drift down on the current to explode the mines and this met with varied success.

The adapted Ju 52s gave better results than surface methods but two were destroyed by exploding mines over a Hungarian stretch of river in June and two more fell to Allied aircraft.

3. *De-magnetising* – a station to de-magnetise vessels was established at Ruse on the Bulgarian bank opposite Giurgiu and a further one at Brăila was planned but never built. Various other efforts to overcome this attack could not be brought to bear in the time available.

4. *Anti-aircraft Defence* – Flak units, mostly of light-calibre, were established on stretches of the river deemed to be suitable for minelaying. Because of the low level of delivery they often fired on full depression, perhaps not their most effective mode. The installation of flak equipment on vessels was never completed but some flak barges were placed at key points on the river. The squadrons of night-fighters based in Romania were never truly effective. They usually had insufficient warning to make a successful intercept of what was a very difficult target to locate and then to engage.

Balloon barrages were deployed between Belgrade and Novi Sad but plans to extend these into Romanian waters never materialised.

Flying Officer D.C. Burcham of 37 Squadron (Wellingtons) observed:

> My crew must have been one of the first to attempt this sort of thing at night. It turned out to be one of the most exhilarating of trips. Having crossed the mountains at 10,000 feet, we then pin-pointed our 'garden' and dived down to 200 feet above the hazily moon-lit river, feeling rather vulnerable as we had no idea what was cooking-up along the dark river banks. In the event, nothing happened and we were able to drop our two mines.

Major J.L. Van Eyssen SAAF, a 31 Squadron pilot, extolled the virtues of the Liberator in its 'gardening' role.

1. It had a radio altimeter which gave the exact, absolute height above the terrain; whether land or water.

2. It carried six 1000 lb mines to the Wellington's two.

3. Liberators had more and heavier guns (six .50 inch instead of four .303 inch) with which to shoot back at gun emplacements on the river banks: an important consideration to keep the enemy ducking and to upset his aim. Moreover, the Liberator's waist guns and top turret could shoot forwards and sideways whereas the tail-gunner of the Wimpey, with his four guns, could only have a crack at guns he had already passed.

4. We were told that the ideal dropping speed for these mines was 190 mph. Could a fully laden Wimpey make 190?

So effective were these operations that the Romanian stretch of the river was not fully cleared until May 1945.

Minelaying – Experience

The silver Danube shimmered under that enormous moon,
It was very wide and clearly in full spate.
So where the banks should be, here and there a drowning tree
As the river wound towards the Iron Gate.

Getting nearer, slowly nearer to the water,
A two-ton load of naval mines to drop,
With our wheels and flaps extended and our speed as recommended
There were 'chutes to make the splash a gentle plop.

At a hundred feet the puzzle became clearer,
The treeless patch must be the waterway.
I contrived to solve the riddle by aiming for the middle,
Slowed the aircraft down and waited 'Mines away'.

We'd avoided wires stretched across the canyon,
We'd missed the barges loaded up with flak.
The mission had gone well, now we'd climb like bats from hell,
Clearing cliff tops where the river doubled back.

But to force the old girl up in such a hurry
Was inviting even 'Q for Queen' to fail.
So, while teetering on the stall I heard the gunner call
'The trees are scraping underneath the tail'.

But here is where those years on Tiger Moths
Presented such an unexpected yield.
Scaling those grim peaks I could use the same techniques
As climbing from some bad forced-landing field.

Flight Lieutenant L.A. Fieldhouse DFC,
150 Squadron, Foggia

CHAPTER 3 - The Defenders

By the summer of 1943, when over 60% of Romania's oil production was going to the Reich, the Germans had moved the 5th Flak (Anti-aircraft) Division to Romania. It was established there before the USAAF low-level raid on 1 August 1943 (Operation TIDALWAVE). At its peak this Division and other Luftwaffe ground units were manned by some 75,000 men supported by a slave-labour force reputedly about the same strength. It was commanded by Luftwaffe General Hans Kuderna.

The Division had radar-predicted 88, 105 and 128mm anti-aircraft guns and their already high performance was augmented by FREYA (FuMG 80) early warning (EW) and WURZBURG-REISE (FuMG 65) ground-controlled intercept (GCI) radars. These were deployed in great depth from Yugoslavia eastwards to give good coverage of target areas and the bomber approaches.

The total number of batteries in 5 Flak Div varied from 40 to over 60 and the total of guns was always in excess of 240. The notorious 88mm and the 105mm flak guns were usually grouped six to a battery (four guns in Romanian batteries). The smaller calibre 20 and 37mm guns were deployed in batteries of four.

The searchlight effort was prodigious. Available information numbers them variously between 200 and 300. They feature prominently in the accounts of the raiding bomber crews. The Division's deployment was supported by Romanian anti-aircraft artillery (AAA) units mostly with a daylight-only capability, as well as by some Austrian AAA units.

The Romanian AAA formations in the main target area were 3 and 4 AA Brigades. 1 AA Brigade covered from Braşov to Timişoara while 2 AA Brigade covered the East of the main target area and was based on Buzău. Co-ordination and control of the ground-based defences in Romania were exercised by a German-controlled National Air Defence Centre in the northern outskirts of Bucharest, while the complex gun, searchlight and fighter defences of the Bucharest–Ploieşti–Cîmpina zone had their headquarters some 7 kms west of Ploieşti itself. The Romanians estimated that there were over 25,000 Germans employed on air defence duties or supporting them. During the fighting which followed the coup of 23 August, over 9000 of these were captured and 1500 killed by their former allies.

Flak

A wealth of information on the deployment and handling of flak defences was gleaned by an Allied evaluation team who went to Romania in October 1944 to discuss the conduct of the defence with Romanian AAA officers, who had taken part.

From April 1944 onwards the flak system in the Bucharest–Ploieşti area was developed and dominated by the Luftwaffe according to their standard defensive practices established for Vienna and key industrial concentrations in the Reich.

Allied Intelligence sought to know the reasons for particular gun deployments and how fighter tactics combined with the flak, to help in the planning of future attacks on the well defended targets still to be attacked.

The TIDALWAVE attack on 1 August 1943 had made the defenders realise that flak alone could not prevent heavy bombers reaching the target, nor from bombing it successfully. Their aim, therefore, became one of making air attacks so costly in a ratio of lost aircraft and crew to results achieved that they would be unwilling to press further.

Among the steps taken to achieve this aim were:

1. A marked increase in the heavy guns included in the defence.

2. Consolidation of heavy gun batteries into *Grossbatterien*.

3. Gun-laying radars had anti-jamming equipment fitted to permit operation through Allied radar countermeasures.

4. Smoke generators – 'Artificial Fog' – were deployed in the Ploiesti area to hinder bombing accuracy. In many cases they succeeded, even to the extent of attacks being aborted.

5. The EW and GCI systems were improved.

6. Alternative positions were prepared and used by the heavier batteries to confuse photo-intelligence and to complicate the selection of correct attack and withdrawal flight paths.

None wholly succeeded, but the defence became formidable and one greatly respected by Allied airmen attacking by day or night. A statistic quoted by HQ MAAF Intelligence is noteworthy. Of nearly 5,490 effective bomber sorties flown by MASAF by day and night between July 1943 and July 1944, almost 160 bombers were shot down by flak, with over 80 lost to other, unknown causes. Thus the flak loss rate is almost 2.9%: over two and half times the loss rate attributed to fighters which was 1.1%. However, in just three attacks on

Ploieşti during the period, the bombers suffered flak losses of over 5%.

On 20 August 1944 the flak defences in the Ploieşti–Cîmpina area comprised a total of 256 heavy flak guns of 88mm or larger in 69 batteries. Six of these were equipped with railway mounted 128mm guns (a total of 24 guns). There were 53 batteries of mobile 88mm flak, totalling over 190 guns. The other ten batteries manned 105mm mobile flak guns. About half of the 88mm guns were deployed in nine *Grossbatterien* arranged symmetrically around Ploiesti or near to the estimated bomb release points.

A typical *Grossbatterie* would consist of two or three gun batteries sited very close together to act as a single fire unit. This gave the fire controller a large concentration of fire at his command, as well as multiple radar sets and other acquisition and control equipments to permit the most flexible deployment of that firepower. A German *Grossbatterie* had 18 guns, a Romanian one 12 guns.

The Romanians described how the two Wurzburg-Reise GCI radars were used. While one set was tracking a formation being engaged, the second was searching for follow-up formations for subsequent engagement. This reduced the loss of firing time while the guns switched to a new wave of bombers to almost nothing. If fire direction equipments were used in conjunction with the Wurzburgs the loss of firing time was measured in the seconds it took to relay the guns on their new azimuth and elevation and re-engage.

The 105mm mobile batteries were sited somewhat beyond the bomb release line to complement the defence provided by the *Grossbatterien*. In general these batteries were well concealed but were re-located from time to time to confuse detection. The siting followed German doctrine for advanced or outer batteries and gave them the task of surprising attacking aircraft by engaging them from advanced mobile positions tactically favourable to the defence. The mobility of these batteries was a key feature: they could be redeployed to augment other defences or to cover frequently used approaches.

The six batteries of 128mm guns were sited closer to the bomb release line in camouflaged positions. Alternative sites were prepared on a scale of at least one per battery and each had duplicate sets of fire control equipment to be used in the same way as in the *Grossbatterien*.

At Ploieşti itself the gun defences were required to deliver effective fire cover out to a range of 10–12 kms from the bomb release line. Outlying defence zones, which were centres on Moreni, Băcoi and Cîmpina, extended the coverage to the North and north-west by some 25–30 kms. It was intended that the flak resources would increase as the length of the bomb-run increased by up to two minutes flying time. In the north-west, however, this was longer and an attack could be engaged for over 4 minutes before it reached its bomb release line.

In German Air Force doctrine the air raid warning service held the key to successful anti-aircraft defence. Weather conditions, visibility and time of day were as fundamental to the defenders' success as they were to the bombers'. The Bucharest–Ploieşti–Cîmpina defence zone was served by an elaborate weather reporting system and protected by an early warning (EW) shield covering all of Romania and most of Yugoslavia. Romania was divided into four Air Defence Regions each with an EW radar and visual observer network linked by telephone to Information Centres. These, in turn, were linked to the National Air Defence Centre outside Bucharest. It was from here that radio-transmitted alerts and attack warnings were sent to military units, industry, civil defence and to local provincial government centres. There were three stages of alarm:

1. *Pre-warning* sent to all EW radars as soon as the attacking force was detected, usually some 400 miles west of Bucharest. In practice this meant that all attacks were well-announced by the time they were over-flying the Yugoslav Mountains.

2. *Increased Alert*: passed to all flak units, fighter airfields and industrial areas when the attacking formations were about 150 miles west of Bucharest – just east of their first crossing of the Danube.

3. *General Alarm* was a universal broadcast made to the entire population when the attackers reached the line of the River Olt in the west or the Danube in the south, at a distance of about 60 miles.

Only the region lying in the direct flight path was alerted, in accordance with normal German practice. The system meant that no one was taken by surprise and there was ample time for civil defence measures to be put in train. The Romanian officials interviewed were in no doubt that the Germans had refined their standard practices during the offensive against Bucharest–Ploieşti and had transferred their experience to the defence of important targets elsewhere in Europe.

The Romanian Air Defence Command made some additional points:

1. The defences were made more effective by the bombers' stereotyped method of attack. Bombing heights hardly varied and avenues of approach were usually predictable in advance.

2. The 'stacked' formations used by the day bombers gave the flak the advantage in that errors in range meant altitude and that gave a dispersion of fire through the height range of the formation. The night-bombers

presented a more difficult problem as the bombing 'height band' was much shallower.

3. 'Barrage fire' was never used. The defence was divided into sectors and all defences in a particular sector would engage all enemy aircraft heading into their sector. In their absence, batteries were required to give support to adjacent sectors already engaged. The aim was to attack the bombers before their bombs were released. Unloaded bombers were usually ignored if there were further incursions in-bound. An interesting statistic emerged at these talks. On average 3,500 rounds of flak were fired for each bomber lost to anti-aircraft fire.

4. The use of Chaff or Window rendered the GCI radars almost useless which could mean that the engagement range of the defences was drastically reduced. The target was lost for the last three to four vital minutes of its approach.

5. The smoke generators producing artificial fog were unpopular. Apart from the nauseating vapour, the smoke obscured optical range finders and generally reduced the effectiveness of fire from blanketed batteries. Nevertheless, the smoke was effective in that it obscured aiming marks and in some cases it undoubtedly saved the designated targets from attack.

Air Defence Deployments

Allied air reconnaissance maintained a constant vigil of the defences during the crucial months of the air assault, here as elsewhere. From the changing dispositions observed it was clear that the defenders' resources were stretched in their endeavours to meet the threats posed by the day and night-bombers and the menace of the prowling long-range day escort fighters. These fighters were frequently diverted to strafe targets of opportunity and were a considerable nuisance. In addition, the enemy had a continuing need to protect his own airfields and other key installations which were primarily dedicated to the support of his ground forces engaged further East.

Anti-aircraft units were deployed and re-deployed around a number of critical target areas, in addition to the Bucharest–Ploieşti–Cîmpina zone, throughout that Spring and Summer.

The map shows the general flak layout around Ploieşti. The smoke generators were integrated into the defences and their deployment was dense and widespread to guarantee effective smoke cover whatever wind conditions prevailed.

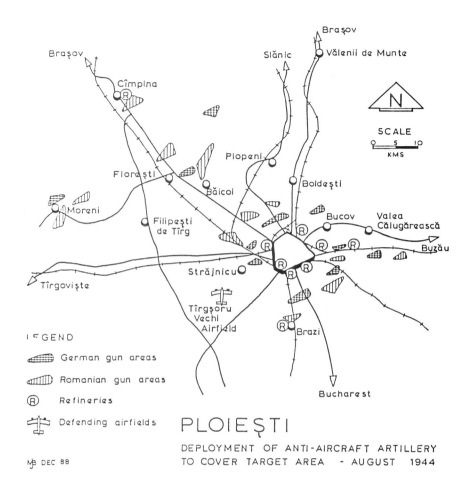

Brașov

Brașov
Slănic
Vălenii de Munte

Cîmplna
(R)

Plopeni

Florești
Băicol
Boldești

Moreni
Filipești
de Tîrg
Bucov
Valea
Călugărească

(R)
(R) (R)
Buzău

Strajnicu
(R)
(R)

Tîrgoviște

Tîrgșoru
Vechi
Airfield
Brazi
(R)

LEGEND

German gun areas

Romanian gun areas

(R)   Refineries

Defending airfields

Bucharest

SCALE
0   5   10
KMS

N

PLOIEȘTI

DEPLOYMENT OF ANTI-AIRCRAFT ARTILLERY
TO COVER TARGET AREA - AUGUST 1944

MJ DEC 88

The Romanian 4 AA Brigade had the responsibility of Ploiești. The defence of Bucharest on the other hand was the responsibility of 3 AA Brigade and its Regiments 1 and 3 were deployed in and around the city, roughly south and north respectively. Romanian artillery units are, unusually, known as Divisions, but they equate to battalions.

Regiment 1 had its HQ in Parcul Libertății (Park of Liberty) in central southern Bucharest. It commanded five AA 'Divisions', No 4 with eight batteries based in Domnești, No 7 with seven batteries at 'Progresul' railway station in the southern suburbs, No 13 – eight batteries at the Gara de Nord, and No 24, four batteries at the Cemetery on Șoseaua Giurgiului (Giurgiu Chaussée). In addition, Divizionul 20 manned five batteries of AA rocket launchers and covered the whole capital.

41

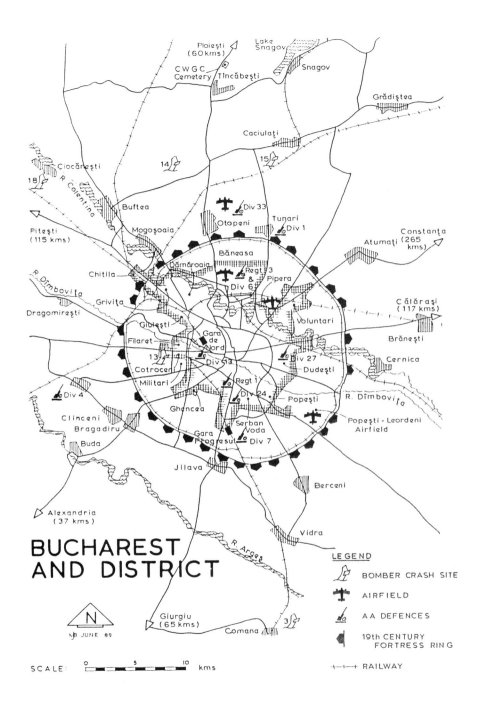

Ploieşti
(60 kms)

Lake
Snagov

CWGC
Cemetery Tîncăbeşti

Snagov

Grădiştea

Caciulaţi

Ciocăneşti

14

15

18

R Colentina

Buftea

Div 33

Tunari

Piteşti
(115 kms)

Mogoşoaia

Otopeni

Div 1

Constanţa
(265 kms)

Atumaţi

Băneasa

Dămăroaia

Regt 3
&
Div 6

Pipera

Chitila

R. Dîmbovita

Griviţa

Dragomireşti

Voluntari

Călăraşi
(117 kms)

Brăneşti

Giuleşti

Gara
de
Nord

Filaret

13

Cotroceni

Div 13

Div 27

Cernica

Dudeşti

Militari

Regt 1

Div 4

Div 24

Popeşti

R. Dîmbovita

Ghencea

Popeşti-Leordeni
Airfield

Clinceni
Bragadiru

Gara
Progresu

Şerban
Voda
Div 7

Buda

Jilava

Berceni

Alexandria
(37 kms)

Vidra

BUCHAREST
AND DISTRICT

R. Argeş

LEGEND

Giurgiu
(65 kms)

Comana

3

BOMBER CRASH SITE

AIRFIELD

AA DEFENCES

19th CENTURY
FORTRESS RING

RAILWAY

N

MJB JUNE 89

SCALE: 0   5   10   kms

Regiment 3 had its HQ at Băneasa Airport and commanded four Divisions. No 1 with seven batteries was based on Tunari Woods, east of Băneasa. No 6 with five batteries, was at the Airport itself. No 27 with ten batteries was at '23 August' Workshops and No 33 with four batteries at Otopeni Airport. Luftwaffe flak displacements around Bucharest are not known, but there was a heavy presence, at least, protecting the Airports.

It would not be unkind to describe the Brigade's equipments as a hotch-potch of AAA pieces. Regiment 1's twenty-seven batteries manned seven different types of gun with six different calibres.

Regiment 3's twenty-three batteries had the same variety of equipments but a somewhat different mix.

The ammunition supply for this armoury must have been a quarter-master's nightmare.

Reconnaissance taken in early May 1944 established the Allied Intelligence base line of flak dispositions although some may have been in place for weeks or even months before that.

A dozen airfields in eastern Romania supported land operations and each had its flak layout, the strengths of which ebbed and flowed through the summer. All these were out of reach of the Foggia-based bombers but, when using Russian bases for shuttle-bombing (Operation FRANTIC), airfields at Focşani, Galaţi and Zilisteanca were attacked.

Defended areas which were close to likely bomber flight paths or in the target area included Giurgiu on the Danube. In May a layout of six guns was noted. A month later that had been increased to sixteen heavy flak guns and, by late July, twenty had been identified. At the end of the conflict this garrison boasted twenty-four guns.

At Orşova, on the Danube north of Turnu Severin, Allied reconnaissance spotted four heavy guns in early May coupled with another four at Turnu Severin itself. These defences had been completely withdrawn by the end of July, leaving the defence to lighter calibre flak. Allied Intelligence assessed that the air attacks appeared to have reduced the target value of communications and port facilities here.

At Slatina, a small town on the main road and railway between Craiova and Piteşti, a defence of four heavy flak guns was spotted in early June but they had been removed a month later and the nearby airfield was deserted.

Timisoara, in the Banat plain, was seen to sport a new defence of eight heavy guns in late May. By early August these had been increased to twelve. This was taken to be in recognition of the importance of the through rail route between Romania, Hungary and Yugoslavia. Further to the east, the small industrial town and rail centre of Simeria, lying on the main rail route to

Hungary sprouted 8 guns during July.

The defences at Braşov, a major industrial and communications centre and a key in both the land and air battle, had 16 guns for most of the period. Four more were identified in early August, emphasising the growing importance of the rail line through the mountains between there and Ploieşti to the south and that leading north and westwards towards Reich territory, which was still intact.

Fighters

In addition to the ample resources of 5 Flak Div, the Luftwaffe Headquarters controlling the whole Balkan region had formidable day and night fighter resources. Known as Jäfu Balkan (Jäfu was military shorthand for Jägdfliegerführer), this HQ had been at Bucharest but it was moved to Pancevo, just east of Belgrade, in May 1944, leaving a subordinate HQ in place to run the Romanian air battle, commanded by Colonel Bernhard Woldenga.

Lieutenant Ioan Dicezare FARR, poses beside his Bf 109. (The inscription on the nose translates loosely "Hello Girls", so allied crews were not alone in painting slogans on their aircraft.) (Courtesy Ministry of National Defence, Bucharest)

By the time 15 AF's attacks had developed into a steady assault, the fighter defenders were organised into five groups. Day fighters were mainly Me Bf 109 G-2s grouped in I/JG 4 and III/JG 27 based at Mizil, 35 kms east of Ploies ti and IV/JG 27 based at Niš and Skopje in Yugoslavia. The day fighter effort was reinforced by the Royal Romanian Air Force (Forțelor Aeriene Regal ale România – FARR) flying Bf 109s, in the main, all under the operational command of Jäfu Rumänien (Colonel Neuman).

The two night-fighter groups operated Bf 110 G-4s – IV/NJG 6 from Otopeni (now Bucharest International Airport) and II/NJG 200 at Zilisteanca, 15 kms northeast of Buzău and safely out of range to all but the 15 AF shuttlebombers on Operation FRANTIC missions. It is interesting that no available German sources mention the subordination of the Ju 88 night-fighters, but they were present and MAAF estimated that there were probably thirty of them in early April.

An Me 110 radar-equipped night-fighter of the type encountered over Romania and other targets in Southern Europe. (Courtesy Imperial War Museum)

A Ju88 night fighter. Radar antennas on nose and wings are evident as is the cannon housing under the nose. (Courtesy Imperial War Museum)

The number of fighters available at any time to meet the air assault varied but, as far as the night-bombers were concerned, Intelligence assessed that, even on a maximum effort night, the ratio could be one to one.

The US Strategic Survey, when studying the enemy economy for the Joint Chiefs of Staff, assessed that the Ploieşti area contained the most important installations, the destruction of which would hurt the enemy most. This is a view apparently shared by the Germans. The Bucharest–Ploieşti–Cîmpina zone remained the most heavily defended target group in southern Europe and third in Nazi-occupied Europe.

CHAPTER 4 - And What of Romania?

The position in which Romania found itself in the war is worthy of some explanation.

The modern state of Romania emerged from the domination of its latest tormentors, the Turks, in May 1877. Carol I, a prince of the House of Hohenzollern-Sigmaringen in Swabia was called to the new throne in Bucharest and the Kingdom was established in March 1881. The Romanian Army had fought valiantly in the war of independence.

Carol I was succeeded by his nephew, Ferdinand in October 1914 – a very difficult and uncertain time. The King found himself in an awkward position, his new country fervently supporting the Entente Powers, led by Britain and France, against the interests of his fatherland and its allies (the Central Powers). In 1916 he broke with his family and his race and, with Allied promises of the coveted lands of Banat, Transylvania and Bukovina, he concluded a Treaty with the Entente, the sole purpose of which, to the Romanian mind, was the achievement of national unity.

On 17 August 1916 the Allies agreed to provide extensive economic and military aid. It was felt that Romania's twenty divisions would have a decisive effect on the eastern front and be a bulwark against the expansionism of post-war Russia.

Romania declared war on Austria-Hungary on 27 August, unfortunately anticipating that the massive Brusilov offensive, launched in June in Galicia would be a success, leaving Romania something of a formality in claiming her spoils. Allied Missions assembling to advise and train the Army were discomfited with what they found: it was wanting in almost all fields of military endeavour. About one third of its 600,000 soldiers were tied to the logistic train and most were illiterate. The officer corps was a disappointment. One observer summed the Army thus:

> . . . soldiers excellent, officers destitute of all military morality, headquarters and command almost worthless.

The Head of the Allied Military Mission, General Henri Berthelot, reputedly commended the Romanian field commander, General Alexandru Averescu, after observing army manoeuvres:

> Congratulations, my dear General, you have completely mastered the art of disorganisation.

After a very brief campaign, in the path of which a British sapper colonel had attempted to sabotage the main oilfield area around Ploieşti, the southern half of the country was quickly overwhelmed. The Central Powers' depredations over the next eighteen months were considerable – more than 1,140,000 tons of oil, petrol and oil products, two million tons of foodstuff and fodder, 300,000 head of livestock and over 200,000 tons of timber, in addition to the daily appetites of the occupation army.

Norman Stone (*The Eastern Front 1914–1917*, Hodder & Stoughton, 1975) concludes that Romania's unsuccessful intervention in the war made it possible for Germany to continue to fight into 1918.

One key factor in Romania's defeat, not lost on either party for the future, was the Central Powers' capability of moving forces, reserves and supplies quickly by rail. In September 1916 they dispatched over 1,500 trains through Hungary and assembled a force equal to the entire Romanian Army within three weeks of the declaration of war. On the other hand there were no rail links at that time between Romania and Hungary through the Carpathian Mountains, so the troops bravely sent forward through the passes into Transylvania to meet von Staussenberg's 1st Austro-Hungarian Army could not be sustained there adequately and were steadily overwhelmed or driven back into the passes.

Romania had expected support from her Allies once she took the field, but this was not forthcoming. The Russians in the East did little and the promised pressures on the Salonika front in Greece did not take place. The result was that von Mackensen, commanding Germano-Bulgarian forces, was able to turn North to meet the new threat posed to his rear by a Romania at war. His offensive began with an unexpected and almost unresisted thrust into Dobrogea followed by a crossing of the Danube at Zimnicea. These moves quickly wrong-footed the Romanian Command who began re-deploying frontline troops and reserves hither and thither. The result was inevitable. Von Mackensen's advance connected with von Staussenberg's – now through into the plains of Wallachia – and Bucharest fell easily on 6 December 1916, with the King and his government fleeing to Iaşi in Moldavia.

Stalemate followed: the Central Powers' advance was halted on the defence line running from Focşani to Galaţi along the valley of the Siret, at the gates of Moldavia. The Romanian Army now needed time to re-train and to absorb the military aid which was at last arriving from the Western Allies via

Russia's northern ports. The Russians, for their part, had had enough and their armies were progressively riven by the advancing revolution. The Germans and Austrians needed to redeploy to face more serious threats.

The October revolution of 1917 reduced Russian influence further until, after the Armistice of Brest Litovsk on 3 March 1918, it was removed altogether. The Peace of Bucharest, signed on 7 May 1918, capped Romania's humiliation. She was forced to cede Dobrogea to Bulgaria and to grant Germany full exploitation rights of her lost oil industry as well as other enslaving conditions.

Fortunately the Allied cause fared better on other fronts and Romania was able to re-assert herself. With her Army re-grouped and re-trained and better led, she went onto the offensive again towards the end of 1918. In November the Army advanced into Transylvania as far as the River Mureş before a general peace descended on all fronts. Post-war treaties granted Romania lands she had sought for generations to unite the Romanian people and they came as a final reward for her sacrifices of 1916. The Armistice of 11 November nullified the terms of the Peace of Bucharest. The Treaty of Neuilly on 27 November restored Dobrogea and the Treaty of Trianon yielded Transylvania and her share of Banat.

Oil

Crude oil in its natural state is a mixture, the constituents of which can be separated in the refining process because they boil at different temperatures. Although crude oil had been known and used for many hundred of years, it was not until the nineteenth century that its nature became fully understood and the distillation process of refining developed. In parallel, the means of extracting oil from the earth were also developing to succeed the quarrying or well-boring techniques formerly used. The first drillings especially for oil were at Hanover in 1857. Romania followed in 1863.

Extracting oil from the ground and treating it in refineries pre-supposed an effective means of onward movement from the wellheads themselves. Initially the oil was handled in barrels, which is how that unit of measurement for oil and oil products became standard. Wagons were inadequate over contemporary roads and the pressing need for railway tank wagons and pipelines was soon recognised. The mid-1860s saw purpose built railway wagons in use on European railways and, once leaks had been overcome, effective pipelines too.

Romania's oil deposits, the largest in Europe by far, lie along the south-eastern curve of the Carpathian Mountains from Băcau in Moldavia round to

Pitești in Wallachia with the main concentration around Ploiești in the basins of the Dîmbovița, Prahova and Teleajan Rivers. In many places crude oil seeps to the surface and had been used for centuries for lighting and lubrication and for some medicinal purposes.

The first refinery was built at Lucăcești near Băcau in 1840, but generally the refining industry grew up in the oilfields, principally centred on Ploiești and Cîmpina. The absence of an adequate transport system at the outset prevented the development of refineries at ports such as Brăila or Constanța. By the time the railways were through (the 10 mile Danube bridge at Cernavoda was completed in 1895) the industry was too well established on site to change. Furthermore, at the turn of the century, the industry was in multiple ownership; for example, in 1898 72 refineries processed nearly 135,000 tons of crude oil.

The international financing of the oil industry, which was vital to its expansion, was only allowed on the basis of concessions since the Constitution barred foreigners from owning land. In the early days the granting of these concessions was a lengthy and tortuous process because of inadequate land survey and complex land holding practices and laws, in the main. This problem was largely overcome by the Mining Law of 1895 which included a provision for the State to intervene in the matter of land ownership. It opened the way for international resources and interests to develop the oil industry to world status. Capital was needed not only for the extraction process itself but also for the development of marketing – tanks, pipelines, railways and oil docks. The first foreign money came from Holland, Germany and the United States. French, British and Italian interests followed. British, American and German involvement would emerge as the largest by the late 1930s.

The Slide into World War 2

In early post-war years the Romanian economy and, with it, the oil industry prospered but, as the storm clouds of war once again gathered, it became clear that oil reserves were becoming exhausted. 1937 is probably the watershed year indicating the beginning of the downturn in Romania's affairs. The increase in the power of the pro-Fascist Iron Guard sharpened nationalist ideals and highlighted the ineffectiveness of the existing political system. The elections of December triggered a chain of far-reaching events. The King dismissed the Prime Minister and installed a rabid nationalist, Octavian Goga. Anti-semitic measures, backed by martial law, followed. Business was paralysed; there was a run on the banks and the stock exchange collapsed. After six weeks the King abruptly dismissed Goga, dispensed with all the political parties and established his 'Royal Dictatorship'. The King's popularity had long since reached its nadir; although clever, he was unscrupulous and the manner of both his public and well-known private life disgusted many of his subjects. For many, this imperious step was a bitter pill indeed.

In the decade from 1930 there had been eighteen different Premiers and nine chiefs of General Staff of the Army.

The establishment of the Royal Dictatorship roughly coincided with the German drive to expand her interests in south-eastern Europe. There was a new-found confidence following the re-militarisation of the Rhineland in 1936. Initially a close relationship was not possible because Romania supported the Czechs against German annexation and because of German support for the Iron Guard and its eccentric and fanatical leader, Corneliu Codreanu. However, the Anschluss in Austria in March 1938 and the Munich Agreement in September established German power in central Europe convincingly. The armament-petroleum agreement in the summer illustrated exactly the mutual wish for a closer alignment. Czechoslovakia looked to Russia as a counter to further German advances but the Romanians still saw the Soviets as their greatest external threat. Furthermore Romania and Czechoslovakia had opposing policies regarding Poland, which had been an enduring ally of Romania.

By 1939 Romanian foreign policy had evolved from a reliance on French influence, which had been in decline since 1934, to one of reliance upon Germany. At the same time, Romanian nationalism was causing concern to foreign investors, particularly those with interests in the oil industry. One result of the King's visit to Germany in the previous November had been an agreement that the major reorganisation to be made in the oil industry would be carried out under German auspices. The days of foreign capital were numbered and trade with Germany blossomed substantially. The continued need for additional investment matched the German need for a secure supply of vital raw materials to support her seemingly unlimited ambitions.

British and French objectives in Romania were less pronounced but, on 13 April 1939, they gave a unilateral guarantee to Romania in the wake of the post-Munich occupation of Czechoslovakia. Although British investment in Romanian oil was greater than that of Germany, the British conceded economic ascendancy in a realistic appraisal of the trend of current events. Western Allied planning only assumed continued supplies of Romanian oil if that country remained neutral. The decline of the oil industry, while marked, still left it as a major world source nevertheless. By June 1939 the continued fall in output had reached 60% of the total refining capacity of 11,000,000 tons and storage was down to some 3,000,000 tons. Throughout the war nine refinery blocks were in operation in and around Ploiești with one more at Cîmpina and an eleventh at Bucharest.

The partition of Poland between Germany and the Soviet Union extended

Romania's frontiers with the latter state, whose territorial ambitions were still feared as the major threat. The British and French guarantees were in tatters after their total failure to save Poland and Germany emerged as Romania's only real guarantor. The perceived Soviet threat was confirmed when the Red Army summarily occupied Bukovina and Bessarabia (that part of Romania all east of the River Prut) on 28 June 1940. Further indignities were shortly to follow. Long standing disputes with Hungary and Bulgaria, now more staunch supporters of Nazi-Germany than Romania, were settled in the Second Arbitration Awards in Vienna on 30 August. Romania was compelled to yield most of Transylvania to Hungary and Southern Dobrogea to Bulgaria.

King Carol attempted to solve the resulting crisis at home by giving General Ion Antonescu almost complete executive authority which the deft general used to force the King's abdication on 6 September 1940. Young King Michael, now aged nineteen, who succeeded to the throne, could be little more than a figurehead. Antonescu's government of this 'National Legionary State' was devoted enthusiastically to the German cause and so it was to remain for the next four years.

Antonescu moved into an even closer dependence on Germany. On 23 November Romania became a member of the Axis when she joined the Tripartite Pact of Germany, Italy and Japan – one day after Hungary had signed. In the same month a German War Economy Commission arrived in Bucharest to aid the Romanian economy with advice and expert knowledge. Antonescu's personal relationship with Hitler allowed him to retain a measure of autonomy for Romania's internal affairs, notwithstanding the presence from October 1940 onwards of a very sizeable garrison of German army and airforce units, which generally observed Romanian Law. Great Britain broke off diplomatic relations in February 1941. The Romanian Army supplied 30 divisions for the German invasion of the Soviet Union, which was launched on 22 June 1941, initially to seek recovery of Bessarabia and the northern Bukovina. Later, as German fortunes took a turn for the worse in losing the Caucasus in 1942, Romania's part in enabling the Germans to continue the war was to become a crucial one.

Britain, incensed by Romania's part in the war against Russia, issued an ultimatum which required the withdrawal of all Romanian forces behind her pre-1940 frontiers. This was ignored and, on 30 November 1941, Great Britain declared war. A month later as a result of the Japanese attack on Pearl Harbour, Romania, with the rest of the Axis, declared war on the United States on 12 December 1941.

Her commitment to the Nazi cause now became total and her isolation from the West was complete, however much many influential Romanians regretted it.

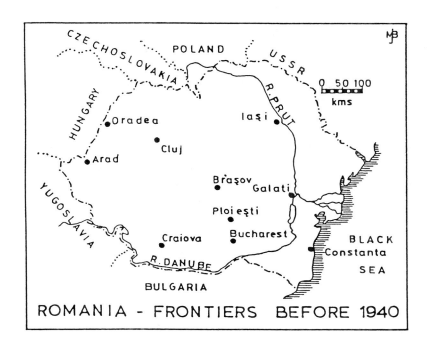

ROMANIA - FRONTIERS BEFORE 1940

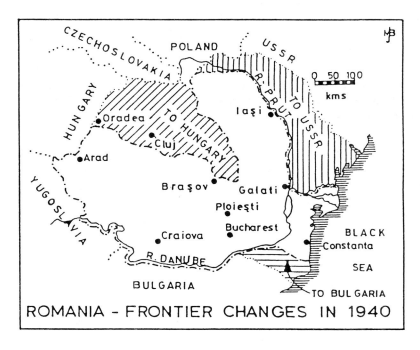

ROMANIA - FRONTIER CHANGES IN 1940

With the Balkans in German hands, the Romanian oilfields were safe from attack for the time being. Her outlets via the Black Sea were closed by Allied naval and air superiority in the Mediterranean. Movement of oil and all other material to Germany therefore had to rely upon the railway systems and on the Danube waterway. The same systems would become vital to the supply of the German armies on the Russian front and they would be exploited to the full. When the time came, they would be targets for the allied air offensive surpassed only by the attacks on the oil industry itself.

As we shall see, the respite was a long one.

When Romanian targets did come under sustained attack, it became clear that her armed forces had learnt many lessons since the humiliations of 1916. Her flak units fought with great determination and resilience and the fighter pilots of the Royal Romanian Air Force (FARR) could be relied upon to press home their attacks against the raiders with skill and courage.

Romanian pilots receive bravery decorations – the Order of Michael the Brave 3rd Class (L to R)

Lieutenants Constantin Cantacuzino, Ioan Milu and Ioan Dicezare. The Romanian Air Force operated principally against the daylight raids. Cantacuzino later featured prominently in the rescue of the Allied PWs in Romania.

(Courtesy Ministry of National Defence, Bucharest)

CHAPTER 5 - Early Attacks on Romanian Targets

This aircraft is the Il-4 or DB-3F used in the 1941 attacks on Romanian transportation and coastal targets. (Courtesy Imperail War Museum)

First blood goes to aviators of the Soviet Black Sea Fleet. Their initial efforts were against targets on the lines of communication of the German invaders, but raids on oil installations were made in July and August 1941. Tupolev SB-2 and Ilyushin DB-3 bombers were used to bomb from levels between 3,000 and 9,000 feet in daylight. On 24 June 1941, two days after the Axis forces invaded the Soviet Union, four DB-3s were intercepted on their approach to bomb Constanţa port installations. Their assailants were reportedly sixteen He-113 fighters which would have been an unusual aircraft in this area. The attack was pressed home and one DB-3 claimed two enemy fighters before he had to ditch in the Black Sea.

Two days later a flight of Tupolev SB-2 attacked enemy shipping in the mouth of the Danube at Sulina. One aircraft had an engine failure after flak had damaged the cooling system. The Flight (Zveno) destroyed the two Me Bf-109s which intercepted them and all returned to base. There is no record of how the target fared.

On 13 July twelve Ilyushin DB-3 bombers of the 2nd Regiment, escorted by six fighters of the 96th Regiment, were sent to attack German troops preparing to cross the Danube. They were met by twelve Me Bf-109s. One damaged DB-3 was brought home and successfully landed by the Navigator, Senior Lieutenant A.F. Tolmachev. For his heroism he received the Order of the Red Banner. He was made a Hero of the Soviet Union in July 1943.

Red Air Force attacks on the oil industry are said to have worried the rulers of Romania and Hitler himself. There were successful attacks between 1 July and 18 August 1941, four involving twenty-five DB-3s. There were also attacks by mixed DB-3 and Petlyakov P-2 forces of 3–6 aircraft by day and a single DB-3 by night. There is no information about *how* successful these attacks were.

One more attack is on record. On 25 May 1943 a Tupolev TB-3 four-engined bomber carrying two I-16 Rata fighters under its wings, each armed with two 500 lb HE bombs raided the 10-mile long railway bridge over the Danube at Cernavoda. The I-16s were released at a great height over the sea and were able to approach at speed in a dive attack, penetrating the defences which had previously proved too much for Il-4 (DB-3) raids. They had adequate fuel to be able to return safely to Soviet-held territory. The Cernavoda bridge was undamaged.

(The account of attacks from the Soviet Union is based on information kindly provided by Wing Commander F.J. (John) French RAF. Soviet bases seem not to have been used to attack these targets again until 15 AF used them for Operation FRANTIC sorties in mid-1944.)

Red Air Force attacks in 1941 were carried out by TB-3 bomber/transport carrying a single-engined Il-16 under each wing. The Il-16's each carried two 250 Kg bombs delivered in a diving attack – were able to return safely to base.

HALPRO

The first raid by the Western Allies on 12 June 1942 was also the first USAAF attack on a European target. In May twenty-three B-24 Liberators, under the command of Colonel Harry A. Halverson, had left Florida for a deployment to South East Asia via the Middle East, with the nickname 'Halpro', derived from 'Halverson Project 63'. Their route took them via Brazil and the Gold Coast to Khartoum. While they were there, Japanese advances in China neutralised the bases from which Halpro would have operated.

On 5 June the United States declared war on Romania (as well as Hungary and Bulgaria: Romania had declared war on the US on 12 December 1941). Colonel Halverson now received orders to attack the Romanian oil refinery concentration at Ploieşti. RAF Middle East (RAF ME) would put fuel and bombs at Halpro's disposal. The force was moved north to the Suez Canal zone base of Fayid. The operation being planned was a brave one. Not one of the aircrews involved had been on an operation to an opposed distant target and the USAAF had never tried the B-24 in action. Because of Turkish neutrality, a complicated route had to be devised to bring the bombers into Ploieşti from the south-east, over Constanţa. Since the range to the targets was some 1,300 miles, the recovery airfields were to be in Iraq, which was, at that time, under allied control.

The take-off was late in the evening of 11 June and thirteen bombers set course individually in the unfamiliar darkness. The leading aircraft arrived over Constanţa at dawn. Twelve bombers reached the general area of Ploieşti but no bomb fell in the target area. No aircraft was lost to enemy action. Four reached their recovery airfield and two more landed elsewhere in Iraq. Two landed in Syria and four were interned in Turkey.

Few Romanians had any idea that a raid had taken place. However, one man in Romania was well aware of what had happened and he began to make plans for the future that very day. General Alfred Gerstenberg of the German Air Force was Air Attaché at Bucharest and Head of the Luftwaffe Mission to Romania. He realised the significance of this attack and began to plan the defences against the follow-up attacks which he was convinced would follow.

Operation TIDALWAVE

The first major attack on the Romanian oil industry was Operation TIDALWAVE, directed against installations at Ploieşti and Cîmpina from North African bases on 1 August 1943. This low-level attack failed to achieve tactical surprise and, as a result, the defenders were able to inflict substantial losses on the attacking force. Of the 177 B-24s launched, 163 actually bombed and the damage was rated as 'severe'. So were the casualties; 54 aircraft and 532 men were lost. Five Medals of Honour were won, three of them posthumously. While the actual damage inflicted was not as great as expected, the attack's main achievement was to eliminate the surplus refining capacity – permanently. The cost of the operation was too high for it to be repeated in that form.

A Romanian Government communique released on 2 August 1943 is remarkably frank and accurate in a world of propaganda distortions – and has not been published in the West before:

> Yesterday, 1st August, the Anglo-American Air Forces carried out their first big raid on Romanian territory. This attack was especially directed against the oil district between Ploieşti and Cîmpina.
>
> The attack was carried out by between 120/130 multi-engined American bombers of the Liberator type, which approached Romania from the south and south-east at the same time. It appears that they came from Tripolitania, as their approach was indicated an hour beforehand by the German forces of occupation in Greece, over which country the raiders flew.
>
> For reasons, which have so far not been explained, the alarm was not given in Bucharest, Ploieşti and the oil region until enemy aircraft were actually over Romanian territory, i.e. at 1300 hours. As a result the precautionary measures were not only put into operation late, but were also inadequate.
>
> This is the first time that Romania had been raided on such a large scale. The raid lasted three hours. The American aircraft, which approached in single groups, made the Ploieşti district their chief target, avoiding Bucharest and flying over the summer resort of Snagov (over the lake of that name) at a height of 200 metres. By a curious coincidence, Marshall Antonescu and the Vice-President Mihai Antonescu were sailing on the lake in a motor boat, but fortunately for them no bombs were dropped there. The aircraft flew over the town of Ploieşti for more than half an hour at low altitude, probably with the object of making a reconnaissance and spotting their objectives. The attack then began in earnest and all important objectives connected with the oil industry were hit with such accuracy that only two bombs fell in the suburbs of the city near to the station, destroying four or five buildings and causing some casualties. The following objectives were destroyed or partly damaged by direct hits, delayed action bombs and, in particular, by incendiary bombs:–

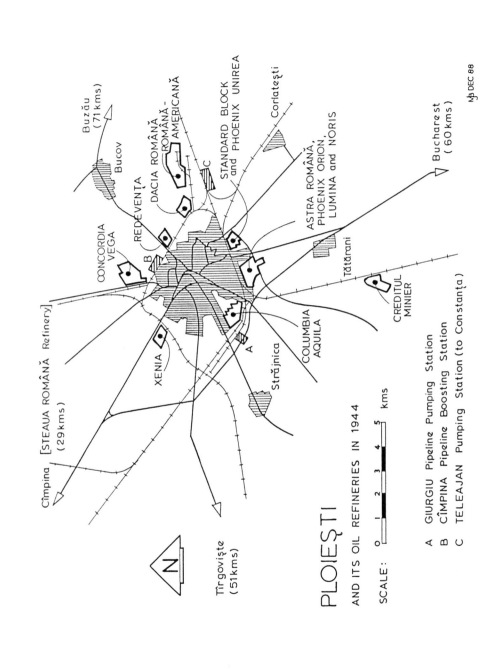

PLOIEŞTI

AND ITS OIL REFINERIES IN 1944

SCALE: 0 1 2 3 4 5 kms

A GIURGIU Pipeline Pumping Station

B CÎMPINA Pipeline Boosting Station

C TELEAJAN Pumping Station (to Constanţa)

Cîmpina [STEAUA ROMÂNĂ Refinery]
(29kms)

Tîrgovişte
(51kms)

Buzău
(71kms)

Bucov

REDEVENȚA

DACIA ROMÂNĂ,
ROMÂNĂ-
AMERICANĂ

STANDARD BLOCK
and PHOENIX UNIREA

Corlateşti

ASTRA ROMÂNĂ,
PHOENIX ORION,
LUMINA and NORIS

Bucharest
(60kms)

CONCORDIA
VEGA

XENIA

Strǎjnica

COLUMBIA
AQUILA

Tǎtǎrani

CREDITUL
MINIER

MAJ DEC 88

The Astro-Română Refinery (regarded as the most important in Europe), Ploieşti	–	Refinery
The Orion Refineries, Ploieşti	–	Refinery
The Creditul Minier, Brazi	–	Refinery
Steaua Română, Cîmpina	–	Refinery
Română-Americană, Moreni	–	Refinery

and fires were burning for several hours. It appears that nothing can be recovered or salvaged from these refineries, which produce 25% of the fuel required by the German army. The number of casualties is fairly low in view of the importance of the attack: 100 persons were killed and 200 injured, half of which were women imprisoned in the Ploieşti Women's Prison. An American aircraft crashed on this Prison with its full load of bombs.

The anti-aircraft defence of Ploieşti, which is in the hands of the German Forces, was extremely poor. It appears that when the alarm was given, most of the anti-aircraft personnel were bathing at Snagov, more than 20 kms away from Ploieşti, having the Sunday off. Most of the American aircraft which were shot down were accounted for by the energetic action taken by the Romanian Air Force. Up to the present, no official details have been issued regarding the exact results of the raid.

In addition to the oil region, various railway junctions – Buzău, Piatra Olt, Piteşti – were attacked as well as the ports of Giurgiu and Olteniţa.

On general lines, the Anglo-American raid can be regarded as a great success from the point of view of the Allies, in view of the very considerable destruction occasioned. Nevertheless this attack was very expensive to the attacking forces, both as regards machines and personnel. It is said that the losses incurred in this raid are proportionately the heaviest suffered by the Allied Air Forces during the whole of the present conflict.

This costly operation could not be followed up until the attacking air forces were better poised to deliver sustained heavy blows. That was not until the spring of 1944, when the recently created Mediterranean Allied Strategic Air Force (MASAF) became firmly established at Foggia and long-range fighter escorts were available to protect daylight operations.

Then began the high-level offensive by day and by night. By the middle of August long-term damage had been inflicted. The Russian advance reached the area on 30 August. They entered Bucharest the next day.

The loss of Romanian oil to the German war machine had a real and immediate impact. In addition, MASAF was released from what has been described as its most onerous commitment. Intensification of attacks on other oil targets followed and this switch of bomber effort was of critical importance. It coincided with a similar effort in north-west Europe which succeeded in bringing the whole of Germany's remaining (synthetic) oil production to a complete halt in mid-September.

Part 2

THE 1944
BOMBER ATTACKS

CHAPTER 6 - April

Summary

Better weather in April allowed Mediterranean Allied Air Forces (MAAF) to field a greater bomber effort than the combined total for the two previous months. The Strategic Air Force's (that is, the MASAF's) contribution was the dropping of over 19,000 tons of bombs by day and over 1,700 by night. 8 USAF and Bomber Command were also able to step up their operations, largely against the German aircraft industry, as were those of 15 US AF from Italy.

In addition, while MASAF played a full part in Operation STRANGLE – an interdiction plan to restrict supplies reaching enemy ground forces in Italy – its bombers ranged in strength into south-east Europe to dislocate enemy communications and to help Russian ground forces who were then pressing hard into the Balkans.

By the beginning of April, troops of the 2nd Ukrainian Front, commanded by Army General R.I. Malinovski, had penetrated the line of the River Prut and entered Romania near Iaşi in Moldavia. This advanced brought them close to the Carpathian Mountains which represented the last ramparts for an Axis defence on the approach into Hungary and Austria from the south-east.

It had seemed as though German Army Group South Ukraine, commanded by Field Marshal F. Schörner, would inevitably be pushed back on to that line; it was threatened further North. However, a stubborn defence held Soviet attempts to carry the critical Iabloniţa Pass (also known as the Tartar Pass) connecting the head of the Prut valley with that of the Tişa, a worthy tributary of the Danube. The Pass is one of the easiest passages through the mountains and had been used many times in history as armies and peoples ebbed back and forth.

In the first week in April, with the Soviet armies stretched to the limits of their supplies for the moment, the Germans launched a local counter-offensive in eastern Galicia along both banks of the Dniester. By the time this surprise stroke had run its course, that part of the front had become stable and was to remain more or less so until the end of July. Malinovski maintained his pressure in northern Moldavia and widened his hold to include a lodgement over the River Siret but here he was checked. The Russian left wing now wheeled towards the Black Sea through southern Bessarabia, the combined threat causing grave concern to the German Command.

Providing support for the Red Army became a high priority task for MASAF's operations. Marshalling yards in Romania, Bulgaria, Hungary and Yugoslavia came under attack and mines were laid in the Danube waterway. The bomber force flew almost 3,000 effective sorties against these targets which included railway installations at Bucharest and at Ploieşti. They each received over 1,600 tons of high explosive.

This Ploieşti raid marked the beginning of the high-level day and night offensive against the enemy's oil and transportation resources which would be intensified in the months to come.

The Raids

Three key dates for 205 Group were 8, 9 and 19 April. The first of these, the evening of Easter Day, was when Romania felt the first touch of the RAF's hand. Nineteen Wellingtons and three Liberators laid forty 1000 lb mines in the Danube between the Romanian frontier, by the little town of Baziaş and Belgrade, without incident.

Easter day itself saw the first use of WINDOW in the Mediterranean Theatre of Operations (MTO). This was on a raid to Budapest. Radar-controlled searchlights, reported one airman:

> . . . wavered and eventually gave up in despair.

Thirdly on 19 April, 614 Squadron carried out its first operation in the Target Marking Force (TMF) role using H$_2$S radar. The target was the railway yard at Plovdiv in south-east Bulgaria. Eight aircraft attacked and the operation was rated as successful.

Tuesday 4 April

15 AF's day bombers opened the offensive against Romanian targets. 220 B-17 Fortresses and 93 B-24 Liberators escorted by 120 fighters dropped over 860 tons of bombs at Chitila in the north-west part of Bucharest. Over 150 enemy fighters were encountered and 10 bombers were lost, but the attackers claimed to have destroyed 50 enemy fighters. The raid began at noon and the main railway station, the Gara de Nord, crowded with refugees from the Moldavian battle area, received a number of direct hits.

FARR fighters were identified among the defenders and US bomber crews rated these Romanians as being just as aggressive and tenacious as the Luftwaffe. Fighter attacks were sustained until the bombers had reached Sofia and there were several reports of air-to-air rockets being fired by the enemy.

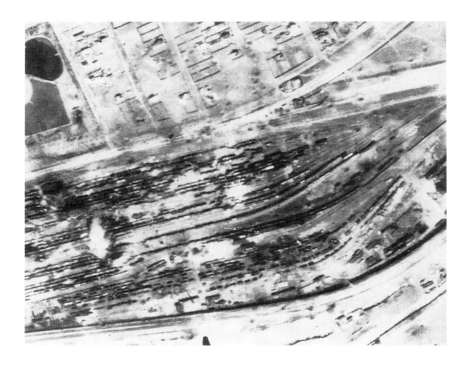

Taken two days after the 4th April raid, this reconnaissance photograph shows clearly the wide scale damage done in the Bucharest railway yards. Detailed photo-interpretation at the time identified at least 1500 rail trucks and 10 locomotives destroyed or severely damaged. In places it appears that the intense heat has melted the railway tracks. (Courtesy Colonel John H. Kirk USAF)

Wednesday 5 April

The next day Ploieşti itself received its first high-level attack when 136 Liberators and 90 Fortresses accompanied by 150 fighters dropped over 580 tons of high explosive on railway yards there and again at Bucharest.

Bombers of 15th AF deliver a tight pattern of high explosive in the railway yards on the Southern outskirts of Ploieşti. Damage and craters from previous attacks are evident. Attempts at a smoke screen can be seen in the top left corner on the perimeter of the Colombia-Aquila refinery. The Astra Romană/Phoenix Orion group are one the right and accepting some punishment. At least one tank is burning and one other has collapsed. (Courtesy Colonel John H. Kirk USAF)

14/15 April

After the RAF's small debut on Easter eve, their next visit was another mining foray, this time deeper into Romania, on this Friday night. 178 Squadron provided eleven Liberators. Four of them successfully mined the Danube between Oriahovo, on the Bulgarian bank and Turnu Măgurele, some 85 kilometres downstream on the Romanian side. Another Liberator laid mines in the navigable channel of the River Jiu, 20 kilometres south of Craiova. However, in this early spring evening, gathering haze and river mist prevented the final four operating aircraft from finding their 'beds' in the river. They brought their mines back. In spite of that, 30 Mark 5 Type A mines were successfully laid without loss by enemy action. The remaining two aircraft crashed badly in Italy. 'R-Robert' (EV 920) captained by Lieutenant K. Shaw SAAF crashed on take-off at Celone killing three crew. His fellow South African, Lieutenant H.E. Rogan's 'D-Dog' (EV 825) crashed 5–6 kilometres north of the airfield, a kilometre east of the small village of San Marco. There were no survivors. Ten men and two aircraft in exchange for 30 mines – not perhaps an encouraging striking rate with which to open an offensive. One thin report suggests that Bucharest, Ploieşti and Craiova also received night-bomber visits that night, but that cannot be corroborated.

Saturday 15 April

The next morning, 271 B-24 Liberators dropped 648 tons of high explosives on Bucharest railway yards. The USAAF's Combat Chronology lists this raid as 448 aircraft and includes Ploieşti railways as a target and so does Rust's History of the 15 AF. Contemporary USSAFE figures, however, show only 271 aircraft attacking Bucharest.

15/16 April

That same night and into Sunday morning, 16 April, 205 Group made its first bombing attack against a Romanian objective. It was launched by the usual signal from HQ 15 AF:

TO AOC 205 GP
FROM TWINING
FE 752
SECRET
15 APR 44
PRIMARY TARGET 15/16 APR 44 TURNU SEVERIN MARSHALLING YARDS AND RAIL FACILITIES. ALTERNATES ARE DIVIDED EFFORT PIOMBINO, LEGHORN, PORTO SAN STEFANO AND SHIPPING. DAY BOMBERS ATTACKING PLOIESTI/BUCHAREST AND NIS

At the same time a single Wellington from 236 Wing dropped over 500,000 leaflets each on Arad and Timişoara to the north of the Carpathians.

The three Wings together launched 92 Wellingtons and, although six returned early, this was the largest night-bomber force to be sent against one target in the Mediterranean Theatre up to that time. The 205 Group ORB remarks that:

> . . . the 83 Wellingtons known to have attacked the target carried out an extremely well-concentrated attack. Many bursts were seen on the yards and across the railway workshops. One 4000 lb HE burst on the East side of the yards, causing a huge explosion followed by fire and a column of black smoke. Another hit the grain silo and started a good red fire. There were three main concentrations of fire – a rectangular mass in the region of the silo with smoke to about 10,000 feet, an intense fire with frequent explosions in the centre of the yards and a fire in the area of the naval workshops. The target was a mass of flames when the aircraft left, visible for 100–150 miles. Over 150 tons of bombs were dropped.

V for Victor of 150 Squadron taking off from Regina in the hands of FO IM Jones DFC
(Courtesy IM Jones)

There were no losses due to enemy action but two Wellingtons from 104 Squadron collided over base on return killing all ten aircrew. They were LP 146 'A-Apple' captained by Sergeant V.R. Chadwick and HE 344 'U-Uncle' flown by Flight Sergeant F.W. Gissing. These two aircraft make up the total of 92.

Warrant Officer Donald C. Twigg, an RAAF pilot in 70 Squadron, recalls that it was his twentieth operation and his notebook for the day recorded

No cloud but very hazy. Told to expect no flak but met up to 30 guns who were really out to get us. Shot up by 12 guns before target. Nearest ever – heard and felt many loud explosions. Target well pranged for over half an hour with good fires started. 5 hours 45 minutes in the air. Took off at 2040 hrs with 9 x 500 lb HE each with .025 second delay. My Navigator, Sergeant Peter Gadbury's de-briefing notes add 'River and Island identified. Bombed in one stick from 8,000 ft at 2327 hrs aimed at east end of railway yards. Good burst seen. Whole of target area left covered in smoke.' New bods on the Squadron often had one trip with an experienced crew and we had a 2nd Nav that night.

Pilots of A Flight 70 Squadron at Tortorella, March 1944

Left to Right:

Standing –FS S. Sinclair RAAF; FS D. Nihill RAAF; FS L. Fallon RAAF; FS R. Shafto (2nd tour); FS D.C. Twigg RAAF; FS Mole RAAF; FS G.A. Seagrove. FS Lawton RAAF.

Sitting – FS Lewis; Plt Offr J.A. Gibson (2nd tour); Lt N.K. Kinkeed-Weeks SAAF; Sqn Ldr E. Pilley – Sqn Comd (2nd tour); Flt Lt H.C. Bownas – 2IC; Lt A.F. Deelman SAAF; WO Smithson DFM (2nd tour);

In Front – FS K.E. Turley RAAF; FS J.G. Custance RAAF

(Courtesy D.C. Twigg)

The Air Bomber in a Wellington has a ringside seat and Flight Lieutenant I.R. (Ivan) Dobson of 104 Squadron took full advantage.

> Our take-off was 2000 hours. The target markers were somewhat off to the left but illumination was sufficient to see the target. We bombed at 2301 hours on a heading of 300° from 7000 feet. Our load was 6 x 500 lb and 1 x 250 lb bomb. The photo flash did NOT function too well. On the return leg we encountered only light calibre flak. The rest of our crew were our pilot, Squadron Leader L.W. Richards who was OC B Flight, *John Elsmore the Navigator, Robert Ford in the rear turret, and the Wireless Operator whose name I cannot recall – he was a 'spare bod'. The aircraft was Wellington Mk X 'T-Tommy' MF 871 and was equipped with a Mk XIV bombsight. We landed at base at 0235 hours. The bombload was relatively small because we had to carry overload tanks.

The Mk XIV bombsight was an important part of the night-bombers's armoury. Ivan Dobson described it as being, 'vastly superior' to the Mk IX CS Bombsight. The principal advantages were:

1. Course, height and airspeed were fed into the sight from the aircraft's instruments. Therefore any variations were automatically compensated for as the bomber approached the target.

2. The windspeed and direction were set manually, as well as the terminal velocity (TV) of the bomb being dropped.

The sighting device had a transparent graticule 4–6 inches long and 1–1½ inches wide pivoted on the longitudinal axis. This was designed so that it would pivot through half the angle of bank of the aircraft so that in a 30° bank the graticule would move 15°. Much of the detail of its operation of the sight is now hazy, but I do recall that it was possible to take some evasive action during the approach to the target and still maintain a reasonable line of sight. A shallow dive would have little effect, nor would a gradual bank. It was easier, however, and I preferred it, if the pilot could fly straight and level immediately before bomb release. A bank at that time could 'throw' the bomb out of the aircraft, as would any other violent manoeuvre.

Above the glass graticule there was a cylindrical device which projected a line and a cross-hair onto the glass. The image of the target came down the line towards the cross-hair, which was, of course, the dropping point. These lines were illuminated and the light could be dimmed or brightened as required. The pivot of the device was controlled by a gyroscope. With the Mk IX Bombsight all settings were applied manually and the ultimate accuracy of the drop depended on all pre-set conditions remaining constant.

142 Squadron fielded sixteen Wellingtons that night, the first of which took off from Amendola at 2100 hours, returning at 0245. The Squadron carried mixed loads: two lifted a 4000 lb HC each, two more carried marker flares only. Nine carried incendiaries and three had nine 500 lb HE bombs with a .025 second delay fuse. Most also carried leaflets. The Squadron claimed the raid to be a success, five crews reporting fires started by the raid to be visible over great distances on the way home. The briefed bombing height was 10,000 feet but it varied in practice. Flight Sergeant Peter Bath's Navigator's Log (Form 441) records that 'K-King' was over the target at 2305 hours at a height of 7,000 feet. The 'blitz' slot was 10 minutes. Squadron Leader H. Langton, the Squadron Commander, flew 'G-George' that night in the marker role with 54 4.5 inch Recce Flares. Just before midnight he saw a violent explosion and estimated that the flames rose to 1000 feet. Flight Sergeant Hill (RAAF), the pilot of 'H-Harry' believed the large fire was from petrol storage tanks: he could see it from 180 miles away. (Hill and his crew were later lost on the raid to Ploieşti on 9/10 August and are all buried in the Sofia CWGC Cemetery.) A New Zealand pilot, Flight Sergeant Blackett in 'U-Uncle' reported that the smoke from the fire seen by the Squadron Commander towered above him to about 10,000 feet. He also, alone, saw a Ju 88 night-fighter in the target area. Lieutenant Koekemoer's 'K-King' was holed by flak and the rear turret damaged. The blast from a large explosion in the target area as Sergeant C. Morgan began his bombing run hit 'Y-Yoke' and blew out the astrodome.

One of the 4000 lb carriers was 37 Squadron's 'R-Robert' flown by Flying Officer Stanton. The Navigator, Flying Officer Hinshelwood recorded in his Log that they began their run-in at 2254 hours through 'moderate accurate light flak' to drop their 'Cookie' from 6,000 feet at 2300 hours exactly. Its explosion started a big fire. They landed safely at 0145 hours after 5 hours 25 minutes in the air.

Flying Officer Roy Billen's rear-gunner, Sergeant Frank Graf, writes of violent evasive action over the target because of 'intense light flak'. The bomber was holed and a window blown out which damaged the tip of one propeller blade.

Warrant Officer Bob Ives DFM, a rear-gunner in 150 Squadron, remembers being briefed to expect a lot of opposition but there was only light flak and no fighters present at all. He adds:

A 250 lb bomb on the confident shoulders of a corporal armourer.
(Courtesy Imperial War Museum)

Some of the night-bombers' repertoire arranged for comparison. The 12,000 lb bomb was not used in the Mediterranean Theatre. (Courtesy Imperial War Museum)

. . . on returning to base, after six and a half hours' flying, we were expecting the same breakfast as we got in England, but no, we had stew.

Flying Officer Denys White DFC, in 150 Squadron's 'U-Uncle' dropped over 800 incendiaries into the fires in the target area. This was his fifth operation.

Mention of the 'blitz' in connection with allied bombing requires some explanation. It was a saturation bombing technique developed by Bomber Command to ensure that the bomber force was over the target for the minimum, most concentrated period of intense bombing. Greater safety for the bombers was an acknowledged advantage, but the principle was simply to overwhelm the target, its defence, the civil defence and rescue services. Day-bombers achieved this concentration of effort by attacking in packed formations, following the visual lead given by a designated formation commander. The night-bomber force could not operate in that way.

Having been given the target, the most critical planning factor to be determined was the 'blitz' time – 'Time over Target (TOT). From this the routes to avoid defended areas were defined and that, in turn, fixed the departure times. With as many as six launching airfields in use and three different types of bomber operating, each carrying varied weights of bombs, the intricacy of the staff-work and the planning becomes evident. Each individual aircraft was given a height to fly to the target and a height to attack from. As one captain put it:

. . . very accurate flying and navigation were essential.

Although no one could be persuaded to describe the detailed work of flight planning and co-ordination, given all these variables it was quite an achievement that operations were completed night after night with so few accidents. This level of proficiency required considerable skill on the part of the planners at their desks and, later, by the pilots and navigators at their controls and chart tables airborne in the dark. How there were not more mid-air collisions is difficult to understand. Except on moonlight nights a bomber crew rarely glimpsed others in the stream.

614 Squadron's Blind Illuminator (BI) aircraft of the Target Marking Force (TMF) or Pathfinder Force were ordered to arrive over the target at 'blitz' minus six minutes to put down flares. These lit up the ground so that the Halifaxes designated as Visual Illuminators (VIs), which followed three minutes later, could mark the Aiming Points (APs). The Target Marking Bombs (TMBs) used by the Illuminator's burst on the ground and burned with a bright colour. This colour was changed regularly to prevent the enemy from lighting false 'TMBs' safely away from the target, to mislead the main bomber

force. It was these TMBs which the individual Air Bombers in each aircraft sought as they guided their captains into their bombing runs during the 'Blitz' period. This could be as brief as three or four minutes or as much as ten to twelve, but the essential trick was to make it as sudden and brief as possible and get away.

614 Squadron's Halifax MK II Series 1A 'Y-Yoke' JN 894 at dispersal at Celone. This is an early model Series 1A: later ones had larger fins. Note the H2S rador scanner bulge beneath the fuselage. A wrecked Ju 88's tail assembly makes a useful workbench for servicing crews. (Courtesy Imperial War Museum)

70 Squadron's Don Twigg remembered that, before 614 Squadron's Halifaxes flew as the TMF, the Wellington squadrons' best crews were given the role 'illuminator' – to drop flares to mark and light up the target.

We had the job a few times.

If there was a delivery sequence specified it would be the lighter bombs first – 250 and 500 lbs followed by the bigger yields, 1000 and 4000 bombs with the incendiary attack bringing up the rear. In the short flash of the 'Blitz' this pattern might not be achieved, with the various yields intermingled.

Wellington crew 70 Squadron Tortorella April 1944

Left to right:

Fg Offr Harry James Air-bomber, WO Ray Gilroy Navigator, FS Ernest Hudson RCAF Rear gunner, Sgt John Bollam Wireless Operator and – in front FS D.C. Twigg RAAF Pilot

(Courtesy D.C. Twigg)

The accuracy of the drop would be recorded by a camera for analysis the next day. Each bomber's camera was mounted in a compartment in the rear fuselage and directed to look down vertically. When the Air-Bomber pressed his Bomb Release, a flash flare fell away with the bombs and the camera's shutter was opened. The flare had a small parachute and its clockwork timer was set for the aircraft's bombing height. The flare would explode with a bright magnesium flash from above as the bombs burst below.

Sunday 16 April

While recovering from the night's attacks, Turnu Severin was subjected to a further air assault the next day. In daylight 124 B-24 Liberators dropped 309 tons of high explosive onto the railway yards, the barracks and the airfield without loss. A further 128 B-24s attacked the principal Romanian aircraft factory at Braşov in the far eastern Transylvanian plain. Post-

strike photography showed that the factory 'Industria Aeronautica' was largely destroyed. Production of the domestic fighter as well as assembly and repair of Me Bf 109s was critically disrupted.

RP 60/PR/504 17JUN44 CROWN COPYRIGHT

By 17 June Turnu Serverin had been raided eight times and over 750 tons of high explosives had been dropped. This 60 Squadron (SAAF) Mosquito sortie photo shows the considerable damage to the railway yards (at top left) and cratering of the grass airfield area (lower right). Revetted aircraft dispersal sites are visible (right of centre) some with aircraft parked within. By now the switch to oil targets was complete and this city was to receive only one more attack, as a secondary target, on 22 July.
(Courtesy Ministry of Defence)

19/20 April

For the RAF's last visit to Romania that month, Flight Sergeant McCallum of 37 Squadron took Wellington Mk X LN 799, loaded with 448,000 leaflets for delivery at Craiova and Pitești. Thick haze in the Danube Plain prevented precise identification of the two cities, but the 'nickels', as leaflets were nick-named, were delivered without any attention from the enemy.

Friday 21 April

The day bombers of 15 AF attacked on two more occasions. On Friday 21 April a force of B-24s was tasked to raid Bucharest, 86 delivered 212 tons of high explosive into the railway/industrial complex in the north west of the city. Turnu Severin was the secondary target and 27 Liberators dropped 39 tons of bombs there. There were no bomber losses. However, the escort of 46 P-38 Lightnings and 48 P-51 Mustangs lost eight and one respectively in dog-fights en route, claiming 35 defending fighters.

Monday 24 April

On Monday 24 April, 290 Fortresses and Liberators attacked the marshalling yards at Ploiești, dropping 790 tons for a loss of 10 bombers. The fighter escort of over 220 P-38s and P-51s claimed 30 defending fighters without loss. Meanwhile 210 B-24s assigned to bomb railway targets in Bucharest, delivered 477 tons without loss.

On 28 April 614 Squadron, working hard to establish their Halifaxes and their crews into 205 Group's Target Marking Force, were warned of a move from Celone to Stornara planned for early May. The ORB talks of problems with the GEE navigational system and with the H_2S installations in the Halifaxes. Many of the problems had been:

> . . . overcome by ingenuity and improvisation. To a large degree the success was thanks to the initiative of 614 Squadron's Radar Officer.

Wing Commander R.R. Banker DSO DFC, OC 70 Squadron, described a typical Foggia-based operation in which they operated tactically as a Group to saturate the defences.

The 456 Bomb Groups target on 24 April 1944 was the Bucharest railway yards. Here smoke and dust from the exploding bombs drifts north-eastward over the outskirts of the city. The racecourse is clearly visible at the top of the picture. This has now gone. On the right is Herăstrău Lake. It and its surrounding parks and gardens form the major recreational area of the city. Standing in its prominent traffic circle is the Romanian Arc of Triumph (Arcul de Triumf) erected by the King after victory in World War I. (Courtesy Colonel John H. Kirk USAF)

On a typical operation the Group would take-off at about dusk. There were two squadrons (a Wing) at an airfield and each would hope to launch about twelve aircraft. It would take some fifteen minutes for the 24 aircraft to get off from each strip. Sometimes we climbed on track, but more often we circled and climbed to set course exactly from our base. It was always an impressive sight, whether from the ground or in the air, to watch 70-odd black-painted bombers climbing into the night sky then all wheel round and fly away in a compact bomber stream. Flying in the stream was a nerve-racking business with gently undulating aircraft above, below and on either side and as the darkness increased these gradually faded from sight, which made it all the more nerve-racking.

79

Air Marshal Sir John Slessor, Deputy C-in-C MAAF with Wing Commander R.R. Banker OC 70 Squadron at Tortorella. (Courtesy Dick Banker)

Dick Banker went on

> *Navigators had an exacting task ensuring that they arrived over a distant target within the designated blitz time. At a well-defended target the whole ground and sky would begin to erupt into a mass of gun flashes and*

bursting shells when the main force was still about two minutes away. Green TIs were dropped by the Halifaxes suing their H₂S radars, as near to the target Aiming Point (AP) as they could. Red TIs would follow to indicate any corrections. At this stage all aircraft had to fly straight and level up to bomb release and hold this for another half minute to allow the photo-flash to drop and for the camera to photograph the AP. After that, bombers were on their own somewhat. Most pilots peeled away in a diving turn,.not always in the homeward direction: it sometimes paid to turn the other way and then doubleback. On the way home, while still over enemy territory, the more alert crews kept going at a good speed and maintained a continuous rolling-search to make it as difficult as possible for radar-equipped night-fighters to home in. With the good GEE coverage over Italy there was rarely any difficulty in finding one's base and landing.

Air superiority over Italy allowed more relaxed conditions, contrasting with the permanent deep blackout which bombers found when returning to English bases.

Flight Sergeant George Carrod, Air Bomber in RAAF Flight Sergeant Geoff Brown's 142 Squadron crew, remarked that he was in the best position to see the target and the opposition.

It was always heavy during our attacks on oil targets, we were not able to identify much – just plenty of flak tracer shells, flares and searchlights. Generally I think our results were good. I personally was very much aware of how much life meant to me, so I was living in a permanent state of anxiety as, apart from being shot at, I was terrified of our bomb load going off during take-off and en route to the target. Quite often we carried delayed action and AP bombs which could be triggered quite easily. Needless to say, I never needed any opening medicines!

One night on the way to the target, we were as usual all tensed up with eyes on stalks looking for enemy fighters when, over the intercom, came the strains of Victor Sylvester. Our Wireless Operator used to play in a dance band and he had been able to tune into a station transmitting dance music – not for long!

The worst part of our trips, especially to oil targets, was the final run up to the target. One night the plane in front of us received a direct hit and just disappeared in a ball of flame so we were literally a few yards away from buying it ourselves.

Sergeant Aleph Palmer, Pilot of 142 Squadron, remembered that the black-out arrangements in the Balkans seemed not to exist:

You could see the lights being switched off ahead marking the advance of the bomber stream.

In spite of losses, Aleph Palmer thought that morale was good in the Squadron. He illustrated the impact of the loss rate simply. When his crew completed its thirty-fifth operation, the next most experienced crew were on number fifteen.

Wellington – Fuel and Overload Tanks

In his account of the 15/16 April Turnu Severin raid, Ivan Dobson observes that 'the bombload was relatively small because we had to carry overload tanks'. These tanks feature prominently in long-range operations and a description of their use would be worthwhile.

The balance of bomb load against fuel in computing the all-up weight for the Wellingtons was critical since the Romanian group of targets was near to the aircraft's limit of range. The 'normal' fuel tanks in each wing and in each engine nacelle had a total capacity of 750 gallons.

A Wellington Mk X in normal trim would consume about 96 gallons per hour (gph), giving the aircraft under eight hours of flying time. Heavily laden, fuel consumption could rise to as much as 100 gph, knocking the flying time down to seven and a half hours.

To increase the bomber's endurance, in addition to these normal tanks, two auxiliary self-sealing 140 gallon tanks could be installed, one in each outer bomb cell. A further 50 gallon tank could be stowed on the crew bed in the fuselage making a full additional 330 gallons available: an overall total of 1,080 gallons. These extra gallons stretched the normal flying time to over eleven hours and, with a full load, to over ten and a half hours.

Sergeant Derek Cashmore of 70 Squadron explained that the twenty-four feet long bombbay was divided lengthways into three compartments or cells. The bays were designed to take three 500 lb bombs in line each. When the overload tanks were fitted, each one occupied the space of three 500 lb bombs. So, on full overload, a Wellington's bombbay would only have room for three such bombs or six 250 lb. It was easy for a fitter and rigger to install the empty tanks using the integral on-board bomb winches but difficult to take down if any fuel remained inside. Robert Ginn of 104 Squadron remembers that, once these tanks were fitted and filled, or if targets were later changed, the crew was faced with taking them out with no means of drainage – and in about fifteen minutes. Using some runway tracking and some baulks of timber, he gingerly lowered the tanks onto the timber and metal and dragged them out from under on this makeshift sledge.

The Pilot's Notes for the Wellington advised that the fuel in the auxiliary tanks should be used early in flight and warns that the:

> . . . use of the tanks should be so arranged that both engines do not run short of fuel simultaneously. In all cases, when one engine fades for lack of fuel, open the pressure balance cock which will revive it immediately.

The Notes go on to recommend that shortly before these tanks run out, the feed is changed to main tanks on one side and the auxiliary emptied on the opposite side. This is repeated to empty the second overload tank. When only one such tank was carried, the Pilot was advised to balance his fuel feed using a wing tank on the opposite side.

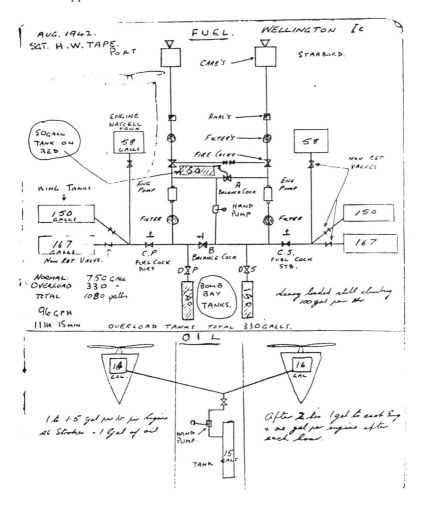

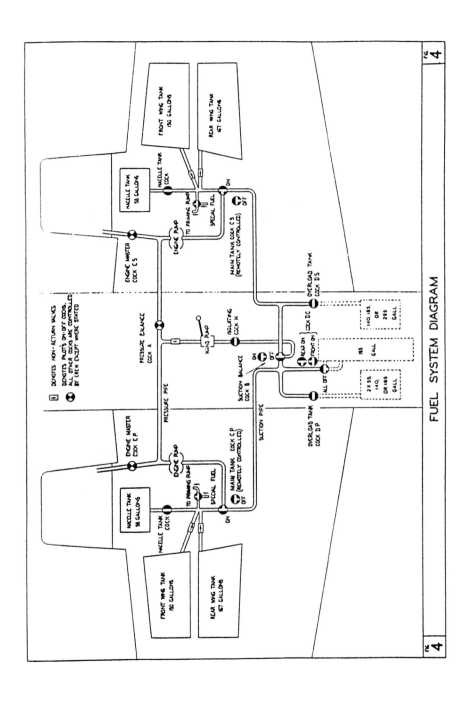

FUEL SYSTEM DIAGRAM

Nickels

The leaflets – or nickels – arrived at the airfield in truckloads and were distributed to the dispatching aircraft in tied bundles.

Pilot Officer F.W.J. Webb, a Wireless Operator of 37 Squadron described how Wellington crews usually delivered their nickels.

> The job was given to the Wireless Operator. The side Flare Shute, which pointed to the rear, had first to be extended into the slipstream, otherwise the nickels would be blown back into the aircraft. Cutting the string and any wrapping was carried out by flashlight because of the blackout. Cold and tired fingers were often the causes of a number of flashlights and dinghy knives being dispatched with the nickels.

In Liberator squadrons they were disbursed via the beam gun ports. Window or Chaff were set forth in the same way.

On one occasion a crew, who had only a few operations left to complete their tour, decided they would not invite unnecessary risks by hanging around alone in the well-defended night sky while some colleague stuffed paper down the flare shoot. So, as this bomber gained height climbing away over the Adriatic, members of the crew completed the stacking of the by now untied bundles of leaflets on top of the closed bomb-doors. Over the target the leaflets would be self-delivering: just open the bomb-doors and turn for home.

However, all was not well with this aircraft and the pilot decided to make an early return. He landed safely and taxied to dispersal where, before anyone could stop them, a willing ground crew winched the doors open from outside. Their intention was to make the bombs safe, but there were none. Instead the wind took the leaflets as they fell to the ground and the Foggia Plain was treated to a free delivery. They were a nuisance to flying for some time to come.

CHAPTER 7 - May

Summary

In May MASAF dropped a record bomb load of over 30,300 tons, 92% by day and 8% by night. Priority targets now included the enemy's oil production, in addition to the continued dislocation of the railways and the mining of the Danube. In the early part of the month 205 Group carried out seven raids against these targets. Allied Intelligence estimated that the refineries' monthly refining capacity of 709,000 tons of oil had been temporarily reduced to 317,000 tons by MASAF's operations in April and early May and that the original surplus refining capacity 'had become an ominous deficit'. Some of the damage was, of course, short-term only but much of it was sufficient to put some installations out of use for the rest of the summer.

Further blows against oil production were being launched by strategic bombers based in England. As a result of these twin offensives, the enemy's May output of finished refinery products was only 74% of the pre-raid level and the comparable output from synthetic plants was down to 80%.

From now onwards the enemy's oil production was to be the first priority bombing commitment.

205 Group's summary of May's operations noted that:

> . . . the most important of the strategic targets attacked this month was Bucharest, which was visited by aircraft of the Group for the first time on 3/4 May. Three attacks were made on this target during the month, the most successful appearing to be that on the night of 6/7 May when the industrial area was subjected to a good concentration of bombing.

The Group's ORB records other activities of note. Between 10 and 13 May 614 Squadron moved to Stornara and passed from command of 240 (Heavy Bomber) Wing to the 'administrative and operational control' of HQ 205 Group. The ORB comments:

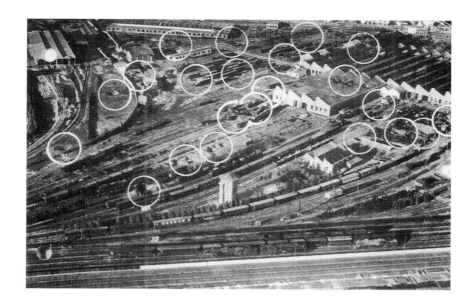

Night-bomber damage. The railway workshops in the Bucharest industrial suburb of Grivița. (Courtesy Romanian Ministry of National Defence)

> . . . 614 Squadron continues to train but are very dispirited because the target-marking technique is not being used on operations. Also, every failure to date has been hailed as proof that they cannot do their job. Until these are overcome and some failures accepted as inevitable, 614 Squadron's training is likely to be dispirited and disinterested.

31 Squadron (SAAF) flew its first operation to attack Kastelli airfield in Crete on Saturday 27 May, under command of 240 (HB) Wing, adding the second Liberator squadron to the Group's attacking power (to 178 Squadron, already operational).

The Group ORB also highlights problems with engineering and supply for the ageing (but much-revered) Wellington force. It noted that the remaining Mk IIIs were withdrawn and transferred to RAF ME. The Mk III had been the main Bomber Command type and was the first to have a four-gun rear turret. It was succeeded by the Mk X. The ORB remarked that a shortage of linen had grounded several operational aircraft.

The Wellington's fabric 'skin' was unusual for that period and earned it such nicknames as 'the canvas bomber' or – from the Americans – 'the goddamned ragbag'. One report, however, proudly tells of the Wellingtons surviving an Italian summer hailstorm rather better than the metal skinned B-

17s dispersed on the same airfield. Wellingtons did survive some heavy punishment from flak and fighters and return home safely, due without doubt to the strength of the geodetic airframe and its fabric covering. Tyres were also noted to be in critically short supply. In 236 Wing at Foggia Main only three operational take-offs and landings were permitted. In other Wings six to nine were acceptable. This shortage also affected the Liberators. Much of the problem was caused by the poor runway surfaces which were in constant and heavy use. Despite the care of the maintenance crews of US Army Engineers, a number of hazards remained. Runways and taxi-ways made of pressed steel planking or wire matting produced sharp edges. The long pins pegging them down could work loose and protrude. Such tarmac as there was would be in poor condition. Damaged aircraft shed bits and pieces at random. One of the less pleasant duties facing aircrew who were not listed in the Order of Battle on a particular night was to inspect the tyres of laden bombers as they turned onto the runway prior to take off. Choked with dust from the revving propeller blades two or three feet away, this was done by torchlight while being stung and bruised by flying debris blown up by the backwash – not to mention the noise.

150 Squadron's MF 244 returns with flak damage to her tail end. (Courtesy Wally Talbot)

The Group ORB had highlighted other problems in keeping the Wellington force operational – engines and aircrews. When supplies of Hercules VI engines were available, they were being issued against demands for Hercules XVI. A March entry had commented that if the situation did not improve mixed installations could have to be resorted to.

When one Mk XVI needed to be changed the practice had been to remove both and replace with Mk VIs, keeping the serviceable Mk XVI for the next engine change requiring that type. The poor airfield surfaces also caused a heavy attrition of propeller blade tips. Rotol Electric blades for Wellington Mk Xs gave the greater concern. Tip vortices sucked up small stones, mud and any other loose rubbish and the blades were damaged. At one time 330 Wing were averaging one breakage a day.

Low-level flying to practise minelaying in the Danube produced some accidents. SAAF Lieutenant Noel Cathrine's 142 Squadron Wellington hit an electric power cable suspended between two Adriatic Islands and crashed into the sea. The Rear Gunner, Sergeant Asplin, could not be saved, but the other four were rescued unharmed. The ORB tells of other Squadron activities which took aircrews away from routine operations and B-24 conversion courses were already featuring regularly, intermingled with other courses, crews completing their tours, leave and so on.

Pilot's instrument panel: Wellington Mk x 142 Squadron. (Courtesy A.B. Harrison)

The Raids

3/4 May

205 Group's attack on Bucharest on the night of 3/4 May was MASAF's first of the month against Romania. The marshalling yards in the north west of the city were the primary objective, to interfere with enemy supplies destined for their front in Moldavia.

205 Group's RAF Form 540 – Operations Record Book – shows that this should have been the third attack of the month. The preceding entry – for 2/3 May – reads:

> On this night 236 Wing were detailed to attack the shipyards at Turnu Severin and 330 and 240 Wings were to have carried out mining operations in the Danube, but both these operations were cancelled by the SASO at 1812 hours, owing to bad weather.

There must have been multiple sighs of relief about the Foggia Plain that evening.

The ORB entry for Wednesday and Thursday, 2 and 4 May, records 62 sorties and describes what must have been a difficult operation.

> 50 Wellingtons of 231, 236 and 331 Wings, 5 Liberators of 240 Wing and 7 Halifaxes of 614 Squadron operated. Unfortunately, a strong crosswind at base prevented 16 further Wellingtons of 236 Wing from taking off and several aircraft had to be diverted to other landing grounds on return for the same reason. Four Wellingtons returned early and one of them, 'N' of 150 Squadron, captain Flight Sergeant Hinchcliffe, is missing.
>
> The first flares were dropped by the Halifaxes in cloud cover by means of their special equipment, the Wellington illuminators were hampered by much haze and illumination generally seems to have been scattered over a wide area of the city. Although the yards received some bombing, it is believed that the greater proportion of the bombs fell in the town area. A big explosion was reported in the centre of the southern bend of the main marshalling yards. 66½ tons of bombs were dropped.

330 Wing's ORB entry for the night ends gloomily:

> . . . Cloud in target areas. Results poor.

Night bombers damage The bombs sometimes spilled over into residential quaters of Bucharest: bomb damage in Griviţa. (Courtesy Romanian Ministery of National Defence)

614 Squadron's Halifax 'W-William', a typical Pathfinder, took off at 2116 hours for the seven hour round trip flown by Flight Sergeant Buchanan. The rear-gunner, Pilot Officer G.J. Shepherd, noted in the Log Book that they dropped their flares into the target area from 19,000 feet, undisturbed by the enemy. Flying Officer Tom Scotland RAAF, a Halifax pilot found the flak defences extremely accurate. His own aircraft was damaged. The searchlights 'had a habit of holding on' on this and subsequent visits. The Blind Illuminators (BIs) were the flare droppers and went in at about 20,000 feet, which was the ceiling for a laden Halifax. Tom Scotland's crew, on the other hand . . .

> . . . thrived on the Visual Marker (VM) work because we could be sure that the target had been marked out. We went in lower than the BI aircraft but we had more freedom to dodge searchlights and flak. BIs had to go in steady, straight and level: not a nice feeling.

Tom Scotland completed 64 operations.

No individual recollections mark this raid as outstanding in the memory

91

although the formidable reaction from the defenders imprinted itself for the future.

The Romanian Army's record of this attack says nothing of that but notes that an unknown number of bombers attacked the capital between 0110 and 0130 hours in three waves. The first entered the country at 2315 hours and left at 0155 hours both over Calafat. The second overflew Bistreţul at 0025 hours and left via Maceşul at 0158 hours. The third was reportedly flying a course further east and entered Romania over Zimnicea at 0040 hours and left Romanian air space over Turnu Măgurele at 0150 hours. All waves left in a south-westerly direction. The report defines a wide area of the city where bombs fell, including the railway station and the industrial suburbs of Griviţa, Chitila, Militari and Dudeşti.

Night-bomber damage. The railway yards at Chitila in N.W. Bucharest.
(Courtesy Romanian Ministry of National Defence)

Warrant Officer K.E. Turley RAAF's Air Bomber, John Bodman, recorded in his Log Book that their 70 Squadron Wellington HE 794 'L-Love' took off from Tortorella at 2115 hrs and returned 8 hours 15 minutes later. Their load was a mixture – three 500 lb HE with a .025 second time delay (.025 TD) and two 250 lb Mk VI HE. 'L-Love' developed engine trouble during the return leg – 'guns and arms jettisoned over land, also all surplus equipment'. 104

Squadron's 'L-Love' also developed engine trouble but it was early in the flight and Pilot Officer K.C. Harrison RAAF made the decision to return to base. His Navigator, Flight Sergeant Peter Bath noted that they were airborne for four hours on this aborted mission.

Flying Officer James Grieve flying as Flying Officer Hugh Morton's Wireless Operator remembers 'slight opposition'. Their bomb load was the same as Turley's but four of them were 'hang-ups'. Flight Sergeant K. Hinchcliffe's Wellington was the only loss that night. All his crew survived, when HE 956 'N-Nan' crashed, to become the first RAF Prisoners of War (PW) of this story. The circumstances of the loss are not known now.

The Second Tour Crew

Sgt A.E. Hutchinson 'Hutch', Navigator

Sgt J.J. Prinsloo 'Dusty', Rear Gunner – from Rhodesia

Flt Hugh M. Morton, Pilot

WO R. York 'Yorky', Air bomber

FO J.F. Grieve 'Shorty', Wireless Operator of 142 Squadron with their Wellington MK X at Regina.

(Courtesy J.F. Grieve)

Friday 5 May

This was 15 AF's largest daylight force to date. Some 640 bombers with 240 long-range escorts attack Ploieşti as well as a German garrison at Podgorica in Yugoslavia. The USSAFE Air Intsum is more precise. 166 B-17s and 320 B-24s bombed Ploieşti, dropping 1,255 tons of high explosive. 185 Lightnings and 48 Mustangs provided the escort and claimed 23 enemy aircraft without loss. However, eighteen bombers were lost. At the same time Turnu Severin was the target for 39 B-17s dropping 177 tons of bombs for a loss of two bombers. A follow-up Intsum reported 'Recce photos following the attack on Ploieşti on 5 May show extensive and heavy damage to oil refineries. All buildings in the Astro-Romană group were severely damaged' – as well as the Phoenix Orion and the Standard Oil block. The assault on the oil industry had begun.

Cîmpina

5/6 May

That same night – Friday 5 May – the RAF joined in when 30 night-bombers sought out the Steaua Româna Refinery, some 30 kilometres north-west of Ploieşti, at Cîmpina. 205 Group's Operation Order reads

To: 231, 236 and 240 Wings. 330 Wing for information.
From: HQ 205 Group   A.269 MOST SECRET   MS61

IMMEDIATE
5 May 1944

Info. The STEAUA ROMÂNĂ Refinery at CÎMPINA is one of the biggest oil refinery plants in Romania and the marshalling yards are a vital part of the whole installation.

Intention. To destroy rolling stock and installations in or adjacent, to the STEAUA ROMÂNa marshalling yards at CÎMPINA.

Date. 5/6th May 1944

Execution
231 Wing, 236 Wing, 240 Wing
231 Wing: 23 Wellingtons
236 Wing: 18 Wellingtons
240 Wing: 10 Halifaxes (Freshmen)

TOTAL: 51 aircraft

Bomb loads

Wellingtons   (i)   500 lb MC TD .025 (with screamers)

          (ii)   4000 lb HC and number of overload tanks at discretion of Officers IC Operations

         (iii)   3 Illuminators from each Wing

         (iv)   NICKELS. 231 Wing C/RA/703
                  236 Wing C/RA/704

Halifaxes   Standard Newhaven complete with 1000 lb GP Tail Inst and 500 lb MC TD .025

Routes   **MAINFORCE.** Base – Lake Salso – Lake Scutari – R. Danube ($43^{\circ}50'N$; $22^{\circ}52'E$) – Point 'A' CRAIOVA – Point 'B' TIRGOVISTE – R. Danube ($43^{\circ}50'N$; $22^{\circ}52'E$) – Lake Scutari – Lake Salso – Base.

                HALIFAXES. At discretion of OC 240 Wing.

                POINT 'A'. Halifaxes will drop 3 x RED TMBs each, one of 6½ minutes and one of 2½ minutes duration, igniting at 3000 feet.

                POINT 'B'. As Point 'A' but GREEN.
                Note: TMBs will be dropped on centre of towns and it is hoped to mark the points over a period. 614 Sqn will notify this HQ direct of estimated times of burning of TMBs at Points 'A' and 'B'.

TOT (Time on Target)
                MAINFORCE:
                Blitz 0100 'B' hours.
                Blind Markers (Halifaxes): Z-5
                Visual Markers (Halifaxes): Z-3
                Halifax attack: Z-1

Illumination: 231 Wing: Z-2, Z-1, Z.
                236 Wing: Z-2, Z-1, Z.

ZERO TIME: 0500 'B' hours. ALL aircraft to IDENT 100 miles from base on Group's Ident Frequency. 'CHAFF' is to be carried Usual emergency airfields and Radio Ranges FOGGIA/TARANTO area. BARLETTA and MANFREDONIA searchlights will be on as required.

TOO 051250 B   Signed DRP Mills
(Time of Origin)   for Air Commodore AOC

The Group's ORB makes almost no attempt to disguise the reality that this was an 'oil raid', the railway yards being integrated into the oil working areas of the refinery. It goes on to record –

> with good weather and no cloud, our aircraft were able to make a successful attack. 7 Halifaxes and 41 Wellingtons operated; 5 aircraft returned early, two with unserviceable rear turrets. The target was attacked by 5 Halifaxes of 614 Squadron, 16 Wellingtons of 231 Wing and 19 of 236 Wing. Blind Marker Halifaxes dropped green and red TIs with great success and all aircraft were to attack the target in excellent illumination. Many direct hits were scored on the marshalling yards, the oil storage tanks NORTH and SOUTH of the yards, loading sidings and adjacent refinery buildings. Bombing seems to have been reasonably concentrated and at the end of the attack the whole area was covered with smoke. One aircraft reported an oil fire among storage tanks, with flames 200 feet high and smoke up to 2,000 feet. Three good fires among storage tanks to the NORTH of the yards were visible 60 miles away.

A post-strike reconnaissance photograph taken after on the morning of 6 May 1944 by a 60 Squadron SAAF Mosquito 205 Group's Wellingtons and Halifaxes had attacked the Steaua Română Refinery and the associated railway yards at Cîmpina. Several oil storage tanks are still well ablaze.

Ground opposition was slight, but several single and twin-engined enemy aircraft were seen, including Me 210s. Two Wellingtons fired on enemy aircraft. One Wellington, 'S' of 37 Squadron, captained by Flight Sergeant Cornwell was forced to ditch on the return journey. All the crew are safe except for the Wireless Operator, Sergeant Mills, who is missing and believed drowned. Two Wellingtons, 'B' of 37 Squadron, captain Sergeant Parkes and 'R' of 40 Squadron, captain Flight Sergeant Royle are missing and may have been shot down over the target. 34.6 tons of bombs dropped.

231 Wing's ORB adds that crews reported big fires still burning in the Ploiesti area after the daylight attentions of the American bombers earlier on 5 May. The sixteen Wellingtons which pressed home their attack delivered thirty-nine 500 lb MC (.025 TD), twenty-six 250 lb USA-Type N1 and 300,000 Nickels.

Flight Sergeant Peter Bath, as usual navigating for Ken Harrison in 104 Squadron's 'B-Baker', has kept his Navigator's Log, which is a fund of data. Their load was six 500 lb HE which they delivered at 0057 hours, three minutes from 'blitz' from 10,000 feet. The illumination markers at two points on the approach went off dead on time and in place. From the flourish of his signature below the entry '0410 LANDED' it seems to have been a satisfactory night.

Night-bomber damage. Another view of the Steaua Română Refinery at Cîmpina early on 6 May 1944. The refinery buildings in the foreground show well the interior walls built to confine damage and fire to the area hit.

The Group's bombers attacked two targets on this night – the action competing with Cîmpina was a Danube 'gardening' operation, which had been postponed on 2 May. Ten aircraft from 142 Squadron laid their mines successfully near Smederovo in Yugoslavia and Flight Sergeant Derrick Burns of 150 Squadron recalls that this was an interesting operation for him because they carried passengers. The BBC War Correspondent, Dennis Johnston and his engineer, Bob Wade, flew in 'Q-Queenie' – along with the standard load of two 1000 lb mines, to make a recording for the BBC's 'Into Battle' programme.

The Cîmpina raiders reported seeing single and twin-engined enemy aircraft in the target area and it is difficult to substantiate these claims or otherwise. Such sightings were not unique, over Romania or anywhere else in 205 Group's inventory of targets – but they were unusual. There were no single-engined night-fighters deployed in this area. Assuming that the sightings were indeed of single-engined aircraft, perhaps it may be assumed that, as it was a clear night, some adventurous day-fighter pilots had been able to join the melée. Some aircrew believed that singles and twins worked together using the latter's radar to direct the former onto a target.

Night-fighters – 'Delayed Confirmation'

Coming out from Bucharest the gunner gave a yell,
'Two fighters, Skipper, closing from the rear'.
One single and one twin and both it seemed to him
Were getting most uncomfortably near.

I praised him for his vigilance and dived away in haste,
But I'd never met night-fighters out in packs.
So I privately considered that the aircraft at the stern
Were Wellingtons and went on to relax.

Thirty-eight years later a reunion at a pub
Turned up a chap researching that attack.
His father, a Rear Gunner, downed a Junkers 88,
But a Focke-Wulf shot him down right after that.

The Junkers had the radar, the Focke Wulf the fire power.
It had taken me some years to find that out.
So my eagle-eyed Rear Gunner had most surely saved our lives.
If we meet again its Champagne – and my shout!

Len Fieldhouse, 150 Squadron, Foggia

Both the Luftwaffe's standard night-fighters were encountered in the Balkan skies. The Me 110 was easy to manoeuvre, climbed well and, being mass-produced, was available in quantity. However, its short tactical endurance prevented long pursuit and was a major drawback. It was gradually replaced by the Ju 88, which though slower and less easy to handle, could remain in the air for five hours. It was constantly being modified and for a time, its crews disliked it. Gradually, however, they came to see that its advantages outweighed its defects and in their skilled hands it became a formidable weapon. It was this type which was more often seen over south-eastern Europe.

A number of crews reported seeing a bomber shot down in the target area. This was Flight Sergeant D.H. Royle's 'R-Robert' of 40 Squadron. All five crew were killed when the aircraft crashed at Valea Lunga, [Crash Site 1] 8 kilometres west of the target: the first of 205 Group's crews to be left to rest in Romania.

The other loss mentioned in the Group ORB was 37 Squadron's 'B-Baker'. In fact it was Wellington HZ 814 'W-William'. Its pilot, Flight Sergeant P.D. Parkes, managed to bring William almost all the way back only to be lost at sea in the Adriatic with all hands. After attacking the target the aircraft reported that it was losing its starboard engine. The last broadcast position put him as crossing the Yugoslav coast south west of Lake Skadarsko – dead on track for home, having succeeded in clearing the 6000 feet high mountains in his path.

Saturday 6 May

Cîmpina's respite was brief. It appeared on the day-bombers' target list for the next day and they struck only eleven hours after the last night raider had turned for home. 134 B-24 Liberators dumped 328 tons of high explosive, escorted by 42 P-47 Thunderbolts. Six Liberators were lost. This was part of a much more wide-ranging sortie into Romania than had been attempted before. The day's main target was Braşov which received nearly 650 tons of bombs from 154 Fortresses and 143 Liberators. Their escort of 94 Lightnings and Mustangs claimed to have destroyed seven defending fighters. One bomber was lost. Three other targets were also attacked. Turnu Severin was raided by 34 B-17s after two had returned to base. There were no losses and 101 tons were dropped. Craiova was hit by 210 tons of high explosive from 94 B-24s. One B-24 was lost when 103 of them took 240 tons to Ploieşti with an escort of 70 Lightnings.

6/7 May

The pressure was maintained – 205 Group returned that Saturday night, 6 May, with an attack on Bucharest's industrial area and with smaller attacks elsewhere. The USSAFE Intsum reports baldly that 65 Wellingtons, 8 Liberators and 7 Halifaxes operated, but that only a total of 57 aircraft were known to have attacked, dropping 76.2 tons within the target area for a loss of four bombers. One defending fighter was claimed. The 205 Group ORB confirms these statistics and identifies the early returns as seven Wellingtons:

> The remaining aircraft all identified and attacked the target, which was well-illuminated. The bombing was concentrated on the industrial area and at least four fires were started, including two big ones. Direct hits were observed on buildings, factories and marshalling yards. Enemy fighters were present and Wellington 'P-Peter' of 150 Squadron, captained by Flight Sergeant Walker, shot down a single-engined enemy aircraft.

Night-bomber damage. The railway yard in NW Bucharest.
(Courtesy Romanian Ministry of Defence)

Another Wellington, 'T-Tommy' of 104 Squadron was followed by an Me 109 from 0044 hours until 0101 hours between 5,000 and 6,000 feet. The fighter opened fire but missed the Wellington. Return fire of four or five bursts of tracer was seen spraying round the nose of the fighter which was not seen again.

The Group ORB concludes:

> Three Wellingtons, 'Q' of 40 Squadron (Flight Sergeant MASTERS), 'O' of 40 Squadron (Warrant Officer COAPE-SMITH) and 'Q' of 150 Squadron (Warrant Officer CLARKE) are missing as is Liberator 'H' of 178 Squadron, captained by Flight Sergeant MOLYNEUX. There were several reports of aircraft, believed Wellingtons, crashing in flames over or near the target area.

The Romanian Ministry of Defence has produced a summary of this operation, starting with the bomber stream concentrations between 2106 and 2212 hours over the Albanian coast to the south-west of Tirana and entering Romanian air space between Bistreţu and Zimnicea in four waves. The enemy put the number of attacking aircraft at about 150 and, as for 3/4 May's operation, the areas bombed show that the attack was spread widely over the city. Some barracks were hit.

Night-bomber damage. The building damaged here is the Headquarters of the Romanian 1st Air Defence Regiment. In the foreground, alongside the line of trees bordering the Cemetry are the Italian Army's graves from World War 1.

(Courtesy Romaian Ministry of National Defence)

The 'blitz' was actually twelve minutes between 0026 and 0038 on 7 May during which time 204 500 lb and 53 250 lb bombs were dropped from 7,500–12,000 feet by the Wellington force. The weather was rated as 'good with some haze' but a number of aircrew recall moonlight bathing the scene. Len (Tubby) Fieldhouse of 150 Squadron recalled that it . . .

> . . . was a full moon and visibility was about 20 miles enabling the enemy
> to send up day fighters. It must have been like shelling peas for them. We
> could see the Danube stretching away for an incredible distance.

231 Wing put up 23 Wellingtons, but three returned early, one using excessive fuel, one with an unserviceable rear turret and one with engine trouble. 236 Wing only had one early return and twenty went on to bomb the target. Sixteen 330 Wing Wellingtons attacked. Enemy opposition was uneven. Some reports spoke of 'intense heavy' flak, while others experienced only 'moderate'. About 25 searchlights, including 'blue masters' were in use, mainly ineffectively. Four to six AA guns were in action at Niš, en route in Yugoslavia and some heavy guns in the Giurgiu defences opened fire. The Group ORB records.

> Two twin-engined and several single-engined aircraft, some showing white
> lights, were seen in the target area.

The several reports of aircraft in trouble were based on some unusual sightings mentioned by crews during de-briefing:

1. At 2328 hours at 10,000 feet north-east of Niš, 'a big red ball of fire seen at 7–8000 feet which fell and burned on the ground for two minutes'

2. At 0018 hours at 11,000 feet over Balta Greacă (a marshy, water meadow area north-east of Giurgiu) 'a believed Wellington was seen to explode at 5,000 feet and drop slowly to earth'

3. At 0029 hours at 9,500 feet, 'in the target area, a parachute was seen just below a Wellington'

4. At 0040 hours a Rear Gunner reported 'air-to-air firing at 10,000 feet just after leaving the target area.'

5. At 0057 hours at 10,000 feet, approximately 70 miles west of the target, 'a Wellington was seen flying south and shortly after, a large dull red glow was seen on the ground, visible for 23 miles.'

6. At 0108 hours, west of Caracal, 'a Wellington was seen in flames at 11,000 feet. It broke into pieces and crashed. Two parachutes were seen to

open'. This was observed by Flying Officer Frank Hinshelwood who was navigating 'N-Nan' of 37 Squadron and taking a sighting through the astrodome at the time. They had delivered their three 500 lb and two 250 lb bombs into the well-lit target at 0030 hours, without incident.

Flying Officer Roy Billen of 104 Squadron flew his twenty-fifth operation that night in MF 238. His Rear-Gunner Frank Graf made a full entry in his Log Book after their 7 hour 40 minute round trip:

> Bombload 6 x 500 lb plus 1 overload of petrol. Excellent weather throughout the trip. No trouble finding pinpoints. Bombed from 12,000 feet on Halifax illumination which was bang on. Opposition 40–50 guns 15–20 searchlights put up very spirited defence until Roy started feeding them CHAFF (WINDOW). Two kites from the Wing failed to return. Seen one shot down in flames. Also one crashed on runway.

That operation completed 215 hours of night-flying for Frank Graf.

RAAF Flying Officer Keen's 142 Squadron Wellington was hit by flak near Turnu Măgurele on the way to the target. The rear turret's hydraulic and electrical systems were damaged and the gunner slightly injured. Keen pressed on to the target only to find that his bomb load remained hung-up. It was eventually jettisoned over the sea on return.

Flight Sergeant Walker's engagement in 'P-Peter' of 150 Squadron was brief but decisive. The enemy fighter was first sighted by the Pilot and Air Bomber at 0011 hours 8–10 miles west of Balta Greacă, some 200 feet higher than the bomber. It passed from port to starboard 500 yards ahead and then turned onto a parallel course to starboard, dived away and was lost to view. The Wireless Operator moved into the astrodome to cover the bomber's starboard side and the Rear Gunner, WO Bob Ives, covered the port side. Two minutes later the Rear Gunner reported an enemy aircraft 600 yards on the starboard quarter. The fighter banked to port then to starboard and came in. The Wellington corkscrewed and Bob Ives opened fire at 5–600 yards . . .

> I had to adjust my guns higher as I saw the tracers going under the fighter. As soon as I lifted the guns I saw the tracers hit the aircraft cockpit and, after a few seconds burst, I could see that the plane was on fire, but the pilot closed to about 100 yards and was still firing his guns. He was diving down on to us but missed and continued until he hit the ground. The fighter broke into two pieces, one of which burned fiercely on the ground. I did not see him bale out. We continued with our duty to bomb Bucharest and we found it was well fortified with anti-aircraft shells bursting all

round us and a lot of searchlights. After we dropped our bombs, the skipper decided to go and see just where the fighter had fallen and we saw it was still on fire. Johnny took a fix and then we returned to base. On being de-briefed, the Officer asked me if I had fired my guns. I said, 'Yes', so he replied, 'It was you who shot down the fighter', as the other crews who had returned before us reported they had seen the fighter shot down. Next day we went to see what damage, if any, we had received but the ground crew had given our plane a good examination had found no bullet holes.

Len Fieldhouse, airborne that night in 'Z-Zebra' LN 792 as an Illuminator with eighteen flares on board, was impressed by the enemy activity in the target area

on the way back, when I saw the situation and realised that there was no chance of the force remaining in a stream, I dropped down to 2000 feet and came home round the contours, chancing the odd aerodrome defences and flak concentrations. I was, by this time a pretty old hand, this being my fifty-eighth operation out of a total of 64.

Ieuan Jones DFM, who was flying 'second dickey' with Len Fieldhouse that night, noted that even low down the round trip still took over eight hours.

240 Wing's sixteen Halifaxes and Liberators brought four 1000 lb bombs as well as over 80 more 500 lb and 32 30 lb incendiaries to the attack, which alone totalled over 24 tons. One aircraft had the discomfort of being coned by eighteen searchlights but managed to fly out before flak or fighters could take advantage. 614 Squadron was pleased with its target-marking for which the Blind Markers used yellow TIs. The Visual markers confirmed these with red and green TIs. They, arriving first, assessed that the defences had up to 40 guns in action.

The Group ORB listed three Wellingtons and one Liberator as being lost that night. Research has been able to amplify what fate did overtake these men and their aircraft. The ORB had one name wrong. 40 Squadron's 'Q-Queen' (LN 982) was piloted by Flight Sergeant K.C.J. Martin (not Masters). This must have been the incident reported at 0018 hours because 'Q-Queen' did crash at Balta Greacă [Crash Site 2A] that night without loss of life. Ken Martin and his four crew jumped clear before the aircraft exploded. They drifted south on their parachutes, were picked up in Bulgaria and spent the next four months as wretched prisoners of war (PW) of the Bulgars.

40 Squadron's other loss was LP 128 'O-Orange'. Warrant Officer John Coape-Smith RAAF was the Pilot. This was the Wellington seen at 0108 hours west of Caracal because 'O-Orange' finally crashed near the village of

Castranova [Site 2], some 30 kilometres west of Caracal. Frank Hinshelwood in the astrodome of 37 Squadron's 'N-Nan' had not seen the other two parachutes. John Coape-Smith and three of his crew survived to becomes PWs in Bucharest. The Rear Gunner, Flight Sergeant Ray Sauerwald RAAF lost his life. Flight Sergeant Gordon Cormie, Navigator and Air Bomber, Flight Sergeant George Dealtry, have given very graphic accounts of that fateful night's adventures. Gordon Cormie sets the scene.

> John Coape-Smith the Pilot, Dick Kilroy the Wireless Operator and Ray Sauerwald the Rear Gunner were the three Australians and unfortunately Ray, who had just been married the day before he left Australia, was killed. George Dealtry was from Yorkshire. We had all crewed-up at OTU in Moreton-in-the-Marsh and from then on we held a very tight sort of friendship with each other and the other crews. There was one other crew who we were especially close to and who actually played an important part in what happened later on. The Pilot was Keith Martin. We used to more or less fly on the same type of jobs.
>
> About a week before we were shot down we were due to go on 'rest' at a place near Sorrento. The Squadron had an old Wimpey Mk I and two crews used to fly to this rest camp and the two crews who were there would fly it back. This was fairly common practice. However, the aircraft had broken down and was delayed at Sorrento, leaving us at Foggia. Two days later the plane still had not come back.
>
> On the day of the 6th we had a new plane, 'O-Orange'. Our regular aircraft, 'W-William', had been lost two days before. We had a busy morning test flying it. About 3 o'clock we went to briefing to be told that we had a Romanian job that night – the marshalling yards in Bucharest.
>
> At about the same time, I think it was the same day, we got a bottle of beer. It was the first time we had ever got a bottle of beer all the time we had been out in the Middle East and North Africa. It was Canadian beer, I remember that, although I never drank it. We left it for the next morning when we came back. This was one of the memories we had later on when we did not come back: there was a bottle of beer waiting for us.
>
> We took off and had a reasonably uneventful flight – a bit of flak here and there, not a lot to get worried about – until we were approaching Bucharest. There was no sign of the target-marking Halifaxes. We were at 12,000 feet and the Halifaxes were going in at about 15,000, and we expected the target to be marked. We were there on time. We may even have been about a half a minute early and, as we hung around, the flak was getting hotter and hotter and there was still no sign of any pathfinders. The night was quite clear, the moon was bright, and as we could see the target,

John decided we would make a run, so the Bomb Aimer got ready and we went in to make our attack.

My position in the aircraft at that time was standing on the Pilot's right, keeping an eye open on the starboard side of the aircraft, while he concentrated on flying straight and level. I had a good view of the fireworks. We had just finished our run and the Bomb Aimer had just said, 'Bombs away', when I saw that there were some dark images like parachutes ahead of us. We had to dive below them when of a sudden these things burst. They were actually the parachute flares which the Pathfinders had dropped. They were about 3,000 feet above us. Somebody had goofed because these flares were supposed to burst 2,000 feet above the ground and some clown must have set them to burst 2,000 feet from the parent aircraft. So here we were right among all these flares like a Christmas cake lit with candles. In the middle of this Ray Sauerwald, the Rear Gunner, called out 'There's a night-fighter below us!'

We were probably about 60 aircraft that night and the Briefing Officer had told us there could be about 50 night-fighters there: more than one night-fighter for every two aircraft. So we were picked up by this night-fighter – I am not quite sure what he was as I did not see him – probably an Me 110. He came underneath us and I think the Gunner had a burst at him but he could not depress his guns far enough because he was right underneath. In the meantime we were trying to do some evasive action as well as getting away from these flares. The night-fighter must have just lifted his nose and we flew through everything he could throw at us. He hit us several times with shells and machine gun fire and pulled away. About five minutes later he came into attack us again. Dick Kilroy called that he had been hit. As the Wireless Operator his position during the raid was in the astrodome where he would look after the top side of the aircraft. I went back to Dick and found him hanging on to the geodetic structure of the aircraft. I took him back to my cabin and sat him down. There was blood all over the place. A shell burst had hit him in the back of his leg and some fragments were stuck in his legs, one had passed right through his kneecap. I ripped his pants up and I went back for some first aid dressings from the kit which was in the middle of the aircraft. Of course, it was completely dark and then I found a hole in the bottom of the aircraft where the first aid kit should have been, just a hole – a whole section of the aircraft missing. The attack had cut all our hydraulic lines, the wheels came down and our gun turret was out of commission. I had to go to the front turret for a shell dressing stowed there. I brought it back and packed up to the wound on the back of Dick's leg, using his ripped-up pants. At that moment the fighter came in again for a second attack and did the same thing again – right underneath us – lifted his nose and again we flew through everything he had to throw. Well, the old aircraft still carried on. We were losing fuel by this time. We were as far home as Craiova when he made his third pass. By this time we were down to about our stalling speed. We were so badly in trouble that it would not have taken much to knock us down anyway, so he used the same tactic as before, but we still flew on with no more injuries. We did not know whether the Rear Gunner was killed in this attack or whether he died later on. At this time I shouted that I could smell smoke. The Bomb Aimer whipped down the fuselage with an extinguisher to discover that it was only a parachute burning. He deftly put that fire out by stamping on it when, all of a sudden, the whole aircraft burst into flames.

The parachute was actually a flare 'chute: one of six parachute flares carried in the back of the aircraft. We had not used them because the target was so well illuminated. This one had been hit by a bullet which had triggered the mechanism. The only thing for it to do was to ignite and it blew its parachute back inside the aircraft, which meant we could not even launch it. The 'chute just held the flare in position. The aircraft now caught fire with this big magnesium flare burning fiercely in the back with oil and petrol all over the place.

Up to now we had been so busy that none of us had our parachutes on, so I went forward into the cabin to get my 'chute and one for the wounded Wireless Operator. He said he was not going to jump and I said 'Damn right you are!' I took him to the front hatch, opened it and sat him on the edge and said 'OK, just remember to pull'. Then I gave the pilot his 'chute. The Bomb Aimer went before me and the Pilot got out later. So that was the end of 'O-Orange', the nice new aircraft.

I landed in some woods near Craiova and started off westward when I heard somebody call my name. It was the Pilot sadly nursing a sore head. He had banged his head when he baled out and he was pretty well shaken up and did not know where he was. He had lost his flying boots and had nothing on his feet. He could not walk – he had sprained or busted an ankle, we were not sure at the time. We eventually settled down for the night together because I realised then I could not leave him and we would see if we could find some help next morning. When daylight came I saw a little peasant boy and I tried to explain that I was an aviator, generalising in language and he beckoned us to go with him. We did not know if we were in friendly hands. We reached a little camp of peasants and gypsies. Before too long the local Home Guard came along and arrested us. We knew that two of us were safe, anyway. While we were counting our blessings we said, at the same time, 'Keith will be away with his crew down to Sorrento today and our beer will be gone. Someone will have taken that'.

We eventually ended up in a police cell in the village near Craiova. They brought in the Bomb Aimer, George Dealtry, and then Dick Kilroy. We had no idea how he had managed it, but he was two miles away from his parachute when they picked him up. How the hell that Aussie had the guts with all his wounds to walk two miles before being picked up I will never know, but he was as hard as nails. Anyway, the four of us were safe, even though two of us were badly injured. They took us to see the aircraft later on and we could see Ray Sauerwald's body still trapped in his rear turret. He probably never had a chance of baling out, he was about 6ft 2in: he was too big for a rear gunner.

That was the end of us. We were taken from there to Craiova, which was not too far away and we were paraded in the police cells, poked at with sticks as if we were bears in a zoo. Then we went on a street-car or train in Craiova from one end of the city to the other.

George Dealtry's recollection matches Gordon Cormie's and he has been able to add an extra touch. When discussing the escape from the burning Wellington with John Coape-Smith in 1986, John had told him:

. . . how amazed and relieved he was to receive the parachute from Gordon's hands as only seconds earlier we had discovered a 'chute badly damaged by fire, leaving us one short. He was also able to shed light on the providential appearance of the sixth parachute. Apparently, one of the ground-crew had been very keen to accompany us on an operation for the experience. Johnny had agreed, expecting the target to be an uneventful milk-run in Italy. When the target was changed to Bucharest the ground wallah's trip was postponed, but his 'chute was left on the aircraft, fortunately for Johnny.

George Dealtry goes on to describe his sensations on baling out:

. . . relief, closely followed by a silence that could almost be felt.

He remembers:

. . . there was a good moon and far below I could clearly see the silvery snake-like outline of a large river which had to be the Danube.

His spell of freedom was more dramatic than that of Gordon and John.

I landed safely in a forest with plenty of soft leaf mould in which to bury my 'chute. I felt it best to travel as far as possible before daylight, but I had not been walking for long when I was startled by the sound of dogs barking, not too far away. My first thought was that these could be Army tracker dogs and my second thought was to find a climbable tree as soon as possible, hoping to escape notice. I found the tree alright, show me an unclimbable tree in that situation, but I did not escape notice. A pack of dogs burst through the undergrowth howling and snarling as they headed in my direction. I was treed. During the next hour or so whenever they appeared to be losing interest, I would loosen my belt, with which I had secured myself to a branch in case I fell asleep and down the tree – and started to descend,hoping to get away before daybreak. However, each time I would be thwarted by one of the dogs barking, which brought all the pack back in snarling pandemonium. As the thin light of early daybreak straggled through the trees and bushes, I heard voices and a couple of figures broke through the scrub looking nervously about them and cursing the dogs milling around them. One thing was sure – they were not soldiers. I could see a couple of olive-complexioned men, one with moustache and beard, wearing black cylindrical fur hats, leather jackets and dark baggy pants, carrying sticks instead of rifles. On spotting me they became rather excited, talking to each other in a language I had not heard before. They waved to me to climb down the tree which I did after they had swung their sticks threateningly at the dogs.

They led me to a poor-looking shack made of branches covered with leaves. Close by was a large sheep-pen containing a lot of sheep and goats. They sat me down near an open cooking fire and members of the family were introduced by means of smiles, gestures, nods and so on. Mum was cooking some kind of stew which she gave to the several children gathered round and to me. After about an hour of this I began to apply myself to the problem of how to leave these good people and be on my way, without upsetting the dogs. One of the large wolfhound types had already sidled up to me and tried sticking his fangs into my leg, tearing my trousers. One of the men chased it away but appeared a little nervous when the dog turned on him with bared fangs. In the event I had no choice – a shout from the forest drew our attention to a couple of figures in khaki uniforms holding rifles. At this my hosts made a wild scramble for the nearest cover, but it did not take long to realise that all was up and I raised my arms in surrender.

I was cautiously escorted inside the peasants' makeshift shack and thoroughly searched by one of the soldiers, watched by an excited and giggling group of peasants. Finding no weapons the soldiers appeared to relax and become quite amiable, accepting one of my cigarettes with obvious appreciation. Much later, smoking some of the Romanian fags, I understood why. While I had been entertained round the camp fire, someone had gone off post-haste to raise the alarm, hence the appearance of my captors. After cheerful farewells from my peasant hosts, I was assisted onto the back of a horse, using my Irvine flying jacket as a saddle, and warned by an ominous charade of loading their rifles of the consequences of trying to escape. I understood perfectly. After several miles of steady progress through forests and country lanes we arrived at a village where I was lodged in the local police station to await further developments. These turned out to be the arrival of three other members of the crew, 'Jed' Cormie, 'Killer' Kilroy and Johnny.

Before they departed from Craiova by train they saw the fascist ruler of Romania, Marshall Antonescu, pass by.

One of our escorts became very excited and yelled at us to salute as he went by. After some delay our train set out for Bucharest. However, when we arrived at a place called Fereşti the train stopped and could go no further because of extensive bomb damage to the railway lines ahead. In the station waiting room for the next six or seven long hours we were the focus of several hostile and unpleasant onlookers blaming us no doubt for the bomb damage.

They moved on from there in a farm cart. They covered many miles in this unsprung wagon over appalling roads and Dick Kilroy was in agony and his untreated wounds were beginning to fester. There was another lengthy delay in a wayside police station. It was, therefore, something of a relief when they moved on by car at night. Their plight was not improved when, in the middle of nowhere.

They stopped the car and we were ordered to take cover in a ditch during a night raid. We could see all this bombing and fighting going on, anti-aircraft guns and searchlights and then when that subsided we were put back into the car and driven on to yet another place.

Then we were transferred to an open truck which was going to Bucharest and we all sat, lay or squatted on the floor, hand-cuffed together. Every time it stopped at a village the driver seemed to take great delight in rousing the crowds. People would climb up on the back of the truck and punch and yell at us and give us a great workover. At one of these stops, in a market place, the crowd gathered round the guard and was practically useless, at the mercy of the truck driver who was enjoying all this. It was not long before a Romanian Army Officer appeared. He drew his pistol and screamed his head off. What he was saying we did not know, but that pistol was wavering about four inches from my head and I was expecting it to go 'pop' at any minute.

However, eventually the journey continued and they reached Bucharest which they then 'toured'. They lay as flat as they could because:

> . . . everything they could see or smell was burning. The streets were chaotic as they had had about three or four nights' bombing in a row as well as some by day.
>
> Eventually we reached the PW camp, a Romanian Army Barracks, and for the first time I would say that we were glad to get inside. At one time we had thought we were about to be lynched.

The first British Prisoners of War had arrived.

There is not quite such a full story about what happened to 150 Squadron's Q-Queen' which had taken-off from Amendola at 2107 hours. No more was heard. It was learned much later that she had crashed at Comana [Crash Site 3], 35 kilometres north-east of Giurgiu. Warrant Officer S. Clarke and his four crew were killed and are now buried at Tîncăbeşti. In August 1992, farmers unearthed some of 'Q-Queen's' wreckage. Inspection revealed that a major component failure had caused one of her engines to seize; the prop blades were feathered. Her load of three 500 lb and 250 lb bombs were also found. It is reasonable to conclude that she crashed on her way into the target as a result of this failure and was not shot down. Villagers recovered the five bodies the next day and they were buried at the nearby Monastery. They recalled that they were very young: one was red-haired and freckled.

Little is known about the fate of 'H-Harry' – Liberator EW 341 – of 178 Squadron. Flight Sergeant W.A. Molyneux and four of his crew lost their lives; two survived and became PWs at Bucharest. The aircraft crashed at Belciug [Crash Site 4], 85 kilometres west of the capital.

Two other targets were attacked on that Saturday night, 6 May, the railway bridges at Piteşti, some 90 kilometres west of Ploieşti and at Filiaşi, 36 kilometres north-west of Craiova. 236 Wing and 330 Wing each detailed a Wellington carrying a 4,000 lb bomb fitted with an eleven second delay fuse to attack the Piteşti bridge. The 236 Wing aircraft made a low level attack at 2320 hours dropping its bomb which burst 25 yards west of the bridge. No damage was observed. It was believed that this may have been the wrong bridge as a road bridge was seen close to it. The 330 Wing aircraft made four dummy runs before bombing, observing that the north end of the bridge was apparently already damaged. The 4,000 lb bomb was dropped from 150 feet at 0025 hours and seen to skid under the bridge near the centre, followed by an explosion, flame and a pall of smoke. No definite results were observed, in spite of two more runs being made over the bridge. So said the official reports. The only eye-witness account comes from Flight Lieutenant J.E. (John) Oram DSO who commanded 'A' Flight 40 Squadron at that time. He flew as Navigator in Flying Officer Ken Dunn's crew in LN 804 'T-Tommy'. He does not mention attacking the wrong bridge and refers to it as carrying the railway over the River Tîrgului, a few miles north-east of Piteşti. There was a railway station near the bridge and the Rear Gunner fired a few rounds at a train in the station as 'T-Tommy' passed over. John Oram was flying a second tour, his first having been with 37 Squadron in Desert Air Force days.

The other railway bridge, at Filiaşi, carried the single-track main line from the oilfield area through the industrial cities of Piteşti and Craiova westwards to the Danube port of Turnu Severin. Thence the railway ran north into Transylvania and on towards the Reich railway system. The damage caused by a successful strike on such a target would have far-reaching effects on rail traffic and take a long time as well as complicated and precious engineering resources to make good.

The Filiaşi railway bridge was attacked by three Wellingtons, two from 231 Wing and one from 236 Wing. The two 231 Wing aircraft attacked first at 0109 and 0128 hours respectively. As at Piteşti each carried a 4000 lb GP with an eleven second delay. Both identified the target, one bombed from 75 feet and although the crew thought they had hit the bridge, no explosion was seen. The second bomb was dropped from 60 feet and it was not seen to burst either. The 236 Wing aircraft was 'D-Dog' flown by Wing Commander H.C. (Harold) Turner, OC 104 Squadron. He spent an hour searching the Jiu valley at heights from 600 to 1,000 feet and only bombed after careful dummy runs from 600 feet at 0157 hours. His bomb was dead on target on the bridge but it failed to explode.

Sunday 7 May

MASAF's steady day and night offensive was sustained with another raid – the third in May – on Bucharest. Over 1,100 tons of bombs were dropped by 155 B-17s and 269 B-24s. Five bombers were lost to enemy action. The 230-strong escort of Lightnings and Mustangs claimed 20 enemy fighters.

7/8 May

That same Sunday night 205 Group's bombers returned to complete the fourth raid on the Romanian capital. This was to be the most costly to date for 205 Group: 34 aircrew lost, of whom twelve only survived to become prisoners and six bombers lost.

The group ORB summarises the raid:

Target: Bucharest Industrial Area. 61 Sorties.

6 Halifaxes of 614 Sqn, 3 Liberators of 240 Wing and 52 Wellingtons from 231, 236 and 330 Wings operated, but 2 Halifaxes returned early. 1 Liberator, 1 Halifax and 4 Wellingtons are missing, and 1 Wellington bombed the marshalling yards at CRAIOVA. The remaining aircraft identified the city, though some of the crews had difficulty in distinguishing the industrial area owing to haze, and the smoke from a number of fires started by the USAAF on their daylight raid. The bombing was well concentrated on the industrial area and on the southern end of the marshalling yards. Though ground opposition was only moderate, fighter opposition was much greater than during previous attacks. Many single and twin-engined fighters were active in the target area and a number of encounters took place. A Halifax was seen with one engine on fire, pursued by a Ju 88 and the following aircraft did not return:

Wellingtons 'D' of 142 Sqn (Flt Sgt Wray), 'H' of 70 Sqn (Fg Offr Hanney), 'G' of 104 Sqn (Flt Sgt Creasey), 'X' of 40 Sqn (Flt Lt Williams).

Halifax 'M' of 614 Sqn (Flt Sgt Dear).

Liberator 'Y' of 178 Sqn (Lt Schuurman).

52.3 tons of bombs dropped by 45 aircraft.

This was another occasion (and their number was steadily increasing) when 614 Squadron's target-marking was good and which did much for morale. The haze and smoke in the target area would have made visual bombing imprecise. The TIs were on time and over the target and the illumination was good. The Markers reported that a number of fires were already burning on arrival. 240 Wing's attack produced 7½ tons of HE as well, comprising two 1,000 lb GP TD .025 sec and 26 500 lb MC TD .025 sec between 2355 and 0006 hours from altitudes between 14,800 and 19,000 feet. The last aircraft landed safely at base at 0405 hours 8 May.

231 Wing had been ordered to provide 24 Wellingtons and 21, including three Illuminators, attacked the primary target, delivering 17 tons of bombs in

mixed 500 and 250 lb loads in a six minute 'blitz' from 2358 hours from 7,500–11,500 feet. Rear gunners were active. One claimed a searchlight extinguished after a 400 round burst at it. At about 0004 hours about 10 miles west of the target another Wellington joined in a Halifax/Ju 88 duel. The Halifax had been attacked and its starboard inner engine set on fire. The Halifax fired back and the Wellington supplied an additional 300 round burst. No strikes were claimed and both aircraft disappeared from view. The same Rear Gunner had already had two other engagements with different enemy aircraft – a Ju 88 south of the target at 2356 hours at 150 yards range and five minutes later over the target a FW 190 with a 500 round burst at 150 yards; no claim in either case. The Rear Gunner of 'P-Peter' of 70 Squadron fired two bursts when a FW 190 attacked at 2356 hours west of the target area at 10,000 feet. He thought he had scored but his attention was diverted by another single-engined fighter attacking from dead astern. The first burst of this attack hit the turret smashing the whole hydraulic system and the perspex of the turret as well as numerous hits in the rear fuselage. The Wellington took prompt evasive action and the enemy renewed his attack from the port quarter, but did not fire. The bomber's corkscrewing evasion must have made that impossible. The fighter made two more separate attacks but was finally lost. 'P-Peter' crashed on landing due to landing gear damage. All the crew were safe. Another rear gunner engaged a single-engined fighter with two 500 round bursts in the target area at 0003 hours, without claiming any hits. At the same time yet another gunner engaged a single-engined fighter at 11,000 feet. The enemy dived away and no hit was claimed.

The Wing's last Wellington landed at 0445 hours 8 May.

236 Wing's experiences were much the same. Their total load dropped was 19.8 tons from their 19 attacking Wellingtons. 'N-Nan' of 40 Squadron was attacked when four minutes out from the target. The Me 110 made two passes, from the starboard beam and from the port beam without success. 'N-Nan''s Rear Gunner returned fire but claimed no hits. Fighter flares were seen at 0007 hours 20 miles west of the target.

330 Wing's ten Wellingtons blitzed last between midnight and 0015 hours. Its ORB recorded areas of the target well alight with smoke thickening the haze.

In addition to the several fighter sightings it seems that 20–30 flak guns and twenty or so searchlights, including blue masters, were at work. 240 Wing rated the ground defences as less active than on the previous visits, perhaps yielding the sky to the fighters? Four or five 'heavies' were in action at Niš en route.

*On the night of 7 May 1944 142 Squadron's Wellington LP 125 made
its second visit to Bucharest, this time as an Illuminator. This
photograph shows the degree of brilliance the flares could produce and
lights up well the select northern Bucharest suburb of Florească. Lacul
(The Lake) Florească lies at the top left and the Dinamo Sports
Stadium at bottom centre.*

*Pipera airfield, used by defending fighters, lies just off the
photograph to the north-east of Lacul Florească. An industrial complex
now covers the old airfield and most of the area of the photograph is
re-built though the road pattern is largely unchanged.*

(Courtesy James Grieve)

The defenders recorded the attack as taking place between 2345 and 0110
hours in three waves, although the number of aircraft remained unknown.
Industrial and residential areas were damaged.

Returning crews reported a number of disturbing sightings en route and,
at the time of the preparation of the ORBs, the ultimate fate of missing crews
and aircraft could not be known. Indeed, some still remain unknown and will

115

probably ever be so. At the time it was believed that the enemy made use of 'scarecrows' – fires on the ground, or even falling to the ground, to resemble crashed or crashing bombers to demoralise aircrew. There are no known records of how much these ruses were actually used in the MTO, but sightings of crashes do outweigh actual losses in numbers and places. Six aircraft were actually lost that night over Romania and all their crash sites have been located. The reported sightings would indicate several more losses and it is not easy to substantiate or discard some of the claims.

1. At 2345 hours, on the way to the target, near Roșiorii de Vede halfway between Craiova and Bucharest, a 614 Squadron Halifax reported a huge orange flash hitting the ground, burning and then dying out. From the general area of this sighting, this could have been the crash of any one of four of the night's losses. However, the only bomber which we know was lost on the way *to* the target was 178 Squadron's Liberator Mk III 'Y-Yoke'. This location is, however, too far west for that crash.

2. At 2348 hours, a 330 Wing Wellington saw an aircraft explode at about 12,000 feet. It fell and burned on the ground near Turnu Severin. Subsequent research has not revealed any bomber lost in this position.

3. A minute later, while still 30 miles West of Bucharest, another Wellington watched an aircraft trailing smoke fall and burst into flames on hitting the ground. This was probably 104 Squadron's 'G-George' LN 663, captain Flight Sergeant T.W. Creasey, which was shot down at Preajba de Sus [Crash Site 7]. He and Flying Officer W.J. Meikle survived to become PWs. A third, Flight Sergeant C.G. Middleton, was seriously injured and died in hospital in Giurgiu on 13 August 1944. He now lies with the two killed that May night, at Tîncăbești.

4. At 2351 hours, again at 12,000 feet, two miles North of Bolintin a stick of bombs was seen to explode on the ground. Burning wreckage was also seen. Bolintin is about 30 kilometres west of Bucharest. This crash is more likely to be Schuurman's 178 Squadron Liberator 'Y-Yoke' crashing at Lungulețu [Crash Site 9], 38 kilometres north-west of Bucharest.

5. One minute after midnight an object was seen burning on the ground and emitting black smoke, three to four miles south-west of Bucharest. If this was not a fire caused by a bomb or a spent flare or marker burning out, it must have been a 'scarecrow'. No allied aircraft crashed near here.

6. Two minutes later, about one and a half miles North of Bolintin, a spiral of smoke was seen 500 feet below the reporting aircraft (at 10,000 feet), followed by an explosion on the ground.

7. At 0005 hours, on leaving the target area, an aircraft flying at 12,000 feet was seen to be attacked by another which was unidentified, from the starboard side. The attacker pulled up and fired a single rocket projectile almost vertically. The rocket exploded into 'five red sticks' which fell to the ground.

8. Two minutes later an aircraft was seen to burst into flames over the target. It broke up as it fell to earth and was seen to burn on the ground. Subsequent searches show that no bomber fell anywhere near Bucharest that night. All six came down roughly along a direct line from Bucharest to Foggia, via Niš.

9. At 0009 hours another aircraft, flying at 9,000 feet twelve miles north-west of the capital was seen to catch fire and break into three parts which burned on the ground: another sighting which cannot be reconciled with what has emerged from later researches.

10. At 0022 hours a 240 Wing aircraft saw what might have been a decoy scheme. Flares and green TIs were seen at a position to the East of Roşiorii de Vede.

11. An explosion was seen on the ground South of Sviştov in Bulgaria, not far from the Danube, at 0024 hours. The fire which followed resembled a burning aircraft, but it probably was not one – there were no losses within miles.

12. At a position near Caracal at 0050 hours, a small amount of flak was seen and an unidentified aircraft flying at 11,000 feet was seen to be hit and fall in flames. This could very well have been 142 Squadron's MF 198 'D-Dog' which crashed at Fǎrcaşele [Crash Site 8] eight kilometres north-east of Caracal and near an occupied defending airfield. The pilot, Flight Sergeant C. Wray and his crew were killed and are buried at Tîncǎbeşti.

Flying Officer G.G. (Geoff) Knyvett RAAF flew in Flight Sergeant Lloyd Fallon's all-RAAF crew taking part in 70 Squadron's Wellington MF 194 'F-Freddie'. Tied to his Navigator's table, he saw little but he heard Lloyd Fallon's battle with a single-engined fighter over the intercom.

Both attacks were from the beam position and we easily avoided them by the traditional manoeuvre of 'turning in'. The fighter gave up and I suppose went looking for a less aware target. I am under the impression that the fighter was single-engined but it was never identified. A few rounds were exchanged but there was no damage. The visibility that night was superb. We were able to see other fighters and our own bombers in the bright moonlight. I believe that Bomber Command in England had given

117

up flying over Germany on such nights. Perhaps they had forgotten to pass on the message. They also forgot to fit out our Wellingtons with warning devices – we had MONICA aerials poking out of the tail but no electronic gear on the inside to match it.

40 Squadron's loss on this operation was 'X-X Ray' ME 878. The captain, Flight Lieutenant G.W. Williams DFC and three of his crew, which included an RCAF Warrant Officer, died with their Wellington which crashed at Vartoapele [Crash Site 5]. This is 11 kilometres from Belciug where Molyneux's 178 Squadron Liberator had crashed the previous night and very much in the developing 'beaten zone' of downed bombers. After the war Flying Officer Douglas Calvert, the Rear Gunner, and 'X-X Ray''s sole survivor wrote *A Romanian Journal* which starts at 0115 hours 8 May when his twentieth operation ended abruptly:

Shot down by fire from ahead or mechanical trouble. Aircraft burst into flames, intercom dead. Last heard conversation re course and height between Navigator and Pilot – then silence.

Got out at 1,500 feet and landed safely near the burning tail – burn parachute – ran into darkness over ploughed field – heard the noise of frogs very loud – heard enemy fighters returning to base now going in westerly direction – threw away flying suit into stream – sweating hard – presumed rest of crew dead in other fire – several explosions. Settled in wood at dawn, and sat by tree and slept a little down by the stream.

Dawn – peasants near – dogs barking – saw two peasants without shoes, wearing light brown coats and sheepskin hats – lay low – voices near by – a man and three women came ploughing – very close – so moved around the wood – dogs suddenly scented me – stood still for fully five minutes behind a tree – three big savage dogs within 50 yards of me – they went away eventually. Hid by field side – now very hot, dried wet clothing, had Horlicks tablets – not hungry – only thirsty.

Estimated to be twelve to fifteen miles from the aircraft. All open fields with no sign of farms. Day endless, feet very sore. About four p.m. set out west – damn the peasants – covered about five miles – several peasants passed – curious looks from them. Had upset water, now terribly thirsty, feet very very sore indeed – slow progress – drank from a pond – came near to a village and crossed the river. Sat down to rest – peasant came up to me and I told him I was English – feet now impossible – must have help. By gesticulating, I managed to get water and he suggested I came to his 'casa' for food and sleep – admirable – got in his buggy and proceeded to village.

I could see he was telling all the neighbours – presently there were about 70 people following. The peasants appeared to be very friendly. He took me to the local wine store, where I was given bread and goat's cheese and wine. There was a large crowd and eventually I noticed a soldier with a rifle who turned out to be a gendarme, so I realised then that I was under arrest. However, very tired and full of food and drink, so proceeded to police station. Met a police officer who seemed friendly. I tried to bribe the officer to set me free – flying boots and 10 dollars for a pair of boots and liberty, he nearly took it, but since there were so many people about, even crowded round the window, I suppose he felt he had to do his duty. Eventually I was taken outside and got back into the buggy, it was very dark, but there was a good crowd to see me off and many hand-shakes.

Dry straw and a blanket were provided, but the ground was very rough and it was difficult to lie down with comfort. A long journey – I carried on an odd conversation with the guards neither of us understanding the other, but it certainly seemed to amuse them. For a time I imagined we were on an airfield, but what I thought were runways turned out to be strips of ploughed field. At long last I dozed off and woke up when we came to a village police station. Here I met two other RAF chaps. The police officers seemed upset because I would not stand to attention. However I managed to convey to them that I too was an officer. They took my things and counted my money. Several children and a woman (wife of the gendarme) were also at the scene. The woman could speak French, she was very voluble. Her main concern was for my parachute, apparently she wanted it for clothing. However, I had the satisfaction of telling her that I had burnt it. Many questions were asked and I gave them a very rough idea of the actual locality of the aircraft. The Lieutenant said that he and I would try and fix it next day – the two RAF men were leaving for 'somewhere' at 3 a.m.

They gave me supper, three fried eggs and plenty of bread and water – very good, only two beds available for three of us, so we put them together – also Lt. and guard in same small room. Unspeakably hot and they could not open the window because of the blackout. In spite of this I fell asleep immediately.

In the morning we set out in the buggy to look for my aircraft. It was a really beautiful fresh morning and I enjoyed the scenery very much. I had no intention of finding the aircraft, so when we were (I estimate) about four miles from it I gave directions in the wrong way. Much to my surprise we did find an aircraft, a B-24. It had burnt out. I did not leave the buggy but when the Lt. returned he said the pilot was dead in the wreckage. On the way back the Lt. stopped at a local wine store for a drink. A few minutes later he called me in and soon I found myself clinking my glass and saying 'Prosit' in the true Romanian style. They provided bread and goat's cheese for which I was ready.

They had sent for a professor who could speak English. He appeared an elderly man from Bessarabia who had been evacuated and was teaching at the local school. He had spent some time at Oxford and had written books on England in Romanian. I could not make him understand why the Anglo-American raids took place. He spoke all the time of the killing of women and children and the Bolshevik menace. He promised that I would be well looked after, that cheered me up – not that I needed it – I had already had a lot of wine and my escort had even more. I was very impressed with the cleanliness of the villages. The little houses were clean and the rooms well painted and adorned with needle work, also, on the whole, the peasants look after their animals well. It was the ploughing season and the peasants set out for their fields at 4 a.m. and return at dusk. The women and children all work on the land, yet for all that they are really very poor and know little of the luxuries of our modern life. Each village has its Orthodox church and, usually, its own clinic. There is also a police station as I found to my cost. Eventually we left, most of the population turning out to see us depart and there were many handshakes and we returned to the police station.

It was now 10 May. I was wakened by the guard at 3 a.m. I dressed and swilled my face at the pump – taken into the office – guard given packet with my meagre belongings – shook hands with Lt. and went outside. Still dark and rather cold. I climbed into the buggy and heard one of the guards say what I believe was, 'he should have a card on his back to say he bombed women and children'. Set off for railway station, a long uninteresting journey, mile after mile. A grey dawn broke. The buggy driver who was a peasant, annoyed me by staring at me as if I were an animal, later I got used to this kind of thing.

At the railway station at Roşiorii de Vede the guard and myself alighted. From then on until the train came in I was the object of interest for dozens of peasants. The train was very, very full with peasants, soldiers and a few women. I had to stand most of the way. It took about two hours, stopping at every station until we arrived at our destination, Turnu Măgurele, where I was taken up the railway track for a quarter of a mile, then up side streets to a barracks.

At another police station later I caught a glimpse of the Danube so knew this could not be Bucharest. This was the Police HQ for the 'county' of Teleorman.

The room behind the police station was bare of all furniture and fittings – apparently I was to stay the night and wondered where the bed was. Nothing to do, nothing to read, except a notice on the wall telling of glorious Romanian victories in Bessarabia – between June 22nd and July 7th 1941 and a German skit on our U-boat losses.

In charge of the three guards was a little Corporal who had served on the Russian front from Odessa to Stalingrad. Evening came and my bed arrived, one rather dirty blanket on a hard wood floor. There was a wash basin but no water. I had of course no soap, or towel, or tooth-brush and I was steadily becoming very dirty. At sundown I made my bed and laid out my trousers to absorb a little of the hardness of the floor – actually I was soon asleep and when I awoke the sun was shining.

Between 11 and 18 May I was kept alone in the room. The waiting nearly drove me mad. Each day they promised I should go to Bucharest, each day I was disappointed.

The guards never seemed to take their clothes off. They just lay down and slept during their time off. Sometimes they washed feet, hands and face, and occasionally shaved. Their food appeared to be entirely bean soup and bread. This bread tasted very sour. The officer spoke a little French so I managed to convey to him most of my wants.

I was introduced to a Colonel who later brought his wife to see me. One day he brought a General to see me who was quite pleasant and told me he would try and obtain a bed, chair and table – nothing happened of course.

I became friendly with the town's doctor or should I say sanitary expert. He was a Greek and had a very poor opinion of the Romanian Army and did not like the Germans. He also brought his wife to see me. She also was a doctor and spoke good English. It was a very nice change to talk with her and through her I again found I was going to Bucharest next day – again nothing happened.

The weather was fine and during the day I used to spend a lot of time in the yard. I walked to and fro and by this means kept myself fairly fit, though the food was pretty monotonous. Even fresh bread and good cream cheese can be very tiring day after day. One day the alarm went and I saw formations of Yank bombers steering West. They had bombed Ploieşti and it made me quite homesick to see them going back to their base. After I had been at Turnu Măgurele a few days the little Corporal was posted to the front. We shook hands before he went. He looked very very sick about it and I don't blame him. He had had his taste of the Russians.

On 17 May I was told I was certainly leaving the next day and that several Americans were arriving. As usual nothing happened, although in the morning he confirmed that I should leave in the afternoon. However, that evening after I had gone to bed, he suddenly turned up with the news that I was to leave at 3 a.m. next morning. I shook hands with him, wished him luck and promised to write to him after the war.

Very early next morning, 19 May, the guard awoke me. It was still dark, I grabbed some bread and cheese that I had left over, then picked up my few belongings and went outside to an open wagon. There were several more soldiers in the wagon and an Alsatian dog. I sat down on a box and very soon we set off on our journey – was I glad? I didn't mind even though I was cold. We were soon on the open road and made fairly decent speed although the road was very bad. It was just coming grey and quite cold. We passed through the town of Alexandria but I did not get off. The road was crowded with peasant buggies going either to the fields or market. The sun came up and soon it was nice and warm. The whole journey was about 70 miles and it was 6.30 a.m. when we approached the outskirts of Bucharest. It was now a beautiful morning as we drove into the city. There were a lot of people about in spite of the early hour. We drove around making various calls. Bomb damage was pointed out to me by the guards. The city had a certain amount of damage but nothing compared with blitzes as we know them, but certain damage to residential property. The Alsatian dog I mentioned we delivered to an Institution for the Blind to be trained to lead.

What I saw of it, Bucharest appeared to be a very beautiful city. I was taken down back streets to a private house that had been taken over by the military and here I got off.

Douglas Calvert was now a prisoner of war.

Little is known of the fate of Flying Officer S.J. Hanney and his crew in 70 Squadron's 'H-Harry' (MF 146). This Wellington crashed at Talpa Bîscoveni [Crash Site 6], 10 kilometres north-east of Vartoapele, where Douglas Calvert survived his crash that night. 'H-Harry' was carrying a spare 'bod' on this final operation. Five airmen were killed and are now buried at Tîncăbeşti. They include a Sergeant A.F. Rowlands whose name is not on the ORB crew list. A sixth airman, Warrant Officer Charles Weppler RAAF, a Navigator, baled out successfully and, following a brief spell of freedom with peasant farmers, was captured and moved to the Schoolhouse prison camp in Bucharest. Charles Weppler died in 1968 and left a tantalising set of brief notes for lectures he gave in Australia after the war. His widow, Eileen, who kindly supplied the notes, served in the RAAF herself as a Corporal.

The first Halifax to be lost over Romania was 'M-Mike' JP 111 piloted by Flight Sergeant N. Dear. The crew baled out when a Ju 88 fired a single rocket which crippled the bomber. It crashed at Spătăreni [Site 9A], 20 kilometres south-west of Alexandria. The crew had been briefed to expect some concealment to be given by cloud cover but the Navigator, Flying Officer D.C. (Dudley) Egles, remembers that it:

> . . . turned out to be clear with strong moonlight. We all baled out and I came down in a field quite close to the Danube, some 60 miles south-west of Bucharest. I buried my 'chute and started walking westward. By about 0400 hours I was very weary and went to sleep in the remains of a haystack. I was woken at daybreak by umpteen barking dogs and several peasants armed with pitchforks. They took me to their farm where the man in charge, owner or manager, spoke French, so I was able to explain who I was. They gave me some bread and 'apă dolce' and the 'boss' then drove me to a nearby village and handed me over to the local gendarmerie. I was of great interest to the local populace – the first RAF officer they had ever seen. I was 'introduced' to the mayor and his daughter – she also spoke French and asked me if there was anything I needed. I asked for some soap to wash with and was given a tiny sliver. It was only much later that I realised what a sacrifice this was on the part of that young lady.
>
> I spent the night in the local lock-up and was collected by an army truck the next day together with other members of my crew and some USAAF aircrew. We were taken to the Central Police Station in Bucharest and there searched and interrogated by Luftwaffe personnel. Later we were all marched off to our 'Kriegie' – a disued High School in Bucharest.

An RNZAF member of the crew, Flight Sergeant Norman Foster, remembers that the attacker was an Me 110. The single rocket was 'a remarkably good shot'. He landed in a field near to a pond and moments later the Flight Engineer, Sergeant Ron Williams, landed safely nearby. They set off westwards but they were not at liberty for long. All the crew had been intercepted by dawn and were handed over to soldiers and taken by truck to some barracks in Alexandria. After a night there they travelled on to Bucharest with the Americans who Dudley Egles had mentioned. Norman Foster casually notes that the . . .

> . . . reception from the population along the road to Bucharest was not the most hospitable.

because of widespread air raid damage. He was the only New Zealander PW until another arrived in mid-August.

Warrant Officer R. Roy Grier RCAF, the Navigator of 178 Squadron's

Liberator 'Y-Yoke' BZ 932, captained by Lieutenant J.G. Schuurman SAAF, has been able to contribute a valuable account of his last operation, which only he and Flight Sergeant W. Parson had the good fortune to survive. This was one of the last Liberator Mk IIIs which the Squadron flew.

On that long ago night, we were running up to the target when the German night fighter opened fire on us. In moments, it seemed our aircraft was a great ball of fire plunging towards the earth. There was an explosion of considerable magnitude when the bomb-laden aeroplane struck the earth. This sudden and violent end to our proposed bombing raid on Bucharest was a traumatic experience for me.

The more routine parts of that night's flight are gone from my mind and for the most part it is those 'never happened that way before' experiences that I can remember. To illustrate this memory gap phenomenon, I will mention a few items that most certainly would have taken place.

An example would have been the afternoon briefing and other afternoon activities. All the aircrews detailed for that night would have assembled for the senior officers and the meteorologist to give us such information as they deemed essential. The Navigation Officer and the Armament Officer would have a special word for the Navigator/Bomb-Aimers.

After the briefing ritual, I would have made out a Flight Plan incorporating all the information given to me – the route to be followed, wind speeds and directions, the designated heights and air speeds to be used. This night the target was the industrial area of Bucharest.

It would be a very rare occasion if the Navigator used his Flight Plan to reach the target area! The Plan was there as a general guide for use on trips when the weather prevented us from using navigational information from the stars, ground observation, or fixes from other navigational aids. If no other information was available the Flight Plan was used as a last resort until something better came along. So on that day, I would certainly have made out a Flight Plan.

After supper, we would have been picked up by a truck and taken out to the dispersal site where our Liberator 'Y' was parked. At a pre-arranged time, with the assistance of the ground crew, the aircraft would have its motors started and run-up before taxi-ing out to take off. When the last plane was safely up, all would set course at the same time for the first turning point on the night's route.

My first clear memory of this flight is a mind picture of the Yugoslav mountains glistening in the moonlight. Their beauty was very great, but I was much more concerned with a lake that we were coming towards. It would provide me with a definite fix of my position and was to the south of the track that we were supposed to be following. We were wandering off track quite quickly, so it was apparent that the winds that the Met people had forecast must have been wrong. There was an unbelievably strong north-west wind out there. Then again, there were the up and down air currents acting upon our aircraft. For a while, we were losing height rapidly and Lt Schuurman, the 1st Pilot, opened up the engines to try and maintain height. This was followed by a rising current of air and we very soon had our height back again. It looked like a lovely clear, quiet moonlight night from our vantage point, but clearly there did appear to be some pretty wild winds in the vicinity.

We were still wandering off course rapidly, but this did not concern me too much because all of the other aircraft would be experiencing the same problem. They would all realise this at about the same time and all would make a correction of heading in order to get back on track again.

The lake that was coming up would be just the thing to make it possible for me to calculate the correct wind speed, which I would use to work out a new course to put us back on our proper track. There is nothing a Navigator likes better than a definite fix of his position – that is, to know that the aircraft is over a known point at an observed time.

We were edging slowly up to the lake; the ground below always moves very slowly. The Pilot's voice over the intercom 'I am sorry, Roy, but I have made a mistake. I put the wrong setting on the compass and have not been flying the heading that you gave me.' My theory of the strong winds that had been putting us off track proved to be incorrect. Our Pilot was an experienced flyer. He had never made such a mistake before. We both had a routine that we followed. I would carefully tell him the course to fly and he would repeat it slowly back to me. There did not seem any possibility of an error. Somehow the wrong setting was put onto the compass and now, instead of being one of the pack, we were a straggler. No matter what we did now we would always be a little behind the main stream of bombers. We could increase the airspeed somewhat to try and catch up, but unfortunately, that uses more fuel and there is no reserve available to use on long flights such as this.

On looking back on this mistake, it is easy to see that I had some responsibility in the matter of the wrong course too. I knew we were drifting off to one side of where we should have been; but I made the wrong interpretation of the facts which I had in front of me. I blamed the unusually strong winds instead of the Pilot who had always been completely reliable in such matters.

I cannot say that, had we not made this error, we would have got safely through, but it certainly did not help.On such a clear moonlight night, the advantage is greatly with the night-fighters. I expect the German pilots would have made about as many kills regardless of where we were placed in the raiding pack. I believe that, if we had been with the main group of bombers, the night-fighter that singled us out might have got someone else, but who knows?

As we approached our target at Bucharest, it was easy to see that there was plenty of activity ahead. Searchlights probed the sky and the anti-aircraft guns flashed below. The Pathfinders' markers then went down and our planes started to drop their bombs. We would be going in when everyone else was coming out. It looked like we were in for a very rough ride indeed! A hot reception was awaiting us and our chances of an unmolested bomb run would be almost zero.

The probability of being caught in the dazzling super light of an unknown number of searchlights would be high. Once an aircraft was coned by the searchlights, the black puffs of the exploding anti-aircraft shells in the bright light would easily be seen. Their bursts would come ever closer as the gunners on the ground adjusted range. Soon, we would be feeling the crunching sound of the exploding shells as they burst all around us. The only thing to do, once coned over a heavily defended target such as this, was to go into a weaving, screaming dive to get away from the searchlights. This tactic had worked before on earlier raids to Athens, and, hopefully, would work again.

It was at this point that the Rear Gunner yelled over the intercom 'A fighter!' That was all he managed. The German night-fighter had us centred in his gunsights and had already pressed the trigger on his weapons. I could see the tracer bullets streaming up from below – they were going into our fuselage and port wing, especially in the area of the inboard motor. Our aircraft shuddered as the cannon shells tore into it. The attack lasted only a very few seconds and stopped almost at once. The Rear Gunner was screaming in agony and sobbing over the intercom. 'Help me for God's sake. I am hit bad.'

The aircraft banked sharply to the left as the two pilots, Lt Schuurman and FS Peter Bisset fought to regain control. I understood from their conversation that one port motor was knocked out, I presumed they were trying to get the propeller feathered. They must have succeeded because we levelled out again.

During this time the Rear Gunner kept calling for help. The Skipper came on the line again and said 'Jettison the bomb load'. I made haste to do his bidding. I flipped on the switch that controlled the bomb door opening. Nothing happened. I reported 'I don't think the bomb doors are opening.' I was almost certain that the doors were not opening because when I next flipped on the switches to jettison the bomb load, they would not work either – something had been damaged. The Skipper did not reply. I suppose he could have ordered the Wireless Operator or the Second Pilot to open the doors manually, but that would have taken some time and there was precious little of that commodity. After a few moments it dawned on me that no one was saying anything and perhaps there was a good chance that the intercom system was out.

I did not know what to do next. I took a few seconds to note in my log an entry of the time of the attack. Then it occurred to me that my intercom was not properly connected. I pushed the connecting plug in tighter and the crew voices came back to me again. I heard the Pilot shouting 'Abandon aircraft, abandon aircraft'. Even as he shouted, the fighter opened on us again and once more the aircraft shuddered as the tracer shells burst into us and flashed by in the night.

Those frightening gravity powers, known as the 'G' Forces, were taking over now. When an aircraft goes out of control, one minute a man would seem to weigh a ton and be held to the floor, the next he might be pinned to the roof. I could feel the gravity forces clutching at me as I quickly knelt in front of the nose landing wheel to open the door. I then dived out, head first, into the wild slip-stream of the plane.

The contrasts were remarkable. One moment I was in the comfortable, though noisy, nose of the aircraft; a second or so later I received a mighty buffet from the slip stream. This was followed by a loud crack that sounded not unlike a rifle shot and I instantly received one powerful body-jerking jolt as my parachute filled with air and the shroud lines slowed me from 155 or so miles per hour to an almost complete stop.

Out of the corner of my eye, I saw our aircraft burning brightly as it winged its way to the ground. There was an explosion of some considerable strength when the plane hit the ground.

This was near the village of Lunguleţu, some 38 kms north-west of Bucharest [Crash Site 9], close to the defending fighter airfield at Titu-Boteni.

This was followed by the sounds of ammunition exploding in the fire. Then there was silence – I would say a startling silence. Except for a very, very faint whine of the rushing air as it filled and spilled out of my parachute, there was not a sound in the night.

If it had not been for the glow of the fire on the near horizon and the faint sound of occasional exploding rounds of ammunition, the experience would by this time have been quite pleasant.

A parachute ride to earth may seem to last a very long time but in reality, it is soon over. Suddenly the ground came rushing towards me, my feet hit the earth and my parachute settled slowly on the field in front of me. My first act when back on the good earth was to bury my parachute. I then set off to put as much distance as possible between me and the burning aircraft – towards Yugoslavia and its famed partisans.

My flying boots were gone. They were the easy-on, easy-off type. I presume that when the parachute opened and I stopped, the boots just kept on going. Walking along in one's stockinged feet on soft ploughed ground on a warm, dry spring night is no great hardship. Having survived through the night unhurt, I was optimistic that most of our crew had done the same, but I was less optimistic of the Rear Gunner's chances.

Common sense told me that I would not have a chance of getting out of Romania without help from the local population. However I was determined to give it a try and I set off at a brisk pace towards the West. I had not gone very far when there erupted in front of me a chorus of barking, howling dogs. I had ventured too close to a village and the dogs did not like me. I did an about turn and ran as fast as I could away from this village. The dogs soon stopped their baying. I skirted the village, staying far enough away to attract no attention. Before long, I was once again on my way to the west and to freedom.

I walked along for a mile or two and then my escape plans received another set-back. I came up to a river. An out-an-out-hero would have dived into its icy spring current and swam across. I did not measure up to this standard. I doubt very much if I even considered this option. I had grown up on the semi-arid plains of Saskatchewan and had never learnt to swim properly. Anyway, there might be a bridge, or a boat, in the neighbourhood and I proposed to try for one of these for the crossing.

I walked along the river and was rewarded after a very short distance with the sight of a bridge. My spirits rose as I walked quickly towards this welcome structure. I was getting very near when I thought I saw some movement in the moonlight. It was a sentry and he was walking towards me. I held my breath and froze in the standing position. Just when I thought it was all up with me, he made an about turn and started to walk back the other way. I made an about turn too and got out of there as quickly as possible.

There are a number of candidates for Roy Grier's river. The Şuţa, or its twin the Sabar, are strong starters because of distance but neither is very substantial. The larger Argeş is 10 kms away. Could he have reached that?

It was starting to get brighter in the East. I had noted earlier that there were bushes along the river bank so I soon found what seemed like a good place to hide in. I made myself as comfortable as possible and was soon asleep. Nine o'clock the next morning found me waking up to a beautiful spring day. Except for a few birds chirping, the countryside was silent. I had my emergency ration packet with me, so I had some chocolate and then settled down to sleep again.

This time, sleep would not come to me. A new element entered my existence; an element I was not used to, nor prepared for by my life in the armed Services. It is called boredom. The activity and motion of Service life were gone and now I had absolutely nothing to do. My Royal Air Force issue watch was set on Greenwich Mean Time and it slowly ticked away the seconds as they came along. The minutes crawled by at a pace that made five of them seem like an hour. At about eleven o'clock or so in the morning, the boredom fled for a short while. Above me on the edge of the river embankment, a shepherd came along herding a small flock of sheep. A short distance down the stream, the sheep came down to the water's edge for a drink. Very soon the man left with his animals. He did not appear to have seen me. For my part, I was back dong my watch watching routine again.

The afternoon wore away. Four thirty, or a little later, found me dozing again. I was awakened by someone calling. Startled, I looked up to see several peasants standing along the river embankment above me. As I stood up, it seemed that I should say something. I said 'Are there any Germans around?', or something to that effect. Back came their voices in a chorus – *Nui Germani – Romani*. Now I do not know any Romanian, but this sounded to me very much like what they were saying – 'No Germans here, only Romanians'. Along with this there was a torrent of Romanian talk, plus many gestures of welcome, inviting me to come up to the high ground.

They were so friendly I just could not get over it. I had difficulty believing my good fortune. It was apparent that I had landed in the centre of a partisan settlement. There were a dozen or more people, both men and women waiting in the field a short distance away. Every one of these people extended to me a handshake and a welcome.

When the welcoming ceremonies were over, one man acted out a tableau for me. One hand became a pretend *Avian* flying along, followed by a rapid descent to the ground and a crash. He then held up five fingers and said *Morti* to indicate that five of my companions were dead. I learned later that, except for FS Parsons and me, all of the crew were killed. Parsons was very badly burned on the face and hands when the aircraft's

129

oxygen tanks blew up before he got out of the plane.

I now became aware of a man seated in a two-seater buggy who invited me by gesture to come up with him. Two of the men got into the back and our group set off across the countryside. The closer we got to the village, the larger the throng of people became; men, women and children, all bidding me welcome.

At the outskirts a young woman, who was walking along beside the carriage, said something to me in French and I got down to talk to her. I do not claim to be fluent in French but I had studied it in school for four years and so had a basic vocabulary. We started to walk along again, carrying on a rather halting conversation in French. She wanted to know about my family: did I have brothers and sisters? Was I married? She was single she said and did not seem saddened to learn that I had no wife. That she was a most attractive girl was easily seen. During a lull in our conversation, I told her that she was pretty. She understood that all right because she blushed and looked away from me. After that encounter, she walked a little closer to me and then I do not know how it came about, but our hands just happened to touch as they swung by our sides. Somehow or other, before anyone had time to realise it, we were walking along hand in hand. Yes, indeed, life among the partisans was going to be interesting, very interesting.

We had reached the centre of the village and everyone stopped walking. The people fell back on one side of me to reveal an army officer and an armed soldier standing in front of me. There were no smiles of welcome from either of them. The officer curtly motioned for me to follow him into the open door of the Police Station. The soldier fell in behind me and we marched into the building.

When the soldier shut the door, I understood then that the hopes for the good life that I had imagined awaiting me among the partisans was no more than an idle day dream. The people who brought me into the village were not the partisan people from whom I was hoping to obtain help for my freedom. They had lost no time in delivering me to the authorities of the realm.

In less than a week, I would be transferred to Bucharest, where I would be living in a school hastily converted into a prisoner-of-war camp.

This area is so dotted with villages that it is almost pointless to conjecture where the villagers took Roy Grier to turn him over to the authorities. Potlogi must be a strong possibility.

Target: Railway Bridge 4–5 kms WEST of FILIAŞI: 2 Sorties

Two Wellingtons of No 236 Wing were detailed for this attack, but only one is known to have attacked the target. One 4000 lb bomb was dropped from a height of 600 feet and seen to burst just SOUTH of the most Easterly span. The bridge appeared to be intact after the attack and the photographs show no damage. The other aircraft, 'T' of 40 Sqn, captain WO Bradshaw, is missing.

The Wing's ORB adds only a little more, that the bomb probably burst under the bridge, 'throwing up a spout of water and smoke'. The Wellington which returned reported no opposition in the target area when it bombed at 2330 hours. This was Wing Commander Harold Turner's second attempt to destroy this bridge.

'T-Tommy' found things at the bridge rather different and it was, indeed, missing.

'T-Tommy' was Wellington Mark X LN 804 and the crew, for whom an adventure began that night, were:

WO T. Bradshaw RCAF	Pilot
WO N.L. Reid RCAF	Navigator
Plt Offr I.B.H. McKenna	Air Bomber
Flt Sgt W. Taylor	Wireless Operator
Sgt R. Somers	Air Gunner

Once again, the load was a single 4000 lb GP 'Cookie' with the same 11 second delay fuse. The bomb was to be dropped from the lowest possible altitude to have the best chance of a direct hit and the time delay ensured that the aircraft would be well clear when the bomb exploded.

Success depended very much on the right weather conditions and the night turned out to be clear with a moon and some scattered cloud. The flight over Yugoslavia was uneventful and, taking a fix at Turnu Severin as they overflew the Danube in the Iron Gates Gorge, Bradshaw began a timed run to the bridge site letting down in height on the way. However, they failed to find the bridge on this attempt and Bradshaw carried out the run again. This time they were lucky the bridge was identified and a dummy run was made.

The other attacking Wellington had found things no easier. OC 104 Squadron, Wing Commander Harold Turner, in 'D-Dog' spent an hour searching for the bridge and after a careful dummy run proceeded to bomb from 600 feet. Before setting course for home they climbed to 2000 feet and took photographs of the bridge.

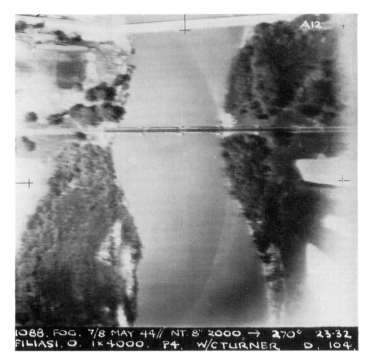

THE FILIAŞI RAILWAY BRIDGE OVER THE RIVER JIU SOME 40 KILOMETRES NORTH-WEST OF CRAIOVA

Among other things the Titling Strip tells that the photograph was taken at 1132 pm on 7 May 44 at a 104 Squadron, captained by Wing Comd Turner and was carrying one 4000 lb bomb. (The strip is along the photograph's northern margin)

The chosen dropping height for this attack was too low for the conventional Mark XIV bombsight to be of any value and Tom Bradshaw's crew had devised a substitute using the guns in the nose turret and the Bomb-aimer, Pilot Officer McKenna, took his place there. The nose guns, trained at a previously calculated angle of depression were his gunsight and he sighted along them. When the Aiming Point passed the muzzles the bomb release was pressed.

Tom Bradshaw was determined to be as accurate as he could be with this one bomb and he let down to a flight level below 200 feet as he flew westward along the line of the railway. During this very vulnerable approach some light flak, probably 20 mm, was encountered from the bridge guard positions. McKenna called out that he had been hit, but he was able to continue to aim his bomb. The last words his comrades heard him say were 'Bomb gone!' The light flak was now making its mark in the final stages and as Tom Bradshaw began to pull the Wellington up and away for home, the Constant Speed Unit (a kind of engine governor) on the port engine began to run away and the engine speed built-up dangerously. At the same time, the crew realised that the fuel tanks on the starboard side of the aircraft were badly holed and petrol was being lost at an alarming rate. The Wireless Operator, Sgt Taylor, went forward to help McKenna but found that he was already dead. It was by this time obvious to everyone that 'T-Tommy' was not going to make it back to Foggia. Indeed, it quickly became clear that there was insufficient power to attempt to clear the Yugoslav mountains.

Bradshaw ordered the aircraft to be abandoned as soon as they were West of the Danube valley and the crew landed near the small Yugoslav town of Zagubica, some 80 kilometres south-west of Turnu Severin. The actual crash site of T-Tommy is not known but since Pilot Officer McKenna was finally buried at Sofia, it must have veered to port and headed south-east before striking the ground either in Bulgaria itself or in Bulgarian-occupied Yugoslavia.

The four surviving members of the crew were picked up individually by the Chetnik resistance groups and local peasants. Filiaşi bridge was forgotten. The only person who would have known that night if the bridge had been hit was Dicky Somers, the Rear Gunner, who ought to have had a ringside seat of the detonation. In the event, no one recalls him saying anything and no one remembered to ask. In fact, the bridge was not hit and there is no record of where the bomb fell or even if it exploded.

Initial relationships with the crew's new hosts were based on mutual suspicion. The Germans had reputedly infiltrated agents in aircrew uniforms to ensnare local people who offered help. For their part the aircrews had been briefed to be wary of Chetniks because it was believed that they were collaborating with the Germans. Aircrews had been told that British supplies had just been stopped and British advisers withdrawn. The Allies had finally abandoned General Mihailovic and thrown in their lot with Tito. However involved relationships might have been at a higher level, as far as this crew was concerned, a warm relationship soon developed.

Another 40 Squadron survivor, Flight Sergeant Bill Goodbrand, describes his first encounter and subsequent adventures with the Chetniks.

Three armed men crossed the field towards me. They were armed to the teeth, with cross belts of ammunition over their shoulders, with knives and guns in their waist belts, as well as rifles. They were bearded and their side caps carried a skull and crossbones emblem at the front. At least they appeared friendly as, with huge grins, they pointed to themselves and said 'Chetnik' and made gestures for me to go with them. This I did with some misgivings . . .

We walked for a long way down dusty lanes and across fields and through woods and I realised that fleece-lined flying boots were not meant for walking. My three escorts chatted away but communication with me was limited to smiles and back-slapping. Eventually we reached an isolated farmhouse and, on being ushered in, I was delighted to see that our pilot was already safely there. We were given large mugs of hot milk into which had been put bread and sugar and left to sit on a bed at the end of the room while all the Chetniks present, now about a dozen, held a heated discussion round a long table. An elderly man came over and told us that he had worked in America for many years, coming home to Yugoslavia to retire. His English was fair and we pressed him about reaching the coast and crossing to Italy. For an answer he pointed at the Chetniks, touched the knife at his belt and making a horribly significant gesture of throat-cutting, said 'you feel nothing – all over very quick'. Not exactly comforting but, if the Germans had been dropping men dressed in RAF uniforms into the area to find out who would help Allied airmen, it was no wonder the Chetniks were taking no risks.

However, apparently satisfied, they gave us our first glass of Slivovic, hands were shaken all round and we set off into the night again. We arrived at a small village and sat down to a meal in what was obviously the village hall. Two other members of the crew were already there. The hall was packed, it seemed that everyone in the district was there and we had a truly memorable meal of roast pig plus the inevitable Slivovic. It was to be our last decent meal for some time. Many speeches were made, unfortunately not completely understood, but a Chetnik with a smattering of French did his best to translate.

The following morning we were taken to another isolated farmhouse where our Bomb Aimer was already – so now our crew was all complete. We set off again and finally, in a meadow almost surrounded by trees, we met a group of Chetniks on horseback. They were to be our escorts and we were to be with this party for about three weeks.

We were now provided with horses and so began a slow trek into the mountains. We moved mostly at night, lying up in farmhouses during the day and experiencing sudden departures. I soon learned to hate the latest words learned – *Nemsky nemsky idamo* (phonetic), which appeared to mean 'Germans, Germans, let's go!' We ate mainly at these farmhouses or in villages. Although food was obviously short we were always given the lion's share by these generous and hospitable people. The standard fare was bean soup, cheese and coarse bread, washed down with Slivovic.

The only Germans we saw at this point were a bit too close for comfort. While travelling late one evening and coming to a village bar, we decided to buy a drink for our friends. Our escape kit contained 50 US dollars which we had converted into dinars. The building was just a large wooden hut with one large room with no bar as such. Our drinks were brought to the wooden benches where we sat. We were enjoying ourselves when a lorry pulled up outside and about a dozen German soldiers came in. We kept a very low profile but it turned out they had come in solely to drink and were soon on their way, much to our general relief. That was one of the few occasions we were actually on a made-up road. Usually we were taken by country lanes or over the countryside.

We were a mixed party. In addition to our Chetnik escort there were a number of others. A large blond Russian, George, had been captured at Leningrad and had deserted from a work battalion in Yugoslavia. There was Nino – a captain in the Italian Army as well as an Austrian Doctor of Music. Conversations were always an adventure into the unknown.

After about three weeks of moving, either by night or day, but always higher into the hills, we arrived at a farmhouse to discover a large party of American airmen, as well as four RAF or, to be more exact, two RCAF and two RAF airmen, Tommy Bradshaw, Pilot, Norman Reid, Navigator, Dicky Somers, Rear Gunner, and Flt Sgt Taylor, Wireless Operator, whose first name I do not recall. Amazingly they were from our own 40 Squadron. Our fates now combined. There was also a Sgt J.E. Turnbull, a Bomb Aimer from 40 Squadron. His captain, Sgt Dicky Sutcliffe, and Sgt Eric Turner had been captured by Bulgarian occupation troops further south in Yugoslavia, having been shot down on 3rd July after bombing Bucharest. The other two members of their crew had been killed.

It was at this point that Bill Goodbrand and his party said 'Goodbye' to their own escort friends and joined this larger group. Although there were now over 200 Allied airmen they did not all travel together but in smaller groups linked by Chetniks bands. Again the pattern was to lie up during the day and move on in the late evening.

Two incidents stand out in Bill Goodbrand's memory.

We had to cross the River Morava which had a road and railway running parallel. There was a long wooden bridge over the river with German sentries on guard at each end. We lay hidden in the hills above the bridge until early evening then, given a quick signal, we ran hell for leather down to the bridge and across, feet beating what seemed like a thunderous tattoo on the wooden roadway. What had happened to the sentries I can only guess, but I imagine their bodies were in the river. We pushed on all night. Shortly after crossing the bridge, the rain began to come down in torrents. Our paths became ankle deep in mud and eventually the spunkas (Yugoslav moccasins with turned up toes) which I was wearing simply fell apart and for most of that night I was barefoot.

The second incident: we were in a farmhouse high in the hills when our guides called us out to move about 3 a.m. We thought that there might be a German patrol about but we were taken to a clearing high up on a hillside and told to wait. Faintly at first then more loudly we heard approaching hoofbeats, and about twenty Chetniks on horseback wearing richly decorated uniforms came at full gallop to where we waited. It soon became clear why we were there – the leading horseman was General Mihailovic himself, or Draja, as he was affectionately known by the Chetniks. Through an interpreter he wished us well and hoped we would soon return to Italy to continue the fight against the common enemy. Then with a salute, they wheeled and were gone in the night.

The group continued to move around to avoid detection and they reached the small town of Pranjani some 130 kms from Zagubica where Tom Bradshaw's crew had baled out. Now came the breakthrough. The airmen had been pressing to find how they might return to Italy.

One of the American officer pilots managed to acquire a radio transmitter and he used it to establish contact with an Allied station at Bari. Various authenticity checks were made and eventually Bari was satisfied and help was promised.

At last the message came to stand-by at a certain time and place. The first night nothing happened but the following night a Dakota flew over and three parachutes were seen to open delivering two American officers and a sergeant with full radio equipment and codes to set up a rescue operation. On the next night boots, K rations, cigarettes and other goodies in large quantities were parachuted in. The senior American officer, a pilot, asked Bill Goodbrand to help to distribute these supplies, although the number of American airmen far exceeded the small RAF and Commonwealth contingent. It was a nice gesture and was appreciated.

Several days now passed and then came the message to go up to the plateau to a reasonably flat area which would be used for landing and take-off. On arrival there, the airmen had a grandstand view as large numbers of P-38 Lightnings wheeled round over a nearby German airfield to keep their aircraft on the ground and distract them from what was to come. At last six C-47 Dakotas appeared and landed quickly one after another. They taxied to their take-off points, with their engines ticking over, picked up all the Allied airmen and took off again. From the landing of the first Dakota to the take-off of the last not much more than six to eight minutes had elapsed.

The flight to Italy was uneventful. At Bari, the British were taken to an army camp. After their clothing had been burned, their bodies de-loused and thoroughly washed, Bill Goodbrand phoned 40 Squadron and they were picked up the next day. The date was 13th August. Tom Bradshaw's crew from T-Tommy had been away for 14 weeks. Bill Goodbrand's adventure had lasted 44 days.

40 Squadron survivors return from the Chetniks.

L to R back row:
Sergeant J.E. Turnbull, Air bomber, of Flt Sgt R. Sutcliffe's crew shot down 22/3 July at Pirot. WO Tom Bradshaw, RCAF, Pilot of T-Tommy shot down 7/8 May. WO Norman Reid, RCAF, Navigator of Tom Bradshaw's crew. Flt Sgt Bill Goodbrand, Navigator of Wally Booth's O-Orange crew shot down 1/2 July.

Front row
Sgt J. Mason, Wireless Operator, of O-Orange's crew. Sgt Dick Somers, Rear Gunner of Tom Bradshaw's crew. Flt Sgt W. Taylor, Wireless Operator of Tom Bradshaw's crew.

(Courtesy W Goodbrand)

Thursday 18 May

There was now a pause while the attentions of MASAF were directed elsewhere. Ten days were to pass until 35 Fortresses and 173 Liberators dropped 499 tons on Ploieşti for a loss of nineteen bombers. The escort of 200 P-38s and P-51s claimed to have downed thirteen defenders without loss.

24/25 May

After a long break from Romanian skies, 205 Group returned on Wednesday 24 May, but only to deliver nickels. USSAFE's Air Intsum No 29 records that three Wellingtons and one Liberator were launched but one Wellington returned early from leaflet raids to Romania and Hungary. The only more detailed information to emerge is that 142 Squadron launched Wellington 'T-Tommy' LN 961, captain Lieutenant W. Wallace SAAF for a delivery to Timişoara and Arad. Take off was at 2125 hours and the load was 520,000 nickels.

'T-Tommy' reached Timişoara at 0037 hours on 25 May and Wallace dropped a flare to identify the ground. However, the cloud base was at 7,000 feet and very hazy beneath. They descended to drop at 5,000 feet and stayed in the area for some two hours. Arad was not visited as a result and Wallace landed safely at Amendola at 0435 hours. There had been no enemy reaction whatsoever.

Life at the airfields does not stop for war. The group ORB for May tells posterity that Air Marshal Sir John C. Slessor KCB DSO MC Deputy Air-CINC MTO and CINC RAFME visited 330 Wing on Wednesday 24 May. He visited both 142 and 150 Squadrons before taking lunch at HQ 205 Group.

28/29 May

The next night-bomber visit was no more aggressive than its predecessor. On Sunday 28 May Sergeant P. Cooke and his 142 Squadron crew took-off in 'C-Charlie' LP 117 at 2105 hours with 600,000 leaflets for Craiova and Bucharest, dropping at 0005 and 0056 hours 29 May respectively. Again, the defences remained silent, there was no cloud but some low-level haze.

Wednesday 31 May

15 AF rounded the daylight raids of the month with a heavy concentration on Ploieşti on 31 May. Turnu Severin was attacked as a secondary target by thirteen B-24s. Refineries at Ploieşti were individually targeted. 105 Liberators attacked Romană-Americană dropping 257 tons. 65 more attacked the Dacia Refinery – 130 tons, while 30 bombed Redevenţa – 48 tons. Unirea received 248 tons from 123 B-24s and 106 bombed Concordia Vega – 245 tons. The only B-17s attacking went for the Xenia Refinery with 53 aircraft and 130 tons of bombs. The 240-strong P-38 and P-51 escort claimed 41 enemy fighters for a loss of three. Fifteen bombers were lost.

21 May/1 June

205 Group's last Romanian objectives for the month were to be the Iron Gates Canal installations, upstream from Turnu Severin. On the previous night 38 sorties had been flown against Feuersbrunn airfield near Vienna. Day fighters based there had been causing heavy casualties to 15 AF operations against military and industrial targets in eastern Austria. One bomber was lost.

Turnu Severin was not the only target on 31 May. The Group was out in force. 34 Wellingtons of 231 and 236 Wings dropped over 67 tons of HE to crater and block the roads in Subiaco, a village East of Rome, behind the German lines. Another 38 Wellingtons and nine Liberators laid 129 Mark V mines in the Danube above Belgrade. There were no losses in either of these ops. As to the Iron Gates operation, the Group ORB records:

Target – IRON GATES CANAL – Sheds, Locomotives and Railway Tracks. *38 Sorties*

25 Wellingtons of 231, 236 and 330 Wings, 2 Liberators of 240 Wing and 11 Halifaxes of 614 Squadron operated. One Wellington returned early with engine trouble, but the remainder attacked the target.

All aircraft clearly identified the target and bombing seems to have been well-concentrated, mainly across the embankment near the main engine shed. Several 4,000 lb bomb bursts were reported well in the target area. 83 tons of HE and 580,000 nickels were dropped. There were no losses.

Sergeant Gurth Addington of 37 Squadron sums his raid briefly.

139

We were told that this was a bottleneck in the Danube transport system and that if we could knock out the mole wall, the engine shed or the railway line, we would cause great delay. It was a good effort. Three 'Cookies' went off together, so I am not sure which was mine. The whole op took 5 hours 20 minutes.

Night raid on the Iron Gates installations at Turnu Severin on the Danube on the night of 31 May 1944.
Flying Officer Morton's Wellington LN 748 explodes its 4000 lb bomb among riverside buildings. (Courtesy James Grieve)

While Flight Sergeant Morgan's nine 500 lb bombs burst a short way inland. (Courtesy James Grieve)

A very good example of night flash photography, showing clearly the canalised section of the Danube at the Iron Gates. A 4000 lb bomb explodes centre left and small ones fall in the vicinity. (Courtesy Gurth Addington)

For RAAF pilot, Flight Lieutenant Victor (Bill) Skehill of 150 Squadron, this raid put the seal on his award of the DFC. That part of his citation reads:

> On another occasion, he was detailed to attack installations at the Iron Gates Canal on the Danube. As the target was small, three bombing runs were necessary before the bombs could be released with precision. On this sortie, five photographs were obtained.
>
> Flight Lieutenant Skehill has fulfilled the duty of flight commander for the past six months and in this capacity has acted in a most able manner and set an excellent example to crews in his flight.

This persistence almost cost them dearly: by the time they landed back at Amendola there was very little fuel to spare.

Flying Officer Frank Hinshelwood, navigating for Flying Officer Stanton in 37 Squadron's 'Z-Zebra' kept another immaculate Log of the operation. The Blitz was 15 minutes from 2330 hours. Their 4,000 lb Cookie was dropped at 2333 hours from 8,200 feet. They arrived safely over Tortorella at 0204 hours and landed sixteen minutes later after a round trip of 1,010 miles and exactly six hours since the engines were started the previous evening.

Flight Lieutenant Bill Skehill RAAF and his crew wish a B-17 crew Good Luck as they set out to raid a Balkan target from their shared airfield at Amendola.

From the right – Flight Sergeant Maurice Jefferson (Wireless Operator) Flight Sergeant 'Gran' Haywood (Air Gunner), Bill Skehill DFC RAAF and Flight Lieutenant Phil Jameson RAAF. (Courtesy Imperial War Museum)

142 Squadron's record adds that the enemy defence's response was non-existent.

Its ten Wellingtons carried a variety of loads, three had a 4,000 lb HC each, one carried two 2,000 lb bombs and the other six each bore nine 500 lb GPs each. The only report of any enemy action came from Lieutenant E. MacDonald SAAF who experienced one close burst of light flak when he was at 8,000 feet.

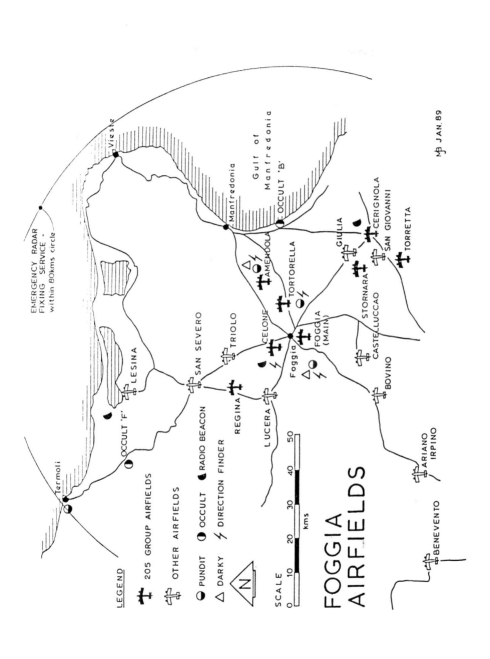

FOGGIA
AIRFIELDS

MB JAN. 89

EMERGENCY RADAR
FIXING SERVICE -
within 80kms circle

Gulf of
Manfredonia

LEGEND

✚ 205 GROUP AIRFIELDS
✚ OTHER AIRFIELDS
◐ PUNDIT   ◑ OCCULT   ◖ RADIO BEACON
△ DARKY   ⚡ DIRECTION FINDER

N

SCALE
0   10   20   30   40   50
kms

Vieste
Manfredonia
OCCULT 'B'
OCCULT 'F'
Termoli
Lesina
San Severo
Triolo
Celone
Amendola
Tortorella
Giulia
Cerignola
San Giovanni
Torretta
Stornara
Castelluccao
Bovino
Foggia (MAIN)
Regina
Lucera
Ariano Irpino
Benevento

CHAPTER 8 - June

Summary

The build-up of MASAF's strength had continued and by June 15 AF mustered 60 Squadrons of B-24 Liberators and 24 of B-17 Fortresses based in the Bari and Foggia areas respectively. The B-24s were formed into four Wings of fifteen Groups, each with four Squadrons. The B-17s were in one Wing of six Groups, each with four Squadrons. The escort fighter Wing by now had seven Groups with nine Squadrons each of P-38 Lightnings and P-51 Mustangs and four Squadrons of P-47 Thunderbolts.

205 Group retained its three Wings of Wellingtons (six Squadrons). Its Wing of Liberators (two Squadrons), now included 31 Squadron SAAF, 614 Squadron (Halifaxes) continued to operate in the Target-Marking Role: a total of nine effective Squadrons.

June 1944 was a month of some highly significant events in the path towards Allied victory. Rome fell on 4 June and D Day in France was two days later: personnel in Italy were 'overjoyed' at the news of the landings. On 13 June the first of the V-1 flying bomb raids on London began. Cherbourg fell to US ground forces on 30 June. It was on 8 June (D + 2 days) that General Carl Spaatz, Commander USSAFE, instructed 8 and 15 AFs that their primary strategic aim would now be to deny the enemy his oil supplies.

During the first half of June MASAF bombers attacked oil targets on six days and five nights involving some 1600 day and 205 night sorties. The net spread to include oil installations in Hungary, Yugoslavia and Italy as well as in Romania where Constanța and Giurgiu were successfully raided.

Spells of bad weather in late June curtailed bomber operations but on four nights 205 Group's bombers flew 325 effective sorties against oil targets delivering some 625 tons of bombs. Targets included two Italian refineries and one at Budapest. The only oil target hit both by day and night was the Danubian oil port of Giurgiu.

The Group's monthly total for operations on twenty-two nights was over 2,000 tons of bombs and 22,000,000 leaflets in 1,600 sorties altogether.

British-based bombers continued the oil offensive: Bomber Command delivered over 1100 tons on two plants while 8 US AF dropped over 3000 tons on eight synthetic production centres. June's efforts produced an estimated cut of 51% in synthetic output and 45% in refined products. However, clearance and repair work now had the highest priority and was classed as vital reconstruction work.

Railway targets were also hit to support the Red Army's ground offensive at Oradea, Simeria, Cluj, Ploieşti, Piteşti, Turnu Severin, Craiova, Piatra Olt and Timişoara. 205 Group made its first sally into the Reich itself with an attack on Munich railway station.

Meanwhile mining of the Danube continued.

The Raids

Friday 2 June

June began with two new developments in the MASAF offensive – Operation FRANTIC and raids on railway and industrial centres in Transylvania. 107 B-17s escorted by 42 P-51s flew the first Operation FRANTIC shuttle mission from their Foggia bases to airfields in the Poltava area of the Soviet Union, making no attacks or contact with the enemy en route. USSAFE Intsum No 30 summarises the raids into Transylvania. 125 B-24s attacked Simeria escorted by 49 P-38s, dropping 306 tons of high explosive. Simeria is an important railway centre at the junction of the East–West route along the Mureş valley, with the North–South lines through the industrial centre of Calan into the Jiu valley. 128 B-24s delivered 252 tons of bombs on Cluj. Their escort was 47 P-51s. 25 B-17s attacked Oradea with 72 tons of HE, escorted by 50 P-57s. Cluj and Oradea, in Hungarian hands at the time, were nodal points on the railway network between the front to the south-east and Germany.

2/3 June

Apart from a single Wellington from 231 Wing dropping 108,000 nickels over Arad without incident on 1 June, 205 Group's first operation of the month was launched on Friday 2 June against the quays and storage tanks at Giurgiu, on the north bank of the Danube. The Group's Operational Record Book notes that 44 sorties were flown and goes on:

Four Halifaxes of 614 Squadron, six Liberators of 240 Wing and 34 Wellingtons of 236 and 330 Wings operated. Six Wellingtons returned early . . . and one, 'N' of 40 Squadron, captain FS HUGHES is missing. Illumination was good and all crews identified the target. Bombing was well concentrated, bursts being seen to straddle the oil depot and loading area and direct hits were claimed on the storage tanks. A very large fire was started, which burnt a deep red colour and gave off black smoke to a height of several thousand feet. Photographs confirm. 52¾ tons of bombs were dropped.

The oil terminal port of Giurgiu on the Danube photographed by a 60 Squadron (SAAF) Mosquito on 25th April. The night-bombers' successful visit on 2nd June was doubtless based on such vivid evidence as this. (Courtesy Ministry of Defence)

256. FOG. 2/3 JUNE 44//NTB" 10,000 '→ 035° 00.4
GIURGIU. X. 3x500. 3x250. P.8. SGT. NEVILL. H. 10

The first night attack on Giurgiu's port installations on the night of 2nd/3rd June was rated a success. This photograph from Sgt Neville's Wellington, H-Harry of 104 Squadron, shows that his bomb release was dead overhead the port's inner basin. Oil storage tanks can be seen at the right. (Courtesy D.C. Hurd)

The three Wing ORBs add little to this and strangely this was one of the successful attacks made by the Group and one which was a highlight for 614 Squadron's target-marking role, for which there have been few contemporary eye-witness accounts. 142 Squadron's pilots all thought that the TMF did a good job. The Aiming Point (AP) was well-marked, the target well-lit and much damage in view. RAAF Warrant Officer S. Bryant could see target fires from 130 miles away on the return leg. He had bombed from 10,300 feet and saw his stick of six HE bombs straddle the AP. Flight Sergeant T. Slade dropped his bombs in the oil quay area. They caused a sheet of flame to flash from a ruptured tank. RNZAF pilot Flight Sergeant Stinson in 'P-Peter' saw burning oil flowing into the Danube with columns of black smoke billowing into the sky. He and a few others commented on meeting 'some heavy flak'. In spite of good visibility there were no sightings of enemy fighters.

Little is known about the loss of 40 Squadron's 'N-Nan' LP 120. The aircraft crashed 15–20 kilometres south of Pirot in Yugoslavia.

Night-bomber damage. Two views of the burning oil-storage area at Giurgiu taken early on 3rd June 1944, after 205 Group's first visit to this key Danubian oil port.
(*Courtesy Romanian Ministry of National Defence*)

Flight Sergeant K. Shaw baled out and survived the war as a PW. He knew that two others baled out with him, but not who they were and he never saw them again. They lost their lives as did the other two members of the crew. These four are recorded as having 'no known graves'.

3/4 June

It is occasionally worthwhile to focus briefly on an attack which did not happen, if only to illustrate the eleventh hour changes which could be and were made to planned operations in responding to the needs of the land battle. On this Saturday bombers of 205 Group were poised for a 'maximum effort' to attack the railway marshalling yards at Timişoara. However, at 2100 hours an order from HQ MAAF, not in this case from HQ 15 AF/MASAF:

> . . . switched the attack to a target in the battle area in support of 5 (US) Army, which had broken through the Colle Laziale position and was now threatening Rome.

148

The 205 Group target was a road bridge over the Tiber between Rome and Ostia. 44 Wellingtons from all three Wings and six Liberators from 178 Squadron delivered 82 tons of bombs. The bridge received five direct hits.

5/6 June

One lone 142 Squadron Wellington, captained by RNZAF Pilot Officer A.R. Harrison, delivered 500,000 nickels over Timişoara and Turnu Severin without any noticeable enemy reaction.

Tuesday 6 June
(D-Day in Normandy)

This date was also a 'first' in MASAF operations; the completion of the first operation FRANTIC mission. The B-17s and their escorting P-51s which had flown through to Poltava on 2 June now returned to attack a deep target in Romania on their return leg to Italy. They dropped 359 tons on the important airfield at Galaţi on the Danube. Twenty-five enemy fighters were encountered and eight were claimed to have been destroyed for a loss of two Mustangs. No bombers were lost.

On the same day 570 more 15 AF bombers hit other Romanian targets. The biggest raid was by 308 B-24s with over 700 tons to Ploieşti. Braşov was attacked by 137 B-24s dropping 332 tons. Twenty-eight B-17s bombed the Iron Gates installations near Turnu Severin (84 tons) while 31 B-24s delivered 70 tons to the railway yards at Piteşti. This was a secondary attack. These Liberators had been directed to bomb Ploieşti with the main force but that was obscured by its smoke screen by the time they arrived there.

8/9 June

Another night when a single Wellington was the only 205 Group presence over Romania. A 150 Squadron aircraft visited Turnu Severin and Craiova with a delivery of nickels. Complete 10/10 cloud cover obscured Craiova so the full load was dumped over Turnu Severin. The defences were silent.

Saturday 10 June

This day's operations were an attempt by 15 AF to overcome the smoke generator defences by sending a fighter-bomber force only to attack

Ploieşti. With their P-51 escort, 36 P-38s, each carrying a 1000 lb bomb, flew low and fast along the Danube valley and up to Bucharest, attacking targets of opportunity on the way. On arrival over Ploieşti the P-38s dive-bombed the Romană-Americană Refinery from low level. It was a costly raid: twenty-four Lightnings were lost. As a result of their strafing sorties en route, the fighters claimed to have shot down twenty-three enemy fighters in the air and destroyed three on the ground. 15 AF did not repeat this experiment.

Sunday 11 June

This was the 'home run' of the second Operation FRANTIC shuttle. 615 B-17s and B-24s attacked three main target areas on their return flight to Italy.

Immediately after 264 of the B-24s had bombed the port installations at Giurgiu, they were set-upon by 70 aggressive enemy fighters and seven bombers were quickly lost. The P-38 escort eventually dispersed the attackers without further losses.

At Constanţa, the principal Black Sea port, 145 escorted B-24s were attacked over the target by twenty-four enemy fighters. The escort claimed to have shot down fourteen for a loss of three bombers, two Mustangs and two Lightnings.

At the Luftwaffe airfield at Focşani, 126 B-17s were greeted by seventeen enemy fighters. This time there were no 15 AF losses. The B-17s claimed two fighters while their escort claimed three.

14/15 June

The ORBs record very briefly the efforts of another singleton: another 150 Squadron Wellington undertook a nickelling mission. This time the delivery was 520,000 and the target was Bucharest.

16/17 June

This was 205 Group's first bombing attack on the railway centre of Timişoara in the Transylvanian plain. Initially, 66 aircraft were detailed but, late in the day, a second force was mounted for a mission in support of land operations in Italy. The number of sorties against Timişoara was reduced to 41. 231 and 330 Wings together assembled 32 Wellingtons and the force was completed by nine Halifaxes of 614 Squadron, of which one returned early.

A 60 Squadron (SAAF) Mosquito photographed Timişoara in Western Romania two days before it received its first night-bomber visit on 15/16 April. (Courtesy Ministry of Defence)

The raid was claimed as a success. The illumination was well-placed and a well-concentrated attack was delivered. The railway yards and the built-up area to the North and South were covered with incendiaries and the yards were described as a mass of flames and explosions. Three good fires were noted to be burning at the eastern end of the yards and the main station was reported to be ablaze. The Damage Assessment Report after the attack confirmed that the operation was 'very successful'. No railway installation of importance had escaped damage. The carriage, wagon and loco repair shops were more than two-thirds destroyed and the ruins were still smouldering at 1500 hours the following day. 50.5 tons, including 47 tons of incendiaries, were dropped. 'Blitz' was 0020 to 0030 hours 17 June. The Group's only loss on this raid was

Wellington 'H-Harry' HF 524 of 37 Squadron flown by Flight Sergeant M.E. Holloway. Gurth Addington also of 37 Squadron remembered that Holloway had Flying Officer D. Watson with them as 'Second Dickey' acquiring operational experience. The crew radio-ed that they were baling out over the Danube, one engine being unserviceable. 'H-Harry' crashed 10 miles south-west of Szeged in Hungary and all six became prisoners of war in Hungary. The ORB records Holloway's Wellington as 'H-Harry' but the Air Ministry file 418869/44 lists HF 524 was 'W-William'.

The enemy air opposition to this attack was summed up as 'meagre'. While the flak was 'scant, inaccurate light and heavy'. The 'light' and 'heavy' refer to calibres in contemporary reporting. Four unidentified aircraft were reported to have attacked one Wellington which shook them off. Bob Ives, 150 Squadron Rear Gunner, remembered that there was a lot of heavy firing and a host of searchlights, but they got back to Amendola safely. John Bodman of 70 Squadron was flying as Air Bomber that night in 'L-Love', as usual. He noted in his Log Book that fires were visible from the Danube on return. Their load had been incendiaries. For Derrick Burns of 150 Squadron this was the last operation of his first tour of operations. He remembered that the target area was ablaze from end to end

> but otherwise it was a bit of an anti-climax. Being our last operation I suppose we were psyched-up but on our return realised that it was just another op or perhaps it was because of the relief of knowing that we would be leading a comparatively normal life for the next few months.

Flying Officer Frank Hinshelwood's Navigator's Log is, once more, a mine of detailed information. At 2340 hours he observed red flares with green stars seen 20 miles South of his track at Belgrade. Then half an hour out from the target he records seeing a flare path lit and then extinguished. This would undoubtedly be for defending night-fighters to take off from their Yugoslav airfields. Such sightings were unusual but not unique.

Flying Officer Bill Burcham, also of 37 Squadron, was flying his twenty-second operation that night in 'Q-Queen'. His diary records:

> ... dead on track all the way – the 614 Squadron route markers went down to time straight ahead and we reached the target beautifully. It was illuminated extremely well, with the whole town lit up like day. Wanted to make our run quickly before fires from incendiaries spoilt our target photo. However, it was a dummy run and we bombed with sticks of incendiaries already covering the target. Light heavy flak not near us. Climbed from

5,500 feet to 11,000 feet and so home. The landing circuit was again the worst part of the op but a very successful raid.

Pilot Officer A.R. Harrison flew 'T-Tommy' that night with a load of 810 4 lb incendiaries, carried in nine Special Bomb Containers (SBCs) at 90 each. His Log Book's brief 'Good prang' conceals a fuller account in his diary

> Briefed at 1830 hours for Timişoara marshalling yards. Trucks at 2015 hours. Ran-up and took off at 2130 hours. Bad cross wind, swung on take off. Climbed to 8,000 feet and set course to a spot 10 miles west of Belgrade and onwards to the target. Climbed to 10,000 feet to cross mountains and dropped down to 6,000 feet on approaching the target. Markers – red TIs cascading green stars went down over the target just as we got near. We went round the outskirts to the South and turned in over the town and dropped our load on the already plastered and burning yards. Other aircraft milled around us in the light of the flares. There were odd burst of heavy (calibre) flak above us but it was well-scattered. Climbed to 10,000 feet on course for home. Landed at base after a 5 hour 50 minute trip. In bed by about 0430 hours.

142 Squadron's ORB lists eight aircraft operating, each carrying a full load of 810 incendiaries and nickels. Two pilots, Flight Lieutenant King in 'R-Robert' and Capt Van der Westhuizen SAAF in 'U-Uncle', reported that surface to air rockets were fired at them somewhere south of Belgrade.

Friday 23 June

Over 100 bombers were lost when 400 plus attacked oil storage tanks at Giurgiu and two of the Ploieşti oil refineries. Thirty enemy fighters were claimed. USSAFE Air Intsum No 33 supplies some further data. 133 B-17s dropped 330 tons on two Ploieşti 'petrefs' and 270 B-24s dropped 486 tons on Giurgiu. Only 46 P-38s seem to have been on long-range escort duties which may account for the high bomber losses.

Saturday 24 June

Another 'first' for 15 AF – the first use of Pathfinder aircraft. 146 B-24 bombers attacked the Xenia and Concordia Vega 'petrefs' at Ploieşti. The escorting fighters also carried out sweeps against ground targets. Seventeen enemy aircraft were claimed. Six bombers were lost. First Lieutenant D. Pucket USAAF won the seventh and last Ploieşti Medal of

Honor on this raid, losing his life. Another 146 B-24s dropped 358 tons on Craiova. 55 B-17s attacked the main railway line at Piatra Olt, 40 kilometres east of Craiova, escorted by 41 P-38s. One bomb severed the bridge over the Olt while two more cut the railway and further damaged the bridge. Fifteen B-24s were lost to enemy action.

Wednesday 28 June

Industrial and petroleum targets in Bucharest were 15 AF's principal objectives. 100 B-24s attacked the railway yards in the north-west suburb of Chitila with 230 tons, 64 more B-24s dropped 147 tons on the Titan industrial area and another 65 put 109 tons onto the Prahova refinery. Three B-24s were lost. The fighter escort for these attacking formations was large: 79 P-51s and 80 P-38s which claimed ten defending fighters. A further 40 P-51s flew sweeps in the Bucharest area and claimed seventeen enemy aircraft without loss.

28/29 June

That Wednesday night, 205 Group returned to Giurgiu flying 105 sorties, 31 Squadron SAAF making its first attack against a Romanian target. It was not an overwhelming success and the Group ORB implies many tales of woe in its few lines.

74 Wellingtons of 231, 236 and 330 Wings, 23 Liberators of 240 Wing and 8 Halifaxes of 614 Squadron were dispatched. Three Liberators of 31 (SAAF) Sqn

'R' Capt T.A.M. Van der Spuy

'Y' Lt D.J.S. Haggie

'F' Maj J.A. Mouton,

one Halifax 'F' of 614 Sqn, Flt Lt T.P.G.G. de Bloeme and one Wellington 'F' of 70 Sqn, Flt Sgt L. Fallon are missing. One Liberator and 6 Wellingtons returned early for various reasons. One Liberator and two Wellingtons jettisoned their bombs, one Wellington brought its bombs back and one more landed away at Brindisi.

Owing to cloud and electrical storms on the route, the Illuminators arrived late and target-marking aircraft were unable to pinpoint the target, because of haze and extreme darkness. Some aircraft identified the target, but the majority bombed on its estimated position in relation to the river, island and harbour installations. Bombing appears to have been scattered over a wide area. One 4,000 lb bomb burst just short of the target.

There were numerous reports of aircraft crashing in flames and some crews believed that two aircraft collided over the target. Several reported fighters. Some aircraft had encounters and one claimed to have damaged a single-engined fighter. 158 tons of bombs were dropped.

The oil installations at Giurgiu attacked on the night of 28/29 June. This a good flash picture of one of the storage areas hit.

(Courtesy Angus MacLean)

The Wing ORBs reflect the same general gloom. That of 330 Wing (142 and 150 Squadrons) sums up the operation as 'poor'. Of the fourteen Wellingtons of 142 Squadron which operated only four claimed to have put bombs into the target area, blaming ground haze and poor illumination. As usual some odd sightings were reported and those of 142 Squadron's crews are typical.

Flight Sergeant P. Cooke dropped his 4000 lb bomb from 10,000 feet at 0149 hours. He and members of his 'A-Able' crew saw a suspect Me 110 head-on at 1,000 feet lower. It was showing its tail light.

Flight Lieutenant J. Long in 'B-Bertie' LN 808 saw blue and green tracer above his height and at 0155 hours he saw an unidentified aircraft shot down. Flight Sergeant C. Hill in 'H-Harry' and Warrant Officer W. Morton RAAF also saw this aircraft shot down. Morton placed the incident as South of the Danube. These three Wellingtons carried six 500 lb and two 250 lb bombs each. Sergeant Aleph Palmer in 'L-Love' saw an aircraft with 'amber lights' attacking another aircraft (could these lights have been exhaust flames?) Half an hour later he saw another aircraft with yellow lights. He was also followed by a Ju 88 which was . . .

> . . . using radar, because many times I took evasive action by altering course 90° in cloud only to find him keeping still keeping station when we emerged. No explanation could be guessed at why he made no attack. Lack of ammo or jammed guns could have meant that he was trying to bring other fighters into contact with us. We believed that the soft orange glow showing in the nose of these fighters originated from the radar display reflecting on the cockpit canopy.

Perhaps it is even more likely to have been the reflection of the screen on the operator's face, dimming or going out as he moved his head or looked up.

Flying Officer K. Jones in 'P-Peter', Flight Sergeant Dean in 'Q-Queen' and Captain Van der Westhuizen SAAF did not find the target. They all saw other aircraft, Jones even reported a dying Halifax at 0219 hours, which could not have been 614 Squadron's loss that night. This Halifax was 'F-Freddie' JN 942. It made its last radio contact at 0442 hours giving a garbled position and saying that its port inner was burning. 'Freddie' did in fact crash at Tetovo, 40 kilometres East of Skopje in Yugoslavia. Flight Lieutenant T.P.G.G. de Bloeme RCAF and the other five members of his crew became prisoners of war.

Warrant Officer W.T.H. (Hugh) Fleckney flew his first operation with 614 Squadron over Romania that night. He remembers that it must have been uneventful because his Log Book shows 'slight flak, fighters active'. His role was a Blind Illuminator (BI) using the H_2S radar to place flares which, in turn, allowed the Visual Markers (VMs) to put Target Indicators (TIs) over the target. This was Flying Officer Denys White's twentieth operation. He flew 150 Squadron's 'W-William' with a standard mixed load of six 500 lb MC and two 250 lb GP.

31 Squadron (SAAF)'s three losses on their first Romanian operation must have jolted morale. The Squadron had only begun to move its Liberators from Jebel Hamzi to Celone on 11 June. The loss of Captain T.A.M. Van der Spuy and his crew in 'L-Love', not 'R-Robert' as the ORB stated, is a total mystery. The aircraft was not heard of or seen after take off and no trace of any of the crew has been found in any post-war investigations. All seven of KG 839's crew are registered as having 'no known grave'. Sadly, the fate of 'Y-Yoke' EW 104 is only a little better in that the dead are known and are buried in the CWGC Cemetery at Sofia. All seven lost their lives when 'Yoke' crashed at a village near Ruse, in Bulgaria. The records show it to be

Woecwage but no such place exists (nor with that spelling could exist!) Major J.A. Mouton DFC and another SAAF officer were killed when their Liberator 'F-Fox' EV 970 crashed in Bulgaria at an untraced site. Three other SAAF officers and a Warrant Officer survived and became prisoners of the Bulgars. Very strangely, the one RAF member of the crew, Pilot Officer A. Gill, became separated from his colleagues and parachuted into Romania to become a PW in Bucharest. He has not been traced since.

'F-Freddie' MF 194 of 70 Squadron was the fifth loss that night. This Wellington crashed at Svistov in Bulgaria. Flight Sergeant Lloyd Fallon RAAF and three of his all-RAAF crew were killed and are buried at Sofia. Flying Officer G.G. Knyvett survived, although injured in baling out. He tells the story well:

> That evening 'F for Freddie' happened to be the last in the marshalling line – we would be the last Tortorella aircraft to take-off. Nothing unusual about that – positions in the line always varied. Unfortunately, just as we were about to line up on the runway, an aircraft which had already taken off called for an emergency landing, so we had to clear the runway and wait. After considerable delay and two or three attempts the aircraft in trouble finally landed and we were able to go. The delay was 30–40 minutes after the last aircraft ahead had gone.
>
> The planned target route to Giurgiu led almost direct from Tortorella with two slight deviations to confuse the enemy as to our real intentions. We cut these corners and increased cruising speed about 5 knots to try to catch up with the main stream (there's some safety in numbers). We were heavily loaded with one overload tank in each bomb bay and just the 250 lb bombs in the remaining space, so we could not risk excessive fuel consumption by increasing our speed too much. We were also a little concerned at the possibility of meeting returning aircraft, particularly if they were a little off track. In all probability we picked up only 10–15 minutes – at any rate we appeared to be alone over the target which we bombed as best we could and turned for home.
>
> Being the Navigator, I was usually glued to my table, but it was our custom when very close to the target for me to stand in the astrodome as an extra pair of eyes, for any enemy aircraft or our own – which could be just as dangerous. I don't recall seeing any aircraft, nor did I see our bomb-strike, just a certain amount of flare and the usual signs of an operation having taken place. Having given the skipper a memorised course for home I returned quickly to my desk. We all realised the danger we were in. About ten minutes later and without any warning there were noises of something ripping through the aircraft and the Rear Gunner calling on the

IC about an attack. Within seconds there was another burst through the aircraft but no one seemed to have been hit, so that I (now) assume that the wings and the overload tanks received the main brunt. We went into a slight dive and the skipper gave the order to bale out.

We went about our parachute drill as practised many times. I moved forward and fastened my parachute (breast type) on the skipper's chest. He was sitting in the pilot's seat, unharmed, but fighting the aircraft. I was aware of flames on the port wing. The bomb-aimer had left his seat and moved back to the area of the main spar, I cannot recall why. I undid the pilot's parachute from its stowage, put it on and opened the forward hatch in the floor near the nose of the aircraft. Up to this point the drill had been quite normal – we were all supposed to drop through the hatch in turn, navigator first and pilot last, except for the rear gunner who exit-ed backwards.

On opening the forward hatch a great wall of flame shot through the space. In hindsight I can only assume that the overload tanks were punctured and that fuel had run forward even against the airstream. At any rate, I did not believe we could get out that way, so I banged the hatch shut, shouted to the skipper, who was still in his seat struggling with the controls and pointed to the rear. He nodded. The emergency exit is a small diamond shaped hole in the floor at the rear of the fuselage. It is quite lightly covered with fabric and some other material like thin plywood. I knew this because we had lost our cased bombsight through it on another operation following severe jinking to shake off a hung up bomb. I passed the bomb-aimer and wireless operator in the passage way, giving each a nudge and pointing to the rear. As far as I am aware they were following me closely. I had just reached the exit when the interior of the aircraft seemed to burst into flame. Remembering the bombsight, I jumped on the exit and went out.

From here until I woke up on the ground, everything is a little dim. I remember passing through a lot of flame; I remember reaching for the parachute rip-cord and I think that I heard an explosion. Then I woke up on the ground and I was unable to get up. There was a burning feeling on my back so I hit the harness release and pulled the pack pad round to the front. It was smouldering and one of the straps had burned through. There could not have been any wind on the ground because I was able to pull the parachute canopy right up. It was cold and I was very sleepy so I wrapped the 'chute round me and went to sleep almost immediately.

I woke at daylight and took stock. I could only raise myself to about a half-sitting position and I realised that my leg was broken. My battledress was sprayed with melted duralumin and there were many holes burned in it. I knew I had some burns behind my ears. I went to sleep again.

Some time later I awoke to the sound of voices and, raising myself a little, I could see some menacing figures about 10 yards away. There were one or two with shotguns and others with farm implements all pointing in my direction. The peasants and I eyed one another until I beckoned with one arm. They approached cautiously and eventually, while keeping me covered, searched me as I lay on the ground, relieving me of my navigator's watch, pipe (a rather good one which I valued greatly) and one or two other items. Satisfied that I was not armed they stood around and we tried to converse. I was very thirsty, I pointed to my mouth, swallowed and said every word for water I could think of. There was no immediate effect. Eventually, however, I was given some of the most beautiful cool water I have ever enjoyed.

Based on what I was told later by other PWs that the only reason why I was not summarily dispatched was because I was injured – human compassion came to the fore and, in any event, I posed no further threat. Perhaps my obvious youth (21) was also showing. Mind you I was asked – and I clearly understood the sign language – whether I wished to shoot myself! I declined.

Geoff Knyvett had become a prisoner of war.

Meanwhile – at Foggia

Crews of 330 Wing (142 and 150 Squadrons) were disappointed at the announcement on 30 June that the Wing would be moving to Regina early in July. They had hoped to stay at Amendola to see out their period of operations. Regina had only a fair-weather runway and its other facilities were even more stark.

The Group's summary of the month's activities throws an interesting light on the operation of a force of this size flying three types of aircraft from different airfields and landing grounds and carrying out the widest range of missions given to a night-bomber force. Under the heading of Training the ORB records that the accident rate at 446.26 hours per accident is the lowest for the year. It attributes this success to recent instructional schemes. Early returns from operations for 'petty reasons' had increased.

614 Squadron was to fly its best crews on each operation, together with 'unproven possible first class crews'. These latter crews would act as BIs and assessment could be made of their H_2S techniques and general efficiency under operational conditions. Squadron training was to concentrate on the team of

Navigator, Set Operator and Pilot, 'an essential requirement for success'. All targets were now marked by the TMF (Pathfinders). New crews were to be trained on operational sorties, their success or failure being photographed at the time of blind release of TM bombs or Illuminating Flares.

HQ 330 Wing at Regina. (Courtesy Wally Talbot)

Main Force bombing was of a very poor standard. The arrival of a new Bombing Leader, Flight Lieutenant D.G. Watson, would see an improvement.

Under the heading of Organisation, apart from noting the arrival of 31 Squadron, the arrival of ten Italian searchlights manned by Italian Navy personnel for duty at three each to Stornara, Tortorella and Celone Airfields was noted. The tenth would be retained at HQ 205 Group. On 13 June the Group learned that 34 Squadron SAAF would arrive and join 2 SAAF Wing. No date was given. On 28 June the future make-up of the Group was announced. It would consist of six squadrons each of 24 Liberators. Two Wellington squadrons would be 'rearmed' with Liberators with the remaining four squadrons 'withdrawn from operations' so that their personnel could augment the Liberator squadrons.

The re-allocation of airfields was settled on 30 June; 330 Wing was not happy with their lot but the move was planned for 3 July. 240 Wing with 178

Squadron would move from Celone to Amendola on 4 July and 614 Squadron would join the Wing from its present base at Stornara. 2 SAAF Wing with 31 and 34 Squadrons would concentrate at Celone from Regina.

Rear gunner's view of Celone as his 31 Squadron Liberator climbs away.
(Courtesy T.W. Timoney)

The Signals part of the Summary was lengthy, much not relevant to operations over Eastern Europe. On 11 June the decision was made to fit MANDREL equipment to 236 Wing's aircraft: enough was now available. Rearranging the GEE stations was also discussed but a decision was postponed.

The Engineering section was primarily concerned with arrangements to support 31 Squadron's arrival at Celone for temporary attachment to 240 Wing.

Equipment was still giving cause for concern. Maintenance was now centralised at Wing level, having been formerly an individual Squadron responsibility, and that arrangement was 'working smoothly and in a most satisfactory manner'. The arrival of 31 Squadron's air echelon before its ground party had caused some difficulties, which included borrowing tents from the USAAF to accommodate the aircrews. The supply of tyres was still a major headache. By 24 June 40 Wellingtons were grounded through a lack of tyres. On that date the arrival of 380 tyres 'greatly relieved' matters. 16 Halifaxes required tyres. The arrival of replacements was unpredictable and erratic. Given the complexities of the supply system into and within the Theatre and the other demands on transport and for the supplies themselves, it is, perhaps, surprising that there were not even greater crises.

Photographic Reconnaissance – 60 Squadron SAAF

Intelligence on enemy targets comes from a great variety of sources. One of the most important of these since the advent of military aviation has been air reconnaissance, visual or photographic. Visual air reconnaissance was not a normal feature of strategic level operations except for that acquired from the detailed de-briefing of aircrews after raids. Photographic Reconnaissance, Photo Recce or PR as it came to be known, was by far the more usual feature of strategic air recce and was a highly-developed art by 1944. There is no need here to explore the complexities of the cameras nor how they were operated. The key to the considerable Allied successes in this field was the development of high-speed, high-altitude aircraft which could intrude enemy airspace at such heights as to defy interception and return with the exposed film.

Deep PR from beyond the Danube to the Alps from December 1943 onwards was the responsibility of 60 Squadron SAAF, flying twin-engined De Havilland Mosquito aircraft based at San Severo, north-west of Foggia.

The Squadron was familiar with Ploieşti. A single Mosquito had flown the post-strike PR sortie there on 3 August 1943, two days after the low-level Operation TIDALWAVE, from an airfield at Derna, Libya. This was a feat of airmanship – 2,860 kilometres in 3 hours 10 minutes.

The next visit was on 24 October 1943. Stopping over the re-fuel at Taranto, a Mosquito made four runs over Ploieşti, only attracting flak on its final pass.

The first comprehensive PR mission of Romanian targets was flown on 20 January 1944 covering Bucharest, Cîmpina, Galaţi and Braşov, in particular.

The Mosquito Mk XVI could give a range of over 3,000 kilometres using droptanks. Their usual operating altitude was in excess of 30,000 feet at which height it could outpace Bf 109 Gs and FW 190 A-4s. It has to be added that these Mosquitos frequently also had to outpace P-51s and P-38s, which seemed determined to press their attacks.

During April the Squadron's tasks took it over a wide arc of targets which included Braşov and Ploieşti. On 24 April one aircraft photographed enemy positions in Moldavia between Galaţi and Focşani opposite which the Red Army thrust was concentrating. In May, 60 Squadron flew over the Ploieşti Refinery areas and other nearby targets on four separate days and, in June, it handed over responsibility for Romanian targets to a USAAF P-38 PR Squadron.

CHAPTER 9 - July

Summary

During July MASAF intensified its offensive against oil targets and 205 Group's contribution was some 680 sorties to drop almost 1,400 tons of bombs. Operations were only possible on seventeen nights, however, compared with twenty-seven in May and twenty-one in June. Bad weather caused operations to be cancelled on three nights.

The biggest effort was directed against Ploieşti installations which received their first visit from the night-bomber force on 26 July. Air reconnaissance had noted signs of recuperation and attacks on five days and one night delivered over 4,800 tons of bombs. There were now over 2,000 smoke generators in the target area which were able to blank it out by day or night before the bombers arrived. It was necessary to resort to pathfinder bombing or off-set visual bombing and by these means considerable success was achieved.

Strategic air forces based in Britain were mainly concerned with operations in support of the land battle in Normandy and the destruction of the V-1 flying bomb sites. Oil targets were attacked, however, and Bomber Command and 8 AF delivered some 3,000 tons each on a variety of targets.

The enemy's oil production was further depressed by these attacks and pre-raid outputs were now cut by over a half in both crude and synthetic products. In Romania, to the enemy's credit, production was stepped-up to 70,500 tons over the June figure, largely due to the successful smoke screen defences and reconstruction work.

Attacks on railway communications were continued but in view of previous successes the effort could be more relaxed. It is worth repeating that the bombing of oil targets often spilt over into nearby marshalling yards and conversely, though to a lesser extent, oil installations were damaged during attacks on railway facilities. Over 12,000 tons of bombs were dropped on railway yards at Budapest through which all rail traffic between Germany and Romania had to pass by this stage of the war. Romanian railways themselves were attended to, at Ploieşti over 270 tons were dropped, with the same at Arad and somewhat less on railway yards and workshops at Bucharest.

205 Group continued to add an additional element to the dislocation of traffic; 427 mines were laid in the Danube waterway.

A new Liberator squadron joined the 205 Group Order of Battle. Aircraft for 34 Squadron SAAF began to arrive at Celone from North Africa on 8 July under the temporary command of Major C.M. Smuts pending the arrival of the CO, Lieutenant Colonel G.T. Moll. 31 and 34 Squadrons came under command of the new 2 Wing SAAF established at Celone on 6 July. By the end of the month 205 Group was operating five Wings. 2 Wing's first operation was on 19/20 July to attack an oil target at Pardubice in Czechoslovakia.

On 22 July, the first all-fighter Operation FRANTIC shuttle to the Soviet Union took place attacking targets in Romania en route. On 25 July Brigadier J.T. Durrant DFC SAAF arrived at Group HQ to assume command from Air Commodore J.H.T. Simpson DSO on 3 August 1944.

In the land war two July dates of consequence were the capture of Caen on 9th and Pisa on 26th.

The Raids

Night-bombers were to operate over Romania on seven nights in July and, towards the end of the month, five of these were on consecutive nights, interspersed with daylight attacks in strength.

The month's operations opened on Saturday 1 July with 76 sorties flown by Wellingtons and Liberators with route-marking Halifaxes to lay mines in selected stretches over a 580 kilometre length of the Danube from Nyergesujfalu, 80 kilometres upstream from Budapest down to Baziaş on the Romanian frontier. The operation was a success, but four Wellingtons, two each from 40 and 104 Squadron were lost. 192 mines were laid.

2/3 July

On Sunday 2 July the Group sent its aircraft against three targets, 'gardening' in the Danube once more – rated as 'a most successful operation', nickelling over Arad and Timişoara and a major effort over Bucharest which involved 53 sorties, making a total for the night of 64. One Liberator and three Wellingtons were lost. Perhaps understandably, the night of 3/4 July was declared to be a Group stand-down.

The Bucharest attack was directed against the Prahova Oil Refinery. The Group ORB summarises the events of the night:

With the decrease of Axis refined oil supplies from 14 million tons to 4.7 million tons annually, as a result of Allied bombing attacks, the Bucharest Prahova refinery had become a target of the highest priority.

31 Wellingtons from all three Wings and nine Liberators operated, while eight Halifaxes illuminated (five also bombed). Three Wellingtons and one Halifax returned early.

The illumination was good and Red TIs were place very close to the AP. Bombing was well-concentrated on the TIs and, though haze made observations of results difficult, three 4000 lb bursts were seen, two at the South edge of the target and one on the road to the north. Two sticks of bombs were seen to fall right across the Refinery and, at the end of the attack, three fires were left burning. 67 tons of bombs were dropped.

Moderate flak and numerous fighter sightings were reported. Ju 88, Me 110 and FW 190s were the types identified. Two bombers were damaged and hits on a Ju 88 were claimed. One Liberator 'D-Dog' of 31 Squadron SAAF (Captain Bird) and two Wellingtons, 'R-Robert', (Flying Officer Tichbourne) and 'C-Charlie' (Flight Sergeant Sutcliffe) of 40 Squadron are missing, but Sergeant J.E. Turnbull, Air-Bomber of 'C-Charlie' has returned to his Squadron. He reports that the aircraft sustained very severe damage after three attacks by a Ju 88 and the crew baled out. He landed safely and contacted the partisans, being evacuated by air after 40 days, but has no news of the remaining members of the crew.

Sergeant Turnbull features in the story of Tom Bradshaw's crew who were shot down on 8 May after bombing the Filiaşi railway bridge.

The seven Halifaxes of 614 Squadron operating that night were successful. Illumination was reportedly excellent and the Visual Markers identified the Aiming Point. Red TIs were dropped on the West and East boundaries of the target area and bombs were also released with the flares. The attack had not fully developed by the time the target-marking aircraft left the area although many bursts were seen. Route markers were also dropped at four key points on the way to the target. The Squadron's opinion of the opposition was that the flak was moderate and inaccurate. 30–40 searchlights with several 'blue masters' were operating ineffectively. However, the Giurgiu defences were alert with . . .

. . . very accurate heavy flak. Fighter flares could be seen for up to 50 miles from the target area bursting at 10,000 feet.

The Squadron's bombload was twenty-eight 500 lb MC TD .025 and 96 Mk II Flares which were dropped from 6,500–10,000 feet between 0125 and 0132 hours. The last Halifax landed safely at Celone at 0500 hours after almost seven hours in the air.

231 Wing ordered 23 Wellingtons but only eight were able to operate. The ninth burst both main-wheel tyres on take-off and blocked the single runway at Tortorella. The remainder, unable to take off, were stood down. 'L-Love' of 70 Squadron had a running fight with a Ju 88 night-fighter at 0106 hours, some 40 kilometres north-east of Turnu Măgurele at 10,000 feet in clear moonlight. The fighter approached from the starboard beam slightly high and fired a short burst from 400 metres range to which the Rear Gunner replied with several bursts without observed results while the Wellington dived steeply into wispy cloud. The Ju 88 followed and dived to attack from the port quarter, giving a long burst again at about 400 metres. The Wellington received no hits and the Rear Gunner again returned fire. 'L-Love' corkscrewed to starboard and the Ju 88 dived below as though to make a belly attack. At this point the Wellington jettisoned its bombs. The Ju 88 was eventually lost at 0115 hours, nine minutes after its first pass. 'Z-Zebra', captained by Flight Sergeant Cliff Bridges RAAF, also of 70 Squadron, had three clashes with a Ju 88. At 0113 hours at 10,000 feet while north-east of Turnu Măgurele a sister Ju 88 climbed to attack from the starboard quarter but was evaded. Then eight minutes later over the target a fighter attacked from dead astern opening fire at about 300 metres hitting the Wellington in its starboard fuel tanks, ripping off fabric and splintering the geodetic airframe. At 0125 hours, after only four minutes, the Ju 88 came into make its final attack, climbing from astern to within 200 metres. The Wellington's Rear Gunner fired first this time and the fighter broke away directly overhead, with the gunner's final burst entering the enemy's belly. The Navigator, Sergeant Peter Gadbury, remembers it as a 'particularly tough encounter'.

These seven 231 Wing Wellingtons delivered twenty-one 500 lb MC TD .025 and fourteen 250 lb GP NI from 8,000–12,000 feet between 0130 hours and 0138 hours. The last bomber was safely home at 0510 hours.

236 Wing operated sixteen Wellingtons, the seventeenth failing to take off through a propeller damaged during taxiing. There were two early returns and two from 40 Squadron were missing. The twelve aircraft which reached the primary target reported that the flares were lighting up to 8,000 feet. Three 4000 lb HE fell into the target area, two at the southern edge and one on the main road to the North. There were five fighter incidents. A Ju 88 made four passes at 'B-Baker' of 104 Squadron at 10,500 feet just West of the target at 0116 hours. Three of these were from port and one was from below starboard. Normal evasive action shook him off. 'B-Baker' was attacked again on the way

home at 0226 hours at 10,000 feet. The assailant was an unidentified single-engine type which opened fire from astern with cannon tracer from 1000 down to 600 metres. Once more the evasion was successful. 'G-George' of 104 Squadron clashed with an Me 110 at 0110 hours at 9,000 feet on his run-up to the target. The fighter opened fire from 600 metres on the starboard quarter with his four cannon. The Rear Gunner returned the fire with two bursts and evasive action was successful. Neither aircraft was hit. There were a number of other sightings of enemy aircraft.

236 Wing delivered 18 tons of high explosive comprising three 4000 lb HC NI, 44 500 lb MC TD .025, five 250 lb GP TD .025 and six 250 lb GP NI from 7,000–10,000 feet between 0131 and 0140 hours.

The third Wellington Wing – 330 – put up twelve bombers and all returned from a successful raid. Seven aircraft bombed on the Red TIs and five bombed visually. The Wing's loads were a usual mixture of 500 lb MC and 50 lb GP all TD .025 totalling 12 tons from heights between 8,500 and 9,000 feet during a six-minute blitz from 0130 hours.

The heavy bomber Wing – 240 – ordered and operated nine Liberators, losing 'D-Dog' of 31 Squadron SAAF. Seven bombers attacked using the well-positioned Red TIs, the others were able to bomb visually. The extra lifting capacity of these aircraft is shown well in the bombloads delivered. The eight aircraft which returned to base had dropped a total of 22½ tons, all 500 lb MC TD .025 in nine minutes from 0130 hours from between 10,000 and 13,500 feet. This Wing's crews also reported that the flak was spasmodic, adding that only 4–6 guns seemed to be firing at the same time. This may have been deliberate, to allow the ever-present night-fighters a looser rein.

Lieutenant H.F. Smith of 31 Squadron SAAF had a serious brush with one fighter. At 0110 hours with twenty minutes to run to the target and at 12,000 feet an unidentified enemy aircraft opened fire from a range of about 1,000 metres from astern and below. Tracer was seen to strike the Liberator's starboard elevator and the rudder which fell away. Even with this degree of damage and difficult control, the fighter was shaken off. During the evasive manoeuvres two 500 lb bombs were thrown onto the bomb doors but Lieutenant Smith determined to carry on to the target. On the final approach the bomb door were raised manually and the six bombs were released onto the target by the Second Pilot, Lieutenant Cairns. He had barely returned to the cockpit to report to the captain when the aircraft was trapped in a searchlight cone. Lieutenant Cairns was able to assist Lieutenant Smith in righting the Liberator after the evasive action, after which he went back to the bomb bay and, without his parachute or harness which would have restricted his movements in the tight space, proceeded to chop away the runners on the port bomb doors and clear the remaining bomb load. This fell away about 130 kilometres down the homeward leg. Lieutenants Smith and Cairns were able to bring their crippled Liberator safely back to Celone.

The Romanian military record of the raid is quite brief. It noted that about 70 aircraft attacked the capital in three waves at 0120, 0130 and 0135 hours on 3 July. The bombers entered Romanian air space at 0050 hours and left at 0215. Bomb damage was inflicted on the suburbs of Grivița (industrial), Băneasa (airport), Chitila (railway yards), Dămăroaia (very near to the target), Bucharest railway junction 'triaj' and Cotroceni (a garrison area in the western suburbs).

Ieuan Jones's 150 Squadron Wellington Mk X was LP 148 'P-Peter' that night. His bombload was three 500 lb MC and three 250 lb GP and two overload tanks. His Log Book shows:

> No target photo. Coned over target. Rear Gunner shot-out two searchlights. 7 hours 15 minutes.

He remembers that the crew:

> . . . regarded it as one of our shakiest trips [their fifteenth operation] . . . about 30 minutes from the target, at about 10,000 feet we emerged from cloud to find a Halifax coming at us from port and only an instinctive reaction from both pilots averted a collision . . . On our approach we were coned by several searchlights with flak being fired up the beams. We were not badly hit and I took evasive action, culminating in a (only partly) controlled dive which, after losing the searchlights, we experienced some difficulty in correcting. Pulling out needed the combined muscle of the Navigator and me, and the manufacturer's speed limits were exceeded quite comfortably. On levelling-out, the Rear Gunner advised me to gain some height as we were rather close to some tree tops (or words to that effect!) As we started to climb, we were again caught by searchlights. At such a height it was easy for the Rear Gunner to open up and extinguish two or three of them. At about 7,000 feet we levelled out and the Rear Gunner reported a night-fighter on our beam on the same course at 500 metres range. So – more evasive action and we lost him (perhaps he had not seen us). As we neared base we were very short of fuel so I obtained a quick clearance for a straight-in landing. As the starboard engine was revved-up to turn onto the taxi-track, it cut – out of fuel! On the ground inspection the fuselage was found to be warped and 'P-Peter' never flew again.

150 Squadron crew and Wimpy before their 25th operation.
Left to Right: Sgt JR Lester (Bomb Aimer) of Tooting Bec, Sgt (later FO) CD Mansfield
DFM (Navigator) of West Norwood, FO IM Jones DFC (Pilot) of Ruthin, Sgt R Tubbs
(Rear Gunner) of Netley Abbey, Hants, and Sgt R Salisbury (Wireless Operator) of
Flint. (Courtesy IM Jones)

On de-briefing, returning crews produced a formidable list of thirty en route and over target incidents and sightings. It is not possible to cross-check or verify most of them from later information. Few incidents were seen or experienced by more than one crew, which, in view of the 'blitz' streaming of the bombers, is surprising and most related to other aircraft crashing. What these sightings actually were may never be known, but, perhaps they do lend credence to the widely held view at the time that the enemy used deceptive fires, explosions and pyrotechnics – 'scarecrows' – to demoralize raiding aircrew. As to this night, only three aircraft were lost and the sites of their crashes and the fates of their crews are known.

40 Squadron lost two Wellingtons that night. 'C-Charlie' LP 253 was captained by Flight Sergeant R. (Dicky) Sutcliffe RCAF. The Group ORB was able to add more to the usual blunt statement that 'C-Charlie' was missing because Sergeant John Turnbull, the Air Bomber evaded capture and was able to return to the Squadron. His report was included in the ORB:

the aircraft sustained very severe damage after three attacks by a Ju 88 and the crew baled out. He landed safely and contacted the Partisans, being evacuated by air after 40 days, but has no news of the remaining members of the crew.

As we saw in Chapter 7 John Turnbull joined up with a Chetnik band and not Partisans and later fell in with two other 40 Squadron crews.

Sergeant E.H. Turner was C-Charlie's Wireless Operator.

Our Wimpey was attacked shortly after we crossed the Danube on the way home. It crashed in open country about 18 kms North of Pirot in Yugoslavia.

Pirot is north-west of Sofia and some 30 kms into Yugoslavia on track for Foggia. Eric Turner remembered that:

the time was about 0200 hrs. Sergeant Harry Beason was killed in his turret at the rear and the remaining four of us baled out. John Turnbull, our Air Bomber, was nearest to the escape hatch and was first out of the aircraft. He made his escape to the Chetniks before the welcoming party, attracted by the burning aircraft in the sky, was organised. Next out was Sgt J.D. (Johnny) Yole, our Navigator. His luck was out because he was shot as he descended on his parachute. The next to go was the skipper, Dicky Sutcliffe, and I followed a few seconds later. We were captured separately during the daylight hours of 3 July. Our captors were Bulgarian cavalry, part of the occupation forces of Eastern Yugoslavia at that time. We were taken by horse and cart and cavalry escort to the local Army HQ at Pirot for interrogation. The Bulgars tended to be bullying louts but the local population were very friendly. Four days later the two of us were transferred by rail to a concentration camp in Sofia.

The bodies of Sergeants Harry Beason and Johnny Yole were buried locally and were moved into the CWGC Cemetery at Belgrade after the war. Two other sergeants who lost their lives that night are also in this Cemetery. Sergeant R. Black and Sergeant D.A. Stephens lost their lives when 70 Squadron's 'V-Victor' was shot down over Yugoslavia on its way back to base from a nickel raid over Arad and Timişoara. The captain, Sergeant H.J. O'Brien and the two other members of his crew survived and became PWs in Germany.

Little is known about how 'R-Robert' ME 990 of 40 Squadron was lost.

It crashed at Maceşul de Sus [Site No 10] some 45 kilometres south of Craiova. Flying Officer J.C. Murphy was killed and his body now lies in the Cemetery at Tîncăbeşti. Flying Officer L.F. Tichbourne RAAF and the other three members of 'R-Robert''s crew became PWs and were held in Bucharest. Two of them were arrested and taken to the HQ of the Romanian 6th Regiment at Bîrca. At the time this was an unusual crew, consisting of four Flying Officers and only one NCO, Flight Sergeant L.J. Goodlet RNZAF.

31 Squadron's fourth loss in two raids to Romanian targets was Liberator Mk 6 serial 199 'D-Dog'. The crash site is recorded in Consular papers as Furculeşti in Vlasca County. Unfortunately Vlasca County disappeared from Romanian local government after the war, and there are two possible places with the same name. The Romanian Ministry of National Defence has been able to confirm that the correct Furculeşti lies some 27 kilometres north-east of Turnu Măgurele, on the road to Alexandria, in the present County of Teleorman [Site No 11]. The Navigator, Lieutenant Ed Irving Nicholson SAAF recalled that night fluently. His first operation to Romania had been to Giurgiu on 29 June. 'We hit this one very hard.' His second and final one was only three days later. He would not forget 2 July 1944:

It was the day on which I woke early and knew, with absolute certainty, that my luck had run out. For the four years in which I had been flying, I was known among my friends to have 'Nicholson's luck'. Where others would get themselves hurt, or written off, I would get off undamaged and in one piece. I had completed two tours on light bombers in Marylands and Bostons in the desert, been shot down twice and walked away from it and had done a hundred and fifty anti-sub and shipping patrols, with never a spot of bother, even with those temperamental Venturas. I had had a good run of luck, but I knew I would not be coming back on 2 July, when we headed for the refineries in Bucharest. But equally well I knew I would survive.

We were at the head of the bomber stream, south-west of Bucharest over the Danube, when we were caught by a night-fighter pair, one of whom dropped a string of flares on the starboard side, while his mate came in from the port side. We had a running fight for ten minutes, with all gunners firing, before they got our tail-gunner, and set the port engines on fire. We were very low at the time when Captain Brian Bird gave the order to bale out. I do not know if the others were alive or not, but Brian and I were the only two to get out.

I had not unclipped my oxygen tube from my parachute harness when I went out of the bottom front hatch and it pulled me up with a jerk, so I was suspended like a spider on its thread. The aircraft was diving steeply and the pitch of the roaring sound was getting higher and higher, so, in desperation, I pulled the ripcord. The 'chute opened with a tremendous 'swoosh', but in doing so, it caught the aerial mast under the tail. I was swinging free but when I looked up, the 'chute was torn and bunched right up the one side. At the same moment I saw and heard the aircraft hit the ground and explode about a mile away but I was more concerned with untangling my 'chute. I gave the shroud cords an almighty jerk and as I did so I remember the rush of air under my eyelids and then nothing.

I do not recall hitting the ground and, though we were shot down at midnight, the sky was already light when I woke up in a cornfield, listening to the peasants excitedly calling to each other across the fields. There was no question of running away. I could barely sit up. Taking stock, my left leg was damaged, my shoulder seemed to be dislocated, something had happened to my back, and my mouth was full of blood where I had bitten scallops around my tongue. I just hoped someone would take me to hospital before they shot me.

The peasant who found me did not shoot me but from the way he waved his hay fork in front of my face, he left me in no doubt that our relationship was far from cordial. He and his friends threw me in the back of his cart which must have been handed down by his ancestors and took us to the local police station. The cart had no springs and I think the wheels were square.

At the police station in the local town, where the excited police sergeant locked me behind bars, I had a surprise. In the next cell, whole, but not very hearty, was Brian Bird, largely unhurt except for a stiff neck and a sore back and a flying boot lost when he baled out. He had been caught early and had already been taken to the remains of our aircraft to identify the bodies. He had not been able to find mine.

Nobody spoke English or French so the hordes that came to peer at us through the bars could give us no answers. They simply stared at us with expressionless faces not spitting, not sneering – just looking. They thought that the red tabs under our pips meant that we were Russians. The least favourite animal for a Romanian is a Russian, so we just sat back waiting for the firing squad and hoping that all those guards with sub-machine guns would wait for official orders and not make a mess in our cells.

It seemed that our visits a few nights earlier had not improved the telephone system. The sergeants spent the whole day – the entire day – screaming into an apparently dead, hand-wound telephone, presumably to get official permission for his squad to have some weapon practice on us.

Fortunately, the instrument remained mute. The sergeant lost heart with the phone, and instead proceeded to demonstrate what happened to 'Russkis'. He slid his forefinger across his throat. Our one meal of dry bread and a mug of milk did little to uplift us.

The following day the telephone did ring, and from the woeful expression on the sergeant's face, he had clearly been denied the 'Russki' remedy. After spending a day and night here we were taken by cart to the station and put on the train to Giurgiu. There an ancient truck arrived, with six soldiers, all armed to the teeth, to escort us to the interrogation centre in the city, where the usual 'name, number and rank' exercise took place. The captain spoke no English, so he tried a few questions in bad French. He gave us a pencil and some paper, to write letters home, and that gave us an opportunity to complain bitterly about the lack of medical attention and the food.

Next morning he came to our cell and in perfect, cultured English, apologised for the poor food, telling me I would be taken to hospital for treatment. By then everything was so sore that I would have welcomed the 'Russki' treatment.

Next morning Brian went off to the PW camp in Bucharest, while I, a little delirious by this time, was carted off to the Giurgiu hospital, where a kind old doctor reduced my shoulder under anaesthetic, strapped my leg and back and gave me two aspirins. Drugs were in short supply but he gave me a sleeping pill that night and next morning, for the first time, it seemed important to stay alive.

I did not feel like that for long. I was in a ward in the Regina Maria Hospital with eight American airmen and eight Romanian civilians who had been badly wounded in an air raid. One of them waved his bandaged arm to me and in a strong American accent, said he was sorry to see me hurt and please accept these Camel cigarettes. He had lost a hand and a leg when his refinery was destroyed by the RAF on the night of 29 June. I might have done that to him and here he was sympathising with my discomforts, while he had lost a hand and a leg. I have never felt so wretched in my whole life. The sleeping pill had no effect because if ever a person was justified in slitting my throat it was him, so I slept with eyes wide open, watching that corner. But I misjudged him completely. He was too big for petty revenge. Over the next few weeks we became firm friends. He was the character of the ward and was the one to raise the spirits when morale was low. I never heard him complain. Even today, when I think of him, I can only feel humble.

The food was awful, the drugs were non-existent, and some of the Americans died despite the compassionate care of the doctors. One of the

173

Americans, a Captain Lawrence somebody, who had no visible signs of injuries – nobody knew what was wrong with him – woke me one night and said 'Nic, I can't go on any longer', turned over and died.

A Romanian sergeant slept in the ward as guard, while his mate, a corporal, slept outside the door and entertained the scullery maids in bed every night. The sergeant would complain every now and again, so they would swop places, but by my count the corporal's scores were way ahead. Occasionally one of their friends would sit in the courtyard and play those haunting folk tunes on a violin. I saw where Ionescu got his material.

The only light relief was the continual passage of the American heavies over Giurgiu in the mornings, when most of Giurgiu jumped on bicycles, carts, trucks or whatever was available and rode out of town. We would watch them from the ward windows, see the silver darts as the Focke-Wolfes and Me 109s harried this huge formation and hear, over the noise of the flak, the rattle of machine guns and thudding of the fighters' cannons. Sometimes a fighter fell, but more often it was a Liberator or Fortress, sometimes in flames, sometimes not, but always the winding up of that noise with the pitch climbing so high you thought your head would burst. And then the 'thunk' and the black smoke as it exploded.

The hospital staff never quit. Every morning the nursing and cleaning staff assembled in the ward, closed the doors, opened the windows, flapping the sheets from our beds, advanced towards the window in a long line shouting *Mouska, mouska* which is the Romanian for 'fly'. When the long line reached the window, they gave a final triumphant *Mouska* and shut the windows. They then opened the doors and let the flies back in again.

We were shown Romanian newspapers from time to time and I had no difficulty in translating the familiar old slanted approach, that the RAF and the Americans were bombing hospitals and schools and that civilians were our major targets. What caught my eye one day was a photograph of a Luftwaffe hero, a night-fighter pilot, who had just been awarded some addition to his Knight's Cross for shooting down an RAF Liberator, his fiftieth kill, over Giurgiu on the night of 2 July. That was me. Our aircraft all had the same markings as RAF aircraft and were indistinguishable otherwise.

I had never believed that leeches were used in the twentieth century, but the doctor put two on a poor emaciated RAF gunner who had his leg in traction. He had had a cannon shell through his thigh and he was in terrible agony. When they put the leeches on his upper leg he went out of his mind and I thought we would all go out of our minds listening to this poor devil. He died a week later. The bones in his thigh had not knit, the leeches had done no good and his mind was gone, but they gave him massive injections so that he went out without pain.

This can only have been Flight Sergeant C.G. Middleton, a member of Flight Sergeant T.W. Creasy's crew from 104 Squadron shot down in 'G-George' on 7/8 May. Middleton died of his wounds in this hospital on 3 August.

Two more Americans and one civilian died, but my friend who had lost a hand and a leg survived. After five weeks I was pronounced fit enough to go to the prison camp in Bucharest on 9 August. It was not a moment too soon.

The 'gardening' of the Danube that Sunday night covered a considerable length of the river almost from the Hungarian/Yugoslav frontier, near Burovo Bukova to 20 kilometres east of Zimnicea, south-west of Giurgiu, in selected 'beds'. The ORB sums it up:

10 Liberators ordered, detailed and attacked primary. None missing. All aircraft 100% successful. 30 tons (made up of 60 Mk 5 mines) dropped from heights between 50 and 200 feet (above the waterway) between 2326 and 0001 hours.

Eight aircraft came from 178 Squadron and two from 31 Squadron SAAF. Five of the 'beds' were in 'Romanian' waters – upstream from Calafat mined by 'Q-Queenie'; at the confluence of the Jiu with the Danube, south of Craiova by 'R-Robert'; at Lom by 'C-Charlie'; east of Oriahovo by 'X-X ray'; and 25 kilometres upstream of Giurgiu by 'K-King'. In every case all mines were seen to enter the main waterway successfully and individual loads of six mines were spaced evenly into 300–400 metres of water.

The Allied Intelligence assessment of the enemy's fighter defences facing operations to and over Romania was updated on 10 July. (MAAF Air Intelligence Weekly Summary No 86.) In Yugoslavia, Albania and extending into Bulgaria, the Luftwaffe was believed to operate only thirty Me Bf-109s. These could be reinforced by up to 125 single-engined fighters of the Bulgarian Air Force, mostly Bf-109s. From bases in Romania itself the Luftwaffe deployed 70 Me Bf-109s and thirty Me 110s or Ju 88s. It could call upon up to 50 others (single- and twin-engined) normally engaged against Russian forces. The first-line strength of the FARR itself was 125 single-engined types, mainly Bf-109s and up to ten Me 110s. The Hungarian Air Force was smaller, its fighter element mustering only about 100 effectives, of which thirty were Bf-109s. The Weekly Summary reported that about 100 enemy aircraft opposed early July operations by day and night and 'were generally very aggressive.'

Monday 3 July

Seven different Romanian targets were attacked by 15 AF day-bombers, supported at one target by 8 AF B-17s operating temporarily from airfields in Italy. The shared target was the railway yards at Arad. 44 B-24s attacked the primary with 122 tons. Two bombers were lost. The 55 8 AF B-17s delivered 155 tons. One was lost. Post-strike photography clearly shows severe target damage. The Arad force was escorted by 100 fighters.

An oil storage depot at Mogoşoaia, on the north-west outskirts of Bucharest received almost 190 tons from 94 B-24s which caused major fires. The navigational waterway at the Iron Gates was bombed as a secondary target. Two B-24s were lost.

34 more B-24s dropped 84 tons on the Malaxa Locomotive Works and the Titan Petroleum Products Plant in Bucharest. Their long-range escorts chased off 50 defending fighters for no loss.

Another 93 B-24s operated against the railway yards at Timişoara for the loss of one bomber, dropping over 220 tons. Post-strike reconnaissance showed clearly that buildings had been destroyed and that both marshalling and through tracks had been severed by craters in a large number of places. Destroyed and damaged rolling stock was evident.

Giurgiu received 280 tons of high explosive from an attack by 112 B-24s on the railway and port facilities. The attack was met by 40–50 aggressive fighters, mainly FW 190s. The 33 P-51 escorts claimed to have destroyed eleven defenders, without loss.

The seventh target this Monday was the Piatra Olt railway bridge on the main line between Craiova and Piteşti. 55 B-17s dropped 165 tons and the bridge was severely damaged, losing one bay of the new pontoon bridge.

Tuesday 4 July

Independence Day was marked by the third consecutive day and night of heavy bombing of Romanian targets. Braşov received 430 tons of high explosive from 148 B-24s for the loss of three. The large escort of 170 fighters claimed to have destroyed ten defending fighters. A good concentration of bombs almost completely destroyed the petrol products depot and reconnaissance several days later showed the depot still to be 'moribund'.

The railway bridge and railway repair shops east of Piteşti were bombed again. 105 B-24s dropped almost 280 tons for the loss of one bomber. A P-38 damaged on a low-level sweep by 84 aircraft against targets between Ploieşti and Braşov crash-landed at base. They also shot down three Ju 52 transports fitted with mine detector rings which were encountered over the Danube south of Craiova.

330 Wing's move to their new quarters on the fair-weather airfield at Regina was completed.

The maximum effort attack on the day-fighter airfield at Feuersbrunn near Vienna on the night of 6/7 July is an example of the versatility of 205 Group's squadrons and cooperation between the day and night elements of MASAF. Feuersbrunn's resident day-fighters were causing unacceptable attrition of 15 AF's day-bombers on their regular operations to the industrial areas of eastern Austria and to Czechoslovakia. 205 Group's attack rendered the airfield 'entirely unserviceable'. 50 enemy aircraft were grounded by cratered runways and taxiways and nineteen more were destroyed on the ground. The success was costly. Of the 57 bombers launched, ten Wellingtons, two Liberators and a Halifax were lost. It was a night to be long engraved on the memories of the bomber crews who came back.

Sunday 9 July

After a five-day pause in the attack, a large force returned to concentrate on two refineries at Ploieşti. 122 B-17s brought over 360 tons to the Xenia Refinery, for the loss of one bomber. 104 B-24s dropped 240 tons on the Concordia Vega Refinery for a loss of seven. The 130 strong escort claimed ten enemy defenders. There was comparatively little fighter opposition against this attack. The bombers themselves claimed three more enemy. There was intense flak. Another 73 P-51s claimed a further defending aircraft while on an offensive sweep in the target area.

Saturday 15 July

600 bombers attacked four Ploieşti refineries and a pumping station. The Română-Americană was the most heavily attacked; a mixed force of 153 B-17s and 125 B-24s dropped nearly 760 tons for a loss of nine bombers. Dacia was bombed by 100 B-24s for a loss of four dropping more than 230 tons. 94 B-24s dropped 200 tons for a loss of one on Creditul Minier. Six B-24s were downed from a force of 38 which dropped 89 tons on the

Teleajan Pumping Station and 36 bombing the Unirea group of refineries. The day's score was a total of 1370 tons for a loss of twenty bombers. Interestingly, the post-strike report asserts that, of the refineries attacked, Concordia Vega was the hardest hit: it was not a listed target. Six enemy aircraft were claimed.

Saturday 22 July

A week later, Ploieşti refineries were attacked once more and another Operation FRANTIC mission was launched.

152 B-17s raided the Romană-Americană Refinery. Enemy fighters were very active and the flak was intense and accurate. The 60 P-38s escorting the bombers claimed five of the sixteen enemy fighters seen in the target area but twenty-seven B-17s were lost. In addition a force of B-24s dropped 57 tons of HE on Turnu Severin railway yards.

This phase of Operation FRANTIC was an all-fighter affair. 73 P-38s and 47 P-51s completed the outward part of the mission. The force attacked Luftwaffe airfields at Buzău and Boboc/Zilisteanca claiming fifteen enemy aircraft destroyed in combat and another 41 on the ground for a loss of five. The force flew on to temporary bases in the Southern Ukraine.

23/24 July

After a break of three weeks, 205 Group's bombers returned to attack Bucharest on this Sunday night, in another attempt to destroy the Prahova Refinery. This was the Group's second heavy raid on a refinery target in three days. On 21/22 July a maximum effort of 94 sorties was flown against the Pardubice Refinery in Czechoslovakia. A Liberator and five Wellingtons were lost and, final blow, post-strike photography did not reveal any fresh damage caused by the 105 tons of bombs delivered. The force had encountered heavy en route flak at Vienna, Klagenfurt, Graz and Zagreb.

The second visit to the Prahova Refinery was not blessed with success but at least all the bombers returned safely. The Group ORB sums up what seems to have been a somewhat messy performance: 76 sorties were flown.

45 Wellingtons from 231, 236 and 330 Wings, 23 Liberators from 240 and 2 SAAF Wings and 8 Halifaxes of 614 Squadron operated but 15 aircraft returned early, 2 jettisoned and 1 Wellington bombed the airfield east of the city. Although one Halifax returned early and two others were unable to identify the target, the first bombers reported good illumination. This

had, however, diminished on the arrival of the later bombers (delayed by adverse winds) and, in general, bombing was scattered, the only results reported being a few small fires in the target area and some bursts on and near the marshalling yards. There was moderate inaccurate flak, 50 searchlights in the target area and several enemy aircraft were sighted. 106.75 tons of bombs were dropped.

Of the eight target-marking/pathfinding Halifaxes which set out, six arrived to mark the target between 0100 and 0108 hours on 24 July. Two Visual Markers failed to identify the Refinery AP and returned to base with their full load. Another dropped his markers accidentally. The Blind Illuminators dropped their flares and Green TMBs using H_2S to the North and north-east of the AP. 'Bombing was very scattered' the Operations Summary reports. Two Halifaxes had brushes with Ju 88s on the return trip, in one case an unusual head-on attack with cannon. In the other attack the fighter used white light in its initial pass. No hits were claimed by gunners who engaged these attackers, who were readily lost by evasive action. One crew watched a formation of four unidentified aircraft take off from an airfield near Bucharest.

This was 2 SAAF Wing's first operation with the Group to attack a Romanian target. Their seven Liberators considered the target illumination to be very good. Aircraft were not 'foxed' by searchlights and they were able to pinpoint the railway marshalling yards and the horse racecourse near to the AP. No results of their attack were observed. The SAAF crews agreed with most others that there were 30–40 searchlights active, including two 'blue masters'. At one point 4–6 Wellingtons were seen to be coned. One was damaged but it did not go down. The Wing delivered 84 500 lb MC TD .025 – 21 tons – in a five-minute blitz from 0110 hours.

240 Wing's dozen attacking Liberators did not agree that the illumination was good, assessing it as 'indifferent'. No crew positively identified the target, the markers having burnt out by the time the first bombers arrived. Near Caracal at 0145 hours a FW 190 flew under one Liberator from port to starboard and fired two rockets which passed about 30 metres behind the bomber. Cannon shells passed beyond the starboard wing tip. The Rear Gunner fired a short burst in retaliation but saw no strike. At 0205 hours, well on the way home, another Liberator encountered an unidentified enemy flying with white light displayed. The Wing's load totalled 36 tons, made up of a gross of 500 lb MC TD .025, in the same blitz as 2 Wing. One aircraft bombed late – at 0128, having searched for the target for over fifteen minutes, because the TIs had burned out.

Adverse winds delayed 231 Wing's eighteen Wellingtons but they reported bombing on the Green TIs which they considered well placed, although little ground detail could be seen. Bombing was scattered. Enemy fighters were active but all were evaded successfully. Once more enemy aircraft displayed lights, varying from white light, such as landing lights, to orange glowing lights, in the nose of the enemy machine. There were a number of theories about the use of these lights. Some felt that the enemy doctrine must be that white light to support a night interception was worth the risk if the initial run-up to the target bomber had been by radar and had been undetected. Others held the view that this display of white light was to provoke the air gunners in the blacked-out bombers to open fire and give away their presence.

One 231 Wing Wellington claimed to have damaged a Ju 88 on this raid. Just after 0200, closing to the Danube, the fighter was seen beneath the Wellington on the same heading. The bomber made corkscrew turns during which there was an exchange of fire. The enemy broke off the engagement and, after emitting a blue flash, dived steeply away into cloud trailing smoke.

The Wing's twenty tons included one 4000 lb HC NI dropped in a blitz from 0109 hours from between 5,500 and 10,000 feet. Over 370,000 nickels were also dropped.

236 Wing's Wellingtons suffered the same delays with corresponding results over the target. Numbers were also a problem. Of 17 Wellingtons ordered, 14 were detailed and 12 operated. However, two failed to take off due to mechanical failures, three more returned early and only seven attacked the primary. One had bombed an airfield east of Bucharest and another dropped its bombs to the North of the city, being unable to locate the target. Unfortunately, these two aircraft were carrying the Wing's only two 4000 lb 'cookies'. Illumination in the target area was rated as 'weak' by the time the bombers made their runs between 0110 and 0121 hours. Only 8.75 tons were delivered anywhere near the AP together with 250,000 nickels.

330 Wing, with the last start time, seemed to have suffered worst from the wind change. Several aircraft had difficulty in reaching the target area at all and others had to cut off a course leg to make up time. The illumination went down on time, but the ORB observes that the aircraft were too far away to see the position.

The twelve Wellingtons to bomb the primary did so using the widely scattered Green TIs. Four more bombed visually because of lateness over the target and were vague as to where the bombs fell. Twenty-one tons of bombs were dropped from between 8 and 9,000 feet to make the Group's total delivery for the operation 106.75 tons from 57 aircraft.

Bill Burcham, pilot of 37 Squadron, flew 'Y-Yoke' to Bucharest on this operation carrying six 500 lb MC TD .025. His diary entry for Sunday 23 July 1944 reads:

The nervous strain is starting to mount after the last op – to Pardubice – not because of the 36 we have done, but because of the four more we have to do. Tonight's op is to Bucharest, an oil refinery, with only one overload tank. Take-off delayed for half an hour, then another hour, because of crosswind, which was equally strong when we did leave.

Went to Yugoslavia at 5,000 feet and climbed to 10,000 feet over the mountains, switching on the overload. Track followed pretty well. Saw the target searchlights dead ahead and bombed nicely on time. Far more searchlights than last time and flak fairly intense, though we were not, ourselves, too bothered. Saw one aircraft coned and he fairly tore across the area going deeper into the defences which helped us as most searchlights followed him and left us alone. We bombed on the Green TIs (thought that the Reds were not on target) at 6,000 feet, rather low, we thought, for this target. Turned immediately right, eluding some searchlights and reached the outskirts at 3,000 feet averaging 220 mph. Went straight down to 1,000 feet and stayed there until re-crossing the Danube. Then a tedious trip to the coast through 10/10th cloud. Engines began to cough over Manfredonia, put on nacelle tanks when there was an immediate drop of 1000 revs on the starboard engine, which fortunately, slowly picked up. Quite a big oil leak from this engine. Careful to do a high circuit for a glide approach, but some clot cut in on us and I had to do a split-arse turn to avoid going round again. Bed at 7 a.m. That same engine was to cause us to make an early return from over the Yugoslav mountains on our way to Ploiești two nights later.

Sergeant Arthur Clarke, an Air Gunner in 40 Squadron, described the operation from his Rear Gunner's position. He was flying that night in Wellington LP 554 'R-Robert' with a bombload of one single 4000 lb 'cookie':

Our day began when we reported to the Flight Commander's tent at about 0900 hours to check if we were flying that evening. If we were we then carried out our various duties. As Rear Gunner my job was to clean the four Browning .303s in my turret, check the hydraulic system lights, see that the electrical circuits were working and polish the perspex of the turret. Once we were satisfied that everything was in order the rest of the day – until the briefing – was ours.

After tea we reported for briefing. We knew nothing until the Flight Commander named the target. You could hear a pin drop. 'Bucharest Oil Refinery'. The route was already marked on the blackboard. The Met man gave his report on anticipated weather and the IO briefed us on defences, searchlights, guns, fighters etc on the route.

Transport took us to the aircraft, where we did our final checks and reported to the skipper, Sergeant Robinson, in turn. After running up the engines we would taxi to the end of the runway. We waited for the green light to clear us for take off and at 2115 hrs we were off.

Across Yugoslavia and into Romania, right up to the target, we were harassed by night-fighters and now and again something would hit the ground and explode. Knowing the situation kept us alert. When I saw a fighter it was time for evasive action: any order I gave my pilot was obeyed immediately. As we approached Bucharest we climbed to our bombing height and searchlights split the sky. The PFF boys had already dropped the marker flares and I now threw out bundles of 'window' from my turret to confuse the radar.

As our TOT approached we altered course to do our bombing run and the flak was bursting all around us. The tracers filled the sky and made a pretty sight. Other aircraft were already bombing when we made our approach. The Air Bomber selected his target and released the 4000 lb cookie.

'Home James and don't spare the horses' – as we left the target area I got a clear view of what was going on from my turret. Fires and explosions every few seconds. The return flight was a repetition – chased by fighters all the way to the Yugoslav coast. When the Wireless Op started to transmit our position once more, I began to feel a little more at ease. Sitting in that turret for over seven hours was no joke. Once we were down we had our de-briefing, breakfast and bed, hoping never to go to Bucharest again. After that raid we had four days' rest until 26 July when we paid a visit to Ploieşti.

Flying Officer Denys White flew 150 Squadron's 'G-George' that night on his twenty-seventh operation. Their load of six 500 lb MC and two 250 lb GP bombs and bundles of nickels went down west of the AP. Flying Officer James Grieve flew as Wireless Operator in Flying Officer Hugh Morton's 142 Squadron crew with the same load. Apart from the failure of the flares, he remembers the night as unmemorable. Both took the average time of 7 hours 20 minutes. Comments by members of other crews bear the same unfortunate theme, that the Wellington force was delayed by the wind and arrived after the TIs had burned out. Flight Sergeant Pennefeather in 142 Squadron's 'U-Uncle' found the flares out at 0114. His RNZAF colleagues, Flight Sergeant R. Blackett in 'O-Orange' arrived a full ten minutes later and could not find the target at all and bombed on dead reckoning (DR). Lieutenant E. MacDonald SAAF in 'J-Jig' had the same frustrating experience.

Flying Officer Denys White's crew at Amendola, Foggia Plain. (before their 18th operation on 22 June 1944)

From left to right:

Sergeants R (Dai) Evans (Wireless Operator)

George Colman (Rear Gunner)

Flying Officer Denys White DFC (Captain – pilot)

Lieutenant GK (Bunny) Hart, SAAF (Navigator)

Pilot Officer Paul Wheatley (Bomb Aimer)

The Romanian view of this attack was that it came in five successive waves. The first crossed into Romania over Calafat at five minutes past midnight and the last left – over Dăbuleni – at 0210 hours. Bombing fell particularly in 'periferal' zones of the capital, Herăstrau and nearby Pipera, Dămăroaia (near the target), Giuleşti (western suburbs), Băneasa and Popeşti-Leordeni (airfields), Voluntari and Chitila (railway yards).

Early morning photographs taken by a FARR spotter aircraft endorsed the claim that the bombing was scattered.

A Different War

The long flight back from Bucharest meant fighting all the way
With that unremitting moonlight turning night-time into day.
With night and some day-fighters up and seizing every chance
I thought if it were possible I wouldn't join the dance.

It seemed to me that the risk of flak and stray airfield defence
Instead of that great duck-shoot made a whole lot better sense.
So I rapidly descended to two thousand feet or so
And went home contour-chasing, sometimes getting very low.

I was thinking I'd outwitted them when underneath the wing
I glimpsed a different side of war, a horrifying thing.
Groups of Serbian villages were blazing in the night
With the fires the Nazis started in their overweening spite.

Then my little war receded at the thought of what they'd paid,
Of the lines of hanged civilians, the reprisals that were made.
I was feeling very thoughtful as I got back to my tent
Of the different kinds of suffering that this wretched war had meant.

Len Fieldhouse, 150 Squadron

24/25 July and 25/26 July

A dozen Wellingtons from 231 and 330 Wings nickelled towns in Italy, Hungary, Yugoslavia and Romania, where the targets were Timişoara and Craiova – 520,000 and Arad – 500,000. The weather was generally poor. Donald Twigg of 70 Squadron remembered that they had been one of the 'early returns' from the previous night's sally to the Prahova Refinery. The intercom had become unserviceable and they had to abort, landing only three and a quarter hours later.

> They did not think our excuse was valid so the next night we were sent out solo to drop nickels . . . a very unpleasant trip – we were chased by fighters and shot-up by the Danube's anti-mining air defences.

The next night 70 Squadron sent another Wellington with nickels for Timişoara and Craiova once more.

Wednesday 26 July

The Operation FRANTIC fighters which had been out-bound on 22 July now returned and attacked 'targets of opportunity' in the Ploieşti–Bucharest area. They claimed to have shot down twenty-four enemy aircraft and destroyed half a dozen on their airfields. While in Russia the fighters operated in support of the Red Army, attacking an airfield in south-east Poland.

26/27 July

This Wednesday evening saw the launch of another maximum effort by 205 Group, attacking a Ploieşti target at last – the Romană-Americană Refinery to the east of the city. The Group ORB introduced its summary of the operation –

> this target had become one of the very highest priority but, owing to a most effective smoke screen, this attack could not be pressed home.

53 Wellingtons, 20 Liberators and 8 Halifaxes operated – a total of 81 sorties. However, the ORB continues:

> . . . six Wellingtons returned early and one Liberator is missing. One Halifax returned and two more were unable to locate the target, but the remainder dropped flares and Green TIs 'on equipment' (ie. using their H_2S radar). Some crews bombed on the Green TIs, but they were quickly obscured in the smoke screen which extended up to 7,000 feet. Bombing was generally scattered, but a few small fires and one large explosion were observed. Ground defences included 50–100 searchlights and moderate, inaccurate Heavy and Light Flak. A few enemy aircraft were seen and one encounter, in which a Ju 88 was claimed damaged, took place. 133.3 tons of bombs and 1,005,000 nickels were dropped.

This summary illustrates well how differently one crew sees the operation from another. A fighter here or a burst of flak there can make the difference between the 'few enemy aircraft' referred to above and the 'met heavy opposition' which the 31 Squadron SAAF ORB recorded. 31 Squadron suffered the only loss that night. Lieutenant E. Rood's 'R-Robert' – Liberator KG 826 was lost at sea. Three of the crew are buried in the Bari CWGC Cemetery. The remaining five, including Rood, have no known graves.

142 Squadron's War Diary has a footnote to this date that the No 9 RAF Gang Show performed. 'Much enjoyed by all.'

The three Wellington Wings seem to have had a frustrating night. 231 Wing launched twenty-one aircraft but only fourteen were able to attack the primary. 236 Wing was more fortunate. Of the twenty-one which operated, twenty attacked the primary. 330 put up eleven, of which nine attacked. No Wellingtons were lost to enemy action. The Liberator Wings, 240 and 2 SAAF Wing, operated 31 bombers, of which twenty-four were able to attack the primary, for the single bomber loss of the night.

The defensive smoke obliterated the flares and TIs, which the seven pathfinding Halifaxes had put down before the main bomber stream could use them. Nevertheless, 156 Mark III flares and four Green TMBs were dropped from 15,000 feet between midnight and one minute past. Ten Red TMBs had been jettisoned but the ORB does not explain why.

Warrant Officer Hugh Fleckney, flying a 614 Squadron target-marking Halifax noted:

> . . . intense flak and many searchlights. In fact, we were coned twice. The first time was during a lull in the battle. I can clearly remember seeing many silhouettes of a Halifax thrown onto a high layer of cirro-stratus cloud above us. At first, it did not occur to me that these silhouettes were us, despite the fact that the flight deck was brightly lit by the searchlights' glare. We were soon brought back to reality when several bursts of flak appeared at our height and not too far away. I dived away and the next group of bursts occurred just about where we had been. We were now out of the cone and I continued on our run up to the target. The next time we were coned was on the way out of the target area and that necessitated a few more aerobatics.

WTH Fleckney of 614 Squadron as a brand new
Pilot Officer Amendola. (Courtesy Hugh Fleckney)

240 Wing's Liberators had begun to arrive over the target before the Green TIs were consumed by the smoke and the first five aircraft bombed on them and the second five picked what they could from a fire discerned through the gloom, bombing on ETA (or by dead-reckoning).

Liberator crews reported several contacts with enemy aircraft. Near Gaeşti an FW 190 was seen to be following one bomber about 500 feet above and behind. Shortly afterwards an Me 109 was seen on a parallel heading. There were no engagements. At 0023 hours a rocket appeared from nowhere and missed its target. At 0037 hours what seemed to be another bomber exploded in the sky and fell to the ground. This must have been some form of 'scarecrow' – the only bomber to be lost crashed in the sea. Another crew reported ethereal air-to-air firing. The Wing's 128 500 lb MCs totalled 32 tons, dropped in a five minute blitz from 0005 hours. The attacking height was well clear of the smoke at 12,500 feet. They assessed the active ground defences to be 60–80 guns and some 100 searchlights.

No 2 SAAF Wing's crews rated the illumination as poor and scattered. However, eight were able to bomb on the Green TIs before they disappeared. The Wing contributed 27 tons worth of 500 lb MC TD .025 in the same blitz spell as 240 Wing from 12,000 to 12,500 feet. One Liberator had the misfortune to be coned in searchlights for its whole bombing run at about seven minutes past midnight. The worst recorded experience of the night befell Lieutenant P.A. Rautenhach's 'J-Jig' serial 825 of 31 Squadron. At 0040 hours the aircraft was rocked by an explosion in the starboard main plane which stopped No 4 engine. The crew then spotted what was probably a Ju 88 below and astern, which climbed to port and delivered a second attack from that side. The Mid-upper Gunner fired a long burst and saw his strike go home into the attacker before the Liberator corkscrewed away. The Rear and Mid-upper Gunners fired again and the enemy aircraft was lost as a result of this evasive action. The aircraft became extremely difficult to handle, full aileron and udder being necessary to maintain any kind of level progress. The Pilot called for a course but could get no response from the navigator on the intercom. The Bomb Aimer found that the Navigator, Lieutenant A. Dickinson, had left the aircraft with his parachute.

No order to abandon had been given. Another enemy fighter was seen, but there was no engagement and eight to ten minutes after crossing the Danube, yet another was encountered. This time the mid-upper and rear turrets opened fire and the fighter broke away astern without any further damage to the Liberator. Over Celone when Lieutenant Rautenbach selected landing gear down, the nosewheel was found to be jammed. Captain Harrison, a 34 Squadron pilot flying 'Second Dickey' that night, investigated and found a pilot parachute, used to pull out the main canopy from its bag, caught on the starboard nosewheel door, with its line trailing beneath the fuselage. Lieutenant Rautenbach, still fighting to control his damaged bomber, ordered the bomb-doors opened. On further and courageous investigation by Captain Harrison, Lieutenant Dickinson, the missing Navigator, was found to be suspended under the belly of the Liberator with the shroud lines of his parachute passing beneath the open bombbay. An attempt was made to pull Lieutenant Dickinson into the aircraft, but the force of the slipstream made that impossible. Captain Harrison then cut away the entangled pilot 'chute, leaving the main canopy complete and capable of full deployment and the Navigator fell away about two kilometres south of Celone. His body was recovered next day.

231 Wing's Wellingtons had running encounters with two possible Ju 88s, two Me 109s and a 110 and, even though fire was exchanged, managed to evade without loss or damage. Flashes and explosions noted en route to and from Ploieşti do suggest some deception schemes in operation. The eighteen bombers dropped 28 tons which included three 4,000 lb cookies in fifteen minutes after midnight from between 9,000 and 10,000 feet. Donald Twigg of 70 Squadron, made a note:

> Cloud over target. Moon on way home in C-Charlie. One overload tank plus six 500 lb GP bombs. Flight Lieutenant Jack Zeeley as Wireless Operator. Very poor trip. Target Indicators useless and late. Lots of searchlights and flak in the cloud. 30th trip.

The twenty Wellingtons of 236 Wing which reached the target bombed through the murk but had no sight of the target. Crews reported a number of fighter sightings along the way, including a possible Me 210. Flak was active at Bucharest and Piteşti as well as in the target area. The Wing's thirty tons of bombs contained a full mixture, three 4000 lb, 93 500 lb and nine 250 lb dropped in eight minutes from six minutes past midnight. 420,000 nickels also fell on Ploieşti.

Sergeant Arthur Clarke of 40 Squadron continued his account from his first raid on Bucharest on 23 July.

> Then on 26 July we took LP 554 'R-Robert' again and paid a visit to Ploiesti. Same bomb load but this time we were routed a different way. We had the fighters again and there appeared to be more flak than on any of our previous trips. It was a night I would like to forget. I was glad when we got back to base. But worse was to follow: next day we were off to Bucharest again. The last bomber landed safely at 0522 but one damaged Wimpey, unable to lower its main wheels, circled the airfield until dawn when it made a successful belly landing with all the crew safe.

Of the nine attacking Wellingtons from 330 Wing, seven bombed on the Green TIs disappearing into the smoke and two which could find nothing bombed the East side of Ploieşti. They encountered no fighters along the way but, like the others, did see some short-lived flares burning in the air above the bomber height. One aircrew saw a flashing morse signal 'NM' on the ground in Yugoslavia and wondered if this might have been a partisan reception committee signal. The Wing's bomb load of two 4000 lb, 41 500 lb and thirteen 250 lb (all TD .025) totalled almost 16 tons and was dropped in the same blitz as 236 Wing. Over 220,000 nickels went down too.

Post-strike photography showed that only twenty-one aircraft had dropped their bombs into the target area. The main weight of the attack fell to the north-west of the refinery, back towards the industrial suburbs of Ploieşti, where storage tanks and other installations were seen to have been destroyed or damaged.

The Romanian account of the raid shows that they were confused too. They estimated that the attack was made by up to 100 Wellingtons in four waves, dropping high explosives particularly on the East side of the town. Incendiaries fell on the Romană-Americană Refinery: the primary was hit, after all.

Second Lieutenant W.R. (Dick) Cubbins, USAAF, (author of *The War of the Cottontails* published by Algonquin Books of Chapel Falls, 1989), a B-24 Pilot shot down on 3 July looks at the raid from the standpoint of the Allied PWs held in Bucharest.

The siren wailed us hurriedly into the basement. After several periods of sporadic anti-aircraft fire, probably vain rounds sent in search of a too distant bomber, I groped my way up dark stairs to see if I could catch a glimpse of the action. There was no way of knowing the cause of the alert.

One of the most curious aspects of those Bucharest nights was the deathly quiet that seized the city during the endless moments following the final moan of the warning wail and the guns commencing their terrifying fusillades. It was as though death hovered quietly, savouring the moment it would seize its intended victims. Our Romanian guards cowered in fear and made little effort to enforce the rules governing our movements.

It was a moonless night but I could make out the group of prisoners crowding the open entrance at the end of the hall. Joining them at the door I arrived in time to witness the final moments of a classic night air battle. A B-24 was trapped in the apex of several powerful searchlights. Searching the sky immediately behind the bomber, I saw it, a German night-fighter making a pass on the bomber from 6 o'clock low. The distance from our vantage was too great for us to see the torrent of tracers from cannon and machine guns that characterise such ghostly duels. To the contrary, the weaving bomber and its trailing fighter were more like toy craft frolicking playfully, or moths flitting in and out of the illumination of a street lamp. The stalking fighter, barely visible to us in scatter light, suddenly shone crystal clear as it entered a beam, then just as suddenly disappeared from view as it danced out of the light and the sight of the bomber's tail gunner. Within moments, a second fighter appeared wraith-like in a slow closing pass from the bomber's rear.

The advantage a fighter has over an illuminated target is great. Even when not illuminated by searchlights, bomber engine exhausts often disclose their position. Once the fighter pilot sights his quarry, it is usually only a matter of moments before the unwary bomber crew is trapped in a flaming coffin that signs its own death knell as it hurtles downward. Trapped as it was in multiple beams of light, we waited for what was certain would be the tragic outcome of the fight.

I could not tell if the first fighter had gotten in a telling blow or if the bomber pilot had added yet another factor to this evasive manoeuvring, but the bomber appeared to have suddenly entered into a shallow dive. Then, as if by magic, it disappeared. It did not explode nor did the lights pinioning it like deadly lances waver from their prey, yet the bomber disappeared as quickly as if someone had flicked a switch and erased it from the dramatic scene.

A sense of relaxation worked its way through our small group as searchlights moved about in sweeping patterns, probing the blackness for the elusive craft. When it became apparent that the bomber had bested the lights and the fighters in the uneven contest, I felt myself relax and realised how tense I had become. I had seen enough of the engagement to know that I preferred the massive violence of day combat to those brilliant fingers of light that singled one out as if to say 'This one. Now!'

Interestingly, the British viewed the night terror as the normal environment of the bomber and thought us foolish for flying in daylight wherein enemy fighters could be massed against us. Each concept had its advantages and disadvantages. Our advantage, and it was an over-riding one, was our ability to find the target and do precision bombing. Precision bombing, particularly on a mass scale, at night, was beyond the state of the art.

From the safety of over forty years later, we know that the Liberator did, indeed, survive the encounter.

The King Watches

It was only after the main account was written that contact was established with Mircea Ionniţiu, King Michael's Private Secretary. He was to be deeply involved in the planning and execution of the 23 August coup. He describes the raid from another viewpoint:

> The most spectacular night raid that I watched was in July. I was together that evening with King Michael in Sinaia when he received word of planes headed for Romania. On a hunch, he drove up the mountain to a spot where we knew we could watch part of the Wallachian plain. It was a clear night and we were just in time to see the marking flares being dropped over Ploiesti. Then the fireworks started. The AA began firing with all available guns (each calibre had a different tracer colour). One could distinguish the bursts of the bombs and of the AA projectiles. And being so far away, everything was so quiet, so clean, so unreal. On a few instances, an occasional plane flew by, headed for the fires.
>
> I remember that one night, late in July, the King had summoned his counsellors to a confidential meeting at the Royal Palace in Bucharest. The meetings were so secret that Marshal Antonescu, who sent needlessly tens of thousands of youngsters to fight in Russia, would not find out that the representatives of the opposition parties were discussing with the King the details of the armistice with the Allies. When the sirens started growling and whining, the King called for a recess. It was not desirable to let the politicians be seen in the Place air raid shelter since it would disclose their presence at the Palace and fail to maintain the secrecy of the meetings. So, following the decisions previously reached, I drove the elder statesmen to their homes in the darkened city without even turning on the dimmed headlights. I drove very slowly guided only by the glare of the exploding AA shells and bombs. Needless to say there was no other human being to be seen, that I was scared stiff, but I was pleased as Punch to carry out this assignment. Most of the time I was not even sure which way I was supposed to drive, as I did not know where I was. And strangely enough, I escaped unscratched from this episode.
>
> I have to confess that when I was caught during the British raids, my so-called bravado was melting away rapidly. I was young and believed myself to be indestructible, consequently no air raid shelter was good enough for me. I always watched in awe the striking and colourful spectacle, sitting where I could have a good view of the night sky. But being also witless, it did not occur to me that this was a serious and deadly show. Only later, when visiting areas where bombs had fallen or where aircraft had crashed, did I understand the reality of the war and what it meant to the human beings on both sides.

191

27/28 July

This Thursday a maximum effort was ordered once more and 205 Group generated 90 sorties. The Group's ORB summarises what must have been an eventful and frustrating night.

> Target: BUCHAREST – PRAHOVA OIL REFINERY
>
> 60 Wellingtons of 231, 236 and 330 Wings, 22 Liberators of 240 and 2 SAAF Wings and 8 Halifaxes of 614 Squadron operated, but only 50 of the Wellingtons attacked the primary target: 5 Wellingtons returned early, 4 were unable to identify the target (2 jettisoning and 2 attacking targets of opportunity), and 1 'E' of 150 Squadron, captain Sgt WILKINSON, is missing. 2 Liberators also returned early.
>
> 9/10 – 10/10ths cloud base approx. 5000 ft, covered the target and flares and Green Target Indicators were dropped on equipment. 1 Visual Marker dropped Red Target Indicators from below the cloud base. Some aircraft observed the Indicators and bombed on them, others bombed on DR. Bombing was in general scattered and few results were observed, although 2 explosions were reported from the target area. 40/50 searchlights and moderate inaccurate Heavy and Light flak were encountered at the target, one aircraft being hit in the rear turret. There were many fighter flares between the target and the Danube and several enemy aircraft, including Me 109s and Ju 88s were sighted, three encounters taking place without damage or claims. 138 tons and 1,147,000 nickels were dropped.

330 Wing's record is typical of all the Wellington Wings. Ten aircraft from each of 142 and 150 Squadrons were detailed. Two from 142 Squadron and one from 150 Squadron returned early. The rest bombed, as reported, on DR through 10/10th cloud from between 6,000 and 13,000 feet – an unusual breadth of altitudes for Wellingtons.

236 Wing's tale was much the same, 40 Squadron put up nine Wellingtons and all bombed the primary without loss, making 146 sorties for the month to date. 104 Squadron's 'Y-Yoke' returned early with a malfunctioning overload tank, otherwise eleven bombers completed the raid to make 145 sorties for July.

240 Wing ORB's summary was quite abrupt.

> Eight Halifaxes drop 253 Mark III flares and seventeen target marking bombs. Twelve Liberators drop 141 500 lb MC TD .025 totalling 35 tons.

Tom Scotland, pilot of 614 Squadron, found the defences extremely accurate on all his five visits to Bucharest as a target marker.

Our 27 July raid was the hottest for us and by then I thought I knew Bucharest defences, but we got an extremely bad time on our run-in to mark the target for the bombers. The fighters could be sudden death on this long seven and a half hour trip. I was not attacked but I saw others go down. There'd be a stream of red coming out of the attacked plane as the cannon shells found their mark and exploded within, then the long trail of fire would arc towards the ground there to spread out on impact. The effect of exploding cannon shells from German fighters was fearsome. Their pilots tried to attack the unprotected belly of our planes so, very often, they were unseen. I adopted a relentless weaving pattern to enable the eyes of our crew to search the area of space beneath us. We had Mid-Upper and Rear Gunners, a Flight Engineer's observation point and the Bomb Aimer crouched in his place in the nose.

40 Squadron's Arthur Clarke continues his account:

At the briefing we learned with a shudder that it was Bucharest again. Same aircraft, same single 4000 lb load. We were airborne at 2030 hrs and we set course. Over Yugoslavia we picked up fighters and some stayed with us all the way to the target. Several times I gave the Skipper orders for evasive action, we lost them, but they found us again. By the time we were near the target and had it dead ahead, the searchlights were scanning the skies. We were just about to settle into our bombing run when a master searchlight with a blue beam picked us out. All the other searchlights homed on us and the flak began to burst all round us. The smell of cordite in the air is something I shall always remember. Tracer was popping all around *and* we still had that 4000 lb bomb. The Skipper started to corkscrew and as he did a salvo of flak exploded just where we had been. Shells still burst too close for comfort and I ordered the skipper to put the aircraft into a diving turn followed by another corkscrew. By now the Air-Bomber had taken his position to bomb and while we were shaking off the searchlights he dropped the cookie – and we flew clear of the glare. We were now alarmingly near ground level and, climbing to a safe height, we set off for base. On looking back the target area was like the Blackpool illuminations. We were shadowed all the way back to the Adriatic by a fighter. This was 7 hrs 20 mins.

Next day the Flight Commander sent us off to the leave hotel at Sorrento for a few days' break.

Wing Commander Dick Banker, OC 70 Squadron, flew that night and recalls it as uneventful seven and a quarter hours, one overload tank, six 500 lb and four 250 lb bombs.

142 Squadron's ORB went as far as writing this off as a failure due to cloud cover. Pilot Officer Coulthard in 'T-Tommy' LN 961 could not find the target so he bombed a road junction east of Caracal. RNZAF Flight Sergeant R. Blackett in 'U-Uncle' and Sergeant A. Palmer in 'L-Love' also failed to find the target. Flight Lieutenant H. Morton in 'G-George' LN 914 had the same difficulty and bombed the target on dead-reckoning using flak and searchlight reflections.

Bob Ives remembers his 150 Squadron crew's adventures on the way home that night:

> We had the cookie kite and on our way back to base we ran short of petrol. Jock got in touch with base and gave them our position. They said we could not possibly reach Base. They would send an air-sea rescue plane to pick us up – we still had to cross the Adriatic. It was a very warm and sunny morning and the sea was very calm, the Skipper told us to throw out anything we could move and I stripped off into just my shorts and Mae West. We were losing height and could see the coast and our runway was not far inland, so the Skipper asked for a landing but was told to do another circuit. He just said, 'I'm coming in', and what a panic there was. The radio was red hot with the Yanks telling him to keep clear as the Fortresses were about to take off, but we landed on the 'drome alright but not on the runway, as we finished up among several Fortresses. How the petrol lasted we never knew.

SAAF Air Gunners. (L to R) WO1 Preez, WO1 I.W.M. MacLachlan, Capt T.W. Timoney, 34 Squadron Gunnery Leader. (Courtesy T.W. Timoney)

It was Captain T.W. (Terence) Timoney's first Romanian operation. Although Gunnery Leader of 34 Squadron SAAF, on this raid he flew as a Beam-Gunner in Lieutenant Bob Klett's 31 Squadron Liberator 'G-George' to gain operational experience. He has remembered it well:

The large wall map in the barn they used as an Operation Room covered the whole area of Southern Europe. Red tape pinned to the map indicated our route and destination that night, the Prahova Oil Refinery, Bucharest.

The route line on the board indicated known concentrations of flak and night-fighter bases. We were to expect strong fighter opposition as well as heavy concentrations of radar-controlled flak and searchlights. The Intelligence Officer advised us what to do should we come down in the various countries we flew over. We each signed for and were given a waterproof sealed pouch containing an escape map, compass, American dollars and chocolate. We never carried or wore side arms.

I was allocated the beam gun position, a single .5-in Browning MG on a swing mounting. The beam positions of a Liberator were simply large openings on either side of the aircraft. On the floor were stacked packets of 'WINDOW', thin aluminium foil strips, which were thrown out by the handful at five minute intervals over enemy territory to confuse the enemy radar screens.

After take off we climbed up through a low bank of clouds on course and started across the Adriatic. The Rear-Gunner tested his guns by firing a few bursts and I followed suit. The Rear-Gunner dropped a few flares, took a sight on them and gave the Navigator some drift readings. At Lake Scutari in Albania, we saw the first pathfinder flare, giving our Navigator a course change.

At this point I started to drop Window. We were flying over the Yugoslav Alps and not too far from Belgrade. At another course change point we started to lose height over the Romanian border. We met our first arcing searchlights, sweeping arcs in the direction of the main bomber stream to assist the night-fighters. I clearly saw the lights of aircraft taking off from two airfields. Then we were approaching the first ring of defences around Bucharest. The pilot and navigator noted that skylight glow from the city. Then this suddenly disappeared and there was a complete blackout. We started to lose more height and met the first probing searchlights. At that stage I saw many night-fighter flares, well away from our bomber stream. I saw what I took to be a burning aircraft, but the Rear-Gunner said it was a 'scarecrow' fire. He had often seen them over target areas.

Comfortable, but very cold, crouching behind my .5 Browning, watching for night-fighters and trying to keep my eyes off the searchlights, I heard the Wireless Operator say that he had hurt his fingers in the heating fan blades. The captain asked me to come forward immediately and take his place. Things then started to go wrong. As I saw him arrive in the murky light, I took off my oxygen connection and intercom plug and started forward. As I was about to turn, my flying boots slipped on the 'Window' strips loose on the floor and I jammed my foot under the .5 gun mounting. I could not release my boot, so had to take it off and pull it out of the mounting bracket. By now I was close to panic because I knew we were approaching the bomb release point. I hurried into the bomb bay. My first task was to turn off the valve isolating the front and rear hydraulic systems. This was done as a precaution over the target area.

This operation required me to stretch my arm over the bomb rack and operate the valve. To my consternation, my Mae West inflation lever must have hooked onto something because it immediately inflated itself and I found myself jammed in the catwalk. In desperation I pulled off the Mae West and hurried forward to the radio compartment. On plugging in my intercom, the first words I received were, 'Open the bloody bomb bay!' This I did immediately, and within seconds I heard the Air Bomber say, 'Bombs away!' In fact, I saw them fall away. I quickly went down the catwalk to see if there were any hang-ups. There were none and I closed the bomb bay doors and sent the call sign back to base, which was acknowledged. It was only then that I realised I had left my parachute back in the beam gun position.

I returned to my gun position. By then the aircraft had set course for base. The searchlights had lit up the area and I could clearly see the tanks of the oil refinery. We were in a ring of heavy ack-ack and flicking starlike shrapnel and black smoke puffs seemed to surround the aircraft. We continued to climb and eventually we got out of the belt. The Mid-upper Gunner reported the occasional fighter-flare. We droned on back to base.

For Sergeant Alan Bates DFM, Air-Bomber of 31 Squadron SAAF, the memory was clear.

We had been listed to fly and already the smart boys who knew how to balance 'All Up Weight' against bomb and fuel loads were trying to forecast the night's target. It was later on at Briefing that we met up with the South African officers of the crew – Lieutenants Bill Norval the Captain, Bob Burgess, Second Pilot, and Noel Sleed the Navigator. The target was revealed as the Prahova Oil Refinery at Bucharest, which produced a buzz of excitement. Bucharest was considered to be one of our major targets, equal in status to Ploieşti.

We were given a course and told to keep to very strict timing. The Pathfinder Force (PFF) would provide route markers and mark the target. The weather forecast was very doubtful and considerable cloud was expected in the target area. If the target was obscured by cloud we were to bomb on ETA and for this purpose we would need to follow an accurate course from the final turning point. From this point, Noel Sleed would time our run-up to the target to the second and let me know the precise moment to drop our load of twelve 500 lb bombs.

Eventually we went out to our aircraft. The summer sun was setting low on the horizon and we were wearing shirts and shorts and carried our flying clothes in kit bags. The aircraft had been standing in the sun all day and was still at oven temperature. We entered through the bomb-bay doors and, while the others took up their normal positions, Noel and I remained on the flight deck. Eventually the bomb doors were closed and the engines started up. We were subjected to an intolerable heat until we reached sufficient height for the temperature to fall. Noel and I then climbed into our flying kit and made our way past the retracted nose wheel to our small compartment in the nose. Noel sat at a small table facing aft where he plotted our course by the dim light of a spot lamp. I occupied a small square of floor between the nose wheel housing and the bomb-sight. I crouched on a rug and tried to make myself comfortable with the aid of two cushions. To maintain my night vision I attempted to read my maps by the glow of a weak torch which had been dimmed by several layers of toilet paper. We crossed the Yugoslav coast on course and obtained a further fix on the Danube before the first of the PFF route markers was sighted dead in position. Shortly before midnight, we located our final turning point. We were at 12,500 feet and Noel gave the Pilot a new course of 127 to follow at an air speed of 190 mph. Noel noted the time and joined me looking down from the nose. The cloud had closed into 10/10th up to a height of 8,000 feet. We soon located Bucharest by the light of the dozens of searchlights which filtered through the clouds lighting them up like one huge electric light bulb. Through this luminous cotton wool sheet broke the green and red dots of the tracer shells which fizzled out in graceful arcs well below. Some heavier flak was bursting up ahead and I picked up the silhouettes of two or three Wellingtons flying just below.

Suddenly a break appeared in the cloud and the city showed up bright and clear in the reflected glow of the searchlights. There below, travelling along the sighting line of my bomb-sight was the main target area just as I had memorised it from the target plan. I hesitated a moment and then pressed the release button and called 'Bombs gone'. I kept looking down and just as the clouds closed in again I saw the red glow of the Target Markers blossom forth. Normally I would have bombed on them. Noel had watched proceedings over my shoulder and I think he was a little bit disappointed to have been pre-empted in his timed-run to the target. The crew was also taken by surprise, by not having to listen to a series of course corrections from me before dropping my bombs, but they were evidently well satisfied to miss the preamble. After a short delay for the photo-flash to operate, the pilot opened up the throttles and we headed for home.

I had been most concerned at the thought of dropping the bombs on ETA. It had always struck me as being a very haphazard method. On this occasion I was most impressed with Noel's navigation and the captain's accurate flying.

In the Bucharest schoolhouse where the Allied officer PWs were held, Dick Cubbins recalled that he had spent the day trying to relax.

It was nearing midnight and 'Pop' Egles – Navigator of 614 Squadron, shot down on 8 May's raid on Bucharest – and I were deep in conversation sitting on the top step in the stairwell when the hated siren sent the first wave of men scurrying for the dubious safety of our half-basement. Although nearly trampled in the rush, Pop, in characteristic manner, hardly interrupted his speech. I fought the urge to follow the crowd but pride won out over discretion. Reluctantly, I remained seated beside the unflappable Englishman.

We had been discussing the courage and skill the South African pilot had displayed in escaping the searchlights and fighters, and the pros and cons of day versus night bombing. Pop explained how the 'Illuminators' were responsible for finding and lighting the target for the following bombers. If the Illuminators failed, as they often did, the subsequent bombs would still be dropped but with little effect. His explanation of RAF target marking procedures was not helping my confidence in British bombing accuracy and my determination to remain with him.

At that point in Pop's unnerving dissertation, a sudden explosion of anti-aircraft gunfire sent me racing for the basement. 'Oh my God, we're the bloody target!' Pop yelled as he catapulted down the steps with remarkable agility and speed for a man of his size.

By the time I reached the doubtful sanctuary at the foot of the stairs, I heard the first onrushing scream. 'The damned Limeys use screamers on their bombs!' I thought, 'It wasn't enough to blow the enemy into oblivion, the British have to terrorize them with screamers that make each bomb sound as though it were right on top of you.' Sympathy for the enemy was lost in the onslaught of explosions of the stick of bombs approaching, then passing, the schoolhouse.

The first string bracketed our building, missing to the east by mere yards. Seconds later, the concerted screams of another stick of death hurtling downward approached with earsplitting accuracy. Again the building rocked from nearby explosions. Between strings of bombs anti-aircraft shells shredded the air overhead and added yet another measure of terror to the night. Muscles ached from the pressure as I squeezed my balled body into an ever smaller compaction.

Following the 'All Clear', the sounds of a deeply wounded city lit by numerous fires reflecting off scudding, smoke-blackened overcast kept tensions at a high level. Few of us returned to our bunks on the floors above.

The Romanian summary of the night's activities was brief – between 70–80 aircraft attacked in two waves damaging buildings in the centre of the city. The report singles out the National Bank, the Romanian Bank (Banca Românească) and Băneasa airport among several commercial streets.

Friday 28 July

This was the fifth time in five days and nights that Romanian oil targets came under MASAF attack. This raid was to be the fourteenth heavy bomber attack on Ploiesti of the so-called high-level offensive. Two main refineries were singled out for attention, the Romană-Americană and the Standard Oil-Phoenix Unirea complex in the south-east industrial suburbs of the city. 71 B-24s and 154 B-17s were launched against Romană, dropping some 590 tons of bombs. The force attacking the Standard group was 68 B-24s and 30 B-17s, dropping 255 tons. Losses were also heavy. Between 110 and 130 defending aircraft were encountered and the long-range escort of 265 fighters claimed eleven. However, the defences, including intense flak brought down seventeen B-24s, two B-17s, a P-57 and three P-38s.

30/31 July

Operations the previous night to send twenty-four Wellingtons to mine the Danube and 69 other bombers to attack the Almasfuzito Oil Refinery, on the Danube on the northern frontier of Hungary with Czechoslovakia were cancelled 'owing to weather' at 1805 hours. The last operation of the month for

205 Group centred on 53 sorties to mine the Danube with two singletons on separate nickelling missions. The 'gardening' beds were in four groups. One was centred on Mohacs in southern Hungary, another was between Kovin (to the East of Belgrade) and Bazias and two more were in 'Romanian' waters. These were respectively from Orşova upstream fifteen kilometres to Ogradena/Dubova and from Giurgiu upstream to Vrata, some 50 kilometres south of Turnu Severin. 34 Wellingtons from all three Wings and eighteen Liberators from the two Heavy Wings operated and dropped 175 mines into a total of thirteen 'beds' in the four groups. Only three mines fell astray. Barges, river traffic and light flak positions were machine-gunned. Light flak was encountered in several places and accurate heavy flak en route at Paracin in Yugoslavia. No encounters with enemy aircraft were reported, although some unidentified planes were seen. There were no losses.

One of the two nickelling Wellingtons was 'F-Freddie' from 40 Squadron, captained by Flight Sergeant Trigg, which dropped 392,000 leaflets over Turnu Severin without incident. The other Wellington, from 231 Wing, dropped 400,000 leaflets over Rimini and Pesaro safely.

Of the mining Wellingtons, all operated except one from 40 Squadron. 'Y-Yoke' captained by Sergeant Patterson failed to take-off from Regina because its main wheel tyres were found to be unserviceable: a familiar problem.

Most crews found it to be a lively night. One 231 Wing Wellington fired 800 rounds at searchlights while coned by seven of them and being hosed by light flak near Florentin. Two lights were extinguished but the aircraft was holed in both fin and rudder. Another was holed in the fuselage and starboard wing by light flak.

A 178 Squadron Liberator strafed some twelve river barges in the main waterway and dispersed in creeks and channels between Vardim and Sviştov (opposite Zimnicea). A Rear Gunner dispensed over 1,000 rounds from his .5-inch Brownings at a light flak site near Orşova. 31 Squadron Liberators noticed the same light flak and machine-gun fire holed one aircraft.

The lowest release height noted by 231 Wing that evening was 125 feet above the river.

236 Wing's 'beds' lay in the channel where the river passed through the approaches to the Iron Gates and where the land on either bank towered steeply hundreds of feet above the water. Low-flying at night is hairy enough without these confining cliffs and the unpredictable air currents in these chasms as well as an alert enemy able to fire downwards at many of the passing bombers. This Wing's logged release heights varied from less than 500 feet to over 3,000 feet, the former over the plain near Lom and the latter in the mountains around Moldova Veche.

Gardening operations did not require a 'blitz' in view of the care needed and the variety of target beds. Mines therefore entered the water over longer spells. All Wings began their drop at about 2300 hours, 231 Wing's being complete in eleven minutes, 236 Wing took fifteen minutes, 331 Wing twenty minutes with the Liberators from 178 Squadron and 31 Squadron SAAF interspersed. Liberator dropping heights matched those of the Wellingtons, with several 31 Squadron aircraft able to fly below 100 feet with the aid of the radio-altimeters. The eighteen Liberators, which mined, delivered a total of 107 1000 lb Mk V mines out of the night's total of 175.

Crews made some interesting en route sightings. A 231 Wing aircraft watched an aircraft's exhaust flames over Yugoslavia but could not identify its owner. Again, over Yugoslavia, another Wellington overflew a lighted flarepath with an unidentified aircraft landing. There was also some air-to-air firing in the area. Perhaps a returning Luftwaffe aircraft was being harassed by a marauding allied fighter-bomber of Balkan Air Force? A 178 Squadron Liberator saw a twin-engined aircraft astern and below but no contact was made and it was lost to view. What this was may never be known, but the time and the reported positions do not totally rule out the exhaust flames spotted by the 231 Wing Wellington being those of this Liberator. At about 2200 hours another South African Liberator saw a letter 'Y' in lights on a Yugoslav hillside below – probably a partisan recognition signal for a supply drop. A 142 Squadron crew saw a flashing beacon below them at Turnu Măgurele, which could have been a navigation light for river traffic.

Captain J.L. Van Eyssen, SAAF, flying a 31 Squadron Liberator remembers the clear bright moon that night. His allotted 'bed' was a stretch of river just west of the little town of Corabia.

The mines arrived in lorries in the early afternoon hidden from view under tarpaulins and were loaded into the bomb bays by very efficient RN armourers and the bomb doors closed – not to be opened until over the Danube. We did, of course, see them as we entered the aircraft and walked between them on the cat-walk on our way to the flight deck. There were six of them – cylindrical, red in colour and so big as to occupy almost all the available space in the bomb bays.

These mines were top secret and certainly ingenious, devastating and difficult to sweep. I gleaned a little technical data and it seems that they operated magnetically and the firing mechanisms clicked one setting each time a tug or barge passed over. Settings were random and made by the RN armourer. A mine set for four clicks would go up under hull No 5 and so on.

We took off singly, crossed the Adriatic and headed straight for our beds. At two points along the way, runway lights were switched on at airfields beneath us, while a single light accelerated along the runway before all lights again went off. Fighters had been launched to intercept us. According to Intelligence these were Ju 88 'Catseye' fighters, meaning that they had to make visual contact without radar aids. Their chances of a successful interception were remote.

On a previous occasion the enemy had been taken by surprise, but on 30 July they were waiting with 35mm flak guns on both banks. As far as I could afterwards ascertain the greatest concentration of guns was in the vicinity of my 'beds'. When I overflew at 1000 feet to identify my bed, tracer erupted from 12 guns on the north bank and 2 from the south. I evaded them with a diving turn to the left and hastily briefed my gunners for full deflection firing at gun emplacements when on our dropping run.

We circled left, lost height and speed and headed upstream (ie. westwards) above the Danube while my radio altimeter, set for 30 feet, showed green. Then it flashed yellow then red indicating that we had reached and dipped below 30 feet. Slight backwards pressure on the control column and we reached and stayed in yellow while our speed settled at 190 mph. The Bomb Aimer called 'ready to drop – ONE' and the Second Pilot came in with 'two three DROP – two three DROP – two three DROP etc' until all six had splashed into the river at 3 second intervals, which spaced them at about 300 yards apart.

Then all hell was let loose as fourteen AA guns opened up and lit the sky with tracers. Our aircraft shuddered as our gunners returned the fire raking the enemy gun emplacements. There was a jolt on the control column and the Liberator no longer responded to fore and aft. The elevator cables had been severed. Using the tail trim, I climbed out of the Danube valley and away from those guns and I eventually got back to Celone, not quite knowing how I would land. Then in a flash I remembered that the Auto Pilot duplicated all control cables and I managed to pull off quite a reasonable night landing with normal aileron and rudder control but by turning a small wheel on the panel to operate the elevators.

My waist gunner had, during the running fight, fired a continuous burst of 250 rounds at the twelve gun emplacements on the North (Romanian) bank. His .5-inch Browning barrel lost all its rifling and was smooth-bore like a shot gun. It was not coincidental that our only damage suffered came from the left – the South (Bulgarian) bank's 2 guns. A man being shot at cannot aim too well.

I was to be associated with the Danube mining offensive again shortly afterwards when I was a guest of the British Military Mission in Moscow, having been shot down on a Warsaw supply drop. The British

Admiral there called me to go to a meeting at the Kremlin to discuss the mining of the Danube. He led me to a conference hall where more than 20 Soviet naval officers were already seated. At once I discovered that this was not a conference but an interrogation and that I was to be interrogated.

The Russian at the head of the table, who was at least an Admiral of the Fleet, called the shots through an interpreter. He soon warmed to his subject and asked how, where, when, from what height, how many mines I had dropped into the Danube. Then came the $64,000 question 'How did the mines work?' To this I answered 'I don't know.' When that was translated my interrogator flew into a rage, while all the others glared at me as if I was the Devil himself.

Before the interpreter could give me the first of his ravings, more were added at a higher pitch and volume. The message coming through was that we were allies fighting the worst tyrant in history and here I was withholding vital information when, after all, Russia had borne the brunt of the war. My anger rose and when I had the opportunity to speak, I briefly explained that the mines were secret and that I was only paid to transport and drop them, not to design, build or maintain them. Back in the British Admiral's office I blurted 'What the hell was all that about?' He replied with a grin 'You see the Russians have overrun Bucharest and some areas to the West of it and your mines are still active and blowing up Russian shipping!' After my morning's experiences I replied 'That's the best news I've heard in months, Sir.'

The success of these minelaying operations is amply illustrated by the simple statistic that one tug, tanker or barge was sunk for every five mines laid despite all attempts to sweep the waterway.

As the month ran out, Allied Intelligence assessed that there were significant flak reinforcements and re-deployments in the Danube plain. At Giurgiu, there were now twenty heavy flak guns, while the Ploiești defences had received thirty more to bring the total to 210. Heavy flak was seen to have been withdrawn from Turnu Severin even though it had been attacked twice by night and seven times by day up to 22 July. Other centres from which heavy flak had been withdrawn were Călăraşi, on the Danube in south-east Romania and Mamaia – an airfield just north of Constanta, where there had been eight and sixteen guns respectively.

Overall in July, 205 Group's bombers flew 1,313 sorties, with a total of nearly 7,200 flying hours – by night. The price was over 200 aircrew killed or missing and the loss of 44 aircraft. 31 July was a Group stand-down: no operations were flown but 15 AF saw the month out with a heavy attack on Romanian oil targets.

Officers of 150 Squadron assembled for a casual group photograph on the roof of their farmhouse Mess at Amendola. (Courtesy Ron Turner)

1	FO Hammond (RAAF)	6	Sqn Ldr Boxwell (Acting OC Sqn)	11	'Doc' Crabbe (MO)
2	FLT Ron Turner (RAAF)	7	Flt Lt Laurie Hodson (Adjt)	12	FO Skehill (RAAF)
3	FO Johnnie Bayton	8	Flt Lt Tubby Fieldhouse	13	FO Thomas
4	FO Max Thompson (RAAF)	9	Flt Peter Scott (Gunnery Leader)	14	Lt G K Hunt (SAAF)
5	'Aggie' Weston (Engr. Offr)	10	FO Bint (RAAF)		

Monday 31 July

More than 360 escorted bombers attacked four oil production targets. It is interesting to note that the long-range fighters were succeeding in keeping the determined defenders away from the bomber force: only two B-17s and four B-24s were lost while the escorts claimed to have destroyed 31 enemy fighters of the 90 they encountered, losing four P-51s.

155 B-17s attacked the Xenia Refinery at Ploieşti delivering 437 tons of high explosives. Two were lost to the defences. The other raids were carried out by B-24s, nineteen attacked Creditul Minier. 47 more B-24s dropped 116 tons at Tîrgovişte, west of Ploieşti. One was lost. Mogoşoaia received 187 tons from an attack by 87 bombers. The 93 escorting P-51s claimed to have destroyed thirty defending aircraft. The fourth objective was the Prahova Refinery where 157 tons of bombs were dropped by 70 B-24s.

204

Group Captain Morris, commanding 330 Wing, briefs on an operation over the Balkans.

Flying officer Ron Turner DFC stands at left. (Courtesy Ron Turner)

CHAPTER 10 - August

Summary

August was a busy month on all fronts. On the 1st the Warsaw Uprising began. Florence fell to the Allies on the 4th. On 8 August Air Marshal Sir John Slessor agreed to provide night relief flights to sustain the resistance in Warsaw. On 13th he diverted 178 and 31 Squadrons from operations in support of the landings in southern France and committed them to supply missions to Poland. Those landings, Operation DRAGOON, began the next day. Two days later the battle for the Falaise Gap in Normandy was concluded. On 19 August the inhabitants of Paris rose and took over their city.

In Romania, Red Army formations in the Iaşi-Chişinău (Kishinev) area went onto the offensive on 20 August when 2nd and 3rd Ukrainian Fronts began an attempt to encircle the German Army Group South Ukraine.

For this account the most significant event must be the *coup d'état* on 23 August, when King Michael and his supporters arrested Marshal Antonescu and deposed his pro-fascist government. The total defection of Romanian armed forces from the Axis cause that night heralded the collapse of the German defence line in Moldavia and allowed Soviet troops an unopposed advance. A week later they entered Bucharest after despoiling the countryside and exacting revenge along the way.

In the Mediterranean Theatre the strategic air effort continued to batter at the enemy's rail communications in Hungary, Romania and Yugoslavia aiding the Russian drive westwards as well as resistance movements in Yugoslavia and Greece.

Oil targets retained their top priority rating and in the first half of August over 8,500 tons of bombs were delivered. The last assaults on the Ploieşti oil installations dropped almost 3,000 tons by day and night. The last three operations of the 'siege' continuously delivered on 17, 18 and 19 August met with increased success due largely to a novel counter measure to outwit the smoke screens. The USAAF positioned a single P-38 Lightning weather reconnaissance aircraft over the target ahead of the bombers. The pilot's task was to observe the screen and broadcast details of its drift and spread to the approaching bombers. This technique allowed some very effective visual bombing.

Three days after the Romanian *coup d'état* day bombers returned to the capital to attack German troop concentrations still holding out in the northern suburbs of Băneasa.

The night-bombers delivered another 212 1000 lb mines into the Danube.

Throughout the four-month offensive Romania's oil production capacity was reduced from over 700,000 crude oil tons per month to 77,000 tons – a cut of 89%. The cut in petrol production was estimated to be even greater at 91%. This was rated as a triumph in strategic bombing. The Red Army's successful advance at the end of the month finally reduced Axis supplies of Romanian oil to nil.

Heavy bomber commanders: Wing Commander Donald Smythe, DSO, GM, OC 178 Squadron: Brigadier J.T. Durrant, CB, DFC, AOC 205 Group: Group Captain John McKay OC 240 Wing (the Liberator Squadrons) and Lieutenant Colonel Dirk Nel, SAAF, OC 31 Squadron. (Courtesy Imperial War Museum)

For 205 Group August began with two operationally barren nights through bad weather. Brigadier J.T. Durrant SAAF became Air Officer Commanding 205 Group vice Air Commodore J.H.T. Simpson on 3 August. (On relinquishing his command of the Group, Air Commodore Simpson completed a long spell in the Mediterranean. He had joined 37 Squadron in December 1941 and became very much a '205 Group man'. He went on to command 70 Squadron and later, in May 1942, 236 Wing. He took command of the Group in June 1943. He now returned to command RAF Marston Moor in England and remained involved with bombers and training until he retired in 1959. John Herbert Thomas Simpson died on 26 August 1967.)

That same night the month's bombing offensive got under way. The target was the railway yards at Portes-les-Valence in southern France against which the Group flew 85 sorties without loss. The operation was another good example of close cooperation between the day and night-bomber elements of MASAF. A 15 AF daylight attack had successfully severed the railway North and South of the marshalling yards and had isolated several hundred railway trucks and wagons of all types. 205 Group's mission was to destroy this rolling stock and over 164 tons of high explosive were dropped in achieving it.

Not only did Romania's capitulation on 23 August signal the removal of Romanian targets from the Group's inventory, it also marked the beginning – quite coincidentally – of a period of operations against 'tactical' targets in support of 8 Army's advance on Rimini. Bologna, Ferrar, Ravenna and Pesaro all received heavy and successful attacks.

On the four nights between 13 and 16 August the two Liberator Wings flew supply missions to the embattled and surrounded Home Army in Warsaw. There were heavy casualties – of the 47 Liberators despatched, thirteen were lost and several more were damaged.

During August the Group would operate on twenty nights and the total weight of bombs would be the heaviest yet at over 2,600 tons.

The Raids

Friday 4 August

The last Operation FRANTIC raid was launched from Italy on this day. It was a 'fighters only' performance and 42 P-38s and 36 P-51s strafed Focsani en route to their temporary USSR bases, claiming the destruction of five enemy aircraft without loss. Bad weather in the target area limited the attack to Focşani.

Sunday 6 August

The return leg of this Operation FRANTIC raid saw a number of fighters left behind in Russia. Of the 78 which had flown in, only twenty-six P-38s and thirty P-51s took off for the home run. They carried out successful strafing attacks at low-level on railway targets at Ploieşti, Bucharest and Craiova. They claimed to have destroyed one enemy fighter on the ground while sweeping the Ploieşti area.

Tuesday 8 August

A force of 73 B-17s was tasked to bomb two Luftwaffe airfields supporting the German front in Moldavia, at Buzău and at Boboc/Zilisteanca. The bombers suffered no losses, nor did their escort of 55 P-51s and no enemy aircraft were claimed.

9/10 August

205 Group generated its largest 'maximum effort' of the campaign against Romanian targets with 81 sorties mounted by all five Wings on this Wednesday night. Allied Intelligence had noted that Bucharest's heavy flak defences now mustered a total of 120 guns – a reduction of 20 which, it was assessed, had been redeployed North to protect railway installations behind the front in Moldavia and Transylvania. Timişoara and Braşov were both seen to have been reinforced. The raiders that night did not notice the difference as they overflew the capital. The preamble to the Group ORB report sets the scene for a most eventful night.

> The target was the Romană-Americană Refinery, just East of Ploieşti which despite persistent attack was still believed to be in full production. It was a most important target. As a result, the defences had been greatly strengthened and this was a most costly operation. 50 Wellingtons from all three Wings, twenty-three Liberators and eight Halifaxes were despatched and eight Wellingtons, one Liberator and two Halifaxes failed to return. In addition, five Wellingtons returned early . . .

The Group ORB goes on:

> The ground defences, estimated at 100 searchlights and 60 heavy guns, concentrated on the illuminating Halifaxes and they were repeatedly coned with the result that, in addition to two which are missing, two more were prevented from making bombing runs because of the need for constant evasive action, one could not open the bomb-doors through flak damage and one was late owing to evasive action over Bucharest. Two Green TIs were dropped on equipment (using H_2S) but their position was uncertain

because of the most effective smoke screen. Most aircraft bombed on the TIs, some on DR from Lake Snagov and a few visually through the smoke on the estimated position of the target. No results could be observed, but one fairly large fire was seen glowing through the smoke.

Many fighters were active form Krusevac, 50 kilometres north-west of Niš, to the target and back. Ju 88, Me 109, Me 110 and FW 190 were identified and persistent attacks were made with tracer and rockets, one Wellington and one Halifax being damaged. Two aircraft were seen coned and shot down by flak and three others were seriously damaged. Of these the most serious casualty was 'W-William' of 614 Squadron, captain Flying Officer Prange, Bomb-Aimer Warrant Officer Fox. On the return journey, just south of the Danube, this Halifax was hit by heavy flak. The nose was entirely wrecked and a Red Target Marker bomb was ignited in the bomb-bay which set the aircraft on fire. After an order by the Captain to don parachutes the intercom failed and in the resulting confusion, four of the crew baled out. Warrant Officer Fox, though wounded, managed to extinguish the fire and Flying Officer Prange brought the aircraft safely back to base.

Details of the missing aircraft are Wellingtons 'C-Charlie' Flight Sergeant Marsh, 'W-William' Lieutenant Cathrine, 'H-Harry' Flight Sergeant Hill – all of 142 Squadron. Wellingtons 'B-Baker' Sergeant Merrick and 'S-Sugar' Sergeant Double of 37 Squadron, Wellingtons 'L-Love' Pilot Officer Futcher and 'O-Orange' Flight Sergeant Ross of 70 Squadron. Wellington 'X-X Ray' Pilot Officer Jones of 150 Squadron (eight Wellingtons).Liberator 'D-Dog' Flight Sergeant Watson of 178 Squadron and two Halifaxes of 614 Squadron – 'I-Item' Flight Sergeant Caldwell-Wearne and 'Q-Queenie' Flight Lieutenant Langton.

'B-Baker' of 70 Squadron (Sergeant Merrick) managed to reach Turkey after sustaining damage to its oil system from flak. The crew all returned safely via the Middle East. Pilot Officer Futcher and his crew baled out over Yugoslavia and all returned safely via the Partisans. Twenty-one members of other crews were taken prisoner and evacuated from Bucharest after the entry of the Russians.

The last sentence is not supported by the facts. Only fourteen members of other crews became PWs in Bucharest.

Even allowing for the military writing style of the ORB this was clearly an eventful, exciting and for many a decisive night, as the accounts which follow bear out. Derek Cashmore, a Sergeant Air-Bomber in 70 Squadron and a member of Flight Sergeant F. Sullivan's crew had a clear memory of the next day.

B Flight 614 Squadron in the Summer on 1944.

Not all the faces have been identified, but Plt Offr J.L. Nicholson is 2nd left front row. On this left is Fg Offr Bruce Prange DFC RCAF, who brought his wounded Air Bomber back from Ploiesti on 10 August. FLt Bob Wilson is next. 6th from left is Sqn Ldr Ben Susan from Southern Rhodesia. Fg Offr Chas Symons is on the right end of the front row. Syd Barlow of Nicholson's crew is behind Ben Susan. The Air Bomber, FS Cartwright, is at the right end of the 3rd row. The Flt Engr, Sgt Wiles, is 2nd left, 3rd row. FS Hitchin, Navigator, is at the right end 4th row. Tom Scotland stands behind Barlow's left shoulder. (Courtesy J. Frank Cowie)

> Our crew 'found each other' at a Reception Centre at Jerusalem and we were welded into a team at Qastina in Palestine from May onwards. We arrived at Tortorella on 10 August and it was clearly noticeable that the raid had been costly: there was much speculation as to the whereabouts of missing crews, even to the view that some had made it to Turkey.

614 Squadron's record shows that they had a hard task in marking this target and the defenders set about the maximum disruption of these key aircraft. The blitz would begin at 2330 hours and the markers and illuminators arrived in the target area ahead at 2323 hours. On the final approach, at 2317 hours, one Halifax was attacked by a Ju 88. It was shaken off by evasive action but re-appeared at 500 metres range. When the fighter had closed to 400 metres, the Rear Gunner opened fire hitting the enemy's tail plane. He dived away to starboard and broke off the attack. The Halifax sustained damage to the starboard inner engine on this encounter. Another Halifax running-in to the target area was intercepted by a Ju 88 over Bucharest. When the fighter turned

in to the attack the Halifax corkscrewed away successfully and the Ju 88 broke away and attacked another bomber. Other pilots reported seeing four Halifaxes coned by searchlights and heavily engaged by flak on the approach and over the target area. The five Halifaxes which reached the target dropped 94 flares, four Green and one Yellow Target Marking Bombs in under a minute from 10,000 feet. One aircraft jettisoned one Yellow and six Green TMBs after an engine damaged by flak caused the aircraft to lose height.

One of the later models of Halifax B Mk II, Series 1A, P-Peter (JP 228) of 614 Squadron arrived in Italy in late April 1944 but was lost on operations on the night of 21 August. This photograph was taken in England before ferrying to Celone.
(Courtesy Imperial War Museum)

The twelve Liberators from 178 Squadron bombed mainly on the Green TIs, although one crew claimed to have identified the target – lit by flares. The smoke screen was effective and some aircraft bombed on timed runs from the last turning point on the route. The last aircraft found no TIs still visible. They all 'blitzed' between 2331 and 2337 from between 10,500 and 11,800 feet dropping some 30 tons of HE. Sergeant Jack Halsall, Rear-Gunner in Flying Officer Pat Boothman's 178 Squadron 'J-Jig' (Serial EV 839) noted in his Log Book that this was their twentieth operation. They were coned by searchlights and fired on by flak and their twelve 500 lb bombs were 'hung up'. They were released manually later over the sea. Two nights later Boothman and company marked their twenty-second operation with a ten and a half hour flight to deliver twelve containers to the Warsaw insurgents.

212

178 Squadron Amendola, Summer 1944.

Flt Ken Trevena of Redruth and his crew with their Liberator B Mk VI. At the waist gun, Sgts George Dalgliesh, Rear Guner of Inverness and Sandy Burnett, Wireless Operator of Gorebridge, Midlothian.

Standing with Ken Trevena (hatted) are – from the left– Lt Alan Graham, SAAF, Navigator of Johannesbury, Sgt Jim Brannan, Mid-upper Gunner of Dundee and Sgt George McCreary, Flight Engineer of Airdrie. (Courtesy George Dalgiesh)

2 SAAF Wing also produced twelve Liberators and eleven attacked the primary target without loss. Five aircraft bombed on the Green TIs which were assessed to have been properly positioned. One stick of bombs was seen to straddle the TIs. Crew sightings en route painted a picture of mayhem for the bomber stream. SAAF crews reported some six incidents which looked like the destruction of fellow bombers. One near Niš in Yugoslavia at 2210 hours, one north of Roşiorii de Vede at 2305 hours – air-to-air firing followed by

explosions and fires was the norm. At 2315, some 40 kilometres west of Bucharest, air-to-air firing preceded a mid-air explosion. Two minutes later another unidentified aircraft exploded in mid-air to fall in a fireball to the ground, 25 kilometres east of Caracal. This, at least, can be matched to an actual casualty. 150 Squadron's 'X-X Ray' crashed at Dodroteşti [Crash Site 16] killing four of the crew including the captain, Flying Officer N.C. Jones. There was only one survivor, Sergeant M.L. Wilson, who briefly became a PW. One Liberator reported two contacts with Ju 88s which displayed lights. One approached from astern as the bomber was leaving the target area, displaying a 'blinking light' in the nose. After being lost to evasive action it reappeared, followed by another showing a red light. No fire was exchanged throughout the encounter which last over twenty minutes.

A 31 (SA) Squadron target photograph taken at 11.32 pm on 9 Aug 44 from 12000' above the River Teleajan from Liberator 'F for Freddy'. Among the points of interest are:

1. *The Wellington a long way below heading due North*

2. *Five of 'F for Freddy 's' load of 12 x 500 lb bombs.*

3. *The smoke pots of the defensive screen with smoke drifint towards the top left of the photograph.*

4. *The pock marks of the bomb craters from previous raids.*

5. *Bombs bursting in the lower left.*

6. *(Sadly, 'F for Freddy' has over-flown the Dacia Romana Refinery by some 3-4 kms before releasing his bombs. The nearest refinery to his impact point is the Concordia Vega 1.3 kms to the south-west)*

The South African Liberators dropped over 32 tons from greater heights than those of 178 Squadron, between 11,500 and 12,200 feet in a long blitz of seventeen minutes from 2328 hours.

The ORBs of the three Wellington Wings tell generally the same story and that no crews were able to identify the target positively through the smoke. Of 231 Wing's twelve bombers over the target, two bombed on the Red TIs, three on Greens and seven on DR or visually. Of course, it was the Luftwaffe's deliberate design that the smoke screen should prevent a direct view of the target. Equally, it was the pathfinder's task to find it in spite of smoke or whatever the enemy did to conceal it, using their radars or by whatever other technique they could deploy, and then to mark it for the following bomber pack. Perhaps, therefore, the fact that the Wellington crews did not see their target is not so calamitous as might first appear. Were the Markers in the right place and did the bombers bomb on the Markers correctly are, perhaps, two much more important points? Crew sightings on the inward and outward leg present a tantalising sequence of instances of aircraft in trouble which are virtually impossible to correlate, substantiate or even de-bunk. The reporting was genuine without doubt but what was seen may not have been what it seemed – or the map-spotting of the place may not have been quite accurate. A sufficient number of sightings are closely related enough to make the post-war sleuthing interesting but, thankfully, not crucial to this account. 231 Wing's crews reported twelve incidents and with a blitz time of 2330 to 2345 hours it would seem reasonable that their sightings would compare favourably with those of other crews. Sadly they do not.

231 Wellingtons dropped 19.5 tons of 500 lb MC TD .025 and 405,000 nickels.

236 Wing could only launch nine aircraft, five from 40 Squadron and four from 104 because of 'contaminated' oil at the airfield. They all bombed the primary and returned safely. They observed the jettisoned flares and wisely assessed them as such and flew on. Six aircraft bombed on the Green TIs, two on the Red and the last tried visual bombing but none was able to observe results.

At 2330 hours, as the blitz began, a Ju 88 attacked 'O-Orange' (Pilot Officer Nielson) of 104 Squadron, from astern and high at 8,000 feet, hitting the Wellington's tail unit. The Rear-Gunner replied with a long burst as the enemy had closed to about 150 metres. It broke away to port and returned later on the port quarter but 'O-Orange' evaded any subsequent attacks and the fighter was lost. 'G-George' of 104 Squadron captained by Flight Lieutenant Johnson had an encounter with an Me 109 over the target at the same time. It approached from the starboard beam high at 8–9,000 feet and closed to 150 metres without firing. Johnson was able to lose the fighter by normal evasive action. These few aircraft produced some precise sightings of downed aircraft.

Two at 2206 hours south-west of the Danube

One at 2257 hours 40 miles south-west of Lake Snagov

One at 2306 hours 30 miles south-west of Lake Snagov

Four between 2315 and 2330 hours between Bucharest and the target.

236 Wing's load included three 4000 lb HC which with their 36 500 lb bombs totalled 15 tons dropped in an eight minute blitz from 2330 hours from 5,750 to 8,750 feet. 350,000 nickels were also delivered.

330 Wing's ORB shows that thirteen aircraft out of the twenty-one launched bombed the primary. Another four were missing. No aircrew saw the target but bombed on Greens and Reds with six making DR runs from Lake Snagov. Crews saw the usual panoply of falling aircraft, as difficult to substantiate at this late date as any of the others. This Wing had the unusual sighting, three times, of a silver coloured single-engined enemy aircraft in the Craiova area. Many fighter flares were reported.

'R-Robert' of 142 Squadron encountered a single-engined fighter at 2330 hours as the blitz began, at 9,700 feet. The fighter turned in from the port quarter and closed to 200 metres when the Wellington's Rear-Gunner fired three bursts which caused the enemy to dive away: no hits were claimed. 'U-Uncle' of 150 Squadron had a similar duel with an Me 109 about 50 kilometres from Bucharest on the home leg. Again the enemy came close without firing and sheered away undamaged after the Wellington's Rear-Gunner had fired 300 rounds and the aircraft had corkscrewed.

330 Wing's Wellingtons dropped twenty-three tons which included two 4000 lb HC NI as well as the standard mixture of 500 lb and 250 lb bombs, in a six minute blitz from 2329 hours from between 7,000 and 9,000 feet, as well as 490,000 nickels.

So much, perhaps, for what the contemporary records said of this night. The recollections of some of those who took part and subsequent studies add a further dimension to what was clearly the biggest and toughest night raid on a Romanian target so far.

The loss of two Wellingtons supplies the first enigma – 37 Squadron's 'S-Sugar' and 70 Squadron's 'O-Orange'. Both aircraft were a total loss and there were no survivors. This book shows that Sergeant W.E. Double and his crew were all killed in 'S-Sugar' when it crashed at Cotroceni [Crash Site 13] in the western suburbs of Bucharest. It also shows that 'O-Orange' with Flight Sergeant A.S.R. Ross RAAF and his crew all perished at Caciulaţi [Crash Site

15], 10 kilometres south-east of Tîncăbești, the future site of the CWGC Cemetery. But the damage to these aircraft on impact was such that it could have been the other way round. The two crews occupy the same collective grave.

A 150 Squadron crew with JN V-Victor. Left to Right Flight Lieutenant Ron Turner, Navigator; Sergeant Leo Grant, Wireless Operator; Flying Officer Max Thompson, Pilot; Sergeant 'Shorty' Crutchmen, Air Gunner (and the only 'Englishman'); Sergeant Arthur Baker, Air Bomber. (Courtesy Ron Turner)

Wing Commander Cameron Mervyn-Jones RAAF of 40 Squadron returned safely to base in 'T-Tommy' – his fourth operation for the month – and recalls that:

> . . . it seems to have been quite straightforward. It was fairly long, navigationally, but we were able to use the outskirts of Bucharest as a fix before turning towards our oil refinery at Ploieşti. The ground defences were quite active and distracting but our bomb drop went off without a hitch. The only incident I can remember of these raids was of the miraculous escape of an Air Gunner from another Squadron in the Group. On the way home his Wellington was attacked by a night-fighter and blown up but the tail section with his turret was left intact. He was unable

217

to reach his parachute which had been stowed in the rear fuselage but the whole tail-unit with turret 'fluttered' to the ground. A few months later he was back in Italy, but I do not know if he was injured.

It is sad to have to record that it has not been possible to bear this story out. It could have happened but there seems to be no evidence of burial of the remaining members of the crew or an unaccounted loss of a Wellington.

The crew of LP 540 'B-Baker' of 37 Squadron had a very real adventure related by Sergeant Tom Killoran, the Wireless Operator in Sergeant Tom Merrick's all-sergeant crew. The others were R. Stanley, Navigator, C. Querrelle, the Air-Bomber and F.H. Best the Rear Gunner. It was a bright moonlit night:

The flight over the Adriatic, Yugoslavia and the Danube plain was uneventful, although one or two aircraft on both sides were seen to go down in flames. It was only as we approached the target that we were coned in searchlights and then the fun really began.

A Ju 88 night-fighter came in three times and at the same time flak began to pepper the aircraft and light from the searchlights shone through the gaping holes. It was at about this time that the Air-Gunner yelled over the intercom that he had been hit and we realised that the port engine had been rendered useless. With a full bombload aboard we immediately went into a steep dive. If we were to save the crew and aircraft, it was obvious that the bombs must be jettisoned. This was done and we pulled out of the dive only a few thousand feet above the target. The raid was at its height by now and the searchlights and fighters had lost interest in us and, no doubt, were searching for other victims.

The aircraft began to vibrate and the pilot found it difficult to keep it in the air. However, as we were not receiving attention from the enemy, I decided to help the wounded gunner from the rear turret. The release mechanism was not working properly so I used the aircraft axe to release the turret doors and was able to pull him onto the bed where he was given a shot of morphine.

We realised that we were gradually losing height and that it would be impossible to fly over Yugoslavia so we set a course for Turkey. During this time 'Baker' was most unstable and all unnecessary articles were thrown out.

As we approached the Bosphorus, we turned on our navigation lights but the Turks opened fire with their guns and, once more, we were trapped in searchlights. At about 2000 feet we stood no chance at all and the other engine was knocked out. The pilot ordered us to bale out and the wounded air gunner was brought to the forward hatch – his hand was placed on his rip cord and he was thrown out of the aircraft.

I jumped shortly afterwards. The guns were still firing and the searchlights lighting up the whole scene. As I floated to earth, 'B-Baker' exploded beneath me. I landed among some bushes on the side of a hill. It was still a bright moonlit night and, as I had no idea where I was, I decided to try and sleep so I rolled myself in my parachute.

When daylight came I took stock of my situation and set off to find some kind of habitation. I soon came upon two goatherds. Using sign language, I explained what had happened and, of course, they had seen it all from a ring-side seat. One of them took a muzzle-loading gun and his dog and we marched for hours over hills and through valleys. From time to time he had a shot at a rabbit. My feet were really blistered when we came upon a gang of Turkish soldiers making a road. I said goodbye to my goatherd friends and was taken in an ancient lorry to Istanbul.

There I was interrogated by a University Professor of English who informed me that some Turks had been killed in a factory that night. They thought we had bombed it, but it turned out that one of their anti-aircraft shells had exploded in the factory. We learned later that the flak which had been our undoing had been directed by British Army Instructors on secondment to the Turkish Army at that time. Sergeant Best was for some time in the American Hospital in Istanbul.

From Istanbul we were taken by train to Ankara which was a great centre of intrigue – Germans, Italians, Japanese, Americans and English all mingled together. We later flew out from Adana to Cairo in a Dakota. Here we were interrogated once more, this time by our own side, before we set off for the Squadron via Marble Arch, Biskara, Maison Blanche, Sardinia, Naples to Tortorella, where we arrived ten days after our adventure had begun. We finished our tour together, although we had a number of air gunners.

The French-language daily newspaper *La République* carried a front page headline about 'Air alert at Istanbul' in its issue of 11 August: the previous day an American bomber had crashed at Izmit about 100 kilometres east-south-east of Istanbul on the road to Ankara, having been engaged by Turkish AAA – so their tails were up.

Following the appearance at 0215 hours of an unidentified aircraft in the sky above Istanbul, the alarm was sounded . . . Anti-aircraft defences opened fire at the unknown aircraft which came down in the area of Alemdagh. The crew jumped to safety by parachute. It has been established that the aircraft belongs to the English Air Force and had a damaged engine following a raid on Romania. One of the shells of our AA fell into a factory at Bomonti slightly wounding seven people.

(Alemdagh is now a suburb of Istanbul, on the Asia Minor side. In 1944 it was a village.)

Flight Sergeant Ian Arrowsmith, pilot of 40 Squadron remembers the night vividly:

I did my first op as 'Second Dickie' with Warrant Officer Mayers. A rather frightening experience for a young fellow who had never seen much fighting. It was Ploieşti, which in those days was number one target in Europe. They had to have the oil so they defended it with everything they had. By the time we arrived it was just a continual sea of blacky-grey smoke and the target markers that had been put down by the pathfinders became lost in the smoke.

I was very impressed with Mayers' crew. They were very, very competent and alert. Sitting in the cockpit with Mayers, as we turned on our last leg and went towards Ploieşti, we could see there, in front of us, the most frightening display of pyrotechnics that anyone had ever seen, dozens and dozens of guns firing up the radar operated searchlight beams. There would be, I suppose, 250 searchlights around the place of which about 20–25 would be the very deep blue types.

We flew on towards this target and it frightened hell out of me, I'd never seen anything like it in all my life. The guns were blasting away in a continual sheet of explosions above the refineries and it was amazing that aircraft managed to fit through them. Our height was about 10,000 feet. Mayers opened up his engines, put his nose slightly down and charged through, straight as a die, hard as he could to get up to speed, wandering up to about 220–230 knots (which was very fast for a Wellington), really pushing it along. We bombed in the middle of the target markers as we were supposed to do and then, when he turned away, he immediately started diving for the ground. He told me that this was the practice and it was quite possible in these areas; it enabled them to dodge the night-fighters. Mayers then flew low over the Danubian fields. I copied his tactics myself later but I tried to get down even lower than he did. He flew over the high-power electricity lines. I would fly under them because the closer one got to the ground the less chance there was of a night-fighter seeing you . . . When we reached the Yugoslav mountains, we put on power and climbed up over them.

The Pilots of 'A' Flight 142 Squadron at Regina in June 1944.

Front Row (L-R)

FO Allen Harrison RNZAF, FO Jones, Flt Johnny King DFC, Sqn Ldr Tubby Woodroffe (Flight Commander), Capt Noel Catherine DSO SAAF, Capt Van de Westhuizen SAAF, Capt Bill Wallace SAAF.

Sitting – Lt Kelly SAAF.

Standing (L to R)

FS Pop Ashwell RAAF, FS Stinson RAAF, PO Coulthard, FS Pennefather RAAF, FS Blackett RAAF, WO Davidson RAAF, FS Charman RAAF.

(Courtesy Noel Cathrine)

142 Squadron lost three Wellingtons on this operation. Very little is known of the fate of MF 631 'C-Charlie' captained by Flight Sergeant R.T. Marsh RCAF except that it crashed at Orac [Crash Site 14] near Snagov, 25 kilometres north of Bucharest. There were no survivors. This Wellington exploded on striking the ground and subsequent identification of the dead was only possible by reference to numbers on one engine in the wreckage. The crew's remains now lie in the CWGC Cemetery. Equally, very little is known about 'H-Harry'. This was Wellington LP 548 flown by Flight Sergeant C.G. Hill RAAF. It crashed somewhere in northern Bulgaria and all five of the crew are now buried in the CWGC Cemetery at Sofia. Lieutenant E.N. Cathrine SAAF, who was the pilot of LN 972 'W-William', that night was luckier. In September 1944 Noel Cathrine wrote of his experiences to OC 142 Squadron, Wing Commander Angus Maclean.

*Captain E. Macdonald MBE, DFC, SAAF and Wing Commander A.G.C. MacLean OC
142 Squadron – taken while on leave in Rome. (Courtesy Angus MacLean)*

'Cocky' [that is Lieutenant W.D.H. Stone, SAAF] had just given me the
last course for home when one of those bloody Danube patrol jobs – must
have been as we had crossed the river only three or four minutes before –
came out of the smudgy part of the horizon with a frontal attack. He had us
sitting against the moon but took a chance even so for he broke away right
above us. I think he knew what he was doing though – bit of a gen boy!
Anyway, he made a sorry mess of 'W-William'. Both motors were dead,
the hydraulic leads were severed just behind the control levers, the
instrument panel was riddled, the second dickey seat was shot away from
under MacDonald [Flight Sergeant W.A.] and fires started from the
cockpit to the turret. And, just for the hell of it, there was no intercom and
no call lights which was grim as I'd no idea how things were going in the
back. As it happened I couldn't have delayed my jump any longer than I
did. Had to side-slip my 'chute to avoid landing in the wreckage.

God, I was happy to see the lads about midday the next day. Cocky
Taylor [Flight Sergeant J.] and Mackay [Sergeant R.W.] were OK: Graham
[Sergeant J.] a twisted ankle. MacDonald was worst off with a 20mm
cannon shell through the fleshy part of his thigh and sundry shrap. I had
shrap in my left foot and head, a twisted knee and a bullet graze on my
right forearm. All mild – but I had a spot of squitters to help along for a

few days. Just at the darnedest time!

Well – that's the story. We were lucky. Sorry I can't report, similarly on another of the squadron's crews. I saw a kite blow up almost on the Danube and the following day was shown a picture of a lad I recognised as one of our gunners. I do not know his name but he was definitely 142. The crew were all dead.

This aircraft must have been Flight Sergeant Hill's 'H-Harry'.

The whole trip was pretty bloody. Into the target and out fellows were in trouble. Over it was just a shambles. We had no peace from the fighter flares and I'd only completed a little gallop away from the blow-up I've mentioned above when the Joe caught up with me.

Oh, one more thing – my salaams to the ground crew of 'W-William'. She was ticking over like a charm when she met her end.

On their return to 142 Squadron, Flight Sergeant Taylor, Wireless Operator, and Sergeant McKay, Air-Gunner, were 'interrogated' by the Squadron IO, on 23 September. Their story tells another side of the night's decisive events. All was well all the way into the target but . . .

. . . for some considerable distance after leaving, fighter flares were seen astern and on track

but no enemy aircraft were seen.

A head-on attack was made by an unidentified enemy aircraft at 0028 hours near Lom on the river, when the Wellington was at about 9,500 feet. The fighter was believed to have been a twin from the engine noise. The firing – of machine gun and cannon – was in one burst of about two seconds damaging the front of the aircraft and the cockpit severely.

Both engines cut and fire broke out almost immediately in the cockpit. A second fire broke out simultaneously on the starboard side of the fuselage, believed to be ignited oil tanks. The starboard ammunition boxes broke away and the ammunition exploded. The Wireless Operator was wounded in the head by a splinter. The second pilot, Flight Sergeant MacDonald, was severely injured in the legs by machine gun fire and wounded in the thigh by a cannon shell splinter. Lieutenant Stone, the Navigator and Sergeant McKay, Air Gunner, were uninjured. Sergeant Graham, Air Bomber, was burned slightly in one leg. Lieutenant Cathrine, the Pilot, was injured in the head and legs by shrapnel and fell forward in his seat.

The aircraft went into a steep uncontrolled dive for about 4,000 feet when the pilot was able to recover and to hold it for some seconds. That he was able to regain some control for this short period despite his severe injuries, undoubtedly enabled the crew to get out and '. . . the two NCOs . . .' pay tribute to the Captain's conduct, presence of mind and skill in handling the aircraft when badly wounded. He was heard by the Wireless Operator shouting to the crew to abandon the aircraft. Shortly after this the aircraft dived steeply to the ground and crashed.

Flight Sergeant Taylor saw sparks and a fire break out in the fuselage and another fire take hold in the cockpit. He saw MacDonald preparing to jump through the forward escape hatch and was then told by Lieutenant Stone to go to the rear of the aircraft as the forward hatch had jammed. He followed Stone to the rear and saw that the starboard wing and the fuselage on that side were on fire. Sergeant Graham, the Air Bomber, was standing by the diamond escape hatch, fixing on his parachute. Taylor, Graham and Stone jumped. The aircraft then appeared to be 'wallowing' at about 5,000 feet. Sergeant McKay, in his rear turret, first knew of the attack when he heard a rending sound and experienced the aircraft shudder. As the Wellington went into a steep dive he tried to bale out of his turret. But he could not operate his doors and only escaped when the aircraft was about 1,000 feet from the ground. He had only been able to secure his 'chute by one hook and guessed that it opened at about 600 feet. He saw the Wellington hit the ground almost immediately and landed in a maize field about half a mile away. McKay, no doubt believing he was the sole survivor, checked his kit and set off for home. After about 4 kilometres he came upon a peasant cottage and found MacDonald who had made his way there despite his severe leg injuries. McKay administered morphia and bandaged the leg wounds but, realising that MacDonald needed medical attention, he set out while it was still dark to find help at the village of Bela Pole – 12 kilometres distant where he arrived at 0600 hours. He obtained the services of a farm wagon to bring MacDonald in but when he returned to the cottage the peasants would not let MacDonald go until the parachutes were recovered. These had to be handed over to the authorities. The 'chutes were retrieved by Sergeant McKay and:

> . . . after some delay he and Flight Sergeant MacDonald returned to Bela
> Pole where a Russian woman doctor attended Flight Sergeant MacDonald.

Flight Sergeant Taylor, the Wireless Operator, also landed uninjured in a maize field, wrapped himself in his 'chute and rested until dawn, when he decided to set off north-west for the escape areas given at their briefing. After about 12 kilometres his feet began to give trouble – he was wearing flying boots – and he was forced to rest. At this point he was approached by two armed civilians enquiring if he was American or English.

> Some misunderstanding was experienced due to 'No' being indicated in Bulgarian by a nod of the head and 'Yes' by a shake of the head!

Taylor was now taken South for about an hour. His guards had become sullen when they found out that he had shredded his parachute. His feet were now in such a state that he had to remove his flying boots. When they came to a village his guards rejected food offered by the locals. The mayor questioned Flight Sergeant Taylor about his crew and he gathered that three more had been found. His march south to Bela Pole continued and there he found MacDonald and McKay, but they were not allowed to talk. The mayor here phoned to Vratsa and eventually an escort of Bulgarian soldiers with an interpreter arrived. Some hours later Lieutenant Stone and Sergeant Graham were brought in. Stone had only superficial injuries but Graham had leg and rib damage. That afternoon – still 10 August – all five were taken to the railway station where they saw Lieutenant Cathrine on a stretcher but they were not allowed to speak to him and he was taken away to hospital at Bela Pole (of which there is no trace on modern maps).

On arrival at Vratsa all five were taken to a military camp where MacDonald and Graham received medical treatment.

They were prisoners of war – but not for long.

In a letter to the author in November 1983, Sir Henry Calley DSO DFC DL (formerly Wing Commander Henry Langton), President of the 205 Group Reunion wrote:

> Noel Cathrine's episode was one of the bravest efforts that occurred, I think. He was very lucky to get out as he waited until they had all gone and at that time the front escape hatch was stuck and the plane was on fire. By the grace of God it opened when he made his effort to get out. He was so close to the ground when he did that he was almost on top of where the aircraft crashed.

Bob Ives DFM remembers an odd sighting on this operation:

> . . . we were returning to base when the Skipper said over the intercom, 'Bob there is a plane coming towards us on the port side, see what kind it is.' I swung my turret to port, fingers on the triggers waiting for it, but it took no notice of us. It was a German troop carrier with four engines and a

225

swastika on its side. I told the Skipper and he replied, 'Shall we go after it?' 'Well,' I said, 'it is better to be safe than sorry, it may have more guns than we have and as it has not attacked us, I think we can let it carry on, but that is your choice. I am game!' So the Skip decided to keep on course and we arrived back at base after seven hours and forty minutes flying.

Flight Sergeant Norman Lord RNZAF was a 150 Squadron Pilot of an all Flight Sergeant crew – Grace, Air-Gunner – Nash, Navigator – White, Wireless Operator and Truckle, Air Bomber. They flew 37 operations between 8 July and 26 September 1944 from Porte-en-Valence to Athens.

He remembers this raid:

> The searchlights were like several rows of a picket fence and we were crazy enough to fly in amongst them in search of our targets – such is the foolishness of youth . . . while dodging through searchlights over the target area and endeavouring to pinpoint our target, a Liberator was trapped by a blue-beamed searchlight and instantly several others coned him. He became the centre of a concentrated ack-ack attack the like of which I never saw again, or before that for that matter. They were literally blasted out of the sky in a matter of 30 seconds and, as they were at about 18,000 feet, the 88mm and the 120mm flak guns were extremely accurate.

The luckless Liberator seen by Norman Lord must, in fact, have been a hapless Halifax and he agrees that this may be so. No Liberator was lost over Romania that night, but two Halifaxes were.

One JP 110 'I-Item' flown by Flight Sergeant C.F. Caldwell-Wearne crashed at Ciocănești [Crash Site 18] and all but one of the crew survived, hardly possible in the battle which Norman Lord described. Indeed, it is known that a JP 110 was hit and set on fire by a Ju 88 which continued to sit behind the burning aircraft firing into it. A Wellington apparently dived onto the German and opened fire from its nose turret. The guns had, apparently, been previously loaded with day tracer (as this turret was not normally used – or even manned – on night operations) and the ensuing firework display so un-nerved the fighter that it broke away, leaving the Halifax crew to bale out. Caldwell-Wearne was about to jump – the last to go – when the aircraft blew up and he was rendered unconscious. He came to hanging under his parachute, having no recollection of pulling the rip-cord. To illustrate the difficulty of reconciling war-time information with that available today, the contemporary record shows that 'I-Item' crashed at Ciscăuţi, of which no trace can be found today. However, the Navigator, Warrant Officer H. Bath, who lost his life, was originally buried at Ciocăneşti, some 20 kilometres north-west of Bucharest on the old road to Pitesti.

Norman Lord is much more likely to have seen the final moments of the other Halifax, JP 282 'Q-Queenie', captain Flight Lieutenant R.D. Langton, which crashed at Corbi Mari [Crash Site 19] some 40 kilometres West of Bucharest. Warrant Officer H.G. Poynton was the sole member of Langton's crew to survive. He became a Romanian PW together with four other 614 Squadron colleagues, members of Flying Officer Bruce Prange's much-damaged 'W-William'.

J. Frank Cowie, an Air-Bomber of 614 Squadron, joined Bruce Prange to make up his crew shortly after this 9/10 August operation. The aircraft was a complete write-off. Al Fox, his RCAF Air-Bomber, was injured and returned to England, where his wife was staying. Fox had over seventy wounds, caused in the main by tiny shell fragments. Both Prange and Fox were awarded DFCs for their bravery that night. Prange's regular Flight Engineer, Steve Elneski, had been unable to fly on that fateful night and he, with Bill Baker an RAAF Navigator, and RCAF Frank Cowie formed the basis of Prange's new crew. They flew their last op together on 22 September.

The Sortie Report (RAF Form 441A) completed by Lieutenant Andy Smith SAAF, captain of 31 Squadron's Liberator 105 'G-George', has an almost nonchalant tone.

> At 2330 hours slight dive attack from 12,200 feet on course 000° at 195 mph. Bombed SOUTH of Green TIs in the smoke bank. 9 x 500 lb MC TD .025 dropped in stick spaced 100 feet. 2 x 500 lb MC TD .025 broke through bomb-doors. 2 x 500 lb MC TD .025 hung up starboard front bay. 1 x 500 lb MC TD .025 jettisoned at 0130 hours.

He also reports:

> . . . explosion like AA burst 100 feet below aircraft and unidentified aircraft at 7 o'clock and 10° below. Corkscrewed to port and lost aircraft.

Sergeant Michael Cauchi, who was Smith's Air-Gunner, adds:

> It was bad. Lieutenant Smith missed out how he stood that Liberator on its wing-tip to slip out of those searchlights.

227

A 178 Sqn Liberator MK 6 photographed at Amendola with Captain "Dooley" Shaw, his aircrew and the ground crew who maintained it. Sergeant Bill Littlemore is standing second from the right. (Courtesy Bill Littlemore)

One of the most poignant stories of this night's work must be that of Sergeant N.A.B. Cooper, an Air-Gunner in 178 Squadron's EV 974 'D-Dog', captained by Flight Sergeant F.M. Watson. Consular records showed that the aircraft was reported to be in difficulties in the target area and that Sergeant Cooper was suffering from serious burns. Accompanied by an uninjured comrade, Sergeant J.C. Milsom, he baled out over the village of Filipeşti de Tîrg [Crash Site 17], 16 kilometres north-east of Ploieşti. They met a Princess Caradja of the Romanian Red Cross who was acting as an interpreter/liaison officer between the hospitals and the PW camp. The Princess arranged for Cooper to be admitted to the hospital in Ploieşti and Milsom became a PW. Sergeant Cooper, aged 35, succumbed to his massive injuries on 13 August. These were second degree burns on his face, head, neck, both arms and both legs. He had difficulty with his breathing, accompanied by much vomiting. Over forty years later, having 'found' Princess Catharine Caradja, her memory was still very fresh. Filipeşti de Tîrg was her family home . . .

> . . . I always got up during the attacks so I saw the plane fly over us. I saw
> the parachute fall and I rushed over with the car. I yelled at the Germans

who were 'questioning' the poor burned man. I took him to our little hospital and we worked on him there as best we could. At 6 a.m. I left for Ploieşti and got my friend, Dr. Petersen at the Schiller Hospital, to take Cooper in. We talked on the way there and I learned that he had a wife and three kids.

At the hospital I was told that he was unsaveable and three days later I was called to come and get the body. I buried him in my plot, next to the American who fell on 1 August 1943 on my land. Later, the two were 'transferred' and the Russians who had also buried two there remained alone, spoiling my plot.

The plane flew on but the flames may have caused it to explode later.

No trace of 'D-Dog' nor of Flight Sergeant Watson and company could be found. With that level of damage over the target it seemed unlikely to have been able to reach Italy. Indeed, it did not because it was reported missing. None of the names of his crew appeared on any Graves Lists in Bulgaria, Hungary, Romania or Yugoslavia. 'No known graves' seemed to be the only conclusion until the Air Historical Branch were able to confirm that the four remaining members had been reported as being 'safe in Allied hands' in September 1944. That suggested that they might have survived with the Partisans or Chetniks in Yugoslavia as so many others had done before. However, the final question mark was firmly emplaced when a face in a group photograph of officer PWs at Bucharest was unerringly identified as belonging to 2nd Lieutenant F.J. Bagshaw SAAF, the only officer of Watson's crew. No roll of the names of all the PWs has been discovered. Were the other three in the NCOs' camp with their comrade Sergeant Milsom who had tried manfully to save Cooper?

Flight Sergeant Norman Foster RNZAF of 614 Squadron, and still a PW in camp in Bucharest at that time, watched the night's events from another standpoint. He kept a diary:

Tonight we had an Alert and saw some 'fun' for an hour or so. Searchlights have some clues now and we saw about six planes caught. One was brought down. Another we saw come right over us and we could see a fighter making passes at him. He finally got away but all hell and fury were let loose on him 'til he did so.

On 10 August we could see smoke rising from Ploieşti and by dusk the whole sky was covered with a smoky haze.

We heard from Langton's Wireless Operator [Warrant Officer H.G. Poynton] that his crew were blown up – he was the only one to get out. So there goes Bob Langton, Will Martyn and Nobby Clark.

Between 11 and 17 August Norman Foster went on to note:

> Caldwell-Wearne's crew came in the other day. They all got out but C-W himself has been sent to the Schoolhouse. Gibson, his Air-Bomber, is with us now.

Bombers of 205 Group flew 81 sorties on the night of 9 August. They delivered over 120 tons of bombs. By dawn the next day 32 aircrew were dead or dying, twenty-two more were PWs and yet another ten were non-effective while they worked their way back to their squadrons. Twelve bombers were lost to enemy action.

The Romanian military authorities' assessment was that one wave of bombers launched high explosive and incendiaries onto the Astro-Romană and Romană-Americană refineries causing only damage of minor importance. More seriously hit were the residential areas of Bereasca, Teleajan and the village of Bucov. Apparently the toll in human lives was two killed and five wounded. The number of bombs which dropped was given as 49 HE and 12 incendiaries. What can have happened to the rest?

Thursday 10 August

Ploieşti's respite was brief. MASAF was back in great daylight force only a few hours after 205 Group's bombers had turned for home. The detail of the raiders is impressive but what was significant on this day was the relatively small response from the defenders. The attrition and the pressure was beginning to tell.

Six refineries in Ploiesti itself came under attack with Steaua Romană at Cîmpină making the seventh.

Romană-Americană and Concordia Vega were the primary targets for 124 B-24s. The long-range escort of 45 P-51 Mustangs claimed two defenders. Three B-24s were lost. A smaller force of 74 B-24s attacked Unirea-Speranta and Standard Oil: six B-24s were lost here in spite of the escort of 40 Lightnings. The Xenia Refinery was singled out by a force of 85 B-24s, for a loss of three. 70 more B-24s attacked the Astra Romană Refinery without loss. These last two forces were escorted by 120 fighters claiming four defenders.

Steaua Romană at Cîmpina was attacked by 85 escorted B-24s for a loss of two.

The flak response was rated as 'moderate to intense'.

10/11 August

205 Group returned to Romanian skies the same night. Thirteen Liberators of 240 Wing and 2 SAAF Wings dropped 78 mines in widely separated beds between Batina, on the Hungarian-Yugoslav frontier and Turnu Măgurele. Twelve aircraft dropped their loads in the correct beds, but one had to make several runs owing to thick ground haze. Two of its mines finally fell on land. Light flak and machine gun fire was encountered at many places along the bank. A Ju 88 was sighted but did not attack.

Flight Sergeant Alan Bates, an Air-Bomber of 31 Squadron SAAF wrote a splendid account of his adventures of this summer Thursday night.

These operations always coincided with the full moon and even today I think of the full moon as the Danube Moon. The hazards of flying alone in bright moonlight rather than in the protection of a bomber stream were easily out-weighed by the absence of a heavily defended target. Three or four aircraft shared each 'Bed' and each of us would plant six 'Vegetables' (mines).

We were rather concerned to find that we would be carrying a passenger from our sister squadron, 34 SAAF, which had shared the airfield with us for some time now but had only just become 'operational'.

The briefing confirmed our guess that the target was the Danube and our 'beds' lay between two small islets near to Turnu Măgurele. Our passenger turned out to be an extremely aggressive youth and, on the assumption that attack is the best form of defence, he told us with some degree of conviction that he would be flying in the rear turret. We all turned towards Bill Cross, the Rear Gunner, to observe his reaction. The deep-set eyes of the Lancastrian gunner glowed and the heavy jowl moved 'Tha'll be on t'beam guns' he said. Our guest appeared to appreciate that although Bill may not have the gift of rhetoric his few words had the ring of finality. He looked for a moment at Taf Lewis, the little Welsh Mid-Upper Gunner and saw that a similar demand was unlikely to succeed. I moved discreetly away lest the cuckoo in our nest should decide that he would like to drop the mines. Beam guns it would have to be. We consoled our friend with the thought that he would at least get into the war before Errol Flynn and John Wayne wrapped the whole thing up.

We took off at dusk and once out to sea, the guns were tested. A couple of short bursts from Bill in the rear turret and his flat Lancashire voice came through the intercom 'Rear guns OK, Skipper'. Then two quick squirts from the Mid-Upper and the sing-song Welsh voice gave the same affirmative.

At this point quite a minor air battle developed as 34 Squadron's representative decided to test the port beam gun. He was in danger of running out of ammunition before a few well chosen words from the captain brought the battle to an end.

We crossed the Yugoslav coast on course and I passed the time taking drift readings and toying with the new-fangled GEE box, both of which I hoped would be of some assistance to Noel Sleed, our Navigator, who busied himself at a small table between me and the nose wheel door.

It was not long before a staccato warning came from the Rear Gunner – 'Fighter, seven o'clock down, Skipper – weave, he's closing.' Taff confirmed the sighting and the pilot started evasive action. We all waited anxiously for things to start humming. The aircraft corkscrewed around the sky and the tension was increased by a burst of fire from one of the beam guns. Our enthusiastic friend from 34 Squadron was silenced by a few uncomplimentary words from Taffy in the mid-upper turret. The silence continued for several seconds and the Skipper's voice came over the intercom enquiring impatiently what was happening in the rear. Eventually Taffy broke the silence with an apologetic chuckle – 'Sorry, Skipper, it was only the moon coming up over the horizon.' The rest of the journey out passed quietly and soon the broad band of the Danube came into sight. My little strip with its two small islets was easily distinguishable. This was my moment of glory. The Bomb-Aimer is somewhat akin to the triangle player in an orchestra who, at some particular moment in the piece, stops smiling at the girls in the stalls, puts on his white gloves and with triangle held high goes 'ting'. Before going 'ting' it was my job to talk the pilot down to 100 feet on a correct line for the mine drop.

Everything was going well until we reached around 100 feet and we were still losing height. It appeared that the pilot was using his altimeter, which had been set at airfield height and the target was a few hundred feet higher. I called over the intercom 'Level out now – we are a bit low'. This did not produce results and we drifted lower still. I saw two large oil drums, one stacked on the other, on the shore of the first islet. I hardly noticed that our passenger was raking the left bank with his .5 Browning as the oil drums came hurtling towards us. All attempts at a calm and assured intercom manner were abandoned as I screamed for height. Fortunately the Skipper must have raised his eyes from the altimeter and he lifted the aircraft over the island, missing the oil drums by a whisker.

I collected my thoughts. We were on target and were far too low. I had rehearsed the procedure for the drop many times. I would drop Number 1 mine and then count 1, 2, drop – 1, 2, drop until all six had gone. I started quite well keeping to the waltz time until Number 4 mine, when I realised that I was rapidly running out of river and the last two mines were dispatched in quick-step. As we pulled away from the Danube a light gun opened up at us and some form of rocket fizzed past under the port wing. We climbed steadily away and set course for home. We were then delighted to hear the plaintive voice of our guest on the intercom complaining that he was wet through. It appears that we were so low that each time a mine hit the river it threw up a column of water which lifted into the bomb bays and found its way to our favourite beam gunner. He was invited onto the flight deck for the remainder of the journey. We landed after a round trip of 4 hours, said 'goodbye' to 34 Squadron after de-briefing and so to bed. Just another little one for the Log Book.

13/14 August

205 Group's next operation over Romania was to send one Wellington from 150 Squadron to Bucharest with 635,000 nickels. There was no opposition but the crew reported seeing much flak in the sky above Ploiești – anticipation or a rehearsal?

Flight Sergeant George Carrod, Air Bomber of 142 Squadron, remembered an occasion which was different – and had a lighter side.

All was nice and peaceful with the Wireless Operator cutting the string and pushing the nickels through the flare chute, when the enemy opened up on us. So from then on the bundles of leaflets went out tied together. We all imagined a parcel the size of several telephone directories hitting someone on the head. Upon opening them up they would be greeted with the words in their own language 'We are your friends, not your enemy!'

It was George Carrod who claims the unique experience of being caught on his Wellington's Elsan chemical lavatory when the aircraft was attacked by a fighter.

The Group was far from idle during this period. On the previous evening 61 sorties were flown against Hadju Boszormeny airfield in Yugoslavia. As well as the singleton to Bucharest, 50 more sorties were flown against port installations at Genoa and twenty Liberators flew to drop supplies at Warsaw.

Thursday 17 August

Four Ploiești Refineries came under MASAF attack from a force of 293 15 AF B-24s. Unirea and Xenia were the targets for one group of 47 bombers. Astra Română was attacked by 107 B-24s and the largest force, 139, bombed the Română-Americană. Intense and accurate flak accounted for seventeen of the eighteen B-24s lost. One P-51 was also lost. Only eighteen enemy fighters were seen – none was claimed.

17/18 August

During the day Air Marshal Sir John Slessor KCB DSO MC Air CINC MEAF visited the Group. In the afternoon he visited HQ 240 Wing and spoke to aircrews of 178 Squadron who had taken part in supply operations to Warsaw. When writing to the Chief of Air Staff in London, Sir John Slessor had said:

> I saw 205 Group in the Foggia area and I was favourably impressed. They have done some amazingly accurate and effective night-bombing out here with none of the usual aids and their reputation stands high with the Americans. I hope that you will do your best to see that our supply of Wellingtons is maintained – they are paying a dividend and our night-bomber resources are far too light as compared with day.

On this Thursday night 205 Group launched another major attack on Ploiesti as part of an intensive day and night assault. It was a period of heavy pressure for the five night-bomber wings with the relief flights to Warsaw and support of land operations in Italy and in southern France also calling on the Group's resources. Xenia was the specified refinery target. The Group ORB's summary sets the scene.

> The enemy had commenced to repair Romanian oil refineries by 'cannibalising' damaged installations. It was, therefore, important to destroy all undamaged equipment in refineries which were temporarily or permanently out of production. The original target for the night was the Standard Oil Refinery, but this had been successfully attacked during the day by American Forces and at 1600 hours the attack was changed to Xenia.
>
> 63 Wellingtons from 231, 236 and 330 Wings, nine Liberators from 2 SAAF Wing and six Halifaxes from 614 Squadron were dispatched, but twenty-two returned early, three landed away, one jettisoned and three Wellingtons are missing.
>
> The remaining aircraft reached the target but the Ploieşti defences were very active, the smoke screen being especially effective and no aircraft were able to pinpoint the target. TIs were dropped (on H_2S) and

most aircraft bombed on them, but no results were observed. A 4000 lb bomb was dropped on the marshalling yards, causing a large explosion and a column of smoke.

Fighters were active, including Ju 88 and Me 109 and two short encounters took place without result. 86 tons of bombs and 845,000 nickels were dropped.

The aircraft missing were 'X-X Ray' and 'Y-Yoke' of 40 Squadron, captains Sergeants Francis and Patterson and 'Q-Queenie' of 70 Squadron, captain Warrant Officer Bridges.

This last aircraft (Q-Queenie) was attacked by fighters near Slatina and sustained damage to the starboard engine. Course was set for Turkey and the Bosphorus reached, flying mainly on one engine. Here, in spite of navigation lights and the flashing of 'SOS', 'England', 'British' etc on the downward recognition light, the aircraft was greeted by intense and very accurate flak. After some time had elapsed lights appeared at an airfield but intense AA practice was indulged in by shipping. On landing the aircraft caught fire and burnt out, but the crew were uninjured.

The individual Wing and Squadron reports each contribute to a picture of another dramatic and eventful night. The importance of a brief and intense 'blitz' to saturate the target and its defences with the maximum number of bombers in the shortest time was stressed often. Achieving this was a considerable feat of planning and airmanship which merged as the bomber stream set out from its airfields. The departure times for this 'maximum effort' show well how complicated the start of the operation must have been and where airmanship took over from the planning.

1910–1956 hrs 330 Wing's 20 Wellingtons leave Regina
1915–1955 hrs 236 Wing's 21 Wellingtons leave Foggia Main
1910–1945 hrs 231 Wing's 22 Wellingtons leave Tortorella
1930–2000 hrs 614 Squadron's 6 Halifaxes leave Amendola
1950–1953 hrs 2 SAAF Wing's 10 Liberators leave Celone.

The Halifaxes, for their part, strove to make their drop at 2300 hours (they were bombing as well) and the rest to blitz as close to that time as possible. The last bomber was to deliver its load at 2315 hours.

614 Squadron's sixth Halifax failed to take-off leaving the other five to mark the target and bomb. The BIs put down twenty Green TMBs but, as before, these gradually became obscured by the effective smoke screen. A violent explosion and a large fire were caused by the first TMB drop and several other sticks of bombs were observed to burst around the markers. The

Halifaxes were operating at heights from 16,500–18,000 feet and the bomb load of almost eight tons included fourteen 1000 lb GP TD .025.

Whoops! An unidentified Liberator passes perilously close beneath 142 Squadron's Wellington MF 423 during the 17 August 1944 raid on Ploieşti. The fate of the Liberator is unknown but the Wellington's mixed load of 500 lb and 250 lb bombs must have passed very close. (Courtesy James Grieve)

Of the ten Liberators of 2 SAAF Wing launched, only five were able to attack the primary. They dropped fifteen tons, all 500 lb GP TD .025 from as low as 7,000 up to 18,000 feet.

231 Wing's night began bravely but two Wellingtons failed to take-off, five from 37 Squadron and two from 70 Squadron returned early leaving fourteen to attack the refinery. Crews reported fires already burning to the east and south-east of the target which must have been started by the daylight attack. The Wing thought that the Green TIs were late, but all were able to concentrate their delivery on them and two explosions were observed through the smoke. Twenty-one tons – all 500 lb GP TD .025 were dropped from between 13,500 and 15,800 feet, as well as 260,000 nickels.

236 Wing's force was also down to fourteen when the target was reached and two were missing. One Wellington was late and bombed on ETA in a heavily defended area, the Green TIs being no longer visible at 2307 hours. The rest bombed on the Green markers with unobserved results. Crews saw the large explosion also noted by 614 squadron, commenting that the smoke from the resulting fire had risen to 3,000 feet. The ORB added that poor quality flash photos show the smoke screen in operation and the Green markers burning in a built-up area. The numerous scattered fires attributed to the daylight raid were also noted. 19.8 tons of HE were dropped from between

12,500 and 15,400 feet, with 285,000 nickels.

Thirteen of 330 Wing's original twenty aircraft completed their attacks. These crews also thought that the markers were late going down. Ten bombed on the TIs, two by DR and one visually. 'Z-Zebra', of 150 Squadron, captained by Flying Officer Denys White DFC on his 33rd operation, dropped a 4000 lb bomb which exploded at 2304 hours in the adjacent railway yards, causing a violent explosion. A fire followed and oily black smoke towered to 7,000 feet. Altogether the Wing dropped two 4000 lb HC NI and a mix of 500 and 250 lb GP TD .025 bombs to a total of over 23 tons and 300,000 nickels from 13,500–16,800 feet. Three 500 lb bombs were hung-up and brought back to base.

Night-bomber damage. Smoke palls rise above the Standard Refinery on the outskirts of Ploieşti. The white smoke wisps are the remains of the defending smoke pots. (Courtesy Romanian Ministy of National Defence)

The weather overall was cloudless but there was 'a lot of ground haze' en route. In the target area the flak reception was as hot as usual. 614 Squadron described it as:

> active and sometimes accurate heavy and light flak. Up to 60 searchlights.

The South Africans counted another ten searchlights and one Liberator was coned for five minutes. Another was holed by flak splinters. The Wellington Wings' estimates of searchlights varied but some were greater – at 100. 231

Wing felt that the flak was inaccurate and directed mainly into the searchlight cones. A 330 Wing crew reported an unusual phenomenon. At 2325 hours when all the attacking aircraft were clear of the target area, all the searchlights were suddenly directed vertically. 236 Wing noted heavy calibre flak from the Craiova area.

The Romanian Ministry of National Defence's archives show that 'about 60' aircraft attacked in three waves dropping high explosive and incendiary bombs on the Standard Oil, Română-Americană, Unirea, Astra and Columbia-Aquila refineries as well as Ploiești South railway station and some residential areas were hit. However, their bomb count was 165 HE of which two failed to explode: no incendiaries are recorded in these statistics. Added to that, the record shows that no one was hurt.

The flight into and home from the target brought forth many reported incidents and sightings, and since only two Wellingtons were lost to enemy action that night, it is interesting to consider the carnage which the passing crews felt they were witnessing.

While still 30 kilometres short of the Danube on the outward leg a SAAF Liberator saw an unidentified twin-engined aircraft on the same track and carried out a successful evasion. The crew later concluded that it was probably a Wellington. Considering how close aircraft were in the main bomber stream, it is perhaps surprising that there were not many more similar incidents.

At 2215 hours, some 130 kilometres south-west of Niš another South African Liberator saw an aircraft on fire, hit the ground and explode. Two minutes later a 236 Wing Wellington crew reported a similar incident – an aircraft appeared to crash into the hillside and burst into flames. The main difficulty in tying these two sightings together is that the later one places the incident in the hills north-east of Lake Scutari, 110 kilometres away – but on track. Either of these sightings could have been the crash of 40 Squadron's Wellington HF 476 'X-X Ray', captain Sergeant D.J. Francis. No trace of them was ever found and he and his all-sergeant crew are listed as having 'no known graves'.

Another bomber stream near-miss is probably behind 'R-Robert' of 70 Squadron's sighting at 2238 hours when about 140 kilometres west of the Danube and at about 15,000 feet. An unidentified aircraft came within 700 feet from the port beam above but no fire was exchanged.

Between 2257 hours and 2310 hours Warrant Officer Fleckney conducted a private battle in 'C-Charlie' of 614 Squadron over the target. The ORB records that he was attacked:

> . . . by a Ju 88 from the starboard beam on run into target, two other
> unidentified enemy aircraft in the vicinity at the same time, opened fire and

evasive corkscrewing action taken – aircraft not hit. At 2304 hours enemy aircraft attacked as leaving target area; at 2310 hours at 400 metres range the mid-upper gunner fired a two second burst at enemy aircraft on the port bow. Red light in nose of the enemy aircraft was extinguished – no hits claimed and enemy broke off attack and disappeared.

At the same time, 2304 hours, 'R-Robert' of 70 Squadron's crew noted a single parachute falling in a cone of searchlights in the target area. A minute later a 614 Squadron crew saw a Wellington coned over the target. At 2307 hours and at 2308 hours 330 Wing crews saw what must have been 'scarecrows' or decoys of some sort. About 5 kilometres West of Ploieşti a possible aircraft was seen burning on the ground and later an aircraft was seen to crash some 30 kilometres to the North of Moreni. The only bomber lost over Romania on this raid was 40 Squadron's 'W-William' (serial LP 327) which crashed at Conteşti [Crash Site 20], 25 kilometres north-east of Piteşti and over 55 kilometres West of Moreni. A 236 Wing crew must have seen one of these fires west of the target area as they set course for home at 2310 hours.

Five minutes later a Halifax crew saw five other unidentified aircraft, which were almost certainly other bombers milling about as they came away from Ploieşti. At the same time the observant crew of 'R-Robert' of 70 Squadron noticed red fighter flares burning in two areas, one ahead near to the Danube and one in the target area. They also watched an aircraft coned by searchlights catch fire at about 10,000 feet and fall in flames. A 330 Wing pilot saw the same incident rating the height at 13,000 feet.

What was more likely to have been 'W-William''s final moments was seen at 2319 and 2320 hours by two crews, from 236 and 330 Wing. The ground position was to the North of the track back to Foggia, between Cîmpina and Piteşti about 25 kilometres from the former. Air-to-air firing was observed, after which an aircraft caught fire and fell to the ground. The 236 Wing crew thought it was smaller than a Wellington. The 330 Wing report was made by Flight Lieutenant Morton in 'A-Able' three minutes after they had left the target area: the air-to-air firing was the common feature. This was not seen in the decoys or scarecrows.

A possibly connected incident followed immediately. A Halifax crew noted firing from a 6-gun flak position somewhere just north of Ploieşti. They saw the shells burst after which an unidentified aircraft was seen to crash and explode on hitting the ground. Two other crews from 614 Squadron made the same sighting. Could 'W-William', after being crippled by a fighter, have been finally knocked down by one of the Piteşti flak batteries?

A 231 Wing crew saw what they believed to be a burning aircraft on the ground in the target area as they turned for home.

There were three sightings of aircraft believed to be fighters on the homeward leg but no determined engagements took place. At 2335 hours a 330 Wing Wellington, flying at 11,000 feet between Tîrgovişte and the Danube, was overtaken by a Ju 88 which passed some 500 feet beneath from the starboard quarter to port. At a quarter past midnight, while South of Turnu Severin, another 330 Wing bomber was approached by a Ju 88. At 19,000 feet – to clear the Yugoslav mountains ahead – a Ju 88 climbed to intercept from the starboard and fire was opened at 300 metres. No hits were claimed and the Ju 88 'withdrew'. At the same time another Wellington, at 10,000 feet reported an Me 109 flying on a parallel course at the same height, 6–800 metres away. After a while it turned away.

At 0029 hours while south-east of Belgrade and flying at 8,000 feet another crew watched an unidentified aircraft showing a white light to starboard at their height. There was no engagement.

Flight Lieutenant Sid Brownless of 614 Squadron flew as Flying Officer Charles Symonds' Air Bomber that night to bomb and mark the refinery. They had taken off at 2000 hours.

> On our first run over the target we had very heavy flak and broke off the run to try again. This time we were caught and coned – even blue-lighted. Fortunately the flak was behind us but very close and we had some scattered hits – we thought we were finished. By this time the enemy had the target smoke-screened and on our third run-in I dropped the four Green TIs and three 1000 lb bombs using the H_2S radar. This was our first time to use this method and we were quite successful. The explanation we had for not being seriously damaged was classed as human error – on the enemy's part – in transferring settings from the searchlights to the guns.

Almost forty years later Hugh Fleckney's recollection of his experiences over Ploieşti was very clear:

> On this trip we had a Mid-Upper Gunner (MUG) who had been posted to 614 Squadron from a Marauder day-bomber unit. (Most of our aircraft were not fitted with mid-upper turrets, so MUGs were drawn from the hat, so to speak). Our 'temp' MUG was used to daylight ops and .50-in Brownings. Night-bombing and our .303-in Brownings were new to him. He also, I recall, had a particularly high-pitched and piercing voice. Anyway, we were running in to the target and were all in fairly high pitch of apprehension due to all that was going on around us. Suddenly, the MUG shouted 'Fighter, fighter, starboard – go!' and at once I pulled a hard bank and rudder to starboard and down in the first leg of a corkscrew. As

we went down to the right the MUG opened fire and I could see his tracer arcing out towards one of the decoys. The tracer was falling well short of the enemy aircraft. I told him to cease firing and, simultaneously, our two starboard propellers ran away. I do not know what revs they reached, but it was well above the 3,000 rpm which was the maximum. By heaving on the stick and pointing our nose skyward we were able to bring them back under control and we resumed our run in to the target.

Shortly after this, the MUG again shouted over the intercom 'Fighter, fighter, port – go!' There was no time to question him, so I had to go into a corkscrew to port, hoping like hell that the propellers would not repeat their performance. He opened fire again, this time at a light, probably a fire, on the ground. While he was spraying tracer all over the place, my own Rear-Gunner – Dickie Billen – who was a permanent and valued member of my crew shouted 'Fighter, fighter, starboard – go!' and immediately opened fire on a Ju 88 which had presumably been attracted to the firework display which our 'temp' MUG had provided. By this time I was a bit hyper-active and I reefed the aircraft into a tight turn to starboard, such that Dickie could not keep his guns on the Ju 88.

Happily the fighter could not keep his guns on us either and, apart from a 20mm shell, which hit just below the rear turret but did not explode, we emerged unscathed if thoroughly terrified. We managed to complete our bombing run and had no more frights on the way home.

As a postscript, I have to report, sadly, that the MUG in question, with all his crew, disappeared a few nights later.

Ieuan Jones made one of the early returns in 150 Squadron's HZ 554 after 2 hours 55 minutes:

There was a problem with the ammo feed discovered when the guns were test-fired over the sea en route to the target. Our previous experiences made us temper dash with discretion since four hours over enemy territory well-known for its fighters, with no turret defences, was too chancy.

Air Bomber Derek Cashmore and his crew had arrived in 70 Squadron on 10 August after the previous night's maximum effort had left prominent gaps in the Order of Battle State. Their settling-in period, during which their skipper had done one trip with another crew, was completed on 16 August.

The 17th dawned and we found ourselves in Operation Orders for that night and that Ploiești was to be our first trip as a 'sprog' crew.

There were many suggestions such as 'when you have bombed, get down on the deck as far as the Danube.' Remarks of fun like 'fancy sending learners out for so long!' This was all in good fun but some of it was rather lost on us because we had no idea what the unknown could hold.

We took off at 1924 hours and arrived back seven and a half hours later, having been coned by radar-controlled searchlights, luckily not set on by fighters of flak, although there was plenty of fireworks.

The bomb load was only six 500 lb HE to make room in one bomb bay for the overload tank. This was to be used for one hour after take-off on main tanks. Climbing over the mountains on course for the Danube, we suddenly lost an engine and the aircraft turned through 90°. The skipper realised that the overload had run out and switched back to main. Luckily the engine picked up. This all took place in a spell of 30–40 seconds I should think, but it seemed an eternity. The ground crew were very pleased next morning as overload tanks were difficult to handle when they still contained fuel.

Ivan Dobson, Air-Bomber of 104 Squadron, remembered the night well:

A late afternoon briefing: the USAAF had warmed things up during the day and our job was to keep up the attack. Take-off was at 1930 hours. The nearer we got the more flak we met. There were many fires still burning from the daylight attack and the target area was hazy. We used a refinery tank-farm as our AP, but I could not observe our own bomb bursts. The load was six 500 lb GP. The photo flash did not work. Flak remained fairly heavy until we were well out of the target area. We sighted no fighters, but there were some fighter flares. We landed at 0210 hours. Once more our load had been light because of the need for overload tanks.

Norman Lord of 150 Squadron, looked back on raids such as this one:

All round, my excursions to Ploieşti were not really notable, except for being young and innocent enough to excuse flying around among searchlights, flak and fighters while we looked for our target. Now I shudder – then we laughed and had another drink! It was on this trip that we had a dust-up with an Me 109 – almost collided head on – another three or four feet lower and he would have taken our port wing off. How close can you go? He came back and our Rear Gunner gave him a short burst at which point he lost interest.

34 Squadron SAAF was now nicely into its stride – Terence Timoney had

flown twenty-nine missions by the end of the month and on this one – 34 Squadron's only operation against Ploieşti – he was a gunner for Major Des Marais.

At our briefing we were told that the target would be the Xenia Refinery at Ploieşti and we could see the red marker tape pinned on the wall. Pathfinder markers would give us course changes and mark the Target Area. The enemy had intensified their defence around the whole Ploieşti area. Night-fighter bases had been increased in Hungary and some of the best squadrons had been sent from Germany at the expense of the defence of their large cities.

After briefing we were taken to our aircraft. I was Rear Gunner in 'J' Liberator which took Walt Disney's cricket, Jiminey, as its mascot. After a signal from an Aldis lamp and we set off down the metal-stripped runway and climbed into the rapidly darkening sky. Our first course was set and we crossed the Adriatic Sea at about 5,000 feet. I tested my guns, dropped a few marker flares and took some drift readings to assist the Navigator in checking the wind speed.

The course had been set to avoid known enemy night-fighter bases and concentrations of flak. We altered course at the first Pathfinder marker. These were usually a coloured flare and were very clear. We passed over Lake Scutari in Yugoslavia, climbed over the Yugoslav Mountains and crossed the corner of Bulgaria and on into Romania, where we dropped down to a lower height as we approached Xenia. I saw my first night-fighter flares. However, we ran into ten-tenths cloud and felt safe for a while. I had my thick armour-plated glass removed from the turret so that my vision was excellent. The cold was intense even with my electric flying suit and boots, but it was vital for me to have clear vision especially at night.

We had dropped well below the cloud ceiling as we were approaching the target area when, in the glare of a very close flare, I caught a glimpse of a twin-engined fighter, well to port and slightly below our flight path. I alerted the pilot and he took evasive action, a corkscrew roll, and I opened fire. The attack was not pressed home and we resumed our course. By now the first ring of searchlights was probing the sky with the inevitable blue master light and up came the heavy flak. It was well below our aircraft: one could clearly see the star-like bright shower of shrapnel around the black puffs of smoke in the searchlight beams. I felt sorry for the Wellington bombers below us. We seemed to fly out of the first ring of flak, but not out of the searchlights. The place seemed to be alight with them. I heard the Navigator warn the Bomb-Aimer that we were close to the target markers and to take over. The Bomb-Aimer now guided the pilot on the final bomb run, which was a testing time for the rest of the crew. It always seemed to take ages before the call 'Bombs gone' came over the intercom and then we felt the sudden lift of the aircraft after shedding its load. At the same time the searchlights below were trying to cone us in their beams. The Navigator gave the pilot a course for home.

A good view of the rear turret of a 31 Squadron Liberator B Mk 6. Note the central perspex panel removed to improve vision and the flash-hiders on the muzzles of the twin .50 Brownings. (Courtesy T.W. Timoney)

The anti-aircraft guns now found our height and the black puffs in the searchlight beams with the starlight flicks of shrapnel were uncomfortably close as we climbed on course homeward bound. A blue searchlight found us and immediately we were coned by more searchlights. The pilot, Major Des Marais, dropped his port wing and went into a shallow dive. I thought he was going to roll the aircraft. We twisted and turned, but it seemed as though we would never lose the lights – and by now we had lost a lot of height. All of a sudden we were out of the cone and the anti-aircraft shells. A new course was set for Celone and home with high hopes. But that was not to be. On the fringe of the target area, I saw two fighters. I immediately warned the MUG and the Beam Gunner to concentrate their search below the aircraft and not to look at the searchlights. The fighter tactics were for the top aircraft to drop the fighter flares and the lower one to attack the bomber brilliantly silhouetted against the bright light of the flares.

Although I depressed my guns to their limit, my downward vision was limited especially if the enemy aircraft came up close and below us. Then, mercifully, we started to fly into ten-tenths cloud as we approached the Yugoslav mountains. After that there were no more night fighters and it was a steady flight back to base, arriving six hours after take-off.

Some pages back, the Group ORB noted the fate of 'Q-Queenie' of 70 Squadron which, having lost an engine, managed to fly on and crash land in Turkey. Sergeant Peter Gadbury was the Navigator in that crew and his recollections of their adventures, perhaps, make a fitting closing scene to this account. It was not an unusual crew for a Wellington Squadron of 205 Group at that time. The Skipper was Flight Sergeant C.A. Bridges RAAF and there were two New Zealanders, Flight Sergeant M. Hanrahan, the Air-Bomber and Sergeant G. Hanchett, the Wireless Operator. Sergeants E.W. Samson, Air Gunner and Peter Gadbury completed the team.

Our crew had completed 35 ops with 70 Squadron before losing an engine on the way to Ploieşti. We made our way on the other one to the Turkish border where we came down just before dawn and were picked up by a patrol from Istanbul Garrison. The British Consul came to see us: he was superb. We were interrogated at the Military HQ in Istanbul where we all insisted that we had lost our way on a training flight from the Middle East (the plane had burnt out on crash landing). We were eventually taken to Ankara and placed in a large house surrounded by barbed wire and guards. However, the British Embassy secured civilian clothes for us and, with our parole, we were allowed out from 10 am to 10 pm daily. After a month we were moved to Adana and from there left for palestine in a Dakota. Then we went on to HQ RAFME in Cairo and we were back at Tortorella within two months of that fateful flight. HQ 205 Group decided that, since 40 ops was then a completed tour, they would let us off the last five and we broke up to return home at different times. I enjoyed a long time in No 1 General Hospital with hepatitis before boarding the *Empire Pride* for Liverpool.

Friday 18 August

411 escorted 15 AF bombers attacked five oil refineries at Ploieşti and Cîmpina – the third successive day and night attack. Twenty-four each B-17 and B-24 bombed Dacia and 129 B-17s and 97 B-24s hit Romană-Americană. A smaller force of 25 B-24s went for Creditul Minier at Brazi and Astro-Romană. The escort claimed nine defenders and nine bombers were lost. Steaua Romană at Cîmpina was attacked by 112 B-24s for a loss of two.

At Ploieşti the post-strike photo-reconnaissance was somewhat obscured but fresh damage from these and 205 Group's raid on 17/18 August were apparent. Later PR showed severe damage at Romană-Americană and extensive new damage at Steaua Romană. The 'usual' flak was encountered but thirty fighters seen were 'not aggressive'.

Saturday 19 August

This third successive daylight raid concentrated on the Dacia and Xenia Refineries and was an all B-17 affair. Twenty-seven attacked Dacia and 46 more attacked Xenia. The long-range escort comprised twenty-three P-38s and 125 P-51s. No enemy aircraft were seen at all and flak accounted for two B-17s, two P-38s and one P-51. The last to be lost over Ploieşti.

Saturday 26 August

Three days after King Michael's coup d'état, MASAF's day bombers carried out raids against residual Nazi forces holding out in the North of Bucharest and at Giurgiu. 123 B-24s bombed the enemy-held airfield at Otopeni and a further 117 attacked Băneasa. In addition P-51s flew sweeps for targets of opportunity in the Bucharest–Ploieşti area.

Five bombers were lost when 53 B-24s attacked Giurgiu.

While 15 AF raids continued into Hungarian-occupied Transylvania ahead of the Red Army advance until 6 September, MASAF carried out no further attacks on Romanian targets after 26 August. The evacuation of the prisoners began on 31 August and is described later in this story.

The night-bombers' August continued relentlessly. On 27 August six Liberators placed 36 mines into the Danube upstream of Baziaş. The next night 40 sorties were flown against enemy troop concentrations in the Pesaro area. Ten more were flown to lay 54 mines in a number of beds extending upstream from Orsova into Yugoslavia and Hungary. For the Danube mining hat-trick, on 29 August, another seven Liberators of 240 Wing gardened from Orsova once again.

The month closed with 74 sorties flown in a successful raid on Ferrara marshalling yards in northern Italy, without loss.

And so the war went on, but 205 Group's night-bombers had flown their last operation against a Romanian target.

The Red Army entered Ploieşti on 30 August, finding a near wilderness of destruction in major areas of the refineries, railways and pumping stations. They entered Bucharest the next day. Between then and December the

Russians removed nearly 51,000 tons of oilfield equipment, achieving as effective a disruption of Romania's oil as any bomber force could have wished.

The night-bomber squadrons of 205 Group soon began a long programme of conversion into an all-Liberator Force. 231 Wing remained at Tortorella until October 1945 when they moved to Palestine. 37 Squadron converted to Liberators by December 1944 and 70 Squadron a month later. 40 and 104 Squadrons converted a little later – by March and February 1945, remaining with 236 Wing at Foggia Main until October 1945 before moving to Egypt.

330 Wing with 142 and 150 Squadrons had been the late arrivals as a Wellington Wing from NASAF. They were the first to leave – in October 1944 – but both went to carry on the war from English airfields. 142 Squadron, having disbanded at Regina, re-formed at Gransden Lodge in Cambridgeshire the same month with Mosquito B Mk 25s as part of 8 Group's Light Night Striking Force (LNSF). 150 Squadron reformed in November at Fiskerton in Lincolnshire to fly Lancasters in the Bomber Command main force.

In 240 (HB) Wing, 178 Squadron already expert in Liberator B Mk 6 operations remained at Amendola until it moved to Palestine in August 1945. 614 Squadron remained at Amendola until July 1945 and had converted to Liberators by March. On leaving Amendola the Squadron was re-numbered as 214 Squadron. The former Squadron number – 614 – was that of a R Aux AF Squadron, the City of Cardiff Squadron.

So, with 2 SAAF Wing fully operational throughout, 205 Group was able to complete its war with four Wings of Liberators.

Brigadier J.T. Durrant continued in command of the Wing until the war's end. In considering him for a two-star post, Sir John Slessor wrote:

> He is a quite outstanding commander with an excellent record who has run 205 Group extremely capably. He has brought its standard of efficiency as a Bomber Group up to a very high standard. He is young and just the type that, if he were in the RAF, we should want to bring on and I think we should do the same for the South African Service.

TAIL-PIECE

> People often ask me what I did during the war and what happened. When I have told them that I was a prisoner-of-war they have turned and said 'Oh, where?' but when I add 'I was in Romania' that is the end of the conversation. Romania did not conjure up any idea of war. The big raids on Berlin, Hamburg and so on got the glory. What we did seems sort of incidental. I assured such people that a bullet is a bullet and a shell is a shell whether it's over Berlin or over Bucharest.

> (Gordon Cormie, Sergeant, 40 Squadron)

Part 3

POSTSCRIPT

CHAPTER 11 - Prisoners' Tales

Between 1 August 1943 and 23 August 1944 some 2,500 American and British airmen were reported missing in action over Romania. The majority of these men – 2,290 of them – were lost during MASAF's great offensive concentrating on Romania's oil between April and August 1944.

By 23 August over 860 men had made their way back to Italy, individually and in small groups, through Yugoslavia and through Turkey and a few more filtered in later. It was known that 1,500 or more remained in enemy territory and it later transpired that 1,162 American and 38 British and Commonwealth aircrew were prisoners of war in Romania. The remainder were held in a camp at Şumen in Bulgaria, although a few had been transported to Reich PW camps elsewhere.

There is no better way to set the scene of PW life in Romania than to quote from the first Report on the Bucharest Camp made by the Swiss Legation, in their capacity as the Protecting Power, after the visit on 19 June 1944.

REPORT NO 1
PRISONERS OF WAR CAMP NO 13
AT BUCHAREST, ROMANIA
VISITED BY MR P. RITTER

The Swiss Legation at Bucharest had to address repeated requests to the Romanian Foreign Office, the first of which was dated 19 April, in order to obtain from the Romanian General Staff the authorisation for its representatives to visit Camp No 13, in which are interned both American and British aviators taken prisoner in Romania since 4 April 1944.

The Commandant of Camp No 13 is Lieutenant Colonel Victor Ioanid.

On the day of the visit Camp No 13 comprised the following quarters:

1. a large schoolhouse on Strada Sfînta Ecaterina No 12

2. the former regimental barracks 'Mihai Viteazul'

3.   two large rooms reserved to Anglo-American wounded in the military hospital 'Regina Elisabeta'.

(607 prisoners were present for the visit, including 18 'British'.)

The names of the 18 British prisoners were communicated. All of them were visited on 19 June with the exception of Flying Officer Louis Rubens RAF No 6950 and Pilot Officer Joseph Marcus RAF No 8304, who are being kept at Mihai Viteazul in solitary confinement for further cross-examination. The fact that the two officers do not speak English and that they were taken prisoner during a night when there was no British air-raid seems to make them suspect as spies to the Romanian General Staff.'

Quarters

In all quarters of Camp No 13 American and British aviators are kept together and treated exactly alike; there is no separation of any kind between them. As far as the prisoners are concerned, they expressed themselves as fully satisfied with this arrangement and good comradeship seems to prevail in the camp. In each quarter visited a spokesman representing American and a spokesman representing British aviators took part in the conversation with the Swiss representatives. The three quarters of Camp No 13 visited on 19 June, which are only at short distance from each other, are located in the centre of the city of Bucharest. In other words, Camp No 13 is in a region which was repeatedly bombed by the Allies.

The Schoolhouse in Strada Sfinta Ecaterina where allied officer prisoners were held. This picture was taken in February 1987 and shows and advanced state of dilapidation overtaking this once elegant building. (Courtesy DA Bucharest)

251

1. Quarters at Strada Sfînta Ecaterina No 12

The large seminary can in itself be said to fully justify requirements. Daylight, artificial light and sanitary accommodation offer no reason for complaint. On the other hand, dormitories on the first floor, although airy and spacy, are filled with beds to such an extent that there is hardly any room left to move between them. Each bed has a dirty mattress and one woollen cover, all of which are infected with bed bugs and lice according to the spokesman. One of the main reasons for complaint in these quarters is that all instructions are given in Romanian and that no Romanian officer speaks English at all. A copy of the Geneva Convention in English has been given to the spokesman. A canteen has been installed on the premises, but prices (official retail prices plus war tax), which prisoners have to pay, are far too high for their means. Moreover sales and accounts are being made by a Romanian and the prisoners are given no information regarding profits. Space for physical exercise in the open air consists of a tiny yard and prisoners are allowed to remain in the open air only a short time every day. Books are available, but not in sufficient number yet. The air-raid shelter is entirely inadequate.

2. Quarters in Mihai Viteazul Barracks

The dormitories in these quarters, formerly used by a Romanian regiment, most certainly do not correspond to what the Anglo-American aviators were used to. They are crammed with superposed beds, even more dirty than the ones in the quarters in Strada Sfînta Ecaterina. The quarters are sufficiently provided with showers and toilets, but the latter are not being kept clean. A copy of the Geneva Convention in English has been given to the spokesman by the Swiss representatives. No canteen is as yet installed in this camp. Space for physical exercise in the open air is sufficient and prisoners are allowed to remain in the open air all day. There is no air-raid shelter.

3. Hospital Regina Elisabeta

The wounded American and British prisoners are interned in two large airy rooms of this military hospital. This lazaret, which is under the command of Medical General Popescu, also hospitalises a large number of Romanian wounded. In one of the two rooms are bedded 34 Anglo-American wounded, in the other 16; according to the physician, the latter are recuperating from diphtheria. Only one of these 50 men is said by the doctor to be still in danger of life, while all the others seem to be definitely on the way to improvement. A detailed list of these wounded prisoners and their state of health is promised to be delivered shortly to the Swiss Legation. Judging by the spokesmen, medical treatment which the Anglo-American prisoners are receiving at the hospital Regina Elisabeta leaves nothing to be desired; yet, the state of cleanliness might at best be termed as barely satisfactory. Only the food seems to offer reason for complaints, particularly with NCOs, who do not receive the same food as the officers. The complaints made in this respect by the prisoners appear to have been effectual temporarily, but so far the question has not been solved satisfactorily. There exists no adequate air-raid shelter.

Property of Prisoners

The majority of the prisoners were at the time of their capture deprived of their personal effects and objects and part of their equipment such as vests, shoes, etc. also of money, without having so far been given corresponding receipts.

Mail

Theoretically, all prisoners are allowed to send one letter and four cards a month, but there are never enough cards available, so that in practice it is impossible for the prisoners to mail the number of cards permitted. The letters may be one sheet side in length. Correspondence between the spokesmen and the Protecting Power did not work at all so far. The spokesmen at Strada Sfînta Ecaterina have informed the Swiss representatives that they have handed several letters of complaint to the Camp Commandant addressed to the Swiss Legation at Bucharest, but none of these letters reached the Special Division.

Food

Food served at Sfînta Ecaterina and at Mihai Viteazul comes from the same kitchen at Strada Sfînta Ecaterina 12. The kitchen is in very good condition and clean; the personnel consist of Russian prisoners of war. The Anglo-American prisoners complain that food is neither sufficient nor of good quality; the spokesmen of the camp seem to make representations in this respect to the Camp Commandant almost daily and this with more or less success. The Camp Commandant has informed the representatives of the Protecting Power that, due to recent difficulties in food supply, the daily ration of bread has been reduced to 300 grammes and the weekly ration of meat from 1,200 to 300 grammes. Potatoes are being served in large quantities. No collective disciplinary measure affecting the food has ever been taken. The use of tobacco is not limited but tobacco is almost unavailable. Attached is the table of menus for the period 18–24 June 1944.

Clothing

The great majority of the prisoners in the camp possess nothing except clothing and shoes which they wore at the time of their capture, which is entirely insufficient. There are numerous complaints from the prisoners, especially with respect to footwear.

Medical and dental care

From what the spokesmen reported to the representatives of the Protecting Power, medical treatment would not seem to have been properly organised at the outset, so that prisoners were but slowly hospitalised even in cases which looked rather serious. Meanwhile, however, an improvement appears to have taken place in this respect. To the day of the visit no dentist had called at Camp No 13, although a few of the prisoners had asked to receive dental treatment. No deaths have occurred, nor are there any blind prisoners of war at Camp No 13.

Religious service

Catholics at Strada Sfînta Ecaterina had occasion to attend regularly religious service officiated by a catholic priest. Protestants, on the other hand, have so far been offered no religious service, although requests have been made to that effect. At Mihai Viteazul religious service has not been permitted at all so far.

Pay

According to the Camp Commandant, the question of pay is on the point of a practical solution. The Commandant assured the Swiss representatives that he had received, a few days prior to their visit, definite instructions as well as the necessary credits. The same as in Camp No 18 at Timişul de Jos, officers and NCOs are to be credited in account their daily pay and debited likewise for food and for pocket money, be it in cash or in the form of chips used in the canteen. The pay to be credited to American and British officers – to quote the Commandant – will be:

Major	Lei 27.700
Captain	21.000
Lieutenant	18.400
Sub-lieutenant	15.000
Flying Officer	13.700

Bucharest, 21 June 1944.

Corpul II   Territorial   Prisoner of War Camp No 13

Menu for the Anglo-American Prisoners of War 18 – 24 June 1944

Date	Breakfast	Lunch	Dinner
Sunday 18 June	Bread and jam	Pea and potato soup, potato stew	Fresh vegetable salad, macaroni with cheese
Monday 19 June	Bread and jam	Potato soup with noodles, beans	White cheese and onions, potato cookies with gravy
Tuesday 20 June	Bread and jam	Meat and vegetable soup, roast beef with potatoes	Fresh vegetable salad, roast beef with gravy
Wednesday 21 June	Tea, bread and jam	Vegetable soup with noodles, vegetable stew	Cheese and green onions, potato cookies with gravy
Thursday 22 June	Tea, bread and salami	Meat and vegetable soup, lamb roast	Peas, lettuce, radishes and onions
Friday 23 June	Tea, bread and jam	Tomato soup, peas	Fresh vegetable salad, white cheese with green onions
Saturday 24 June	Tea, bread and salami	Vegetable cream, lamb and potatoes	Green peas, macaroni and cheese

Of the 205 Group PWs, Flying Officer Douglas Calvert of 40 Squadron was one of the earliest arrivals at Camp No 13 after being shot down on 7/8 May.

He arrived in Bucharest on 19 May and his diary gives an excellent window onto the humdrum life of captivity and of an intelligent man striving to make the best of his lot. Clearly the division of the PWs – officers to Strada Sfînta Ecaterina and NCOs to Mihai Viteazul did not happen at the outset. As Douglas Calvert's diary reveals, twenty PWs were moved to the Schoolhouse on 25 June.

> Life from now on became routine. At dusk we were locked in until morning. A canteen was available for those with money. I had none, nor had I any saleable clothing, so I was not able to buy anything. However, I borrowed some to buy a tooth brush.
>
> After about three weeks I was paid 1,000 lei. This did not last very long, since I was badly in debt, but I straightened myself up.

24 May

> Called for interrogation before Lt. Valjean, I was asked a number of questions followed by an interesting conversation on current affairs. This officer had studied for two years at London University and appeared to be a very decent fellow, which I later confirmed by becoming a real friend of his. After the interrogation my name was put on a list for transmission to Geneva and then to London. This was a relief to my mind. I was also given a Red Cross postcard which I addressed and sent home.
>
> Several attempts to escape were made. A few men succeeded in getting out of the barracks, though all were picked up sooner or later, mostly sooner. In my opinion, sufficient preparations were not made. One must be independent and have civilian clothing, to make a successful get-away. In any case I intend waiting to see how the expected Russian offensive goes before I seriously contemplate trying to escape.

Sunday, 17 June

> A pleasant break – I went with two Yank officers, Tom McInernay and Ed Ulrich, to the house of Mrs Bragadiru. Had a very good time but rather unsettling.

Douglas Calvert's visit to the Bragadiru house in Allea Modrogan, Bucharest.

L-R: Mr Bragadiru, 2Lt T.M. McInerney of 459 BG (B-24), Alexandra Bragadiru (Princess Alexandra Caradja), Douglas Calvert and 2Lt E. Ulrich of I FG (P-38) (Courtesy Mrs Douglas Calvert)

20 June

Capt. A.M. [Douglas could not remember his name and no name on the 205 Group list fits] arrived so relieved of my duties as CO. On the same day we had a visit from the Swiss Legation to enquire into conditions. I was given a booklet on International Law applying to POWs.

I organised PT classes each day. These went very well for a short time, then fell off. I was pretty fed up with some of the fellows. After all, these things were done for their benefit, so decided not to bother about them in future.

The air-raid sirens blew on several occasions and as the room overlooked the road, we would all crowd round the windows watching the people in the street running to the shelters. On occasion we had some demonstrations against us, such as women shaking their fists and spitting towards us. On the whole, however, people smiled at us more often than not.

On Sunday mornings a Concert Party came to the camp to entertain

257

the Romanian soldiers and we were allowed to go. The first time was nothing very exciting, but the second and third times were much better. There was a small band, girl dancers and singers and a tumbler. After the dancing, etc., the band gave a few hot numbers including 'Vienna, City of my Dreams', 'Lily Marlene' also 'Sweet Sue' and 'Dinah'. The second Sunday, when they repeated their performance the Germans present left as soon as the American tunes commenced. I suppose it was a protest against playing enemy music, anyhow, they gave their usual fan-fare of Nazi salutes and heel clicking. The dance music was very popular.

22 June

Around this date there were numerous attempts to escape, largely I think because a very easy way out had been found, which the Romanians had overlooked. We had a variety of roll-calls and counter roll-calls to find the names of six men who had gone the previous night. Because of this we were locked up and lost the privilege of going to showers or canteen, but later in the day these were restored. Someone called one of the guards 'Cigan', which means 'gipsy'. He cocked his rifle and fired at him, but fortunately missed. This episode nearly started a riot but everything calmed down eventually. Later in the evening we noticed that a double guard was posted and also a machine gun was mounted. This sort of thing – escapes at regular periods – weighed heavily on the mind of the officer who was in charge of us, Lieutenant Traian. He was a soft flabby type, who, I don't think had ever been near the front. One day after several chaps had 'taken off' he had orders for the front, gosh! – did he look sick. However, he managed to crawl out of it by seeing the General, who made the stipulation that he should learn English, and gave him a month in which to do it. He asked me to help him with his pronunciation. This went on quite well, 'til one day he hit one of the recaptured fugitives. After that I refused to tutor him.

About June 22nd, the bread ration was cut by half. This meant quite a lot to us excepting, of course, the fortunate chaps who had money. Then a few days later the volume was increased slightly but quality was changed to 'sour' bread. This was horrible stuff, so in future my limited 'borrowed' money was used to buy loaves at 35 lei a time.

23 June

Another alert today. One of the characteristics is the rapidity with which the Huns leave the town. They have several motor buses and lose no time in driving out into the country, with the exception of a few who have special air-raid shelters. On this particular day Bucharest was not the target. Rumours come through that we shall move shortly – most of them are wrong – anyhow, the destination at the marshalling yards seems pretty certain?

An amusing incident happened when we first arrived in the barracks. There was a severe shortage of toilet paper. In the barrack rooms were pictures of Antonescu, King Michael, Queen Helena, each garnished with coloured paper flags and bunting in the Romanian colours, blue, yellow and red – just the thing – very soft and gave a certain psychological satisfaction.

Saturday, 24 June

Air-raid warning this morning. Many aircraft heard, but none seen. We have been invited to the Bragadiru's, I hope this alert will not interfere with the plans. John Egan is going with us this time. The four of us were called for by Mr Bragadiru and we went out to his house in a Cadillac. It was a beautiful afternoon. On arrival we were introduced to Bragadiru's brother-in-law, a rather big fellow who spoke a little English. Princess Caradja, Alexandra Bragadiru's mother, arrived and we were introduced to her. She spoke English like a native and it was not till later that I found out why. She was a woman of maybe 50 years, going slightly grey, but very active. She had that quiet manner of authority and judgment that is often found in people of 'blue blood'. At the same time she was very kind and congenial. She spoke of generalities and it was not until lunch was served and I sat at her right hand that I had an opportunity to find out more about her. Briefly and so far as I could gather, she and her daughter, Alexandra, were directly descended from the old line of Byzantine Kings, her grandfather had been King.

Apparently there was some intrigue just after she was born and she was sent to England to an Orphanage and brought up as an orphan to the age of 15. This accounted for her fluent English. Her father had died and her grandfather brought her back as the heir. Obviously there is more to this story but this is what I gathered at the party. Thus the young girl returned to her native country in 1908. She settled down into her rightful position, her grandfather being one of the richest men in Romania. Then came the 1914–18 war. She had married and moved around with her husband and gained her hatred and contempt for the Germans. She also held the Russians in abomination. She lost two children in post-war Russia and now has just the one daughter, Alexandra Bragadiru. In 1929 her grandfather died and she was left with the responsibility of the estate including an Orphanage of 300 children. Since then she has continued the work, and now has 3,000 children up to 15/16 years old, a big responsibility in war-time and a full time job at any time. If and when the Russians come to Romania, I have no doubt she will stay with her children. She is not the type of woman to keep her mouth shut, her only hope is that the Russians will shoot her and not torture her. That is her only fear if, of course, the worst happens. This she told me at lunch. She was very sincere. I could only compliment her on her courage – a brave woman. She spoke of small things, too. She and Queen Helena had on several occasions tried to grow primroses in Romania. The summer, however, was too dry for them and they died off. The same with violets.

She had to leave shortly after lunch to do some shopping and return to her orphans. She had managed to make time to visit the PW camps and give lectures. I think part of her loathing for the Russians was that she saw the atrocities of the Reds during the Revolution and had seen brutal shootings and beatings. So it was that I met a very brave and remarkable woman, with a very strong personality. I certainly had plenty to think about, it was a pity I had not more time to hear her story and ask questions.

Returned to camp about 8 p.m. Supper – potatoes and beans – O Hell!

Sunday, 25 June

Had a very restless night, probably due to too much food and drink, which I am certainly not used to. During the afternoon orders came for 20 of us to move to the school. We marched down at dusk, there I met several RAF men and two Yank Majors. The curiosity of the crowds on the way down was not embarrassing. I quite enjoyed the walk and we were rewarded by a hot shower. My bed was not very comfortable, yet the whole place was much cleaner than the Barracks and I was really glad of the change. Next day I found my way around and got the impression that although there was not so much liberty outside (two hours a day) yet we were able to stroll round the building at will. The latrines were clean. There was a nice little auditorium for religious services or lectures. During the day a good supply of books came from the Red Cross at Geneva. These were very welcome and we think clothes parcels are on the way, too. These will be particularly welcome as some of us are badly in need. We are allowed some credit for the Canteen, but there appear to be only cakes today the 27th.

On the 28th there was an air-raid, just after breakfast the sirens went and we all moved down to the dining room which is in the basement.

Presently we heard the roar of formations and loud explosions, none near, though some of the men were panicky. After the all clear, we saw great columns of smoke from the railway yards, the Royal Barracks also had a very close shave. During the night there was another warning, we again went to the dining hall. The all clear went in about an hour. Afterwards we heard that Giurgiu was the target. Have been taking quite a lot of exercise of late, mainly of course PT, but I seem to be keeping my waist line under control.

2 July

All the NCOs were moved up to the barracks yesterday, where their treatment won't be so good, I think. I spend quite a time each day doing exercises, they make me feel a bit stiff, but certainly do me good.

3 July

During the night there was an air-raid on the city, it was quite brisk and it appeared that the marshalling yards were the target. I stayed under the table. At lunch-time the yards were again hit by American formations, maybe they will give us a rest now for a time, big column of smoke seen after the raid.

I understand that the conditions of the NCOs at the Barracks is very bad indeed – food very, very poor – about 100 to a dormitory, which is very unhygienic. I hear that one or two of the men are cracking up a bit through nerves – there are no air-raid shelters – one or more cases of food poisoning thought due to bad bread containing hair, flies and often maggots. (Appeals made to the Romanian authorities and to the Red Cross.)

5 July

I understand that enlisted men are being moved to Military Hospital near the marshalling yards, at least it should be clean. Food is gradually improving, some more greens and fewer potatoes, also an egg for breakfast on one memorable occasion, fresh fruit and milk sometimes available. Together with our credit at the Canteen we are doing OK and I feel, I think, better for it. I still do a certain amount of exercise each day trying to keep fit.

7 July

This evening had a pleasant surprise in some ways. I was called to the window to see Tichborne, Poole and Goodlet in the yard. Had a sketchy conversation with them. Apparently poor Murphy had been killed. I was indeed sorry to hear that, he was a very, very decent egg. Duff was still at large, probably hiding amongst the wheat somewhere. It was quite exciting to see some new familiar faces and am looking forward to seeing them when they come down here after interrogation.

The Romanians, true to style, have sent 20 more officers down from the garrison, we have no available beds, mattresses, or blankets, it looks as if they will have a somewhat miserable night.

8 July

The food has improved during the last few days, whether the removal of the Sergeants has anything to do with this I do not know, however, we have had egg omelettes for breakfast on two occasions – very welcome, also fresh apricots and cherries with some of the other meals.

During the last two days I have been bitten by various bugs, this is the first time for a while, however, I managed to capture a white louse so maybe that will have done the trick.

11 July

Tichborne, Duff and Goodlet arrived here from the garrison.

13 July

Spent the morning in the office working on some pay lists – at least it helps to pass the time. In the evening I replaced my bed and mattress, as mine was terribly uncomfortable. Today more of the Sergeants were moved to the hospital so I swopped my bed for one of theirs. It is much more comfortable.

18 July

Some good rumours around these days – Russians in East Prussia – a drive started around Iaşi. Turkey coming in at any time – I wonder if there is any truth in them – I hope so.

21 July

The whole place put into a state of uproar. Apparently two of the Yanks beat up a civilian and a soldier when they were captured two months ago. The authorities knew they were here, even their room number, but owing to incredible Romanian stupidity they cannot be found. We were hauled out of bed at 7.30 a.m. for roll-call, even then the culprits were not caught. There were numerous countings and check ups and there the matter rests for the moment.

22 July

Nothing much new today. Heard an American Lieutenant Colonel recently arrived, remark that his salary was 725 dollars per month – ye Gods – even my equivalent rank receives 250 dollars (£15 per week) over twice my salary, obviously I am in the wrong outfit.

What appears to be a very satisfactory air-raid on an airfield outside the town, lots of searchlights and guns, I wonder if any chaps I know will arrive as a result of this. Red Cross supplies reported to be ready for distribution.

23/24 July

Various re-arrangements in the running of the prison, all for the good really, the Canteen to be re-organised. Still waiting for Red Cross clothes parcels. Some good war news – Mr. Churchill said the war should be over this year. I hope so.

26 July

Another night raid, appeared to be Ploiești, one or two RAF over the city, but no bombs. Saw an aircraft in the searchlights. Ugh! It got away, however.

27 July

Sirens at about 11 p.m. An hour later flares dropped, through overcast, directly over us, the Green T.I. Oh boy! Beat a hasty retreat to the basement as bombs began to fall. Evidently the bombers could not see the target owing to the weather, so bombed flares, several sticks much too close to be comfortable. Raid over 12.20 p.m. A lot of windows in the building were knocked out. The nearest bomb being about 80 yards away. Five very reasonable fires were started, mostly in residential districts.

28 July

We had numerous foul looks and fist shaking from civilians, 9 o'clock, sirens again, but evidently it is a distant target, as no flak was heard, only the distant drone of aircraft, probably Huns. At one of the houses opposite the courtyard lives a bedridden old lady. At each alarm she has to be put on a stretcher and carried over to the shelter – the soldiers from the camp do this duty.

The long expected visit from the Romanian Minster of War again fails to materialise.

Beautiful weather, not excessively hot, the mornings like warm spring days. Food now definitely on the upgrade, egg omelettes, fried cheese and stewed apples, doughnuts and cakes after meals, three or four times a week. The latter help to complete a meal, particularly if ice-cream is also available. Food is also being sent over for relief of the enlisted men, whose condition appears to be rather better than it was.

Sunday, 30 July

Heard this morning that Warsaw had fallen and that Turkey would probably be in the war very soon.

Captain Arthur Staveley bought a few bottles of *Tuica* over, so in the afternoon we had a small party, which ended disastrously as one bottle broke. However, a good time was had by all, though certain members of the room were rather upset.

31 July

The alarm went this morning, a perfect summer morning, aircraft were heard and five large formation of B-24s swept over the city, and bombed the marshalling yards. We saw one go down, possibly out of control and disappear behind a cloud. In the evening the Russians sang for us, very good too, mostly martial airs accompanied by a balalaika. I did an extra amount of PT today and am very stiff and tired. Heard today that Romania was hit at numerous places by the USAAF.

1 August

A dull morning for the start of the month. I wonder what this month will bring. Everything appears to be going well though this sector of the Russian front is static so far as we know. The Turkish parliament is meeting today in secret, the result may have very definite bearing on us so we are all very interested. More beer in the Canteen today.

2 August

Delighted this morning to see Pilot Officer Joseph Marcus and Flying Officer Louis Robens. Evidently the Romanians had, after 92 days, given up their case as a bad job. They had been in solitary confinement, and on several occasions threatened with shooting and their food was bad. Very considerable credit is due to them that they kept their mouths shut and their spirits up. They tell me they were kept 28 days in darkness and for two days were fed on salted food and given no water. Fortunately, in the same prison were several 'liquidated' Romanian civilians of means, who helped Marcus and Robens by getting them food, after bribing the guards.

3/4 August

Big day, the Red Cross packages have come in. Clothes from the American Red Cross. Dudley Egles, the supply officer, got on to the job and within an hour or so distribution was in progress. I got trousers, towel, vest, under-pants, socks, shaving kit, soap – a very welcome gift indeed. The British Red Cross food parcels have also arrived. These are to be held awaiting the arrival of the Yank food parcels, then all will be pooled. More books have also come this afternoon.

9 August

I decided to keep my food parcel in case of urgent need. Princess Caradja came in one afternoon and I spoke to her for a while – still my first impression stands – a great woman – she promised to help us in various small matters. Major Yaeger USAAF and Captain Ferguson USAAF arrived from Sinaia changing places with two others. They, having been here a year, have lots of good ideas which they hope will be in effect shortly.

Night raid but no bombs on the city, though two aircraft apparently 'nickelling' came over. One poor chap was in the searchlights for five minutes, seemed totally lost, everything let loose at him, and he was attacked by fighter. It was an interesting sight but I was sorry for him. He was believed to have gone down to the South of the city. The bulk of the raid seemed to be on Ploieşti or airfields in that direction.

10 August

Air-raid again this morning, it lasted 2 hours, evidently Ploieşti was the target, several groups seen, and some seen to fall. A vast pall of smoke darkened the sky all the afternoon, apparently the whole of the 15th was involved, maybe that will settle that place for a while.

We hear that Romania and Bulgaria are asking for peace terms, what will become of us?

11 August

Heard some startling news today of conditions in the Romanian political circles, some danger for us if Germans occupy the place. If they do not, all should be well for us.

12 August

Received today from the Red Cross, 20 Players cigarettes and two small packages of candy. Weather beautiful – Bert Whitley received a postcard today from home, so I hope to receive some mail in the near future.

13/15 August

None of the great events relative to this country, which seemed to be impending, have taken place. However, we have a new cook – Ted Lancaster of the Sherwoods, taken in Norway, and had an adventurous career through Europe. He makes tea for the British boys and very good too, particularly after getting a proper teapot.

16 August

A very good impromptu concert this evening.

17 August

Air-raid during day on Ploieşti, also at night on same place.

18 August

Alert. Bombers seen north of the city.

By the way on the 17th I collected 500 lei from Major Haas after a bet made a fortnight previously on the 17th being the date when Romania would be out of the war. I said not and won.

19/20 August

Seem to have been quite busy these last few days what with one thing and another, also had a sharp cold in the head, but early to bed with aspirin, soon got rid of that.

21 August

Heard the news that the Russian offensive on the southern sector has started in earnest. This is really good news for us, maybe it won't be long now. This news, together with the incredible successes in France, and our improved food makes us in quite optimistic spirits.

The attitude of the people so far appears to be complacent – I suppose they are told only half the news – afraid I have little sympathy for them, they little know what they are in for. Girls in summer dresses out shopping in busy streets. I suppose soon the evacuation chaos will start if things go as we hope, although it is too early yet to speculate.

In a letter that Bert Whitley received, his mother said that the first intimation of his being a PW was the first card – so much for the telegrams that the Romanians and the Red Cross are reputed to have sent.

Princess Caradja came to speak to us. I thought her very sincere, though of course she gave the Romanian side of the question, coupled with her own experiences. The Russians, even at that moment were driving further into the country, what will her chances be if she stays – she is altogether too outspoken for the Russians I am afraid – or will she quietly slip out before they come? I think not.

23 August

A fine day. American Red Cross parcels arrived and we got some Camel cigarettes and chocolate.

Just got to bed at 10.15 p.m. when I was called to the CO's room and heard the news that Romania had accepted unconditional surrender terms (Radio 10.45 p.m.) Slight panic as the men were told in the auditorium. Major Yaeger announced the news, all were told to stand by. We hurriedly dressed and got all food packed up. Special duty party assembled – various vague rumours about. Assembled 'A' party in auditorium. Have doubts about our chances. Later find that more guards have arrived, machine guns erected, roads barricaded, evidently these precautions are to defend us. This was later confirmed by the Romanian Colonel. I told crew to disperse to bed and hung about the CO's room.

Orders came that the Romanian Colonel had got parole from our CO that we would not attempt to escape during the night. Everyone settled down and sleeping (in clothes). News from outside vague, no shots heard. Think it pretty impossible that the Germans will be able to handle 1,000 men in the present circumstances with the Russians advancing. Odd shot heard now and then – hear that coffee is available, so go down to kitchen – hand shakes with the Russians and one even kissed me.

Then interruption – all are wanted in auditorium – very packed – ping pong table collapses – all at attention. Romanian Colonel and staff and our senior officers. Extraordinary lull – short speech – claim us as Allies and ask for co-operation against 'common enemy'. Yanks go crazy, cheering and shouting, though why, exactly is somewhat difficult to see. Fortunately the farce ends soon – hang around a few minutes, some shots are fired, evidently nervous guards. Go to bed, but little sleep for singing and noise generally. Get up at 4 a.m. for breakfast, why, goodness only knows, some odd arrangement misconstrued. We had egg and spam then back to bed, short doze then awake again at dawn, 5.30.

24 August

Everyone up and about, a beautiful morning. Some Yanks display a lack of discipline by wandering on the street directly contrary to their CO's orders.

6.30 a.m. Aircraft of doubtful origin heard and seen over the city, but no opposition, so presume Russian. Me 109 fighters, probably Romanian.

7.30 a.m. The aircraft we saw were German, so warned to lie low for a bit.

10.30 a.m. About 30 Heinkel 111 bombed the city, followed, just after the all-clear, by FW 190 dive bombers. We begin to realise that we are going to be bombed and better bombed. Immediate panic to get out of the city, orders given and countermanded. Eventually we stay since the Huns are in the neighbourhood. Spend afternoon in basement shelter, very tired and slept a little between bombings. Siren alerts from 2.30 p.m. to 7.30 p.m. Took my bed to the dining hall for the night, living on tinned food, water reported poisoned.

Many fires in city – 8.30 p.m. another alert, bombs about 9.30 p.m. Too tired, get more or less a decent night's sleep, though intermittent bombing, lots of long delay bombs, civilians certainly suffering. What a b . . . y day as an anti-climax to evening before. Several men getting panicky.

25 August

Get up 6.30 a.m., apparently an alert on, bombers and dive-bombers over city at 7.30 a.m., Heinkels and 190s, no bombs near, it would appear that they are bombing in support of their beleaguered ground troops. No real news though lots of rumours, one NCO killed at hospital, no injuries here yet.

Aircraft over city during morning, dive-bombing marshalling yards. Same old rumours. NCOs to be moved here apparently. See Valjean, took him two days to return to the city from leave. Yaeger doing good job with Romanian H.Q. More bombs from Heinkels after lunch, no alert sounded, now population on perpetual alert. Getting work organised now, have mess going again. 6.30 p.m. military situation still vague but getting better, city being badly damaged. Several chaps living out with Romanian families.

26 August

Slept in Mess Hall. Good night's sleep, no bombs, no bombers at dawn so hope situation is clearing up. We are supposed to be moving from the city today, don't want to go personally, but decided by Romanian authorities. I should think they are fed up with us.

11.00 a.m. 15 AF came over, hundreds of bombers bombed north of the city apparently in support of Romanian Army – Yanks shout their heads off, certainly a very welcome sight.

Afternoon. Everyone told to stand by – move to camp outside town. Personally did not think transport would turn up, however, lorries arrived and we piled in. Just as they got ready the alarm sounded and the lorries moved off. After another raid, bombs fairly near, the lorries got moving at

269

about 6.30. Myself and Bert Whitley put in charge of rear party, a lot of Red Cross clothing to go in this, so got everything ready. Siren goes again and men pile off the lorry in sheer panic, ashamed that I belong to the same crowd. After much shouting and bawling, we manage to coerce them into the lorries again, as it is nearly dusk and transport stops at dark, off they go. Finally, give last check to rooms and then we piled everything into last lorry and departed.

7.00 p.m. Arrived at camp, dark, grabbed all my stuff and found room in staff building. No lights. Had a spot of supper and retired for the night without washing or anything.

27 August

Fine day, organise room, coffee made about 9.00 a.m. Meet several Sergeants I know. Command of camp still in doubt. Haas is CO at moment. Set out for Bragadiru's to arrange for food supply. Have not heard of Princess Caradja who is at Ploieşti. Return to camp 5.30 p.m. Dudley Egles turns up in civilian clothes, minus moustache.

28 August

This morning, camp organisation explained to us by Colonel, slowly becoming organised at last. Had a talk with British chaps, two meals a day now. Military situation obscure, possibility of Germans approaching city. All Yanks required to return to camp, this is easier said than done, since at least 20% are somewhere in the city. In the afternoon, Captain Brian Bird and I drove to town in taxi to see the British Intelligence Officer. Went to hospital and then to H.Q. (Banca Nationale). Had taken two Wireless Operators with us to work there. Captain Porter not there, so waited down in basement where Radio boys were working. Was introduced to several people, most of them 'intelligentsia' including Professor Hurmuzescu of the University who had just been released from detention. Beer and wine were liberally provided during the long talk. At last Captain Porter arrived. Had a talk with him and he explained our situation to us. On the whole he was non-committal though optimistic and I agreed to call and see him again soon. Back to camp at dusk.

29 August

Made coffee in field at day-break. Paraded at 8.30 a.m. Not much new. CO optimistic and talked of passes to the city in the near future. Bragadiru

270

called in the morning and I went to his house for lunch. I learnt that the Russians are approaching the city, a rather jittery feeling amongst the company. After lunch we heard planes and saw two B-17s with escort. This bucks us up as obviously VIPs. Russian units passed through the city, no ill behaviour, local Communists staged demonstration. Military situation cleared, remaining Germans, North of Bucharest encircled and being cleared up.

30 August

Meeting in CO's room. Plan operations for mass evacuation by B-17s commencing August 31st. Parade – news announced amidst cheers. Find that seven Britishers are missing, presumably in town. My plans for seeing a little of Bucharest may go by the board unless I can remain behind, shall try to work it, but doubt whether it is feasible.

Go to town to see Captain Porter who has moved to a new place, so have to take tram which is very, very crowded. Meet Bert Whitley and go out to lunch with various officials and one typist. Met Professor Dan Hurmuzescu and Captain Porter, who want me to stay and agree to take the responsibility. Back to camp where everyone is getting ready to evacuate.

31 August

Everyone up at 4.30 a.m. and though not directly involved, get up to say my adieus. Buses provided and they leave with remarkably little fuss. Russian infantry convoy passes with American vehicles. Dudley Egles turns up with several more British boys.

During the next six weeks Bert Whitley and I worked under Captain Porter of British Intelligence and saw something of Bucharest and Romania generally. We were ordered home when the British Military Mission arrived and were flown to Bari in a Dakota. From there, by air to Naples and then by sea to Algiers, and eventually arrived in Glasgow aboard the *S.S. Tegelburg*. From there to London for interrogation and arrived home December 3rd, 1944, at 6.00 a.m.

(Author's Note: Princess Catharine Caradja died on 26 May 1993 100 years old, home again in Romania after a long, happy and purposeful exile of 41 years in the United States.)

A late arrival at the Strada Sfînta Ecaterina Schoolhouse was Lieutenant Ed Nicholson SAAF, who had been shot down on 28/29 June and in hospital at Giurgiu since. He was moved to Bucharest on 9 August and once he had settled down, set about plans to escape.

*Dudley Eagles, Princess Catherine Caradja and
the Author, Febraury 1988. (Author's collection)*

Most of the Americans flew in ordinary issue army boots – which they called 'shoes' – and as a result, they were well-shod in camp. We were never quite sure whether this constituted commendable foresight or regrettable pessimism, but we nevertheless each scrounged a pair for ourselves. That started off our escape plans. If you have boots, you can walk, but the SAAF issue flying boot was hardly the dress for an escape trying to pass off as a native.

Brian Bird found some brown overalls that we wore over our battledress uniforms. We had decided to wear our full uniforms under the overalls, as there would be less likelihood of being shot as a spy. We had silk maps sewn in the back of the jacket, compass buttons and a small length of hacksaw in the seam of the pants, none of which had been detected in the hospital. What I could have cut with that hacksaw blade, I still can't imagine.

Our friends arranged a diversion with a ball game one evening while we slipped into a dark patch against the fence, hidden from the guards. They were all ordered back into the building while we lay with ears

272

cocked, against the tall wooden fence, gently digging away in the soft earth. It seemed like a hundred years, and our heartbeats sounded like a tattoo beaten on bass drums, but we soon had a hole big enough to slide through. For one agonising moment I got hooked, but I wriggled free, and there we were, with no pedestrians in the street, looking like a pair of dirty labourers, trying not to run. We must have walked all of six blocks before the air raid warnings sounded. We had passed people in the street and no one had shouted for the police, but now the pedestrians were moving quickly towards the shelters. We followed a group into the shelter where we huddled behind our paper which we could barely read in the dim light. After an hour or so, the all-clear sounded and we made sure we were the last out. Well, nearly the last. Two girls gave us the glad eye, and we were left in no doubt as to what they were. And they fancied us. We decided that we would be Germans. At least we knew a few words of German. The Romanian phrases we knew were not going to help us much. But, as it turned out, nor were the German!

Our firm '*Nein, danke*' didn't seem to impress them, because they stuck to us and started talking German. The brush-off hand signals had no effect and they seemed to smell a rat, because one girl slipped off into a side street while the other one hung behind. We quickened our pace and headed south but we knew the worst when a motorcycle with side car came screaming round the corner. Hands on head we were marched back to our camp, Lagerul 13, followed by the motor cycle and a pair of smirking girls.

They would have smirked a little more had they seen us later being beaten with rubber hose pipes and stuck in solitary confinement for ten days. Of all the unpleasant things people can do to you, short of actual torture, 'solitary' is definitely the worst. We did not have it as bad as the two Jews who had parachuted into Romania on a night when no raid took place. They each had 40,000 in gold on them, as I found out later, to organise anti-Nazi resistance, but they had been captured before they could make contact. They were tough but their punishment – 'solitary' and their hose pipe treatment was even tougher.

Flying Officer Dudley Egles, who had been shot down on the same day as Douglas Calbert – 7/8 May – was separated from his all-NCO crewmates a day or so after arrival in Bucharest. While his routine was generally the same as the other PWs, Dudley Egles was not idle.

I was made SBO even though I was only a Flying Officer and I shared a room with the senior USAAF officers. The SAO was Major Chester Haas.

The guards were all Romanians – mostly middle-aged – and the

273

Camp Commandant was a short, obese, colonel whose French was quite as bad as mine. There were a couple of German 'ferrets', of course.

I 'got on' quite well with the Camp Commandant. I always paid the respect due to his rank and RAF chaps all kept their beds, bedspaces and themselves tidy. For my sins I was made Camp Supply Officer and my main duty was issuing toilet paper! The Yanks could not appreciate shortages – the majority of them had only recently left the US. I was also Chairman of the Escape Committee. We managed to get a few bods *out* but never *away*. I 'left' myself but only for a short time. We started a tunnel, stowing the debris under the stage but it was never completed.

Each month I had to sign for the non-USAAF cigarette ration and there were two names on their own at the foot of the list who were not in the camp. When I asked who these two officers were I was told that they were being 'looked after in another place'. Eventually these two types (Marcus and Robens) turned up in RAF uniforms. They were most unforthcoming at first. After much questioning over several days I found that they were Romanian Jews who had been dropped to attempt to organise a Romanian 'underground'. They still had some sovereigns which had been hidden in the heels of their flying boots – they gave me three.

As Supply Officer I was allowed out on parole and under escort to purchase odd items in town. The two newcomers told me which was the predominantly Jewish area of the city and I was able to change their sovereigns for large amounts of lei. My escort consisted of an officer, who only spoke Romanian, and a soldier, who had to walk 10 paces behind us officers. I was not accompanied *into* any shop, nor was I searched on return to Camp.

About a week before the Russians came I managed to 'get out' unofficially. This time I sacrificed my issue Bomber Command moustache – that type of appendage was only worn by the older native – and I was only 23. From instructions given by the two Jewish bods, I contacted a Romanian architect who helped me with accommodation, better civilian clothes etc. My idea had been to get to Constanţa and hope somehow to get to Turkey. The Russian Army's arrival altered my plans. The architect introduced me to a friend who spoke French and Russian and together we approached a Russian captain who had a Willys Jeep.

I told the Russian that I was a British officer and he laughed and said that the British were all 'armchair soldiers'. Since I had been shot down twice on my *first* tour, I felt a little upset. I said that I was pleased to see that he was using an American vehicle, but he insisted that it had been made in Russia. The fact that 'Willys-Detroit' was stamped on the back panel did not impress him at all.

When I heard that the Americans were sending aircraft to collect the PWs, I 'rejoined' the Camp and we were flown safely back to Italy.

A group of British and Commonwealth prisoners of war at Camp No 3 in Bucharest taken on 20 August 1944.

Left to Right (front): Flying Officer L. Tichbourne 40 Sqn, Pilot Officer A. Gill 30 Sqn (SAAF), Madame Ioan, Romanian Red Cross worker, Warrant Officer J. Coape-Smith RAAF 40 Sqn, Flying Officer A. Duff 40 Sqn, Captain R.D. Bird SAAF 31 Sqn (SAAF), Lieutenant E.I. Nicholson SAAF 31 Sqn (SAAF), Warrant Officer H.G. Poynton 614 Sqn.

(2nd row)

Unidentified Romanian Officer, Flying Officer D.C. Egles 614 Sqn, Warrant Officer R. Kilroy RAAF 40 Sqn, Flight Sergeant L.J. Goodlet RNZAF 40 Sqn, Flying Officer Louis Rubens (not aircrew), 2nd Lieutenant F.J. Begshaw SAAF 178 Sqn, Unknown Pilot, Flying Officer A. Poole 40 Sqn.

The two civilian clad persons at the back are not know. (Courtesy H.D. Clavert)

Flight Sergeant Norman Foster RNZAF, a member of Dudley Egles' crew, was among NCOs originally held at the School. Later he and others were moved to Mihai Viteazul, near the railway marshalling yards.

Our straw mattresses were the abode of lice. Life was not hard for us. We did not work as the Russian PWs had to – in general their treatment was far worse than ours. However, our ration of rye bread and some mysterious substance called *mamaliga* a sort of pease-porridge made from maize (polenta in Italian) was supplemented occasionally by a little meat and melted cheese . . . We kept as fit as we could by walking about the compound and playing soccer and basketball . . . We felt quite sorry for the Romanian guards. Their treatment by their officers was appalling. They were peasants and the officers were a privileged class who were determined to keep the lower order in their place.

When the capitulation came Norman Foster and his crew mates did not join the general exodus into the countryside, electing rather:

> . . . to stay behind and act as guards over the wounded Americans in the hospital. We were able to walk the streets and on one such walk I saw bodies of dead soldiers all in a heap in the central square – not a pretty sight. On another occasion my Skipper, Norman Dear, and I were invited out to dinner – a most sumptuous meal.

Although they did not realise it at the time, the crew of 40 Squadron's 'O-Oboe', which was shot down at Castranova [Crash Site 2] on 7 May, became the first 205 Group PWs in Romania. We last saw them in Chapter 7 with the accounts of Flight Sergeants Gordon Cormie and George Dealtry, Navigator and Air-Bomber respectively. They had left their Rear Gunner Flight Sergeant Ray Sauerwald RAAF dead in the wreckage, their only fatality, when they began their adventures as prisoners.

On arrival in Bucharest they were separated from the two RAAF Warrant Officers in the crew – John Coape-Smith and Dick Kilroy who were taken off to the Hospital. Later they were moved to the Schoolhouse. Their hospital treatment was very poor. Gordon Cormie noted that the treatment for the Romanian sick and wounded seemed to be no better.

Meals seemed to be a minor ordeal. The tables seated six each side and filling them at each meal acted as a head count. Gordon Cormie relates how:

> . . . there were three tin cups and when I say tin, I don't mean enamel, they were just plain tin, like a can with a handle, and filled with cold water. The bread was an oval shaped loaf cut into 12 slices. The people at the top end of the table got the loaf first. They picked two of the largest pieces and passed the rest of the loaf down and by the time it reached the end, the man at the end of the table had only the heel. The bread was dry, black and very

stale. Four people shared a tin cup of water. Lunch was similar. Supper was the big meal of the day. We existed and that's all you could say, but we couldn't complain because these were the same as the garrison rations of the Romanian army.

Looking back, it's quite amusing because when someone new came into the camp, we would befriend him which would mean that you would try to sit next to him in the dining hall. Of course, when he saw the stuff dished up, he wouldn't be able to face it and so we 'helped' with their food. Because of this bad diet there was a lot of dysentery or 'gyppy tummy'. We had to queue up for the lavatory and a guard would take six of us there at a time. It was only a hole in the ground, typical of the continental lavatory and because there was no toilet paper, personal hygiene was at a very low ebb. The guards would take us back to the barrack rooms.

When we went through the streets of Bucharest we saw the posters depicting Jimmy Cagney-type gangsters who were flying the bombing missions. The propaganda was that the Americans had opened up all the gaols giving any criminals who would fly these bombing raids an amnesty. I remember seeing other posters of the Russians. One showed a Russian soldier with a bayonet through a baby and the woman's breasts were all slashed and blood was pouring from them. That was the propaganda given to the people. We had a price on our heads and that is why we were turned in. The peasants received a bounty for anybody they turned in.

We saw the German pilot who shot us down. He came into the camp and we were brought out and shown to him. We were his prize: he just wanted to confirm that we were his kill.

It wasn't until very late on that the American Red Cross parcels arrived with food and clothing which they shared with everybody. The camp was growing so fast that there wasn't enough time for the Red Cross people to keep up with the count. So there was enough for one parcel between three people.'

Gordon Cormie's crewmate, George Dealtry, found camp life equally frustrating. He had his 21st birthday in Bucharest and blew all his camp shop coupons on 14 June on a small sticky sugary sweet thing instead of extra bread. He had decided to live it up and enjoy something special. As he says:

. . . enjoyment and appreciation are only relative.

He also remembered Colonel Victor Ioanid, the Camp Commandant vividly:

. . . a fat puce-faced figure of a man. One night he waddled into the dormitory where we were being entertained by one of his peasant soldiers playing lively gipsy music on his violin. The music stopped. The enraged Colonel gave a loud bellow before slapping the petrified soldier almost to the floor.

George Dealtry and another RAF prisoner, Sergeant Ken White of 178 Squadron:

. . . were approached by a group of four Americans to join them in an escape attempt which we agreed to do. The plan was pretty simple for getting out of the prison camp, but after that luck and stamina were to be the order of the day and night. We scrambled through a small window into a storeroom from a corridor where a Romanian soldier was on guard, a few yards from the window. He was surrounded and distracted by a mob of fellow prisoners making fun of him and jostling him, while we slid through the small opening one at a time. Once inside, we hid behind tall cupboards until nightfall, stuffing our pockets and battledresses with carrots, potatoes and the like. The room had one window opening onto the outside wall. The Americans left first with Ken White and me following after a few minutes. I believe one American was carrying a .45 automatic pistol which looked like a small cannon. I don't know how they obtained it. They climbed through the window cautiously and then quietly made their way across a darkened stable yard and out of sight without trouble. Having waited a couple or more minutes we decided to move and slowly crawled through the window and lowered ourselves to the ground. We took half a dozen steps to a nearby fence then froze when we heard a voice shout a challenge and the click of a rifle being cocked. It was all over, we were marched back into the central courtyard where lights were blazing. Great activity, soldiers on parade. Brought in front of an Army officer, who promptly showed his displeasure by yelling and screaming at us and grabbing us by the hair. We were then handed over to an escort of soldiers who marched us across the barrack square to the lock-up. They helped us on our way with the odd fist, boot and rifle butt. We were shown our quarters for the night, one of a row of about half a dozen cells, referred to as sweat-boxes and not quite as large as a common or garden loo. I remember measuring the walls using my forearm as a ruler and finding each wall to be about 2'3". My partner in crime and myself were locked in one of these, but the peace was soon broken by a short swarthy Romanian guard who after opening a small square mesh trap near the top of the door, started lashing out at us with a longish thin bayonet. Fortunately for us, this was rather difficult. After venting his spleen in this way for a short while, he was dragged away by his amused fellow guards. Later that night or early next morning we were disturbed by shouting, yelling and finally a rifle shot outside the guard room. Our American friends had arrived home after a short spell of freedom before capture. During the welcome home ceremony, I believe one of the Yanks had clobbered a guard which didn't improve matters.

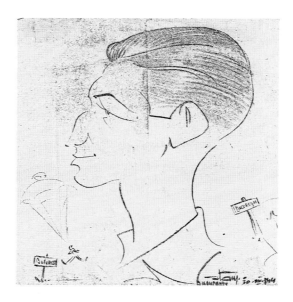

George Dealtry as sketched by a Bucharest Café artist on 30 August 1944, before his evacuation to Bari five days later. (Courtesy George Dealtry)

Gordon Cormie and George Dealtry, like Norman Dear's crew, volunteered to stay in Bucharest to look after the wounded once the PWs were released. They carried out whatever duties were necessary. Some of the wounded had bad burns and lost limbs as well as other injuries and could not easily be moved. All this meant that they were among the last to leave for Bari – on Friday 1 September. George Dealtry comments:

> We British had a low key arrival . . . We were pretty glad to be free and alive and our one thought was to return home as soon as possible.

They had no stomach for a return to active duty. By various and sometimes devious means the ex-PWs returned to their homes, some quicker than others.

Their operational tours with 205 Group were complete.

On 27 September 1944 George Dealtry married his WAAF fiancée, Lilly, at Hensworth Church. Gordon Cormie was best man. That was the last time they met until 1988 after researches for this book and a 40 Squadron history had brought them into contact again, George from Australia and Gordon from Canada.

CHAPTER 12 - Rescuing the Prisoners

Romania

The manner of the rescue of the Allied prisoners of war in Romania is unique. The account of it here is based on the report made by Lieutenant Colonel James A. Gunn III USAAF who, at the time of the Romanian surrender on 23 August, was the Senior Allied Officer (SAO) in the PW camps in Romania. (The full report was placed on Congressional Record in May 1967 having first appeared in the magazine *Aerospace Historian* in the autumn of 1966. I am most grateful to Colonel Gunn for his permission to quote freely.) After only one month in command of 454 Bombardment Group (= RAF Wing), Colonel Gunn was shot down on a raid to Ploiesti on 17 August, his thirty-third operation. During the final run to the target four of the eight B-24s in the leading squadron, including Colonel Gunn's, were shot down by unusually accurate flak. He and his crew abandoned their burning aircraft at about 24,000 feet which resulted in them being widely dispersed on landing.

Colonel Gunn was quickly captured by civilians and taken initially to the small town of Cornu, some 22 kms south-east of Ploiesti. On arrival at Camp No 13 two days later he discovered that he was to be SAO. Hardly had he settled into the camp routine when, on 23 August, PW life changed dramatically:

> A radio had been procured somehow. It was kept hidden during the day and brought out each night to listen to the BBC news broadcasts. That night we learned that King Michael had announced his nation's capitulation to the Allies. Later we learned of the overthrow of Antonescu, the Nazi puppet, and the establishment of an interim government under Dr. Maniu. Upon receipt of this joyous news the camp went wild. Many of the PWs had been there for months, and a few had been there more than a year. The prospect of liberation was exhilarating.
>
> The next morning we were visited by a Romanian Army colonel who spoke favourably of the turn of events. He advised us to remain at the camp until further instructions were received. Soon after his departure we were

visited by Princess Catharine Caradja, who asked for an opportunity to speak to us. I assembled the officers. She did not speak with the joy shown by the Army colonel. As a matter of fact, this lady showed great distress because she feared the day would come when her country would be overrun and occupied by the Russians. This very forceful talk was received rather strangely by some of our young officers because, after all, the Russians were our allies in this effort to beat down the Nazi war machine.

About 9 a.m. on 24 August, only a few hours after King Michael's announcement, we were greeted with the sound of air raid sirens, which were followed shortly by the bursting of bombs. For more than two days and nights the Germans bombed the city of Bucharest almost incessantly. The formations of Stukas and the HE 111s were small, and the bombs they were dropping appeared to be about the equivalent of our 250 pound HE bombs. As soon as the bombing began, what had been mere disorder became chaos, which continued in Bucharest as long as I was there. I had been unable to locate a single Romanian individual in authority. On visiting the Barracks, I found the same situation there. I did not restrict the PWs at either camp to the confines of the prisons, but instructed them to stay within the city and take refuge in shelters or basements during bombings.

Several of us began to search for any Romanians with authority. I planned to make two requests: first, that our prisoners of war be removed from the city of Bucharest to somewhere in the country to be away from the area being so severely bombed by the Germans, and, second, I wanted some means of getting in touch with the Allied authorities in Italy to begin arrangements for evacuating the prisoners.

I soon learned that all of the major means of communications in Bucharest had been bombed by the Germans and there was no operative radio or wire service through which I could communicate with the Allies. The telephone building in downtown Bucharest had received several direct bomb hits. The War Department building was in a shambles and had been completely evacuated. For a considerable time, I could locate no one ranking higher than a staff sergeant. The hierarchy of authority had collapsed. Finally, through the services of a sergeant on a motorcycle (who spoke English), I was put in touch with an officer and, ultimately, was taken to a temporary War Department HQ which had been established in woods several miles outside Bucharest.

I soon found that the senior man present was the Secretary of War, Lieutenant General Racoviţa. He saw me almost immediately. When I described the miserable circumstances of our PWs, General Racoviţa immediately agreed to arrange for the evacuation of Americans and Allied prisoners to another camp a few miles away.

Once this agreement had been concluded, I broached the subject of borrowing an airplane so that I might fly to Italy to arrange for the evacuation of our prisoners of war. I also promised to arrange for a strike against the German bombers which were dumping bombs on Bucharest around the clock. The airfield from which the Germans were operating was at Băneasa just north of Bucharest. At this General Racoviţa, for the first time, began to look with some favour upon my proposal.

I was anxious to get started right then and there. I asked for a plane that very night but was told that it was not that simple, that approval of several high level officials must be obtained.

Somewhere along the way I had previously met a Mr. Rico Georgescu, Secretary of State and Minister of National Economy. At the conclusion of my conversation with General Racoviţa with the assurance that I would hear from him again soon, Mr. Georgescu appeared on the scene and I was invited to spend the night at his residence. Incongruously, that night we had a beautifully prepared steak dinner in a downtown restaurant – and with the sound of ground fighting between the Germans and Romanians on all sides. This was punctuated by the occasional wail of sirens followed by the German bombings.

Throughout the night there were many telephone calls on what appeared to be a 'field phone' system at the Georgescu residence and several visitors came to discuss my proposed departure for Italy.

We retired about 4 a.m. I was awakened early to be taken by Mr. Georgescu for an interview with the Secretary of the Romanian Air Force, who told me that arrangements had been made for me to be flown to Italy in a Savoia Marchetti (an ancient model of an Italian twin-engined aircraft). Soon we were on our way to Popeşti-Leordeni airfield for the take-off. There I found that a Romanian commander and a crew of two enlisted people were to fly me to Italy. I later was told that the enlisted men, who were wearing sidearms, had been put on board to guard me, fearing that I might attempt to murder the pilot and take over the aircraft. I had no such thought.

Unfortunately, some 20 minutes after take-off, the pilot, who spoke no English, returned to Popeşti. I was told he said he had engine trouble although I detected none. Either he had no stomach for the mission or he was called back by radio.

As I stepped out of the aircraft I was met by a Romanian captain by the name of Constantin ('Bazu') Cantacuzino. He proved to be a member of the royal family (and a first cousin of Princess Caradja) and commander

283

of the fighter group in Bucharest. He spoke to me in excellent English, saying, 'If you will ride in the belly of a Messerschmitt, I will take you to Italy.' I agreed without hesitation. The Germans were still bombing and, as far as I knew, the Allied PWs were still in the prisoner of war camps in the city. (I was told later that they had actually been evacuated on 26 August in accordance with General Racoviţa's promise.)

As Captain Cantacuzino and I began talking about the trip to Italy, Secretary of State Georgescu again showed up, saying that the Interim President of the new government wished to see me. So I was taken to Dr. Maniu, who, through an interpreter, made a most impassioned plea that, upon arriving in Italy, I immediately made recommendations in the name of the Romanian government for occupation of the country by either British or American forces. On every side there was evidence of terror at the prospect of Russian occupation, and President Maniu was no exception. I promised to carry out his request and did so upon returning to Italy.

I was eager to be off and somewhat perturbed by the insistence of Captain Cantacuzino in planning the flight with great and meticulous care. He continued to point out that I would be buckled inside the fuselage and in the event of being shot down or a crash landing, my lot would be none too good. We sifted through the store of maps and to my dismay there was not a single useable map of Italy to be found. So I sat down and drew a detailed map of Italy on a piece of cardboard. From this I briefed Cantacuzino. Then I sketched a smaller and more detailed map on which I noted the barrage balloon locations and AA gun positions, together with outstanding landmarks which would be used for pilotage after crossing the Adriatic. I advised crossing the Adriatic at minimum level to avoid radar detection, but Cantacuzino objected. After considerable discussion, I reluctantly went along with Cantacuzino's plan, which was to begin the crossing at the maximum altitude. As I would have no source of oxygen, we agreed on an altitude of 19,000 feet. His plan was to proceed at this altitude to a point approximately half way across the Adriatic and then nose down into a long shallow dive but with enough power to make the last portion of the flight as fast as possible, thus reducing the possibility of interception by American fighters.

Another part of our plan was the painting of an American flag on each side of the Me 109G to lessen the possibility of an attack by American interceptors. While the painting was being done, Captain Cantacuzino pulled me aside and expressed some alarm that the plans for our proposed flight were now quite widely known. We were in the heart of an area where allies and enemies intermingled and on some occasions it was difficult to tell one from the other. Captain Cantacuzino understandably feared that we might be shot down by German fighters soon after take-off.

He cleverly suggested that we broadcast the news that we would be leaving at dawn the next morning, 28 August, but we actually would leave that afternoon as soon as the painting of the flags was finished. I agreed to this and only Mr. Georgescu, the Secretary of War, and the Secretary of the Air Force were told of the true take-off time.

I was outfitted with heavy leather flying clothing and the radio equipment was removed from the belly of the Messerschmitt to make room for me. The means of access into the fuselage was an inspection plate about 18 inches square by the left side of the fuselage. When the painting of the American flags was almost completed, he fitted me into the fuselage on the pretext of just trying out the space. However, once I was inside, he slipped the cover on, jumped into the cockpit, and in a matter of moments we were on our way to Italy.

The flight to Italy was uneventful and according to plan.

In accordance with my instructions, Captain Cantacuzino (who was a superb pilot with 54 fighter victories to his credit), followed the plan I had put on cardboard with great precision. As I had directed him, he followed a stream until coming to a specific landmark on the left side, and then turned to the right to a heading of 340, which took him directly over San Giovanni, home of my 454th and the 455th Bomb Group.

As we had British-manned 40mm guns around the perimeter of the airfield, I had instructed Cantacuzino to lower his gear and flaps upon approaching the airstrip and make a slow, straight in approach while rocking his wings slowly.

I felt sure that no one would fire even at a Messerschmitt coming in in this manner. However, upon reaching the airstrip, Cantacuzino made the decision that a straight-in approach would be too great a risk because of a tail wind. Consequently, he circled the airdrome with gear and flaps down and nose high, rocking his wings slowly as I had instructed him to do.

I felt a great sense of relief when I felt the aircraft rolling down my home runway. Upon being pulled from the fuselage of the Me 109, I found that I was hypoxic and dizzy. As soon as I gained my equilibrium I telephoned HQ 15 AF at Bari asking for General Twining. In his absence I spoke to Brigadier Charles Born, Chief of Operations.

As soon as we had a hasty bite to eat, Cantacuzino and I were hustled off to Bari, which was about an hour's drive. Planning was begun that night for fighter strikes against the Luftwaffe unit at Bǎneasa and for evacuation of the prisoners of war from Romania. A strike was made against Baneasa the next day by the 99th Fighter Group, which was followed on subsequent days by other fighter and bombardment units of 15 AF.

Mrs Alexandra Bragadiru looks on as Lt Cornelius Valjean (PW Camp 13 Staff Officer/Interrogator) bids farewell to released PWs awaiting airlift at Popesti-Leordeni airfield.

Colonel Gunn's part in the operation was almost completed but Bazu Cantacuzino's had some way to run yet. Their arrival at Bari late on 27 August sparked off detailed planning for the rescue of the allied prisoners. Having no authority to initiate such an operation, Brigadier Charles Born called on the Air Rescue Section of the Office of Strategic Services (OSS) who could. The initial element of the plan, which was code-named Operation GUNN, was for Cantacuzino to return to Bucharest and arrange for the reception of an OSS Evacuation Party. The Romanian realised a long-held dream when he was given a P-51, which he mastered in very short order, for his return.

On 29 August at about 0800 hours, escorted by three other P-51s he flew back to Popeşti where he landed. The escorts circled overhead until they received a Verey light signal that the airfield was safely in Romanian hands. The P-51s transmitted this information by radio to Bari and, at 1215 hours two B-17s took off with the twelve strong OSS party under the command of Colonel George Kraiger of HQ MAAF.

Reaching Popeşti-Leordeni at 1530 hours they were cleared to land by Cantacuzino. The 32-strong P-51 escort remained aloft throughout, vigilant to any threat from the Luftwaffe who were still active locally. An OSS office was set up in the home of the Bragadiru family in the Bucharest suburbs and attempts were made, without success, to establish radio contact with HQ 15 AF at Bari. To complete the arrangements for the full evacuation, code-named Operation REUNION, Bazu Cantacuzino was therefore dispatched to Bari in his new P-51 at 1715 hours on 30 August to brief the staff on the details.

Meanwhile Colonel Kraiger briefed the assembled PWs that the incoming B-17s would take 20 of them at a time. The bombers would taxi in, keeping their engines running, the men were to board quickly and the aircraft would take off straightaway in case of Luftwaffe intruder attacks.

Operation REUNION began in earnest on Thursday 31 August and continued over the next two days. Three formations of 12 B-17s each followed by two B-17s converted as ambulance aircraft evacuated 739 ex-PWs, including ten stretcher cases and 29 other sick or wounded on the first day. The turnround using this small airfield was impressive, the first twelve aircraft landed at 1000 hours and were clear by 1030. The half-hour turnround continued with successive formations arriving at 1115 and 1215 hours. The 'ambulance' B-17s arrived at 1315 and were safely airborne again at 1425 hours.

On 1 September one formation of sixteen B-17s landed at 1145 hours and took off an hour later with a further 393 ex-PWs.

That left a mopping-up operation for Saturday 2 September. Three B-17s and one C-47 (Dakota) landed at 1130 hours. The Dakota brought a repair crew and equipment to repair one B-17 damaged on landing the previous day. On this occasion thirteen P-51 escorts for the return trip landed at 1315 hours. Finally, the small party, carrying the last 29 ex-PWs and including the recovered B-17, took off at 1530 hours completing Operation REUNION. In all 1161 men were evacuated, including 29 aircrew of 205 Group. One American, too sick to be moved, was left behind with two USAAF doctors and adequate medical supplies. The operation had been completed by 38 B-17 sorties, escorted by over 230 P-38 and P-51 fighters.

While the evacuation was proceeding, other members of the OSS team visited selected refineries at or near Ploiesti to assess damage and to determine lessons to be learned in the attack of what remained of Germany's oil sources. Much film was shot of the damaged installations and plant at Astra Romană, Romană-Americană and Concordia Vega. The OSS party noted that the Germans had managed to destroy Columbia Aquila before the Romanian Army could establish an effective guard.

The RAF ME report on this unusual feat of airmanship and staff work observed that almost 50% of the Allied aircrew lost in raids over Romanian targets were brought back to Allied bases. Over 1000 USAAF dead remained behind.

In an issue studded with reports of Allied victories, The Daily Express of

Saturday, 2 September 1944, included a feature front page story by James Cooper, who had accompanied Operation REUNION in one of the B-17s on the previous day. He described the operation as an armada and gave a vivid picture of his brief visit to Bucharest. He told of how the seventeen B-17s in his group had landed with some difficulty, how it clearly became a festive day for many Romanians who crowded to this little airfield and how a Red Army horseman had made an appearance. For James Cooper, this man and his horse highlighted the differences between East and West as he rode skilfully among the silver B-17s.

Other headline events in The Daily Express that day were:

1. the Canadian capture of Dieppe

2. Verdun falls to the US Army without a shot fired

3. Giurgiu is captured by Red Army

4. Gothic Line is broken in Italy by 8 Army

5. US 7 Army advances into northern Italy from the French Riviera

6. Germans execute twelve Italian priests in Cremona as a reprisal for the killing of two German soldiers.

Each flight as it landed in Italy was given a riotous welcome back by the USAAF, with Generals and military bands in attendance. British and Commonwealth ex-prisoners were caught up in these joyous celebrations but once the initial euphoria had evaporated, they found nothing and no one. Even though they were aware of what was happening neither HQ 205 Group nor RAF ME nor any other British organisation had made any arrangements to receive these men. Many contacted their Squadrons to be told that they were no longer on strength and no one seemed prepared to help or show interest in their dilemma.

Colonel Gunn retired from the United States Air Force in 1967. Captain Bazu Cantacuzino died in exile in Spain having failed to be admitted to the United States.

Bulgaria

Nothing quite as dramatic was to befall the 320 or so PWs who had been held in Şumen. The Senior Allied Officer, Colonel White USAAF, on learning that the Bulgarian Government was seeking to capitulate to the Russians, established contact with the local Red Army Commander. Normal Russian practice seems to have been to backload prisoners from the war zone and to arrange for their repatriation later. This was not the case in Bulgaria. Their overloaded and strained rearward road and rail communications may have led them to decide to take an easier course – to shunt these somewhat embarrassing dirty, infested and malnourished allies to neighbouring neutral Turkey. (She was not to join the Allied cause until 1 March 1945). No record is available of what deliberations took place at official level.

On the evening of 7 September, Sofia Radio announced that the Bulgarian cabinet had authorised the release and repatriation of Allied PWs. The Government surrender took place the next day and arrangements were promptly put in hand to evacuate these unfortunate men by train to Turkey.

They were taken to Şumen station and herded onto a train which set off, with many wayside stops, first towards Sofia and then to the south-east: Operation FREEDOM had begun. At Stara Zagora there was a long halt and many PWs left the train. There were parades in the town as the populace celebrated their surrender and deliverance from an oppressive regime. PWs remarked on the extraordinary sight of Bulgar soldiers kissing each other while others demonstrated with slogans and placards. There was plenty of drink about and many PWs had to be dragged back to the train. After their prison diets, alcohol soon knocked them out.

The train finally reached the Greek frontier at Svilengrad at 1620 hours on 10 September. It crossed into Turkey at Edirne at 1730 hours. Border officials had, at first, been disturbed by the unannounced arrival of this rabble, none of whom had any recognisable means of identification. The escorts clearly were persuasive because, after loud arguments, the train was allowed through. They were given most welcome food and drink at both frontiers. They reached Istanbul at 0900 hours on 11 September. Those requiring medical attention were taken to hospital. All were given baths and issued with Turkish uniforms in place of their own tattered clothes and moved to two Turkish ships moored in the Bosphorus. Here they received excellent treatment and good food but Geoff Knyvett remembers that they also found a new torment. In camp in Şumen they were all infested with lice and almost all suffered from the most debilitating dysentery and these had travelled well to liberty in Turkey with their hosts. Now bed bugs joined the pestilence.

Fortunately, their stay on the ships was brief. On 14 September they moved onward to Syria by train. At the border they were met by American Red Cross and British Army personnel: more medical attention was available and Geoff Knyvett had a painful abscess lanced by a British doctor.

There were assembled over 300 souls of whom 20–30 were British or Commonwealth. Eighteen of these were 205 Group aircrew who had been shot down during raids against Romanian targets between 7 May and 10 August.

The next step towards real liberty was a flight to Cairo from Aleppo in American C-46 Curtiss Commando transport aircraft. From there the USAAF and some British airmen were taken onward to Bari where the whole party was welcomed by Major General Nathan F. Twining. The British who remained in Egypt were given medical examinations in hospital.

Allied Prisoners of War arriving in Syria in September 1944 from Turkey and Greece from camps in Bulgaria. (Courtesy Noel Catherine)

The evacuation was completed by 17 September nine days after Bulgaria's surrender.

After his spell in a Bulgarian hospital, Geoff Knyvett's injuries were diagnosed as a broken leg and neck. He had lost four stones in weight. At last, in mid-October, he returned to Australia on the New Zealand hospital ship, *Maunganui*. (His colleagues were similarly repatriated.)

Noel Cathrine, 'Cocky' Stone and Sergeant Graham remained at Cairo and went home to South Africa from there.

Sergeant Eric Turner, Wireless Operator, and his captain, Sergeant Dick

Sutcliffe RCAF of 40 Squadron had been flown back to Bari, where they separated. Dick Sutcliffe was repatriated to Canada. Eric Turner was admitted to hospital for treatment of his dysentery 'and other complaints'. He was transferred to Naples and flew home via RAF Hendon on 8 October.

The American report on Operation FREEDOM concludes:

> Two weeks before, the officers and men from Romania had arrived at this same airfield (Bari). They had been jubilant, demonstrative; there was singing and cheering. But the men who came back from Bulgaria walked from the airplanes quietly and without enthusiasm or display. They were tired and weak and subdued.

A week later General Eaker dispatched a special team to Sofia to investigate Bulgarian maltreatment of PWs and to apprehend the perpetrators. The report does not disclose how they fared. One can guess that it was probably fruitless. There was a good deal of summary justice being handed out in post-war Bulgaria.

Reception in Italy

After all the adventures, hardships and privations endured by the prisoners in Romania and Bulgaria, it should have been possible to end their story on a note of acclaim as heros, of brass bands and generals and welcomes home. True, all that did happen as they set foot on Italian soil but that was 15 AF's joy. Once that circus had moved on, the British and Commonwealth ex-prisoners found, at best, a disinterested and unwelcoming reception. At worst, there was none at all.

This generally off-hand and perfunctory treatments ends the story on something of a sour note. The majority of 205 Group's ex-PWs survived their repatriation by their own guile and wits. Perhaps these adventures will be taken up by another chronicler.

The Graves in Romania, Bulgaria and Yugoslavia

The Missing Research Section of the Air Ministry was inaugurated in December 1941, with a staff of three. Initially investigations were conducted from London, but in December 1944 SHAEF (Supreme Headquarters Allied Expeditionary Force) authorised work to begin in France. That was the beginning of No 1 Section – another seven were to follow spanning all areas of the RAF's wartime operations, with the clear and simple mission:

> Find and identify all RAF graves and attempt to trace ALL missing RAF airmen of the Second World War

(This Chapter is based on an article 'The Missing Research and Enquiry Service' in *Air Clues* published by MOD (Air) in May 1986 and other papers kindly provided by the Air Historical Branch (MOD). Notes were also made from the relevant Bucharest Consular files, supported enthusiastically by HM Consul, Mr. John Balchin. The Graves Lists have been compiled from information kindly supplied by the Commonwealth War Graves Commission.)

In July 1945 the Missing Research and Enquiry Service (MRES) was formed with three units known as MREUs. Each was to have 40 search officers working in eight sections of five officers – a Squadron Leader and four Flight Lieutenants. All were volunteers and a number were from the Commonwealth. The task facing them was immense. RAF Bomber Command alone lost over 47,000 killed or presumed killed over Europe.

Middle East Command formed a section known as MRES MED/ME in 1946 operating initially from Naples and later from Treviso. On 1st July 1947 it was reformed as No 5 MREU covering Italy, the Balkans and the Mediterranean area.

When Allied aircraft crashed in enemy or enemy-occupied territory, it became common local practice to bury deceased aircrew in a cemetery near to the crash site. All reports from Romania indicate that the eighty who lost their lives there were buried by the parishioners with dignity.

Civilian Police and Service Intelligence personnel examined crash sites meticulously. Documents, maps, personal papers and belongings found in or near the wreckage were removed for examination by Intelligence Staffs.

Equipment in the aircraft was also studied and radio frequency settings, radar sets and guns were of particular interest. First aid equipment and any medicines found were very popular as local supplies were scarce. Searchers normally removed both identity discs from the bodies.

Once the post-war search for lost aircrew began in Romania, the MREU staff were assisted by the Consular Staff of the British Mission in Bucharest and by the Romanian authorities. However, post-war Romania was in turmoil. The retreating Germans had wreaked a vengeance whenever they could: a staunch vassal-state under Marshal Antonescu's seemingly unshakeable rule had been toppled and the bottom of the Balkan front had been irrevocably holed. But that, which ought to have been enough in itself, was not all. Romanian forces had shared in the invasion of the Soviet Union. Their country's capitulation at the eleventh hour was not to save the nation from its new ally's wrath. Once the land was in the Red Army's grip, normal life became difficult and the movement of members of Western Allied missions and agencies was put under heavy restrictions, many petty in the extreme. The work of No 5 MREU was not easy.

Once a crash site was accurately located, the bodies in their temporary graves had to be positively identified. A crashing bomber often exploded or burst into flames on hitting the ground with the result that its crew were frequently injured beyond recognition. The important initial step therefore was the identification of the aircraft. Squadron records could then pinpoint who the crew were on that fatal operation. Even that was not straightforward. In at least one case in Romania all that survived to identify one Wellington was an engine serial number. A search of the records revealed that this engine belonged to no Wellington flying that night. After more intensive investigation it was discovered that since the raid was a 'maximum effort' the maintenance organisation had made their maximum effort too and found a replacement engine to make one more bomber serviceable. Its records were not completed at the time and when it failed to return there seemed to be no point in doing so. However, the issue of the engine had been properly recorded even if its installation had not.

Once the particular crashed aircraft was identified, the search was narrowed to a named aircrew and the Section had a clearer idea of who it was looking for. If the identity discs and personal papers had indeed been removed, the Search Officers had to look for name tapes in clothing, flashes, badges of rank and other items on uniforms. This was often complicated by the widespread habit among British servicemen in the Mediterranean area of wearing odd items of clothing, especially items from other nations. A Romanian example was the case of the parish grave record of a young man known by his initials 'A.M.41'. The Search Officer discovered that this was the

Air Ministry label from the man's flying suit which had survived, charred, from the fire which had swept through the bomber as it crashed.

Search Sections had the medical and dental records of missing aircrew and frequently these were used to confirm identities. However, it was often the case that, although the wreck was identified and the crew named, the teams could not positively distinguish individual crew members one from another. These were buried in Collective Graves.

In other sad cases, in spite of exhaustive investigations, some dead could not be identified at all. These were buried as 'Unknown Airman': there was not one such in Romania. All the dead have been identified.

After the war the British Government decided that the graves of all British Servicemen should be concentrated into British Military Cemeteries so that they could be tended in perpetuity by the Imperial (now Commonwealth) War Graves Commission. It was during this process that the identifications were carried out.

The Graves Lists

The Commonwealth War Graves Commission Cemetery at Tîncăbeşti, Remembrance Day, 1953, showing the temporary grave crosses.
(Courtesy Commonwealth War Graves Commission)

Romania

The hectare of land near the village of Tîncăbeşti in which the British Cemetery lies was generously provided by the Romanian Government in 1946 and the graves were concentrated there over the next eighteen months. The Cemetery is beside the main road to Ploieşti 25 kms north of Bucharest. It is the only cemetery in Romania containing British and Commonwealth 1939–45 War dead. The total number of burials is 83 of whom 80 are 205 Group aircrew who lost their lives in operations against targets in Romania. 65 of them were RAF(VR), 5 each were RAF and SAAF, 2 each RAAF and RCAF and 1 RNZAF.

The Cemetery at Tîncăbeşti in June, 1964, showing the final arrangement of the headstones and the Cross of Sacrifice. (Courtesy Commonwealth War Graves Commission)

The 80 for whom this book is written

5th/6th May Target – Cîmpina

Wellington LP 191 'R' of 40 Squadron:

Flight Sergeant D.H. Royle (24)	Pilot	Collective Grave
Flight Sergeant J.A. Smith (22)	Navigator	
Warrant Officer A. Brown	Wireless Operator	1.E.2-5
Sergeant G.W. Ward	Air Bomber	
Sergeant A.R. Wood (18)	Air Gunner	

The aircraft crashed at Valeă Lunga, 10 kilometres south-west of the target area. (Marked as Crash Site 1* on the map)

6th/7th May Target – Bucharest

Wellington LP 128 'O' of 40 Squadron:

Flight Sergeant R.G. Sauerwald RAAF (22)	Grave 1.A.1

The aircraft crashed at Castranova, 30 kilometres south-east of Craiova (2*). The other four members of this crew became prisoners.

Wellington JA 525 'Q' of 150 Squadron:

Warrant Officer S. Clarke (27)	Pilot	Grave 2.B.5
Sergeant L.W. Cox	Navigator	Grave 2.B.4
Sergeant R.P. Scott	Wireless Operator	Grave 2.B.2
Sergeant C.G. Walker (21)	Air Bomber	Grave 1.B.7
Sergeant G.S. Vaughan (39)	Air Gunner	Grave 1.B.8

This aircraft crashed at Comana, 15 kilometres South of Bucharest (3*).

Liberator EW 341 'H' of 178 Squadron:

Flight Sergeant W.A. Molyneux (23)	Pilot	Grave 2.A.7
Sergeant H.S. Langley (23)	Navigator	Grave 1.B.3
Sergeant C.G. Rhodes (24)	Wireless Operator	Grave 1.B.1-2
Flight Sergeant J.R. Velzian (19)	Air Gunner	
Sergeant H.J. Tucker (18)	Air Gunner	Grave 2.A.8

This Liberator crashed at Belciug, a hamlet 16 kilometres north-east of Roşiorii de Vede (4*). Two members of the crew survived and became prisoners.

7th/8th May Target – Bucharest

Liberator BZ 932 'Y' of 178 Squadron:

Lieutenant J.G. Schuurman SAAF	Pilot	Grave 2.D.2-3
Flight Sergeant J.A. Phillips (22)	Wireless Operator	Grave 2.D.1

Lieutenant D.P. McGee SAAF	Air Gunner	Grave 2.D.2-3
Flight Sergeant P. Bisset (22)	Pilot	Grave 2.D.1-4
Sergeant K.W. Brown	Air Gunner	Grave 2.D.4

The aircraft crashed at Lunguleţu, 38 kilometres north-west of Bucharest (9*). Two members of this crew survived and became prisoners.

Wellington LN 663 'G' of 104 Squadron:

Flight Sergeant D.A. Eld (26)	Wireless Operator	Grave 1.C.6
Sergeant A. Smith	Air Gunner	

died in the crash at Preajba de Sus, 25 kilometres north-west of Videle (7*). Two crewmen survived but a third, seriously injured, survived in hospital at Giurgiu only until 13 August.

Flight Sergeant C.G. Middleton (23)	Grave 2.B.3

Wellington MF 198 'D' of 142 Squadron:

Flight Sergeant C. Wray (30)	Pilot	Grave 1.A.6
Flight Sergeant O.G. Griffiths (22)	Navigator	Grave 1.A.4
Sergeant R. Padgett (21)	Wireless Operator	Grave 1.A.5
Sergeant C.P. Whalley (22)	Air Bomber	Grave 1.A.7-8
Flight Sergeant P.A. Scott (27)	Air Gunner	

This bomber crashed at Fărcaşele, 8 kilometres north-east of Caracal (8*).

Wellington ME 878 'X' of 40 Squadron:

Flight Lieutenant G.W. Williams DFC (21)	Pilot	Combined Grave 2.C.2-5
Warrant Officer L.F. Dutton RCAF	Navigator	
Flight Sergeant F.W.A Head	Air Bomber	
Sergeant L.J. Carey (23)	Wireless Operator	

The Rear Gunner survived this crash at Vartoapele, 11 kilometres south-west of Belciug (5*) and became a prisoner.

Wellington MF 156 'H' of 70 Squadron:

Flight Lieutenant C.H. Masters DFC RNZAF (25)	Air Bomber	Grave 1.D.6
Flying Officer S.J. Hanney	Pilot	Grave 2.C.6
Flying Officer P.R. Billingsley (20)	Air Bomber	Grave 2.C.8
Sergeant C.F. Pope (33)	Wireless Operator	Grave 1.C.5
Sergeant A.F. Rowlands (19)	Air Gunner	Grave 2.C.7

This is a complete crew (5) but a RAAF WO, A.C. Weppler (Navigator) was also on board and was the only survivor. The aircraft crashed at Talpa Bîscoveni (6*), 10 kilometres north-east of Vartoapele.

2nd/3rd July Target – Bucharest

Wellington ME 990 'R' of 40 Squadron:

| Flying Officer J.C. Murphy (21) | Air Gunner | Grave 1.A.2 |

'R-Robert' crashed at Maceşul, 45 kilometres South of Craiova (10*). The four survivors became prisoners of war.

Liberator 199 'D' of 31 Squadron SAAF:

Second Lieutenant E. Nowers SAAF (35)	Co-Pilot	Grave 1.C.8
Warrant Officer L.A. Preston SAAF (20)	Air Gunner	
Warrant Officer J.V.P. Robertson SAAF	Air Gunner	Grave 2.C.1
Flight Sergeant F. Ryder RAF (VR) (21)	Air Gunner	Grave 1.C.7

The Pilot, Captain R.D. Bird SAAF and the Navigator survived when 'D-Dog' crashed at Furculeşti 26 kilometres north-west of Turnu Măgurele (11*).

27th/28th July Target – Bucharest

Wellington LP 196 'E' of 150 Squadron:

Sergeant B.F.W. Wilkinson	Pilot	Grave 1.B.4
Sergeant E.L. Price	Navigator	Grave 1.B.5
Sergeant G. Kirby (22)	Wireless Operator	Grave 1.B.6
Sergeant R. Turner (22)	Air Bomber	
Sergeant G.J. Crawley (22)	Air Gunner	Grave 1.A.3

Crashed at Crucea de Piatra, 10 kilometres east of Caracal (12*) and burned out.

9th/10th August Target – Ploieşti

Wellington LP 465 'S' of 37 Squadron:

Sergeant W.E. Double (21)	Pilot	Grave 1.C.1-4
Sergeant J.E. Cushing (22)	Navigator	
Sergeant A.J. Currin (22)	Wireless Operator	
Sergeant J.S. Wilson (21)	Air Bomber	
Sergeant B. Bell (21)	Air Gunner	

The records are not clear but this aircraft probably crashed in Cotroceni, a suburb of Bucharest (13*).

Wellington LN 963 'O' of 70 Squadron:

Flight Sergeant A.S.R. Ross RAAF (21)	Pilot	Grave 1.C.1-4
Flight Sergeant H.J.A. Rogers (22)	Navigator	
Flight Sergeant A. Gleason	Air Bomber	
Sergeant W. Butler	Wireless Operator	
Sergeant W.M. Jones (20)	Air Gunner	

This aircraft crashed at Caciulaţi, a village some 10 kilometres south-east of where the Commonwealth Cemetery now lies (15*).

(Note that these two complete crews share the same Collective Grave. An extract from a letter from the Air Attaché's office in July 1948 explains, on the next page)

(left) The first collective grave cross of Sgt Brian Bell's crew. The Squadron number is wrong: they belonged to 37 Squadron. (Courtesy Mrs Marjoie Greening – Sgt Bell's sister)

(right) The permanent headstone on Sgt Bell's grave. (Courtesy Defence Attache Bucharest)

The only two remaining crews unaccounted for are therefore Wellington LN 963 'O' of 70 Sqn (FS Ross and crew) and Wellington LP 465 'S' of 37 Sqn (Sgt Double and crew). Perusal of [a previous letter] has revealed that the only two aircraft not so far identified are those which crashed at Caciulaţi and Cotroceni. There can be little doubt therefore that the missing Wellingtons are in fact these two crashes and all aircraft lost over this country are therefore accounted for. The fact that the aircraft which crashed at Caciulaţi was reported originally to have been a four-engine type can probably be discounted. The No 5 MREU Report of March 1948 reports it to be a twin and that it exploded on striking the ground.

It is strongly submitted that there is no chance of identifying the crews if exhumed at this late stage. No 5 MREU's Report states that, in the Caciulaţi case, few remains were found and the graves Concentration Officer found nothing to establish any identities when he exhumed the graves for concentration in the War Cemetery. Similarly, the bodies in the other crash were badly burned and nothing was found on exhumation to establish identities. While there is little doubt therefore of the collective identities of these two crews, individual identification is considered out of the question.

The letter recommended the concentration of the remains into 1.C.1-4 and have a multiple grave for both crews.

This course would enable complete clearance of all known crashes in Romania to be effected.

The re-interment of the remains of five aircrew into 1.C.1-4 took place on 10 December 1948. A brief service was conducted by a member of the Consular Staff, who was a lay-reader, in the presence of HM Consul and the Assistant Air Attaché.)

Wellington MF 631 'C' of 142 Squadron:

Flight Sergeant R.T. Marsh RCAF	Pilot	Grave 2.B.1
Sergeant W.F. Chambers (22)	Navigator	Grave 1.D.2-5
Flight Sergeant J. Watts (23)	Air Bomber	
Sergeant W.F. Bullard	Wireless Operator	
Sergeant M.J. Watts (20)	Air Gunner	

This aircraft crashed at Orac (14*) near Snagov, 25 kilometres North of Bucharest and just a few kilometres from the cemetery where they now lie.

Wellington LP 507 'X' of 150 Squadron:

Flying Officer N.C. Jones (21)	Pilot	Grave 2.A.1-4
Sergeant E.G. Berry (22)	Air Bomber	
Sergeant W. O'Donnell	Wireless Operator	
Sergeant A.H. Hudson (28)	Air Gunner	

Sergeant Mark Wilson survived when this Wellington crashed at Dodroteşti, 22 kilometres North of Roşiorii de Vede (16*).

Liberator EV 874 of 178 Squadron:

Sergeant N.A.B. Cooper (32)	Air Gunner	Grave 2.A.6

Sergeant J.C. Milsom survived and became a prisoner of war. The fate of the rest of the crew is not known in detail, but they were all reported 'safe in allied hands' later. One, at least, was a PW in Romania.

Halifax JP 110 'I' of 614 Squadron:

Warrant Officer H. Bath (24)	Navigator	Grave 2.B.6

The Pilot, Flight Sergeant C.E. Caldwell-Wearne, and three others survived the crash at Ciscăuţi (18*) about 20 kilometres north-west of Bucharest to become prisoners of war.

Halifax JP 282 'Q' of 614 Squadron:

Flight Lieutenant R.D. Langton (25)	Pilot	Grave 2.D.5
Flying Officer T.J.R. Turner (22)	Navigator	Grave 2.B.8
Flight Sergeant H.G. Jones	Flight Engineer	Grave 2.B.7
Fight Sergeant J.W. Clarke (22)	Air Gunner	Grave 2.D.6
Pilot Officer W.J. Martyn (20)	Air Bomber	Grave 2.D.7
Flight Sergeant P. Brunton (21)	Air Bomber	Grave 2.D.8

This Halifax crashed at Corbii Mari, 40 kilometres West of Bucharest (19*).

17th/18th August Target – Ploieşti

Wellington LP 327 'W' of 40 Squadron:

Sergeant E.E.R. Paterson (22)	Pilot	Grave 1.D.1
Sergeant W.T. Quinlan (28)	Navigator	
Sergeant W.D. Mackenzie (22)	Wireless Operator	
Sergeant G.V. Lea	Air Bomber	
Flight Sergeant I. Campbell (28)	Air Gunner	

This Wellington, the twenty-second and last to come down on Romanian soil was totally destroyed when it crashed at Conteşti, 25 kilometres north-east of Piteşti (20*). The two other aircraft had crashed without loss of crew, who had all become prisoners.

*VE Day at the Commonwealth Graves Commission Cemetery – 'The British Cemetery'
in 1981. Members of the Romanian Government lay their wreaths. (Author's collection)*

Bulgaria

The Sofia War Cemetery is part of the Protestant Cemetery, 2 kilometres
north of the city's railway station. It contains war graves from both World
Wars. The 1914–18 burials number 160 while British and Commonwealth
1939–45 War burials total 27. Of these 24 are 205 Group aircrew, 19 of
whom lost their lives while on operations against Romanian targets.

7th/8th May Target – Filiaşi railway bridge over the River Jiu, north-west
of Craiova

Wellington LN 804 'T' of 40 Squadron:

Pilot Officer I.B.H. McKenna (23)	Air Bomber	Grave 2.A.11

The other four members of this crew survived and 'walked back to Allied
lines' via the Chetniks in Yugoslavia.

303

28th/29th June Target – Giurgiu

Wellington MF 194 'F' of 70 Squadron:

Flight Sergeant J.R. Burgess RAAF (21)	Air Bomber	Grave 2.B.10
Flight Sergeant L. Fallon RAAF (24)	Pilot	Grave 2.B.8-11
Flight Sergeant R.E. James RAAF (20)	Air Gunner	
Flight Sergeant T.R. Lowther RAAF (21)	Wireless Operator	

Flying Officer G.G. Knyvett RAAF survived the crash near Sviştov on the Bulgarian bank of the Danube and became a prisoner of war.

Liberator EV 970 'F' of 31 Squadron SAAF on the Squadron's first operation against a Romanian target.

Major J.A. Mouton DFC SAAF (21)	Pilot	Grave 2.A.10
Lieutenant H.H. Bunce (or Bounce) SAAF (31)	Air Gunner	Grave 2.A.9

The five remaining members of this crew became prisoners of war. F-Freddy's crash site is not known.

Liberator EW 104 'Y' of 31 Squadron SAAF:

Lieutenant D.J.S. Haggie SAAF (21)	Pilot	Grave 2.C.1
Lieutenant D. Lindley SAAF (35)	Observer	Grave 2.C.2
Lieutenant R.G. Southey SAAF (21)	Pilot	Grave 2.C.3
Warrant Officer 2 W.S. Barrett SAAF (21)	Wireless Operator	Grave 2.C.4
Warrant Officer 2 D.T. Flynn SAAF (21)	Wireless Operator	Grave 2.C.5
Sergeant B.O. Brazier RAF (VR)	Air Bomber	Grave 2.C.6
Flying Officer A.F. Paton RAAF	Wireless Operator	Grave 2.C.7

This Liberator crashed at a village near Ruse on the Bulgarian bank of the Danube, opposite Giurgiu. The name is recorded as Woecwage, but there is no trace of such a place.

9th/10th August Target – Ploieşti

Wellington LP 548 'H' of 142 Squadron:

Flight Sergeant C.G. Hill RAAF (20)	Pilot	Grave 2.B.4
Flight Sergeant P.A. Shepherd (20)	Navigator	Grave 2.B.1-3
Flight Sergeant R. Thurlow (21)	Air Bomber	
Flight Sergeant W. Grisdale	Wireless Operator	
Sergeant G.R. Pond RCAF	Air Gunner	

No record of the crash site of this aircraft has been discovered.

Yugoslavia

There are four Cemeteries in Yugoslavia which contain the graves of British and Commonwealth war dead. Three of them, Belgrade New Cemetery in Belgrade, Dunta Doli Civil Cemetery in Dalmatia and Trbovlje Civil Cemetery near Ljubljana contain no graves of 205 Group aircrew.

Belgrade War Cemetery contains 492 burials of Second World War dead, of whom 348 are airmen. Over 145 are 205 Group aircrew graves. Four are of aircrew killed on operations against Romanian targets on the same night.

2nd/3rd July Target – Bucharest

Wellington LP 253 'C' of 40 Squadron:

Sergeant H. Beeson (19)	Air Gunner	Grave 9A.D.2
Sergeant J.D. Yole (2)	Navigator	Grave 9A.D.1

Flight Sergeant R. Sutcliffe and Sergeant E. Turner survived and became prisoners of war in Bulgaria. Sergeant E. Turnbull was looked after by a Chetnik group and returned to the Squadron 40 days later.

Wellington LP 348 'V' of 70 Squadron which had been alone on a leaflet raid to Arad and Timişoara:

Sergeant R. Black (20)	Air Bomber	Grave 1.C.9
Sergeant D.A. Stephens (25)	Air Gunner	Grave 1.C.8

305

The other three members of the crew survived but no more is known of their story.

No Known Graves

A total of 26 further aircrew lost their lives on operations to Romanian targets and have no known graves.

5th/6th May Target – Cîmpina

Wellington HZ 814 'B' of 37 Squadron:

Sergeant P.D. Parkes	Pilot
Sergeant A.R. Mitchell	Air Gunner
Flying Officer D.M. Margison	Navigator
Pilot Officer T.J. Pullin	Wireless Operator
Flight Sergeant R. Cairns	Air Bomber

B-Bertie is known to have crashed at sea on the way back from the raid, having lost the starboard engine.

2nd/3rd June Target – Giurgiu

Wellington LP 120 'N' of 40 Squadron:

Flight Sergeant F.R. Hughes RAAF	Pilot
Flight Sergeant A. Millar	Air Bomber
Sergeant W.E. Samler	Wireless Operator
Sergeant W.E. Sweeney	Air Gunner

This aircraft crashed 20 kilometres south of Pirot in Yugoslavia. The Navigator was the only survivor – as a prisoner of war.

28th/29th June Target – Giurgiu

Liberator KG 839 'L' of 31 Squadron SAAF:

| Captain T.A.M. Van de Spuy SAAF | Pilot |

Second Lieutenant G.B. Mills SAAF	2nd Pilot
Lieutenant W. Dodd SAAF	Navigator
Warrant Officer G.W. Trezona SAAF	Wireless Operator
Lieutenant D. Fietze SAAF	Air Gunner
Sergeant H.J. Kelly	Air Bomber
Flying Officer W.P. Walden	Air Gunner

Nothing was heard of this bomber after take-off and she disappeared without trace.

26th/27th July Target – Ploieşti

Liberator KG 826 'R' of 31 Squadron SAAF:

Lieutenant E. Rood SAAF	Pilot
Lieutenant B.V. Gesundheit SAAF	Navigator
Second Lieutenant V. van Rooyen SAAF	2nd Pilot
Lieutenant K.V. Essery SAAF	Pilot
Sergeant L. Adams	Air Gunner

R-Robert crashed at sea. Three bodies were recovered and were buried at the Bari British Military Cemetery – Flying Officer F.W. Shepherd, Warrant Officer E. Raeburn SAAF and Sergeant H.L. Grieg.

17th/18th August Target – Ploieşti

Wellington HG 746 'X' of 40 Squadron:

Sergeant D.J. Francis	Pilot
Sergeant S.S. Goddard	Navigator
Sergeant D.R.W. Moore	Air Gunner
Sergeant J.W. Davies	Wireless Operator
Sergeant D.A. Beaven	Air Bomber

Nothing was heard from this aircraft after take-off.

CHAPTER 14 - The Balance Sheet

Ploieşti

Over the length of the high-level day and night offensive between 5 April and 19 August MASAF launched attacks on 30 days involving 5,479 bomber sorties to deliver over 134,400 tons of bombs. Aircraft of 205 Group attacked oil targets in the Ploieşti area on four nights making 241 bomber sorties which delivered over 370 bons of high explosives as well as many thousands of incendiaries for the loss of 16 aircraft.

At the outset of the offensive Ploiesti's collective potential throughput of crude oil was 709,000 tons per month. Actual production did not make full use of this capability and was about 480,000 per month. Of this some 177,000 tons were petrol/gasoline and that was rated to be one-third of the total production capacity in German hands.

Early attacks took a heavy toll, reducing the potential in six raids to 44%. Over the whole period the original capacity was reduced by 89% to a mere 77,000 tons per month. Petrol/gasoline production dived by 91% to 15,400 tons per month.

Enemy reaction to these raids showed that they attached as much importance to this target area as the Allies did. In the first 3 months more enemy aircraft were encountered per 100 sorties to Ploieşti than over any target in the Theatre. However, as a result of the air attacks of the CBO continent-wide, German fighter production fell sharply in the last 7–8 weeks up to mid-August. Over the whole period the enemy (including FARR) lost 13 fighters for each 100 sallies made against the attacking bombers, by day or night.

Romanian records of the attacks might be described as incomplete. The night-bomber attacks apparently killed only two civilians, while two men, two women and one child were wounded. The bombers of 205 Group are listed as having dropped a grand total of 221 HE bombs, of which four failed to explode. There were twelve incendiaries. Before one scoffs, perhaps the conclusion could be that these were the totals which fell on Ploieşti itself; the rest fell astray in the countryside. Statistics for the destruction of buildings and installations are inseparable from the overall MASAF totals.

The Creditul Minier refinery at Brazi SW of Ploieşti as seen by a 6 May daylight photo-recce flight from 60 Squadron (SAAF) Mosquito. Evidence of earlier raids is difficult to detect. (Courtesy Ministry of Defence)

The oilfield's agony was not yet complete. Between September and December, Romania's new-found Soviet allies removed over 50,600 tons of equipment. Naturally, such actions impaired refinery repairs and drilling programmes and, in so doing, delayed the restoration of the industry after the Allied bombing offensive. All this was counterproductive: the Soviet offensive into central Europe needed Romania's oil products at this stage as much as Germany had done. Their actions insured that they were not available.

Romanian Transportation Under Attack

In October 1944 Allied de-briefing of Romanian General Staff Officers showed that these attacks achieved significant successes.

Military Movement and Supply

The bombing of railway yards and railway choke points between April and August reduced the capacity of Romanian State Railways – *Calea Ferate Român* (CFR for short) by 45%. Before the opening of the Red Army advance towards the Danube Plain in mid-August, the flow of German personnel and supplies to the front had not been critically interrupted by this damage: surviving rail resources could carry enough to sustain the conditions at the front at that time. Temporary checks had virtually no effect because the German supply system always strove to maintain adequate stocks well forward, together with the Wehrmacht's policy of living off the land. However, once the Red Army's advance began, the Germans tried to re-deploy six motorised divisions by train from central Moldavia, north-east of Bacău. This required 60–75 trains for each division and, when the Germans attempted to concentrate some 500 trains, their only success was to choke the available routes, mainly in Hungarian-occupied Transylvania and units in Romania were forced to rely on road transport. When the Wehrmacht pressed the Romanians for additional trains and traffic facilities, the Romanian General Staff suggested use of already over-crowded routes and were of no help.

Rail Damage and Oil

Before the high-level day and night-bomber offensive started on 4 April, some 24 trains of oil products left Romania daily. By August, the Romanian General Staff's assessment held this to be no more than 5 per day as a result of damage to refineries, refinery sidings, pipelines and railside pipeheads. Continuous and repeated damage in these areas made it impossible to outload all the oil products which the refineries were still capable of producing in spite of bomb damage.

At first, Air Intelligence Staffs were reserved in accepting these figures until more detailed reports were available. These statements might only indicate that the refineries etc were unable to move finished products held in undamaged storage tanks because of damage to railway equipment and rolling stock, rather than to an actual cut-back in production resulting from an inability to outload refined products. Conflicting evidence from de-briefed refinery managers lent some support to this tendency to reticence. For example, Astra-Romậna belittled the effects on transport whereas Romận-Americană and

Xenia were convinced that reduction in siding capacity prevented full use of facilities.

Bombing reduced the CFR's locomotive capacity to 30% of the pre-attack level. The attacks on railway yards at Ploieşti and Braşov (not itself ever a night-bomber target) reduced the capacity on this key route through the Carpathians into Hungarian-occupied Transylvania from 30 to 10 trains per day. In addition, the length of trains on this route had to be reduced. This added calamity was because new trains could no longer be made up to full length at either end. The only other place which might have been used to marshal the usual trains was Bucharest, itself severely damaged.

When asked for an overall view of the effectiveness of air attack on railways and installations, one Staff Officer believed that the bombing of bridges was the most effective form of interdicting attack because of the difficulties in repairing such damage. The restoration of traffic in marshalling yards or over cratered through-lines was relatively easier to effect. The normal delay imposed by such damage was 48 hours. However the Piatra Olt bridge, just south-west of Slatina, was closed for over a week because a near miss had displaced and twisted one span. After some bridge attacks the structure was so weakened that no locomotive could cross: trucks were pushed loose to coast over to the other side. Here another locomotive would take onwards the re-formed train.

Railway Defence against the Attack

In an attempt to minimise the loss of rolling stock and the goods in transit, CFR's policy was to move all made-up trains, which were in and around the Bucharest-Ploieşti area out of key yards and away from choke points, out into open country as soon as the 'general alarm' was given. That gave CFR about 45 minutes' notice. Priority for dispersal was given to oil, military and munitions trains. This practice was made easier because most air attacks were made at the same time of day or night.

Another interesting ruse to combat strafing by the daylight bombers' escorts was to position the locomotive in the middle of the train, in some cases camouflaging it to look like an ordinary rail wagon.

Danube Mining Successes

The Admiralty's Directorate of Torpedoes and Mining produced a brief report, 'The Mining of The Danube – Summer 1944' in January 1946, making a 'more or less final assessment' of the operations carried out by MASAF in the Danube. Mining was the principal attack used against Axis river traffic.

Strafing sweeps were also made by other aircraft. The more important ports which, in Romania, were Turnu Severin and Giurgiu were also bombed on a number of occasions by day and night. Other key ports attacked were at Vienna, Budapest and Belgrade.

The first mining operations in April had, apparently, caught the enemy unprepared: his mine-sweeping equipment was totally inadequate at that time. The result was that river traffic came to a halt over a greater part of the river and, although the Germans were able to organise their countermeasures within a few weeks, subsequent minelaying operations in May and June again increased his problems. Later mining was so intensified that it became impossible for the sweeping forces to meet the strain imposed upon them.

In this book's context, the transportation of Romanian produce and enemy military movements by river to support his operations in Moldavia are of primary interest. These, of course, came to an abrupt end on 23 August but the flow of material was such that it was some time after that before the loss of the Romanian and Bulgarian stretch of the Danube became finally evident.

The Allied Intelligence estimate was that between April and October 1944, minelaying operations in the Danube waterway caused at least a 60% reduction in priority river traffic. Ordinary commercial traffic suffered still more seriously to the extent of 'complete interdiction' of some categories of cargo. The Admiralty report particularly cites supply to the German armies in the south-east which almost entirely ceased. Axis troops defending the Galaţi gap were made short of supplies of every kind and, in the opinion of the *Wehrmachtstransportleitung*, mining of the river was one of the main reasons why the Germans failed to hold the Red Army in this sector that summer.

The effect on up-river traffic was at least equally great, and is illustrated by the following figures (in metric tons) of petroleum exports from Romania during 1944:

	Total rail and Danube exports	Exported via Danube	% of total exported Danube	Amount actually reaching Germany Austria and Slovakia via Danube
January	257,000	103,000	40%	96,000
February	248,000	117,000	47%	113,000
March	262,000	172,000	65%	134,000
April	137,000	90,000	65%	80,000
May	105,000	61,000	58%	21,000
June	100,000	31,000	32%	20,000
July	134,000	59,000	44%	39,000
August	84,000	33,000	39%	46,000

Ice usually brings river traffic to a standstill during January and February but in 1944 the weather was mild and traffic continued for most of these months. The figure for March actually gives a more accurate indication of the petroleum products the enemy planned to transport by river. There is evidence that the German military laid down a total of 200,000 tons as the monthly norm.

The fall in petroleum exports after March, shown in column one, was caused mainly by successful air attacks on Ploieşti, but . . .

> . . . it is quite clear that Allied mining seriously reduced the amount of petroleum products which actually reached Germany between mid-April and October 1944.

The comparatively high figure for April – 80,000 tons – was made possible by the fact that the river above Budapest was not mined at that time and the large number of tankers which had passed Budapest were thus able to continue to their destination without interference. It is worth mentioning that later in the summer the Czech tanker SDP 5, for example, took 125 days over the return voyage Giurgiu–Baja instead of the normal 35–40 days for the round trip Giurgiu–Vienna. The DDSG motor tanker 'Kainach' required 112 days for the latter round trip, and the Customs records at Turnu Severin suggest that the average time required by vessels laden with a priority cargo was well over 100 days. Reports from German, Austrian and Czech ports confirm that, in fact, very little river shipping succeeded in reaching the upper Danube after May.

Enemy Shipping Losses

	Passenger ships	Tugs	Motor Barges	Motor tankers	Barges	Tankers	Total
Mines	6	41	6	–	132	72	256
Bombing	5	11	–	2	174	51	243
Strafing	–	–	–	–	18	7	25
Total	11	52	6	2	324	129	524

The figures for barges and tankers include those seriously damaged, which later became total losses through inadequate salvage arrangements and the virtual impossibility of effecting repair.

Summary

The mining operations carried out by MASAF appear to have succeeded in their general objective, and the following particular results were obtained:

1. Enemy priority traffic was reduced by at least 60%.

2. The effect of the bombing offensive against German road and rail communications in south-eastern Europe was materially increased.

3. The supply of the German armies of the south-east was curtailed at a particularly important time.

4. A significant amount of German and/or German-controlled shipping was destroyed.

CHAPTER 15 - Life at Foggia

Flying

To summarise the deployment of 205 Group on the Foggia Plain:

1. 231 Wing and its two Squadrons, 37 and 70, were based throughout at Tortorella, also known as Foggia No 2.

2. 236 Wing, with 40 and 104 Squadrons, were at Foggia (Main) – the only permanent airfield of the group at the time.

3. 330 Wing – the 'inglese' new arrivals in the Group from north-west Africa, with 142 and 150 Squadrons, were based at first at Cerignola and Torretta (also known as Cerignola No 3), then Amendola, but moved to Regina, near San Severo, in July.

4. 240 Wing's heavies were at Celone, but 614 Squadron moved first to Stornara and later to Amendola, coming under command of 240 Wing on 15 July.

15 AF's Liberator Bomb Groups (BGs) were based largely on a more southern group of airfields: only a few were shared with 205 Group, whose partners were mainly Fortress BGs. 99 BG shared Tortorella with 231 Wing. Torretta was home to 461 and 484 BGs (B-24s). Amendola was shared with 2 and 97 BGs (both B-17s). 463 BG, also operating B-17s, was at Celone with 240 Wing, while 456 BG's B-24s were at Stornara. Although fighter squadrons seemed to use the bomber airfields, their bases were generally to the North of Foggia.

Living and operating conditions are unreservedly described as primitive. Aircrew conceded that their lot was better than that of the soldiers fighting to the north, but only just. Many compared their existence with that which they firmly believed to be enjoyed by their comrades in Bomber Command, but it was not usually with any sense of envy. It was more often with a sense of some pride in their more rugged way of life.

Members of 150 Squadron's ground crew pose with their 'Regina-pattern' bungalow. Improvements and timber by courtesy of the USAAF and disused bomb crates. Living conditions were a bit al fresco! (Courtesy IM Jones)

Len Fieldhouse recalled some of the confusions of flying at night from these airfields:

> . . . the only control at take-off was an Aldis lamp flashed by a sergeant housed in a caravan at the end of the runway. During an operation various coded messages were sent out by radio and consisted usually of TOT (time over target) and ETA (estimated time of arrival). Recalls were passed in this way. To assist in bad weather, the Army would put up a number of searchlight beams in a cone over our radio beacon. These could be seen through cloud. Landing instructions were passed by radio only when the aircraft was actually in the circuit. At times all the squadrons would arrive back at once and begin milling around the area, the circuits of some fields being 'opposed' to those of their neighbours. I saw two aircraft go down inflames and I, myself, missed another Wellington by feet while in the circuit. Of course, no navigation lights were shown – the enemy was not much more than 100 miles away. The take-offs of the various squadrons were at staggered times and it was hoped that they would not all arrive back together, but this was more of a pious hope! Even in daylight, control tended to be a bit rough and ready. My first arrival at Foggia coincided with the return of B-17s from a raid. I had permission to land from the American Air Traffic Controller and was on finals when I was literally elbowed out of the way by a stream of Fortresses landing on the parallel runway.

There were some aids to navigation and the system improved as the summer and the land battle developed. 'Occult' beacons flashed a single morse letter in white-light from sunset to sunrise daily. There were two in the Foggia area, 'B-Baker' on the coast north of Cerignola and 'F-Fox' inland south-east of Termoli. Len Fieldhouse had no recollection of using the 'Occult' lights, but he did remember:

> ... the 'Chance Light' which was a powerful white-light beam powered by a mobile generator and producing several million candlepower. It was positioned at the end of the runway to assist night landings and only used sparingly, as it could be seen for miles. Usually a pilot had to request it and it would only be switched on just before his touch-down to shine ahead of him down the line of the runway. The 'Pundit' was a mobile lamp system flashing two code letters in morse in red. They were placed some distance from the airfield at a bearing and distance from it notified to crews before take-off. In clear conditions it could be seen for 50 miles.

Four 'Pundits' were available, based one each at Amendola, Tortorella, Foggia Main and Termoli.

> 'Darky' was a radio service to give bearings and positions to lost aircraft. It had a very limited range. The drill was that a pilot, on discovering that he was lost, would call Darky – Darky' on his radio and leave the set at transmit for a brief time. At least three ground stations would triangulate his position from this transmitted signal and pass it to the pilot. Sounds simple but in practice it only had short range and was subject to interference.
>
> Incidentally, old hands never flew directly over these and other navigational aids because of possible congestion and the risk of lurking enemy fighters.

Allied fighters could cause excitement too. On arrival at Foggia, 70 Squadron's Wellingtons were parked either side of the landing strip awaiting proper dispersal. John Bodman recounted how:

> ... a trio of Mustangs came in to land in formation and one of them ran straight into a Wellington, slicing it neatly in half. The pilot stepped out of the wreckage and remarked 'I guess I just didn't see it!'

Re-fueling and maintenance on the taxiway at Cerignola in early 1944 before 330 Wing's move to Amendola. (Courtesy A.B. Harrison)

Wing Commander Dick Banker described the airfields:

> All except Foggia Main started out as single-strip airfields: running about north-south and made by US Army Engineers out of well-rolled local soft rock with pierced steel planking (PSP) on top. They were raised up about nine inches above the surrounding ground to keep them above water level in winter. At Tortorella the B-17 Fortresses of 99 BG were encamped on one side of the strip and our Wellingtons were on the other.
>
> USAAF ground crews began their daily inspections at about 0300 hours. It appeared to consist of belting-up all four engines in every aircraft. About an hour later the aircrews came out and did the same and then they taxi-ed out and took off. Somewhere around this time, our night-bomber force landed and taxied in. By about midday something like peace descended on the airfields, apart from an occasional air test. Then the Americans would land and taxi in and at about dusk 205 Group's aircraft would warm-up and take off and the whole cycle repeated itself again. All this on unpaved black cotton-soil and throughout the summer we lived in a permanent dust haze. No wonder it was known as 'Filthy Foggia'.

330 Wing did not use Cerignola for long and, from Ron Turner's description, it seems clear why.

> It had a fairly short and narrow runway and several aircraft had to swerve onto the taxiway at the end. One did not make it and finished up in the ditch. Another slid off the camber on take-off: a but un-nerving with a full bomb load.

150 Squadron's P for Peter bogged having run off the taxiway at Cerignola on return from an operation. (Courtesy A.B Harrison)

For Dennis Hurd there were problems even with the concrete runway at Foggia Main. After heavy use and allied air attacks it had broken up in places and had holes in it.

> At least the metal runways were whole, but they certainly moved a great deal when aircraft landed.

Another Foggia Main experience from Tom Parker, concerns the interminable problem of Wellington tyres:

> We had no less than three tyre checks between dispersal and the head of the runway – all done with an ordinary flashlight. On one occasion a Wellington taking off had a tyre burst. The undercarriage collapsed and friction and sparks caused the dope-soaked canvas skin to ignite. 'Abandon aircraft' was ordered and we all scampered to the slit trenches alongside the perimeter track while the aircraft, which were nose to tail, blew up one after the other, I witnessed the greatest display of pyrotechnics ever as we were pinned down while bomb loads, photo flashes, flares, fuel tanks and ammo were exploding in all directions. So a lack of supplies on this occasion caused more damage and havoc than all the enemy flak and night fighters could have done.

Peter Payne of 40 Squadron experienced this for himself. Foggia Main was littered with metal fragments:

. . . from its bombing and shelling by both sides . . .

He was a member of the crew of 'K-King' (JA 509) which had a full load of six 500 lb and six 250 lb bombs when a tyre burst. They managed to escape before it all exploded, but we were all burned.

Crash on Take-off – 'Ploughing'

When we flew across to Italy the weather behaved bitterly
And we hadn't got a single truck or tent.
So we commandeered a farm without the slightest qualm
When we heard the owner was a fascist gent.

Where the field had once been ploughed the Yankees did us proud
By carving out for us an instant strip.
But when we had some rain, back it went to plough again
And our undercarriage wheels began to slip.

We operated nightly but it got a bit unsightly
With the mudbound wrecks on each side of the run.
Taking off between the hulls and the wheeling clouds of gulls
Loaded up with bombs and petrol wasn't fun.

Standing in the wooden tower, feeling slightly drunk with power,
I was Officer in Charge of Ops one night
When a Wimpy opened wide, hit the mud along the side,
Collapsed his undercart and veered off right.

I thought it for the best when the aircraft came to rest
On our line with only fifty yards to spare.
We'd begun to breathe again when from underneath the plane
A great two-ton bomb came bouncing through the air.

Some fell flat upon the floor, others stuck right in the door.
To get to hell away the common aim.
The human logjam on the ladder simply couldn't have been gladder
When the almighty explosion never came.

The bomb stuck in a rut a few feet from our hut
And it seemed as if the safety fuse held good.
But when we gave it close inspection our ideas needed correction.
It was held safe by a small stray piece of wood.

Len Fieldhouse, *Foggia Plain*

Two views of 150 Squadron's HQ at Amendola. (Courtesy Wally Talbot)

Amendola became a permanent airfield and Derrick Burns of 150 Squadron flew over it after the war from the comfort of a Comet en route to a holiday in Corfu.

> It looked much the same with its parallel runways although these were clearly concrete now.

Sergeant Ieuan Jones recalled that:

> . . . the B-17s took off using both runways to speed up assembly in their formations, but only one of the runways was lit for night-flying. 150 Squadron's camp was 3 miles away on the side of a hill with the USAAF's bomb dump nearby. The constant stream of trucks ferrying bombs to the airfield raised clouds of dust, but the wooden crates were easily adapted to make beds.

142 Squadron's tent lines were pitched round a farmhouse taken over as a headquarters. Allen Harrison remarked that they lived very much as squadron families and saw little of 150 Squadron's aircrews, let alone those from other

squadrons. As a Pilot he found the steel mesh runways a bit tricky in wet weather because there was no grip.

An accident had grounded Tom Fannon and while awaiting his commission he was assigned to the 37 Squadron Intelligence Office. Tortorella airfield had been levelled out of a former olive grove and vineyard and its PSP runway was maintained by an American Advanced Service Park (ASP). The Squadron Commander was always at hand to see the bombers away and to argue with OC 70 Squadron as to which squadron would get the most 'tails up' – a singular point of honour and prestige. One pilot got a rocket for being late on getting his 'tail up'. The next time that pilot operated he held the brakes on so that he almost pranged his props. When he did release his brakes he was airborne in about 100 yards.

Returning safely was essentially the Wireless Operator's job, to get instructions for the pilot's final bearings as we neared home. Those of us up front would search for our searchlight cluster, known as Sandra Beacons. Ours was a trio of lights coned overhead at Tortorella. Foggia Main had two vertical lights and I think that Amendola was a solitary vertical beam.

In the early days, when a dawn intruder was still a possibility, we dispersed the aircraft round the so-called perimeter, but later on we just parked up behind each other and dispersed in the morning. There were no hangars at any of the airfields and our ground crews did sterling work in the conditions they had to work in but we could always rely on a maximum effort when it was called for.

Derek Cashmore, 70 Squadron, remembered that the main PSP runway at Tortorella was 2000 yards long and that there was a wide dirt 'runway' running parallel for 'belly' landings. On arrival over the airfield:

> . . . you flew along the runway line and flashed your recognition letter to the ground. If that was acknowledged a green light was flashed back and we would go round and come in to land. If a red was flashed back, you went round again and repeated the process.

There were hazards. Don Twigg, 70 Squadron, told of the bad luck of his colleague Bob Custance:

> . . . he hit the railway embankment at the end of the runway on landing one night. On another, he blew a tyre on take-off and ran over a fire tender. They all got out and ran away before it all blew up. One night, over Budapest, Bob collided with another aircraft and, although ten feet of port wing was chopped off, he limped home and landed safely. He was cited for his courage and airmanship. He was killed on the 6/7 July raid over Feuersbrunn.

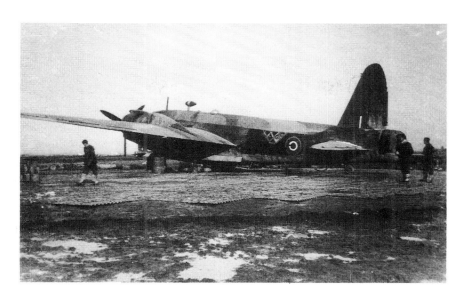

Wellington Mk X MF 475 'F for Freddy' at Tortorella of 70 Squadron at dispersal on a PSP island in the mud. The crew walking away from, Freddy's muddy belly are (L-R) Sergeant Price (Navigator), Flight Sergeant Sullivan (Pilot) and Sergeant West (Wireless Operator) Sergeant Cox (Air Gunner) is in the rear turret. Sergeant Derek Cashmore (Air Bomber) took the photo. (Courtesy Derek Cashmore)

614 Squadron's Halifax Mk II Series 1A 'F-Freddy' JN 978 at dispersal at Celone. Heavy rain quickly produced these giant pools of water on the compacted ground.
(Courtesy Imperial War Museum)

Bill Burcham remembered that the Americans would evacuate their quarters when the Wellingtons took off, after one had crashed on take-off and exploded at the end of the runway.

104 Squadron's LP 364 'M for Mother' is prepared for raid while her crew pose for a snap. On the left is John Elsmore RNZAF and on the right Bluey Cameron, a RAAF WO. Note at left a 4000 lb 'Cookie' waiting to be loaded and, beyond, the tail of a USAAF B-24 of 459 Bombardment Group, 5th Wing. (Courtesy I.R. Dobson)

Crash on Take-off – Four Minute Mile

The new and improved Wimpy gave the Wingco bright ideas.
He could load a few more bombs along the rack.
He could aggravate the Hun with an extra half a ton
And give the squadron that much more attack.

But our Teddy sort of rushed at things and didn't give much thought
To a runway lately carved from splintered rocks,
To synthetic rubber tyres which thwarted his desires
By exploding under extra take-off shocks.

To give all their due there was not a single crew
Who didn't want to give the thing a go.
But when the tyre went and the undercarriage bent
The engines would emit a nasty glow.

324

As she crunched along the ground the anxious aircrew found
They could leave the wreck in nearly record time.
As the bombs were lost in flames, even those 'not good at games'
Could emulate an athlete in his prime.

Four minutes was the guide, after which you all got fried
And separated into little bits.
So, dressed in all the gear you did your best to clear
A mile inside the time – or call it quits.

Len Fieldhouse, *Foggia*

A much decorated 42 operation veteran Wellington of 142 Squadron. The heraldry
suggests Australian and South African crew members. Two enemy fighters are claimed.
Note that the front turret is not in use in this aircraft and is taped up to reduce drag.
(Courtesy Noel Catherine)

Living

While some squadrons were more fortunate than others in their living
conditions, it was all sub-standard. Local improvements were the result of
individual initiatives and guile and, seemingly, not a little rivalry: keeping up
with the Joneses tented-style.

Sid Brownless RCAF of 614 Squadron recalls:

> We lived in tents which some of us had converted into huts . . . They were heated with a 5-gallon tin in which we burned fuel oil. The Squadron Adjutant learnt of some trucks being assembled at Brindisi so, on stand-downs, I would go off with a driver to pick up the material which had been used in shipping these vehicles. Our first project was an Airmen's Mess, then a theatre, then the Sergeants' Mess and finally, our Mess. By the time I left the Squadron, we had a wooden floor and sidewalls with a canvas tent roof.

Living conditions at Foggia airfields tended towards the primitive! Here is a 178 Sqn ground staff shack at Amendola. The oil-fired heating is prominent in the background. (Courtesy Bill Littlemore)

George Carrod in 142 Squadron believed that:

> . . . compared with the USAAF, life was pretty grim; we had a small ridge tent for five of us to sleep in, you either slept on the floor or made your own bed. I managed to find two planks of wood which I balanced on two

empty ammo boxes using my parachute as a pillow. I later managed to find a stretcher from a blown-up Red Cross vehicle. We had no toilets, facilities for washing were non-existent and most of us went down with dysentery or jaundice but morale was very high. I do not think that, had we had to bale out, our 'chutes would have opened as they were never checked or re-packed. In fact one pilot refused to fly for that reason and was promptly court-martialled for Lack of Moral Fibre (LMF).

Don Twigg recalls:

> At Tortorella, 37 Squadron were camped in an olive grove and we (70 Squadron) camped nearby in a wheatfield . . . The Italian olive pickers started work at dawn singing operatic arias which were not appropriate after flying all night. The only way to shut them up was to discharge a .38 into the trees . . .
>
> One day, sitting on the loo in our wheatfield, an old Iti turned up trying to sell us eggs and oranges – when we had our duds down! Another day there was a loud bang as one of these local women trod on a butterfly bomb which Jerry had left for us. We spent the next few days looking for more.

Even though Foggia Main was a 'permanent' airfield, aircrew living conditions were the same as in the other squadrons. Dennis Hurd of 104 Squadron:

> Sudden summer thunder storms were not uncommon and on one occasion every tent was flooded. This was unfortunate because in some cases crew had dug out the ground beneath the tent to give extra headroom. They suffered soaked possessions more than others.

Peter Bath quoted a different 104 Squadron experience in the late spring.

> All of our tents were in a bad way, old and tattered and our ground crews were worse off than we were. Then one day new EPIP tents arrived – a much better design – and were erected. But – believe it or not – not one officer, WO, NCO or other rank was allowed to use them. They also appeared on other Wing sites and we were told that they were for the use of aircrews 'shuttle-bombing' from their UK bases. They never came and the tents eventually disappeared back into their unknown stores depots. Not, however, on 70 Squadron where the 'irks' captured them for their own use and only gave them up after a special promise from the CO that he would do something about it.

Living conditions on the Foggia airfields were a little primitive. Sgt Joe Thurston RAAF finishes his lunch outside the tent while a homemade bed gets an airing.
(Courtesy A.B. Harrison)

For 37 Squadron at Tortorella, at least, accommodation for the officers was a little different. Bill Burcham recalled that their quarters were in a *casa cantoniera* at the roadside and in a vineyard owner's house opposite.

> I sketched a well from my room which was in an old stable inches deep in DDT powder as there were bugs.

Feeding must surely stand as an equal with housing in any military morale context and, at the Foggia airfields, that was generally sub-standard too. If any blame attached to that, most would agreed that it was to the resources, equipment and rations and not to the cooks and their helpers.

Ieuan Jones of 150 Squadron summed it up well:

> . . . the diet was adequate but boring. The food was prepared in a Field Kitchen (oil/sand and metal grill) and there was much reliance on fried corned beef and Spam, supplemented by private venture eggs (swopped with the locals for cigarettes). The cooks had an inexhaustible supply of tea – dark brown, well-stewed with condensed milk. Thus, after night-flying, breakfast was always available!

A covered well in a Tortella farmyard where 37 Squadron had its Officers' Mess. A sketch by Bill Burcham from his room.

Tom Fannon of 37 Squadron explained some improvements:

> The food was mostly from dehydrated concoctions of potatoes, onions and even meat. Later on, unofficially, we made a deal with one of the nearby American Messes. We exchanged our 'hard liquor' ration for US delicacies such as tinned chicken, ham and a twice daily offering of doughnuts – a change much appreciated.

Alcohol was in limited supply, indeed, some veterans spoke of having none at all at the airfields. From others there were dark mutterings of the old aircrew advice 'eight hours from bottle to throttle' to caution would-be drinkers. But it was not all a world of abstinence. Ron Turner remembered that local wine was bought by the cask and it was sold for a penny for a large glass in the Mess. What beer they did have was passed to the ground crews. In 614 Squadron, Hugh Fleckney thought that the drinks 'were limited in range. Locally made 'Cognac' and 'Vermouth' were the mainstays.'

Barter was widely employed to improve the airmen's lot. Peter Bath of 104 Squadron knew of an American who reportedly surrendered a Jeep for a bottle of Scotch but not on 104 Squadron!

Their practice was to send:

> transport into the hills laden with soap, chocolate, tins of bully beef and
> cigarettes to barter.

It seemed to succeed well.

The variety of uniforms worn by British and Commonwealth servicemen
in the Mediterranean Theatre has become almost legendary. By all accounts
members of 205 Group contributed to the legend in good measure. Even before
individual touches were added, there were some wide national differences
which, Len Fieldhouse believed, puzzled people.

> The RAAF battledress was a much deeper blue than ours. Most people
> tried to beg, borrow or steal an RNZAF battledress because it was made of
> finer material and was khaki. That seemed more appropriate for a stroll in
> the desert or even the southern European plains. The South Africans also
> wore khaki. The RAF's blue was too near to field grey to be worn in
> comfort in partisan country.

Relaxation

Dennis Hurd (104 Squadron) and his friends used to walk into Foggia for some
refreshment on some afternoons. After a whole there was a Malcolm Club
there.

> Some evenings we went to San Severo, where there was a theatre, to see an
> ENSA show. I even saw an opera there. On occasion we were transported
> in a 'Liberty Truck' but more usually we thumbed a lift from any passing
> service vehicle.

For Donald Twigg there was the beach at Manfredonia.

> In the summer a truck was laid on to take us there for the afternoon. It was
> nothing to see a hundred naked men and still the old Iti women trying to
> flog their oranges and eggs.

And Peter Payne remembered

> the rest camp at Rodi on the Manfredonia peninsula reached after a long
> and dusty journey in the back of a truck. We made occasional trips into
> Barletta where there was nothing much to do and once we went duck
> shooting on an Italian Count's estate near Rodi.

Spring of 1944 and the officers of 142 Squadron posed with an ENSA party outside their Mess at Amendola. Kay Cavendish is seated in the centre and Florence Desmond is sitting one from the right, next to Wing Commander Angus MacLean. The tallest figure in the back row is Lieutenant Noel Cathrine and Captain Macdonald is on his right. Sir Henry Calley, President of the 205 Group Reunion is standing fourth from the left. (Courtesy Angus MacLean)

One of Hugh Fleckney's abiding memories is of the open-air camp cinema at Celone.

> The introductory music was always *Rhapsodie Espagnol* which was played in march time. It remains a most evocative piece for me. We also had a few live shows – I can't remember much of them except a hard-working Yank comic who sang a song entitled 'Who threw his overalls in Mrs Murphy's chowder?' I also recall the pressing need to learn the reply to the challenge of Yank sentries, who were pretty quick on the trigger.

Leave at Sorrento

Many airmen were able to take a break at the RAF's leave hotel at Sorrento – the Hotel Minerva. Dennis Hurd pointed out that it had been used by the Germans for the same purpose not many months before. For Donald Twigg it represented

> nine hours of hitch-hiking but worth it – real beds too!

Derrick Burns of 150 Squadron enjoyed a break there:

> . . . and had it on good authority from a holidaying relative that the hotel withstood the onslaught of frustrated aircrew and is still open to visitors.

No 2 RAF Rest Camp, Sorrento
The Officers' Club (Courtesy of James Grieve)

No 2 RAF Rest Camp, Sorrento
The Beach (Courtesy James Grieve)

Perhaps the best account is from Bob Ives also from 150 Squadron.

> The Hotel overlooked the bay – we just had to walk down some steps across the road and we were into the sea. During the day we just wore shorts and sandals but for dinner, at seven o'clock, we had to change into uniform. The meals were very good. There was always plenty of fruit and a maid brought us a cup of tea in the morning. The first few days were spent sightseeing in the town. We visited the local workshops where they made us jewellery boxes with the Squadron crest on. We also bought boxes of nuts, gave them our home addresses, paid them and asked them to send them home for us. They were certainly honest because they all arrived home safely.
>
> Some nights after dinner we changed out of our uniforms into khaki jackets and shorts and went to the dances on the patio. The roof was covered with grapes which we could reach and the young Italian girls taught us to dance the Tarantella, (the girls being between 12 and 14 years of age).
>
> After one glorious week we were taken back to Regina to get our clearance from 150 Squadron. We saw most of our pals and then – one more crew had finished their tour.

Morale

It would be tempting to assume that given all the adverse conditions in which the squadrons lived and the hostile environment where they work-ed, morale would suffer. No report bore that out in any way: quite the contrary.

For Hugh Fleckney:

> . . . morale was generally very high and there were, with a few exceptions, excellent relationships in 614 Squadron with our officers and with our ground crews. The latter could be a pretty hard-bitten bunch at times: most had been with the Squadron since Western Desert days. When I was commissioned, conditions did not change much, except that I was issued with a camp kit, which was very useful.

Sid Brownless agreed that morale on 614 Squadron was good. He also cited the long-serving and patient ground crew.

Some of 178 Sqn's original groundstaff photographed at Amendola in the sunshine of the spring of 1944. (Courtesy Bill Littlemore)

Dennis Hurd's illustration of good morale on 104 Squadron was simply stated:

> . . . although after 36 operations I had had enough, within a short time I should have been pleased to go back to another tour of operations.

However, Tom Parker, also of 104 Squadron, had reservations on morale.

> Frequently we would return from ops to find tents flooded and personal belongings awash or lost. Sandfly fever and dysentery added to the general discomfort.

Peter Payne of 40 Squadron thought that

> morale was pretty good and there was a feeling that we had a good chance of completing our tour. The weather and poor navigation were more likely to get us than flak or fighters.

Derrick Burns of 150 Squadron learned the true meaning of *esprit de corps*. He rated the Squadron's morale as magnificent; crews tended to fly their operations in one aircraft and kept:

. . . very close contact with the fitters responsible for that aircraft. The level of serviceability, achieved under their primitive working conditions and with very inadequate facilities, was nothing short of miraculous. During our tour we did not experience one engine failure or other component in flight and never had any doubts about making it there and back.

Groundcrew of A Flight 70 Squadron pose together at Tortorella in the Summer of 1944. 'A for Apple' provides the backdrop. (Courtesy Derek Cashmore)

Tom Fannon of 37 Squadron illustrated the importance of leadership and example in maintaining high morale which:

. . . was a little down as we joined the Squadron, but on the arrival of a new Wing Commander, Henry Langton (later to be Sir Henry Calley) this rose rapidly. A local farmhouse (of the Mussolini Regime) was taken over for a Mess bar and a heated room for our flying clothing. I remember asking if we could organise a football team to play the other Squadrons – next thing I knew I was on my way to Naples to collect all the equipment possible.

And – not the least of the reasons for good feeling, in fact a real reason, was the work of our Padre, Rev A.B. Jestice. Off the record he must have flown on many 'ops', as quite often he would say 'put a 'chute in for me tonight'. He was responsible for a lot of the improvements – so much so that I know that his care and understanding resulted in one of our wireless operators receiving the DFM. He did this, ran Musical Appreciation evenings and organised electricity for our tents.

There were some instances where superstition helped to maintain morale – the 'rabbit's foot syndrome'. George Carrod's view as a 142 Squadron Air-Bomber was typical.

> I remember that there was a lot of dysentery about but none of us would go sick . . . we thought it unlucky to fly without all the crew being together.

Sid Brownless put another slant on it.

> After joining the Squadron, our Pilot, Dave North, developed an inner-ear problem and was grounded. The crew split up. The pilot of the one I joined was having a hard time keeping a crew together because of his press-on tactics. He was a good pilot but, unfortunately, he went round the bend. So – I completed my tour with anyone who needed a spare Bomb-Aimer or H_2S operator.

Lack of Moral Fibre

One of the many personal tragedies in war is the individual fighting man's private struggle with fear. This is not the place to consider or discuss the matter in any depth. There are many theories and there have been – and always will be – endless pronouncements on cowardice. The failure of a man under these pressures goes under some extraordinary names but this story's contemporary tag was 'lack of moral fibre' or LMF. There was almost no defence from the accusation and a man whose courage had failed him was surely his own worst advocate. Many lives were wrecked and the whole subject produced very heated emotions.

> Who really showed LMF between:
> 1. one fit young man who volunteered for aircrew and whose nerve failed and
> 2. one fit young man who volunteered for ground duty and a safe life?

asked a Sergeant Pilot in a Wellington Squadron. George Carrod of 142 Squadron remembers the night

> when we were all lined up for take-off and inching our way forward. The pilot in front of us pulled the wrong lever and his wheels began to come up. The plane settled on the runway like a great swan. He was court-martialled for LMF.

Sir Henry Calley, who commanded 37 Squadron handled the case of a Flying Officer Air Bomber who found himself at the bottom of the Danube with a dislocated shoulder when doing a low-level mining mission.

> Luckily the current took him to the Yugoslav side of the river and he joined up with his crew. He got back to his own Squadron and then came over to me on 37 Squadron because he had fallen out with his CO. He had made a fairly reasonable request that, when he returned from his three weeks' leave, he would do one or two high-level attacks before reverting to mining. His CO took a dim view and talked of LMF. I was short of a bomb-aimer and asked for him to be posted to me to finish his tour and he made no more low-level attacks.

Medals

There was some ill-feeling that the Aircrew Europe Medal was not awarded for operations over the Continent undertaken from Mediterranean bases. One RAAF Pilot of 70 Squadron put it:

> Looking back, a lot of bods gave their lives and when one looks at it today, one sometimes wonders why. No recognition was ever given, yet I flew my bomber over nine European countries on operations.

An RAF 104 Squadron Navigator added,

> I must admit to a little bitterness at the time and consequently I have never applied for the medals which were due to me.

Others felt the same.

Relations with the Americans

The thread which has run through personal accounts of these far-off days is one of good relations and some firm friendships between the principal allies, on the ground and elsewhere – in the prison camps, with the partisans or with the Chetniks. There was an understandable sense of rivalry, but equally there was considerable mutual respect. No examples of jealousy or rancour about the superior living and working conditions which American servicemen enjoyed came to notice. Perhaps it was because 'being overpaid and over-sexed' did not matter much in the circumstances and, as to 'over here' , – all were in the same boat.

Navigator Peter Bath of 104 Squadron thought that:

> . . . it would be unfair not to mention the help we received from our US Allies. On one occasion we had to land at a US airfield because of a fuel shortage and we were promptly filled up and given an excellent breakfast. They showed great interest in the Wellington and were amazed how we had managed to find a target at night. Later we were serviced and fed by them again in Corsica. They were very courteous and obliging.

Wing Commander Angus MacLean, commanding 142 Squadron:

> . . . spent a short leave in the late summer of 1944 at the USAAF Aircrew Rest and Leave Centre in the hills in the toe of Italy. The place was called Villagio Mancuso, not far from Catanzaro at an altitude of 1300 metres. I went there with Group Captain A.H. Smythe who was at the time the RAF LO with HQ 15 AF. He and I had served together on the same squadron in Norfolk in the winter of 1940/41. During our stay the Russians captured the Romanian oilfields and we became involved in a great party. In view of the casualties which they had taken in their raids on those targets, you can imagine that large quantities of alcohol were consumed at the party.

At airfield level, relations seemed to be based mainly on the barter worth of rations and drink, and whisky clearly rated highly.

The memories of George Dalgliesh, Air Gunner with 178 Squadron, are gastronomic.

> Occasionally we were invited over to 98 Bomb Group's parachute silk festooned mess in which we indulged in icecream, real fruit juice and table tennis. Their hospitality was tremendous. They also arranged for Joe Louis to include us in his exhibition tour.

Mediterranean Allied Air Forces (MAAF)
Mediterranean Allied Strategic Air Force (MASAF)
Fifteenth Air Force (15 AF)
205 Group RAF

AIR CINC MAAF	Lt Gen Ira C. Eaker
DEP AIR CINC MAAF and CINC RAF ME	AM Sir John Slessor KCB DSO MC
CG 15 AF	Maj Gen Nathan F. Twining USAAF
RAF Staff Officers	Gp Capt J.A. Powell DSO OBE RAF
	Gp Capt A.H. Smythe DSO DFC RAF
AOC 205 GP	Air Cdre J.H.T. Simpson DSO RAF
	Brig J.T. Durrant CB DFC SAAF (from 3 Aug 44)
SASO	Gp Capt D.I.P. McNair RAF
	Gp Capt L.E. Jarman DFC RAF (from 19 Jun 44)
231 Wing 37 Sqn	Gp Capt P.R. Beare DSO DFC RAF
	Wg Cdr R.P. Widdowson DFC (from 22 Apr 44)
	Sqn Ldr P.E.B. Forsyth DFC (temp from 28 Aug 44)
	Wg Cdr Henry Langton DSO DFC (later Sir Henry Calley) (from 12 Sept 44)
70 Sqn	Wg Cdr C.P. Barber DFC
	Wg Cdr R.R. Banker DSO DFC (from 27 Jun 44)
236 Wing 40 Sqn	Gp Capt P.I. Harris DFC
	Wg Cdr J.D. Kirwan DFC (from Mar 44 but Sqn Ldr C.F. Mervyn Jones DFC was Acting OC from mid-Apr to 24 Aug because Kirwan was ill)

104 Sqn	Wg Cdr H.G. Turner DSO DFC (from 2 Dec 43)
	Wg Cdr C.F. Mervyn-Jones DFC (from 31 Oct 44)
330 Wing 142 Sqn	Gp Capt J.C. Morris
	Wg Cdr A.R. Gibbs RAAF
	Wg Cdr A.G.C. MacLean (from 29 Mar 44)
150 Sqn	Wg Cdr E.R.A. Walker (from 26 May 44)
240 Wing 31 Sqn (SAAF)	Gp Capt J.J. McKay DSO DFC RNZAF
	Lt Col D.U. Nel DFC SAAF
178 Sqn	Wg Cdr Donald Smythe DSO GM
614 Sqn	Wg Cdr J.S. Laird

APPENDIX 2 - The Aircraft

A summary of the performance and capabilities of the aircraft involved

Performance figures quoted are typical and would almost certainly vary, particularly with weather conditions, from one machine of the same type to another.

Luftwaffe, FARR and Bulgarian Air Force

Type	Maximum Speed (at about 20,000')	Ceiling	Rate of Climb (time-height)	Armament
Junkers (Ju) 88	347 mph	33,200'	10 to 18,500'	7 x 7.9 mm 3 x 20 mm
Messerschmitt (Me) Bf 109 G	400 mph	39,750'	6 to 19,000'	2 x 7.9 mm 3 x 20 mm
Messerschmitt (Me) Bf 110 G	368 mph	36,800'	7 to 18,000'	6 x 7.9 mm 4 x 20 mm

No 205 Group

Type	Maximum Speed (mph at height)	Ceiling	Range and typical load (miles-lbs)	Armament
Halifax Mk II Series 1a	264 at 18,000'	21,000'	1,900–7,000 (but 13,000 lbs max)	8 x .303-in
Liberator B Mk 6	270 at 26,000'	27,000'	2,290–4,000 or 990–12,800	10 x .50-in
Wellington Mk 10	255 at 14,500'	18,250'	1,885–1,500 or 1,325–4,500	6 x .303-in*

*In the Wellington Squadrons of 205 Group many crews removed the 2 nose turret guns leaving only the 4 in the rear turret.

The aircrews' views and memories of their bombers are a valid element of this account.

The Halifax

As 205 Group's Target Marking Force (TMF) – or Pathfinders – 614 Squadron flew Halifax Mark II Series 1A equipped with the H_2S centimetric radar in a ventral dome. It was the first type to carry this radar.

The Halifax was a formidable deliverer of bombs and much respected by its crews. It had bomb cells in the wing centre sections as well as in the fuselage giving a total lift of 13,000 lbs over a range of 1,770 kilometres (about 1,100 miles).

It was powered by four liquid-cooled Merlin XXII engines, each delivering nearly 1,400 hp but which were rated by some to be only just tough enough for the job. Nevertheless, a speed of 264 mph at 18,000 feet compared very well with its rivals over its full range. There were some over-heating problems in the airless summer heat but they never reached the state of the Luftwaffe's Bf 109s. Frequently they had to be towed to the end of the runway, to be started for an immediate take-off – or the glycol coolant would boil.

Later Series 1As were fitted with larger tail fins which improved stability and, consequently, bombing accuracy.

The front turret had been removed from this version, being replaced by a smooth perspex nose-dome with a single hand-operated .303-in Vickers K machine gun. The mid-upper turret was a four-gun .303-in Browning Defiant type and the rear turret also had four .303-in Brownings.

Warrant Officer Hugh Fleckney flew Halifaxes throughout and gained a great respect for them.

> I reckoned, probably erroneously, that if I saw a fighter first, I had a good chance of evading his attack due to the manoeuvrability of the Halifax. They were also very strongly built: I survived a mid-air collision in one and I have seen another that had been hit by a rocket and had an enormous hole in the fuselage – and had come home.

Flight Lieutenant Sid Brownless RCAF recalls simply:

> I did my first tour of ops in the Halifax Mk 2 and my second on the Liberator Mk 6. I preferred the Halifax by far.

Flight Sergeant D.C. Hurd flew Halifaxes for a short time.

The general feeling in the RAF was that the Lancaster was a superior aircraft, but I do not think we as a crew had any complaints about the Halifax.

Lancasters did not operate in the Mediterranean so its 'rivalry' with the Halifax was not a regular feature of professional debate.

Flying Officer Tom Scotland RAAF remembers a Halifax returning to base with the body riddled from the wing trailing edge rearwards.

How the tail-plane and rear turret hung on is a mystery. A night-fighter's cannon shells had found their mark.

He related the experience of a colleague, Flight Sergeant Claude Caldwell-Wearne RAAF shot down raiding Ploieşti on 9/10 August and who probably owed his life to the robust construction of the aircraft. Tom Scotland felt that they found it

generally able to take a bashing and keep going. One crash we had, the body broke behind the wing but the rest stayed together in the ripping and tearing of the crash.

The Liberator B Mk VI

By the middle of 1944 the Liberator was widely used in British and Commonwealth hands, particularly in the MTO. In Britain its principal role was with Coastal Command. It was only used as a night-bomber in the Mediterranean with 205 Group in MASAF. RAF and SAAF Liberators were commonly flown by a smaller crew than the nine or ten of the USAAF. A B-24 could be flown (as distinct from fought) by two or three men. The RAF habitually deleted waist and nose gunners as being of little value in night operations and second pilots were often dispensed with, the right-hand seat being taken by the Flight Engineer. In the USAAF the Flight Engineer fought in the top turret just abaft the cockpit.

Sergeant George Dalgliesh, a Rear Gunner of 178 Squadron, was very happy to fly in Liberators:

. . . it was a fine aircraft and comfortable to a degree after the OTU Wellington. It did everything we asked of it regarding fire-power, 'corkscrew evasion' and taking severe flak punishment well.

Squadron Leader Ron Turner, 150 Squadron, who had started on Wellingtons, found the difference remarkable:

> . . . 22,000 feet was no trouble: they were faster and had better heating.

He remembers that:

> we did have trouble with exhaust flames which showed up at night. We tried fitting flame suppressors but they decreased speed and sometimes made it difficult to get off the ground.

Warrant Officer Hugh Fleckney, 614 Squadron, which later in the war flew Liberators, also comments on the exhaust flame being visible for miles. The turbo-supercharger discs glowed red and there were sometimes a lot of sparks. He thought these may have accounted for a number of losses of Liberators to night-fighters which could home-in on this tell-tale from a long way off.

Len Fieldhouse of 150 Squadron observed:

> . . . we were supposed to fly in the stream with the Liberators but our Wellingtons could not attain their height, nor speed. They suffered badly from night-fighter attacks as they were not built for night-bombing and had a bright flame visible from the exhausts.

Flight Sergeant C. Con Leahy of 178 Squadron was not so euphoric about the B-24. He thought his Squadron's aircraft were all re-built American cast-offs and were slow and cumbersome. No one else made this point so strongly. Of the three types used, he would prefer the Halifax.

Wing Commander Dick Banker, OC 70 Squadron, described the Liberator well:

> The engines were 1200 hp Pratt and Witneys with turbo superchargers. It had four twin-gunned powered turrets and two free guns at the waist positions: all .5-inch Browning machine guns. The aircraft was very sensitive to its centre of gravity and the ventral (ball) turret was often removed to move the CG further forward.
>
> It was modified many times to meet changing operating conditions and like all such aircraft it grew steadily heavier. The Liberators we flew were from the vast Ford factories at Willow Run, near Detroit. They could not take off or climb as well as some models made by the Consolidated Aircraft Company. Nevertheless, it was a good and serviceable aircraft and we grew to like its sturdy reliability and the excellence of its equipment.

The crews for all RAF four-engined bombers at this time did their operational training on Wellingtons, after which they did a short conversion course on the type of aircraft they were to fly. The Liberator was the only one with tricycle and undercarriage (nose-wheel instead of tail-wheel), but since OTUs had given up teaching the tail-down three-point landing, in favour of a powered approach, letting the aircraft sink on to the main-wheels only, crews had no difficulty with this type of landing in a Liberator. RAF heavy bombers were designed to be flown by one pilot, on the basis of only 500 hours' pilot-training per aircraft being available. It was better to have one pilot with 500 hours' flying than two pilots each with 250 hours. The Liberator was designed for two pilots and the Americans and South Africans flew them with two. The RAF flew them with one.

The Liberator had, perhaps, one fault that it could not be 'ditched' satisfactorily because the bomb-doors collapsed on impact and the water had direct access to the rear of the fuselage.

Petrol capacity was 2,250 gallons with a further 350 gallons in wing-tip tanks feeding to the main tanks. Additional overload tanks totalling about 700 gallons could be fitted into the bomb-bays. The aircraft consumed about 200 gallons per hour at 200 mph.

Some of the excellent and unusual equipment with which it was fitted was:

1. The Auxiliary Power Unit (APU) to make the Liberator independent of ground power supplies. This was a built-in generating set with an electric-start 2-stroke engine. It provided enough power to energise the starters of the main engines. The APU was kept running while taxi-ing and it provided plenty of power for the hydraulic brake booster-pump, radio, supercharger, controls, lights, cowling gills etc. Used in conjunction with the electric fuel pumps, the aircraft could even refuel itself from drums of fuel.

2. The Minneapolis-Honeywell Automatic Pilot was far and away better than any auto-pilot we had seen to date. It was remarkably accurate, and at the turn of a very small knob would do beautifully banked turns of almost any rate. The aircraft could be landed with it and it was later used for experimental automatic landings. The sensitivity on all planes could be adjusted.

3. The main fire-risk on any aircraft and its main vulnerability was the mixture of petrol-vapour and air in its tanks. The Liberator had its fuel in groups of collapsible cells, without air vents, which subsided as the fuel was pumped out of them. This very much reduced the

345

fire-risk, as did the flexible hoses through which the fuel was pumped.

4. The Radio Compass gave the best presentation of radio direction-finding to date. It comprised a simple tuning-knob in the roof and a large compass-rose dial above the centre of the instrument panel. This had a single needle which pointed to the station to which it was tuned. It would home the aircraft to right overhead of the transmitting mast.

5. The Radar Altimeter was sensitive and accurate and very useful for flying over mountainous country. Although there must have been a thousand aircraft a day flying over Southern Italy there was no 'Let-Down' system whatsoever. By the use of GEE, the radio compass and the radar altimeter, Liberator crews could do their own 'let-downs' with a reasonable degree of safety.

6. At a time when most RAF aircraft had wheel-brake linings that 'faded' after a few hours' use and which were operated by compressed air, the supply of which was rarely adequate, it was a pleasure to have hydraulic wheel-brakes of such power and reliability as the Liberator's. These were toe operated and if the need arose, they could grind this heavy aircraft to a standstill in a remarkably short distance. Hydraulic pressure was maintained whilst taxi-ing by an automatic electric booster-pump which took power from the APU.

The Liberators were returned to the Americans late in 1945 under reverse Lease/Lend agreements and we were sorry to see them go. They were ponderous and heavy to fly and they may have lacked some of the agility of the Lancaster, but their serviceability was high, they were reliable and well-equipped and we grew to like these qualities.

The Wellington

Like so many others, Flight Lieutenant Ivan Dobson of 104 Squadron flew all his operations in Wellingtons. He thought:

. . . they were a good aircraft, very hardy and could come back shot-up quite badly. As long as there was fabric on the main plane and the tail, it usually managed to get down.

Halifax Mk 2.

1. Pilot
2. Engineer
3. Wireless Operator
4. Navigator (faces port side)
5. Bomb Aimer
6. & 7. Gunner

B24 Liberator

1. Pilot
2. 2nd Pilot
3. Navigator
4. Bomb Aimer also acted
   as Front Gunner
5. Wireless Operator
6. Top Turret Gunner/Engineer
7. Waist Gunners
8. Rear Gunner
9. Ball Gunner
   (not always on RAF planes)

Vickers Wellington. Crew positions 1943-5

1. Pilot
2. Wireless Operator
3. Navigator (faces left)
4. Rear Gunner
5. Bomb Aimer
   (also acted as Front Gunner)

Flight Sergeant Tom Parker also of 104 Squadron remarked that the Americans 'regarded the Wimpey with awe.' In his opinion:

> . . . prejudiced or not, it was one of the finest and most versatile aircraft of the war.

Another 104 Squadron pilot, Flight Sergeant Dennis Hurd, was:

> . . . happy to fly in it. The strength and superior construction . . . was demonstrated when one of our aircraft returned minus its rear turret, which did not seem to upset the flying performance in any way. Regrettably, the gunner was lost with his turret.

Flight Sergeant Derrick Burns of 150 Squadron felt that most crews had a deep affection for the Wellington although he was sure that:

> . . . they longed for a modern Lancaster or Halifax with their four engines and better operational speeds, heights and bombloads. Many became frustrated with the comparatively small bombload, on the grounds that they were often not worth the risk involved.

Flight Sergeant Peter Bath, 104 Squadron cited simply that:

> . . . only one early return in 33 operations is a good enough example of the Wellington's reliability.

He rated shortages of spares and assemblies as the greatest cause of unserviceability. Flying Officer A.R. Harrison RNZAF, 142 Squadron, remembered that the older Mk IIIs which had been modified to lift the 4000 lb bomb 'Cookie' were not as fast as other Marks because the bomb doors had been removed, leaving the bomb protruding.

Flight Sergeant Tom Fannon, 37 Squadron, observed that:

> . . . taking off with one of these 4000 lb bombs aboard was a little tricky as was flying back with the bomb gone.

He was very attached to the type and declined to attend a Liberator conversion course in the Delta.

Harrison concluded that the Mark X was safe and reliable:

. . . a good one would cruise at 150 mph with a full load and manage 170 on the return empty.

Flying Officer Bill Burcham, a 37 Squadron pilot, described the heating system as:

> . . . rather primitive and it was virtually impossible to maintain a temperature to suit all the crew. If the pilot was happy, the wireless operator and the navigator would be overheated.

He also remembered that the aircraft was:

> . . . heavy to handle and quite tiring after a long trip. The automatic pilot was unpredictable and rarely used. The intercom could also be patchy and, on my 21st birthday, failed altogether. We went over the target with the bomb-aimer guiding me by raising one or both of his legs as he lay prone at his bomb sight.

Sergeant Ieuan Jones, 150 Squadron, recalled some:

> . . . inflammatory tendencies.

He praised the Hercules engines, remarking that:

> . . . they would take the aircraft off at 105 mph with a run of 1,200–1,500 yards with a full load.The controls were fairly heavy but could be trimmed to fly 'hands off'.

Wing Commander Dick Banker, OC 70 Squadron, also extolled the two Bristol Hercules 18s which could . . .

> . . . deliver 1650 hp each and had two-speed superchargers, giving maximum power at 7,000 feet and 14,000 feet with that amount of power they took off and climbed well. The maximum all-up weight (AUW) was 36,000 lb at which, with full main tanks, the aircraft could carry 4,500 lb of bombs, plus guns, ammo, etc. For shorter trips we reduced the fuel load and carried up to 6,500 lb of bombs. For longer trips, overload tanks were carried.

Blackout or concealment in the darkness of the night is important for a night-bomber. The darker the night, generally, the safer the bomber, but, equally, the greater the need for the pilot to be able to fly on his instruments. He had to be able to see and read them. These conflicting interests were met in the Mk X Wellington by using an ultra-violet light source. This was fitted behind the pilot's shoulder from where it played on and illuminated the white, slightly luminous paint on the instrument panel, without ruining the pilot's natural vision when he came to look up and outwards into the night sky beyond.

Squadron Leader Ron Turner RAAF, a Navigator of 150 Squadron, although preferring his later Liberator, boasted proudly that the Wellington:

> . . . could take a beating and still fly home, although in a panic dive, with indicated air speed off the clock, there was a tendency for some of the fabric to peel off. Many were under-powered when fully laden and unable to clear obstacles such as the Alps en route to Munich.

APPENDIX 3 - Record of Aircraft and Crews Lost

Date	Target	Sqn	Aircraft	Crash Site	Fate of Crew Captain (bold type) († = Captain Survived Crash)
14 Apr 1944	Mining the Danube	178	EV 825 'D'	On take-off	**10 Killed –** **Lt H.E. Rogan (SAAF)** Sgt D.A. Bennett Sgt B.E. Hart Sgt J.C.W. Martin Sgt J. Atkinson Sgt G.H. Evans Sgt J.B. Baskerville
		178	EV 920 'R'		**Lt K. Shaw (SAAF)** Sgt R.H. Birch WO M.R. Wishak
15/16 Apr	Turnu Severin	104	LP 146 'A'	Collided over base on return	**10 Killed –** **Sgt V.R. Chadwick** Sgt D.J. Corlyon Sgt J.S. Beeley Sgt F. Ashbee Sgt J.W.H. Rimmer
		104	HE 344 'U'		**FS F.W. Gissing** FS E.N. Emberson Sgt G.B. Hall Sgt J. Bunyen Sgt R.D. Cunningham
3/4 May	Bucharest	150	HE 956 'N'	Not known	**All 5 became PW –** **FS K. Hinchcliffe†** 2 Lt C.B. Franz (SAAF) Sgt C.W. Finlayson Sgt T.G. Lindsay Sgt J.S. Walker

Date	Target	Sqn	Aircraft	Crash Site	Fate of Crew Captain (bold type) († = Captain Survived Crash)
5/6 May	Cîmpina	40	LP 191 'R'	Valea Lungă (1)	**All 5 KIA – Tîncăbeşti** **FS D.H. Royle** FS J.A. Smith WO A. Brown Sgt G. Ward Sgt A.R. Wood
		37	HZ 814 'B'	At sea on return leg	**All 5 KIA – No known graves** **Sgt D.S. Parkes** Sgt A.R. Mitchell Fg Offr D.M. Margison Plt Offr T.J. Pullin FS R. Cairns
		37	ME 827 'S'	Ditched	**1 Drowned** (Sgt Mills) **FS Cornwell†**
6/7 May	Bucharest	40	LP 128 'O'	Castranova (2)	**1 KIA – Tîncăbeşti** FS R.G. Sauerwald (RAAF) **4 PW – Bucharest** **WO J. Coape-Smith (RAAF)** † FS G. Cormie WO R. Kilroy (RAAF) FS G. Dealtry
		40	LN 982 'Q'	Balta Greacă (2A)	**All 5 PW – Bulgaria** **FS K.C.J. Martin** † FS G.M. Groat FS G. Carey FS K.G. Chambers FS R. Tyrell
		150	JA 525 'Q'	Comana (3)	**All 5 KIA – Tîncăbeşti** **WO S. Clarke** Sgt LW. Cox Sgt R.P. Scott Sgt C.G. Walker Sgt G.S. Vaughan

Date	Target	Sqn	Aircraft	Crash Site	Fate of Crew Captain (bold type) († = Captain Survived Crash)
		178	EW 341 'H'	Belciug (4)	**5 KIA – Tîncăbeşti** **FS W.A. Molyneux** Sgt H.S. Langley Sgt C.G. Rhodes FS J.R. Velzian Sgt H.J. Tucker **2 PW – Bucharest** Sgt K.M.A. White Plt Offr B. Whitley
7/8 May	Bucharest	40	LN 878 'X'	Vartoapele (5)	**4 KIA – Tîncăbeşti** **Flt Lt G.W. Williams DFC** WO L.F. Dutton (RCAF) FS F.W.A. Head Sgt L.J. Carey **1 PW – Bucharest** Fg Offr H.D. Calvert
		70	MF 146 'H'	Talpa Bîscoveni (6)	**5 KIA – Tîncăbeşti** **Fg Offr S.J. Hanney** Flt Lt C.H. Masters DFC (RNZAF) Fg Offr P.R. Billingsley Sgt C.F.Pope Sgt A.F. Rowlands **1 PW – Bucharest** WO A.C. Weppler (RAAF)
		104	LN 663 'G'	Preajba de Sus (7)	**2 KIA – Tîncăbeşti** FS D.A. Eld FS C.G. Middleton Sgt A. Smith **2 PW – Bucharest** **FS T.W. Creasey†** Fg Offr W.J. Meikle (RCAF)

Date	Target	Sqn	Aircraft	Crash Site	Fate of Crew Captain (bold type) († = Captain Survived Crash)
		142	MF 198 'D'	Fărcaşele (8)	**All 5 KIA – Tîncăbeşti** **FS C. Wray** FS O.G. Griffiths Sgt R. Padgett Sgt C.P. Whalley FS P.A. Scott
		178	BZ 932 'Y'	Lunguleţu (9)	**5 KIA – Tîncăbeşti** **Lt J.G. Schuurman** **(SAAF)** FS J.A. Phillips Lt D.P. McGee (SAAF) FS P. Bisset Sgt K.W. Brown **2 PW – Bucharest** WO R. Grier (RCAF) FS W. Parson
		614	JP 111	Spătăreni (9A)	**All 6 PW – Bucharest** **FS N. Dear†** FS N. Dear Fg Offr D.C. Egles FS P. Godfrey Sgt R. Williams FS P. Beevor FS N.L. Foster (RNZAF)
	Filiaşi	40	LN 804 'N'	Zagubica (Yugoslavia)	**1 KIA – Sofia** Plt Offr I.B.H. McKenna **4 evaded capture** **WO T. Bradshaw†** WO N. Reid FS W. Taylor Sgt R. Somers

Date	Target	Sqn	Aircraft	Crash Site	Fate of Crew Captain (bold type) († = Captain Survived Crash)
2/3 Jun	Giurgiu	40	LP 120 'N'	20 kms south of Pirot (Yugoslavia)	**4 KIA – no known graves** **FS F.R. Hughes** FS A. Millar Sgt W.E. Samler Sgt W.E. Sweeney (RAAF) **1 PW –** FS K. Shaw
16/17 Jun	Timişoara	37	HF 524 'H'	Shot down SW of Szeged (Hungary)	**All 6 PW – Germany** **FS M.E. Holloway†** FS H. Cartwright Sgt D.F. Harrington FS W.G. Wastell Sgt A. Grant Fg Offr B. Watson
28/29 Jun	Giurgiu	70	MF 194 'F'	Sviştov (Bulgaria)	**4 KIA – Sofia** **FS L. Fallon (RAAF)** FS J.R. Burgess (RAAF) FS R.E. James (RAAF) FS T.S. Lowther (RAAF) **1 PW – Bulgaria** Fg Offr G.G. Knyvett (RAAF)
		614	JN 942 'F'	Tetovo (Albania)	**All 6 PW –** **Flt Lt T.P.G. De Bloeme† (RCAF)** Flt Lt P.W. Fels (RNZAF) Fg Offr G.J. Brigden (RAAF) FS E. Young Fg Offr N.R. Ellison (RNZAF) Sgt W.H. Hay

Date	Target	Sqn	Aircraft	Crash Site	Fate of Crew
					Captain (bold type)
					(† = Captain Survived Crash)
		31	EV 970 'F'	Not known	**2 KIA – Sofia**
					Maj J.A. Mouton DFC (SAAF)
					Lt H.H. Bunce (or Bounce) (SAAF)
					4 PW – Bulgaria
					Lt Beaumont (SAAF)
					Lt Clack (SAAF)
					Lt Hendricksen (SAAF)
					WO Miles (SAAF)
					1 PW – Bucharest
					Plt Offr A. Gill
		31	EW 104 'Y'	Woecwage (near Ruse) – Bulgaria	**All 7 KIA – Sofia**
					Lt D.J.S.Haggie (SAAF)
					WO2 W.S. Barrett (SAAF)
					Sgt B.O. Brazier
					Lt D. Lindley (SAAF)
					WO2 D.T. Flynn (SAAF)
					Fg Offr A.F. Paton (RAAF)
					Lt R.G. Southey (SAAF)
		31	KG 839 'L'	None traced	**All 7 KIA – no known graves**
					Capt. T.A.M. Van der Spuy (SAAF)
					2 Lt G.B. Mills (SAAF)
					Lt D.W. Dodd (SAAF)
					WO G.W. Trezona (SAAF)
					Lt D. Fietze (SAAF)
					Sgt H.J. Kelly
					Fg Offr W.P. Walden

Date	Target	Sqn	Aircraft	Crash Site	Fate of Crew Captain (bold type) († = Captain Survived Crash)
2/3 Jul	Bucharest	40	LP 253 'C'	Pirot (Yugoslavia)	**2 KIA – Belgrade** Sgt H. Beeson Sgt J.D. Yole **2 PW – Bulgaria** **FS R. Sutcliffe†** **(RCAF)** Sgt E. Turner But Sgt J.E. Turnbull, Air Bomber returned to the sqn after 40 days with the Chetniks.
		40	ME 990 'R'	Maceşul (10)	**1 KIA – Tîncăbeşti** Fg Offr J.C. Murphy **4 PW – Bucharest** **Fg Offr L.** **Tichbourne†** A. Poole A. Duff FS L.J. Goodlet (RNZAF)
		31	199 'D'	Furculeşti (11)	**4 KIA – Tîncăbeşti** 2Lt E. Nowers (SAAF) WO L.A. Preston (SAAF) WO J.V.P. Robertson (SAAF) FS F. Ryder **2 PW – Bucharest** **Capt R.D. Bird†** **(SAAF)** Lt E.I. Nicholson (SAAF)'

Date	Target	Sqn	Aircraft	Crash Site	Fate of Crew Captain (bold type) († = Captain Survived Crash)
	Arad– Timişoara (Leaflets)	70	LP 348 'V'	Yugoslavia	**2 KIA – Belgrade** Sgt R. Black Sgt D.A. Stephens **3 survived –** **Sgt H.J. O'Brien†** Sgt R. Grimshaw Sgt D.F. Newsham
26/27 Jul	Ploieşti	31	KG 826 'R'	Lost at sea	**All 8 KIA – (3 Bari** **CWGC)** WO2 E. Raeburn (SAAF) Fg Offr F.W. Shepherd Sgt H.L. Greig **5 – no known graves** **Lt E. Rood (SAAF)** Lt B.V. Gesundheit (SAAF) 2Lt V. van Rooyen (SAAF) Lt L.V. Essery (SAAF) Sgt L. Adams
		31	825 'J'	Not lost	**1 KIA –** Lt A. Dickinson (SAAF) **Lt P.A. Rautenbach†** **(SAAF)**
27/28 Jul	Bucharest	150	LP 196 'E'	Crucea de Piatra (12)	**All 5 KIA – Tîncăbeşti** **Sgt B.F.W. Wilkinson** Sgt E.L. Price Sgt G. Kirkby Sgt R. Turner Sgt G.J. Crawley

Date	Target	Sqn	Aircraft	Crash Site	Fate of Crew Captain (bold type) († = Captain Survived Crash)
9/10 Aug	Ploieşti	37	LP 540 'B'	Turkey	**All 5 escaped to** **Turkey** **Sgt T. Merrick†** Sgt R. Stanley Sgt. T. Killoran Sgt C. Querrelle Sgt F.H. Best
		37	LP 465 'S'	Cotroceni (13)	**All 5 KIA – Tîncăbeşti** **Sgt W.E. Double** Sgt J.E. Cushing Sgt A.J. Currin Sgt J.S. Wilson Sgt B. Bell
		70	MF 421 'L'	Yugoslavia	**All 5 survived and** **returned via Partisans** **Plt Offr N.R. Futcher†** **(RAAF)** FS G.W.A. Ward FS W.D. Rogers Sgt J.W. Elliott Sgt S. Fryer
		142	MF 631 'C'	Orac (14)	**All 5 KIA – Tîncăbeşti** **FS R.T. Marsh (RCAF)** Sgt W.F. Chambers FS J. Watts Sgt W.F. Bullard Sgt M.J. Watts
		142	LP 548 'H'	Bulgaria	**All 5 KIA – Sofia** **FS C.G. Hill (RAAF)** FS P.A. Shepherd FS R. Thurlow FS W. Grisdale Sgt G.R. Pond (RCAF)

Date	Target	Sqn	Aircraft	Crash Site	Fate of Crew Captain (bold type) († = Captain Survived Crash)
		70	LN 963 'O'	Caciulati (15)	**All 5 KIA – Tîncăbeşti** **FS A.S.R. Ross (RAAF)** FS H.J.A. Rogers FS A. Gleason Sgt W. Butler Sgt W.M. Jones
		142	LN 972 'W'	Bulgaria	**All 6 PW – Bulgaria** **Lt E.N. Cathrine†** **(SAAF)** Lt W.D.H. Stone (SAAF) FS W.A. Macdonald FS J. Taylor Sgt J. Graham Sgt R.W. Mackay
		150	LP 507 'X'	Dodroteşti (16)	**4 KIA – Tîncăbeşti** **Fg Offr N.C. Jones** Sgt E.G. Berry Sgt W. O'Donnell Sgt A.H. Hudson **1 PW – Bucharest** Sgt M.L. Wilson
		178	EV 974 'D'	Not known	**1 KIA – Tîncăbeşti** Sgt N.A.B. Cooper 5 of crew were reported as 'safe' and all survived the war. No more is known. **FS F.M. Watson†** Sgt A.L. Gunn Sgt G.D. Bramley **2 PW – Bucharest** Sgt J.C. Milsom 2Lt F.J. Bagshaw (SAAF)

Date	Target	Sqn	Aircraft	Crash Site	Fate of Crew Captain (bold type) († = Captain Survived Crash)
		614	JP 229 'W'	Not lost	**4 PW – Bucharest** FS G.S. Squire FS E.M. Steel Sgt J. Forshaw Sgt Jamison baled out in error when the aircraft was damaged. WO A. Fox was injured and remained with Prange to return to base. **Fg Offr B.W. Prange†** **(RCAF)**
		614	JP 110 'I'	Ciocăneşti (18)	**1 KIA – Tîncăbeşti** WO H. Bath **5 PW – Bucharest** **FS C.F. Caldwell-** **Wearne† (RAAF)** FS R.C. Jones FS R.B. Collins Sgt D. Sambrook Sgt R.L. Cote
		614	JP 282 'Q'	Corbi Mari (19)	**6 KIA – Tîncăbeşti** **Flt Lt R.D. Langton** Fg Offr T.J.R. Turner FS H.G. Jones FS J.W. Clarke Plt Offr W.J. Martyn FS P. Brunton **1 PW – Bucharest** WO H.G. Poynton
17/18 Aug	Ploieşti	40	LP 327 'W'	Conteşti (20)	**All 5 KIA – Tîncăbeşti** **Sgt E.E.R. Paterson** Sgt W.T. Quinlan Sgt W.D. Mackenzie Sgt G.V. Lea FS I. Campbell

Date	Target	Sqn	Aircraft	Crash Site	Fate of Crew Captain (bold type) († = Captain Survived Crash)
		40	HF 476 'X'	Not known	**All 5 KIA – no known graves** **Sgt D.J. Francis** Sgt S.S. Goddard Sgt D.R.W. Moore Sgt J.W. Davies Sgt D.A. Beaven
		70	– 'Q'	Turkey	**All 5 safe – return to Sqn via ME 2 months later.** **FS C.A. Bridges†** **(RAAF)** Sgt P. Gadbury Sgt G. Hanchett (RNZAF) FS M. Hanrahan (RNZAF) Sgt E.W. Samson

Summary

Aircraft Lost 46

Aircrew Lost:	Dead	154
	PW	73
	Evaded	27
	TOTAL	**254**

APPENDIX 4 - Leaflets dropped on Romania

LEAFLET C/RA/704

(donated by D.G. (Bill) Burcham, 37 Sqn)

THE OBVIOUS TRUTH

In order to survive the GERMANS decimated, exhausted, demoralised.

They will continue their retreat.

They will scorch Romanian land.

They will transform Romania, whose resources they use, making it a target for the bombers of the United Nations.

They will demand that the Romanian soldiers continue to die 'for Europe'.

In order to survive as a nation ROMANIANS,

Harass

the Germans in their retreat through your country,

Cut

the vital artery of supply to the Germans and destroy their resources,

Prevent

by any means the Germans using your resources against the United Nations

Ask

Romanian soldiers to live for Romania!

[Reverse]

HAVE YOU STILL NOT UNDERSTOOD?

The Germans, in this stage of their lost battle, can plan only the senseless destruction of your property.

You, Romanians, must plan wisely and light-heartedly (sic!) a new phase of your nation's existence.

'The help' given by Germany to Romania in the end means the desertion of Romania.

The help given by Romania to Germany in the end means the devastation of Romania.

The breaking of the nefarious alliance with Germany is the only hope for Romania.

SILENCE AND PASSIVITY MEAN DISASTER!

ADEVĂRUL EVIDENT

Spre a supraviețui, GERMANII, decimați, istoviți, demoralizați

Vor continua retragerea lor.

Vor pârjoli pământul României.

Vor preface România, de ale cărei resurse se slujesc, într'un obiectiv al bombardierelor Națiunilor-Unite.

Vor cere mai departe ostașilor Români să moară "pentru Europa".

Spre a supraviețui ca națiune, ROMÂNI,

Hărțuiți pe Germani în retragerea lor prin țara voastră.

Tăiați artera vitală de aprovizionare a Germanilor și distrugeți resursele lor,

Împiedicați prin orice mijloace pe Germani să se slujiască de resursele voastre împotriva Națiunilor-Unite,

Cereți ostașilor Români să trăiască pentru România!

Lansat de Aviația Regală Britanica și Aviația Armatei Statelor Unite.

C/RA/701

OARE N'AȚI ÎNȚELES ÎNCĂ?

Germanii, în această fază a bătăliei pierdute, nu pot plănui decât distrugerea nebunească a avutului vostru.

Voi, Românii, trebuie să plănuiți cu chibzuință și seninătate o nouă fază a existenței voastre naționale.

"Ajutorul" dat de Germania României va însemna până la sfârșit PĂRĂSIREA ROMÂNIEI.

Ajutorul dat de România Germaniei, va însemna până la sfârșit DEVASTAREA ROMÂNIEI.

Ruperea alianței nefaste cu Germania este singura NĂDEJDE A ROMÂNIEI.

TĂCERE ȘI PASIVITATE ÎNSEAMNĂ DEZASTRU!

365

LEAFLET RA/710

(dropped in early June 1944)

THE ASSAULT FROM THE WEST

6 June is the day when the Allies started the first landing on the coast of northern France.

. . . the day when the assault from the West began.

. . . the day when the huge Allied Expeditionary Force gathered in England has launched onto the European continent the assault to annihilate the Nazi armies.

It is the day which has been awaited by all freedom-loving people in Nazi-occupied Europe, the day when the liberation from Nazi tyranny has begun.

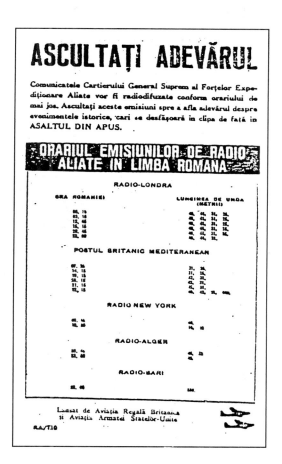

LISTEN TO THE TRUTH

The communiqués of the Supreme Headquarters, Allied Expeditionary Forces will be transmitted according to the programme below. Listen to these broadcasts to find out the truth about the historical events which are taking place at this time in

THE ASSAULT FROM THE WEST

THE HOURS OF TRANSMISSION OF ALLIED RADIO IN THE ROMANIAN LANGUAGE

LEAFLET RA/712

(donated by E. Neale, 37 Squadron)

WHO IS AFRAID OF PEACE?

The Germans describe peace in such a way as to frighten you. Why? Because they themselves are frightened. Peace means the end of expansionist Germany.

IT MEANS NEW LIFE FOR ROMANIA

'The Soviet government declares that it has no intentions of annexing parts of Romanian territory, or of changing the existing social structure in Romania.' (Molotov declaration 2 April 1944, the day the River Prut was crossed)

'We will punish with utmost severity the true guilty party, the criminal leaders of the Axis. The ordinary people in the Axis countries though have nothing to fear'.

(Roosevelt, 13 February 1943)

Dropped by the British Royal Air Force and the United States Army Air Force.

ROMANIANS

You know very well that . . . the alliance with Germany brought you over 500,000 deaths

. . . Hitler brought the war over your land and the allied aircraft over your towns . . .

. . . Germany has lost the war

BUT

it is not enough to know the truth if you put your faith in miracles.

Good sense tells you that . . .

. . . you are on the wrong side of the barricade.

. . . the barricade will be broken. Romania will be broken with it.

IF

you do not break your links with Germany immediately and

you do not oppose the Germans with all possible means

Without Germany – you would not have had war

With Germany – you will not have peace

". . . the longer the satellite nations continue to fight the war on the side of Nazi Germany, the more disastrous the consequences for these nations and the harder the terms imposed."

(From the joint Anglo-American-Russian declarations towards German satellites)

LEAFLET RA/711

(Dropped 23/24 July 1944)

The war has entered its decisive stage

EVERY HOUR BRINGS NEWS OF VITAL IMPORTANCE FOR ROMANIA

LISTEN TO THE TRUTH

[Here follows a programme of broadcasts to Romania from Allied radio stations]

Five years of Nazi lies have drawn Romania into war and disaster.

Romania cannot be saved except through facts based on reality, so

LISTEN TO THE TRUTH

FIVE YEARS OF NAZI LIES

Have you listened to the German Radio?

CAN YOU REMEMBER . . .

England now remains our last enemy. England has two choices: either to perish or surrender.

Goebbels, 26 October 1940

American armament cannot be produced in sufficient quantities, nor can it be shipped intact across the ocean to England.

Radio Breslau, 26 May 1941

For the first time in history, the people of the Balkans can look with calm and hope to a future of security and economic co-operation.

Radio Danube, 10 May 1941

Red Army resistance is obviously crushed.

German High Command Communiqué, 3 July 1941

The German soldier is the victor wherever he attacks. The German soldier is today tougher and better prepared. The troops and their leaders are overwhelmingly superior to the Soviets.

Radio Berlin in a broadcast to Germany, 18 May 1942

We have attacked Stalingrad and we will take it, that's assured!

Hitler, 30 September 1942

On the Dnieper, Europe will be defended as firmly as in any other place on our continent.

Ribbentrop, 6 April 1944

LEAFLET RA/713

(donated by E. Neale, 37 Squadron)

ROMANIA IN FOG

As you have seen, the German fog cannot prevent the destruction of the oil refineries at PLOIEŞTI

BUT

Romanian lives can still be saved, if you know how to impose an end to this kind of camouflage.

Also the fog of the German lies, made up specially to keep Romania at war, cannot prevent the United Nations smashing any resistance on Romanian land.

BUT

Hundreds of thousands of Romanian lives can still be saved, if you can impose the ending of the policy of sacrifice of Romania for Germany

THE FATE OF YOUR COUNTRY LIES IN YOUR HANDS REMOVE THE GERMAN FOG

Dropped by the British Royal Air Force and the United States Army Air Force

PLOIEŞTI IN FOG

The Germans cannot defend the Ploieşti oil refineries against the air attacks. This is why they are trying to divert the bombs towards the residential areas. This and only this is the purpose of the artificial fog curtain which enveils the whole city of Ploieşti during air raids.

The German fog has caused unnecessary victims and destruction. The people have raised their voices; Ion Antonescu was forced to intervene. Here is the answer given by the German Command to the Ion Antonescu proposal to lift the fog camouflage of Ploieşti.

'THE OIL FROM PLOIEŞTI IS MORE IMPORTANT THAN THE WHOLE TOWN AND ITS WHOLE POPULATION'

Faced with this answer, what measures did Antonescu take? Not one! Ploieşti is still camouflaged with German fog during air raids. Antonescu, satisfied, remains the leader and his politics remain unchanged.

'WE GO ALONG ONE HUNDRED PER CENT WITH THE AXIS TILL THE END WE EITHER TRIUMPH WITH THE AXIS, OR WE FALL WITH IT'

(Ion Antonescu, 21 September 1940)

ABBREVIATIONS/CODEWORDS

AA or AAA	Anti-aircraft or Anti-aircraft Artillery (Flak)
ACM	Air Chief Marshal RAF (Four-star level)
AF	Air Force (as in 8 AF, 15 AF etc)
AHB	Air Historical Branch (RAF) Ministry of Defence, London
Air Cdre	Air Commodore RAF (One-star level)
AM	Air Marshal (Three-star level) or Air Ministry, London
AOC	Air Officer Commanding
AP	Armour-piercing (bomb, rocket or bullet)
AVM	Air Vice Marshal (Two-star level)
BI	Blind Illuminator (in Pathfinder operations)
CBO	Combined Bomber Offensive
CCOS	Combined Chiefs of Staff
CFR	Calea Ferate Român – Romanian State Railways
CG	Commanding General (US usage only)
CINC or C-in-C	Commander-in-Chief
CMF	Central Mediterranean Forces
CO	Commanding Officer
COS	Chief(s) of Staff
CWGC	Commonwealth War Graves Commission
DAF	Desert Air Force (RAF)
EPIP	A small marquee tent (English pattern Indian personnel)
ETA	Estimated Time of Arrival
EW	Early Warning (of air raids)
FARR	Forţelor Aeriene Regal ale România – Royal Romanian Air Force
Fg Offr	Flying Officer RAF (= Lieutenant)
Flt	Flight
Flt Lt	Flight Lieutenant (= Captain)
FREYA	German early-warning (EW) radar
FS	Flight Sergeant (RAF)
GAF	German Air Force (Luftwaffe)

GARDENING	Aerial Mine Laying Operations
GCI	Ground-Controlled Intercept – of AA
GEE	Radio navigational aid using three ground stations
GP	General Purpose
Gp Capt	Group Captain (RAF) (= Colonel)
HC	High Capacity (refers to explosives – as '4000 lb HC' bomb)
H_2S	Centimetric radar used for navigation and target marking. The operator looked at a map-like display of the ground beneath his aircraft. USAAF version referred to as H_2X
IC	Intercom – the intercommunication system between crew members in an aircraft
INTSUM	Intelligence Summary
KIA	Killed in Action
km(s)	kilometre(s)
LICHTENSTEIN	German night-fighter borne intercept radar
MAAF	Mediterranean Allied Air Forces
MANDREL	Electronic jammer to counter the FREYA EW radar. In service December 1942
MASAF	Mediterranean Allied Strategic Air Force
MC	Medium capacity (refers to explosives – as '500 lb MC' bomb)
MONICA	Rearward search radar to give EW of following aircraft giving an audible warning on the IC. In service June 1943, but disused in Summer 1944 because night-fighters were homing on its transmissions
MRAF	Marshal of the RAF (Five-star level)
MRES	Missing Research and Enquiry Service (RAF)
MREU	Missing Research and Enquiry Unit (RAF)
MTO	Mediterranean Theatre of Operations
MU	Mid-upper (turret) – on Halifax and Liberator
MUG	Mid-upper Gunner – on Halifax and Liberator
NAAF	North-west Africa Air Force
NCO	Non-commissioned Officer eg. Flight Sergeant
NICKELS	Leaflets dropped from the air
OBOE	High precision blind-bombing aid controlled by two ground stations – not available in MTO
Ops	Operations
ORB	Operational Record Book (RAF Form 540)
ORBAT	Order of Battle
Plt Offr	Pilot Officer (RAF) (= Second Lieutenant)

PSP	Pressed (or Pierced) Steel Planking – used in construction of runways and taxiways
PW	Prisoner of War (formerly POW)
RAAF	Royal Australian Air Force
RAF Form 441	Navigator's Log Sheet
RAF Form 540	Operational Record Book
RAF Form 541	Appendix to 540 recording details of flying operations
RAF(VR)	RAF (Volunteer Reserve)
RCAF	Royal Canadian Air Force
RNZAF	Royal New Zealand Air Force
SAAF	South African Air Force
SAO	Senior Allied Officer (in a PW Camp)
SASO	Senior Air Staff Officer (RAF)
SBC	Small Bomb Container – as in '9 SBC x 4 lbs incendiary'
SBO	Senior British Officer (in a PW Camp)
Sgt	Sergeant
SHAEF	Supreme Headquarters Allied Expeditionary Forces
SOA	Senior Officer Adminstration (RAF)
Sqn	Squadron
Sqn Ldr	Squadron Leader (= Major)
TD	Time Delay eg. '500 lb MC TD .025 secs'
TI	Target Indicators (in Pathfinding)
TMF	Target Marking Force (Pathfinder role)
TOO	Time of Origin (Signals terminology)
TOT	Time Over Target
USAAF	United States Army Air Force
USSAFE	United States Strategic Air Forces in Europe
VM	Visual Marker (in Pathfinding)
Wng Cdr	Wing Commander (RAF) (= Lieutenant Colonel)
WINDOW	(US – CHAFF) Aluminium strips dropped from aircraft to confuse the WURZBURG GCI and gun-control radar
WO	Warrant Officer (RAF)
WURZBURG	German GCI and gun-control radar

ACKNOWLEDGEMENTS

Individuals

Addington, G.F.N. (Gurth) The Hon, Air Bomber 37 Squadron

Arnott, G.E., RCAF Navigator 40 Squadron

Balchin, J.S. (John), HM Consul Bucharest (1982)

Banker, R.R. (Dick), DSO DFC, OC 70 Squadron

Basher, W.F.W.H., SMTO Desert Air Force

Bates, Alan, Air Bomber 31 Squadron (SAAF)

Bath, C.P., Navigator 104 Squadron

Bell, T.D., Air Gunner 178 Squadron

Billen, R.A. (Roy), Pilot 104 Squadron

Bodman, J.L. (John), Air Bomber 70 Squadron

Brenner, Roy, 31 Squadron (SAAF)

Bridges, Clifford A., RAAF, Pilot 70 Squadron

Britton, Guy, Chairman 205 Group Reunion

Brown, G.J. (Geoff), RAAF, Pilot 142 Squadron

Brownless, Sid RCAF, Air Bomber 614 Squadron

Bruce, J.M. (Jack), ISO MA FRHistS FRAeS, Keeper of RAF Museums

Burcham, D.G. (Bill), Pilot 37 Squadron

Burns, Derrick, Air Gunner 150 Squadron

Calley Sir Henry, DSO DFC DL, President 205 Group Reunion, OC 37 Squadron

Calvert, Douglas, Air Gunner 40 Squadron

Caradja, Princess Catharine

Carrod, C.G. (George), Air Bomber 142 Squadron

Carstens, Klaus, Colonel, Luftwaffe, Defence Attaché FRG Embassy, Bucharest (1980)

Cashmore, D.S. (Derek), Air Bomber 70 Squadron

Cathrine, Noel, DSO SAAF, Pilot 142 Squadron

Cauchi, Michael, Air Gunner 31 Squadron (SAAF)

Chalmers, David, Pilot 40 Squadron

Chappell, F.R. (Frank), Author of *Wellington Wings*

Chesshyre, W.J. (Bill), Lieutenant Colonel, Defence Attaché, British Embassy, Bucharest (1988)

Clarke, Arthur, Air Gunner 40 Squadron

Cormie, Gordon, Navigator 40 Squadron

Cornwell, John, RAAF, Pilot 37 Squadron

Cowie, J. Frank, RCAF, Radar Operator 614 Squadron

Cranmer, Tom, Hon Secretary 205 Group Reunion

Cubbins, W.R. (Dick), 2Lt USAAF, Capt of 15 AF B-24 and PW Bucharest

Dalgliesh, George, Air Gunner 178 Squadron

Dealtry, George, Air Bomber 40 Squadron

Dinerstein, G., Wireless Operator 37 Squadron

Dobson, I.R., RCAF, Air bomber 104 Squadron

Durrant, J.T., CB DFC SAAF, Brigadier AOC 205 Group

Dudley C. Egles, Navigator 614 Squadron

Elias, Gwyn, Expert advice, Romanian oil

Elsmore, John, RNZAF, Navigator 104 Squadron

Fannon, T. (Tom), Air Bomber 37 Squadron

Fieldhouse, L.A. (Len), DFC, Pilot 150 Squadron

Fleckney, W.T.H. (Hugh), Pilot 614 Squadron

Flewelling, Gareth W., RCAF, Navigator 614 Squadron

Foster, Norman, RNZAF, 614 Squadron

Fraser, J.M., Air Gunner 178 Squadron

French, F.J., Wing Commander, information on Soviet air raids

Gadbury, Peter, Navigator 70 Squadron

Goodbrand, W. (Bill), Navigator 40 Squadron

Goodhand, P.L. RNZAF, Radar Operator 614 Squadron

Ginn, Robert J., MBE, Engineer Officer 104 Squadron

Green, Peter S., Air Gunner 178 Squadron

Grieve, J.F. (Jim), DFC, Wireless Operator 142 Squadron

Grier, R. Roy, Navigator 178 Squadron

Gunby, David Professor, Researching 40 Squadron History

Gunn III, James A. Colonel, USAAF, Senior Allied Officer PW

Halsall, Jack, Air Gunner 178 Squadron

Hagues, A., 614 Squadron

Harris, P.I. (Paul), DFC, OC 236 Wing

Harrison, A.R., RNZAF, Pilot 142 Squadron

Harrison, Ken, RAAF, Pilot 104 Squadron

Higham, Robin, Historian, Kansas State University

Hoare, George, RAAF, Air Gunner 37 Squadron

Hodson, Laurie, 150 Squadron

Host, Bruce J., Colonel USAF Air Attaché, US Embassy, Bucharest (1980)

Hurd, D.C., Navigator 104 Squadron

Ives, G.R., DFM, Air Gunner 150 Squadron

Jenkins, Peter, Wireless Operator 40 Squadron

Johnson, Henry, RAAF, Pilot 37 Squadron

Johnson, J.C. Rev, DFC MA, Pilot/Flight Commander 104 Squadron

Jones, I.M., DFC, Pilot 150 Squadron

Killoran, Tom, Wireless Operator 37 Squadron

Kirk, John H., Colonel USAF Air Attaché, US Embassy, Bucharest (1982)

Knyvett, G.G. (Geoff), Navigator 70 Squadron

Leahy, C.C.O'N., Air Gunner 31 Squadron (SAAF)

Lewis, Hilda Mrs, sister of Sgt R. Padgett 142 Squadron, buried at Bucharest

Line, H.L. (Lloyd), 178 Squadron

Littlemore, H.P. (Bill), Engine Fitter 178 Squadron

Longdon, G.M. (Graham) OBE, Lieutenant Colonel, Defence Attaché, British Embassy, Bucharest (1987)

Lord, Norman RNZAF, Pilot 150 Squadron

Luckhurst, A.T. (Lucky), 231 Wing Maintenance

Madelin, I., Group Captain, Air Attaché, British Embassy Rome (1985)

MacLean, A.G.C. (Angus), Pilot, OC 142 Squadron

Matthews, D.F. MBE, Air Gunner 31 Squadron (SAAF)

McGregor, P.M.J. (Peter), Colonel, SAAF Association

Mervyn-Jones, C.F., DSO MC, Pilot OC 40 Squadron

Morrison, J. Max, RCAF, Pilot 178 and 614 Squadrons

Mount, C.J. (Mickey), CBE DSO DFC, Pilot, OC 104 Squadron

Murdoch, Ian, Aircrew Association, North West Essex Branch

Naylor, Ron, Wireless Operator 40 and 104 Squadrons

Neale, E.A., Navigator 37 Squadron

Newby, Leroy W., USAAF, Author *Target Ploieşti*

Nicholson, E.I. (Ed), SAAF, Navigator 31 Squadron (SSAF)

Niekerk, George van, Colonel, South African Air Attaché, London (1986)

Norris, Len, Pilot 150 Squadron

Oram, J.E., DSO, Navigator and Flight Commander A Flight 40 Squadron

Palmer, A.G. (Aleph), Pilot 142 Squadron

Parker, T.R. (Tom), RNZAF, Wireless Operator 104 Squadron

Payne, E.P. (Peter), 40 Squadron

Popa, Cornel, Colonel Romanian Army, Defence Attaché, London (1982)

Ralph, J.M., DFC, Pilot 37 Squadron

Reid, N.L. (Norman), RCAF, Navigator 40 Squadron

Ridgway, R.E. (Dick), DSO, Pilot, one-time OC 40 Squadron, Liaison with Gwyn Elias

Robson, G. Mrs, widow of Sgt W.A. Robson, 37 Squadron

Rogers, E.H., 37 Squadron

Sampson, R.F.R. (Reg), Ground crew 231 Wing, Artist

Scotland, Tom, DFC RAAF, Pilot 614 Squadron

Sharpe, L.J., Navigator 614 Squadron

Sheppard, G.J., RCAF, Air Gunner 614 Squadron

Skehill, Mary Mrs, widow of Flt Lt V. Skehill DFC RAAF, Pilot 150 Squadron

Slater, A.N. (Aubrey), RNZAF, Navigator 37 and 104 Squadrons

Stamp, I.C., DFC, Air Gunner 37 Squadron

Sterrett, S.J., 104 Squadron

Stockford, S., 178 Squadron

Talbot, Wally, Squadron Photographer 150 Squadron

Tape, H.W. (Bert), Pilot 104 Squadron, Notes on Wellington overload tanks

Timoney, T.W. (Terence), SAAF, Air Gunner 31 Squadron (SAAF)

Turner, E.H., Wireless Operator 40 Squadron

Turner, R. (Ron), DFC RAAF, Navigator 150 Squadron

Twigg, Donald C., RAAF, Pilot 70 Squadron

Van Eyssen, J.L., DFC SAAF, Pilot 31 Squadron (SAAF)

Vial, Allan J., DFC, President Pathfinder Force Association (Queensland)

Walters, S.P. (Paul), Lieutenant Colonel, Defence Attaché, British Embassy, Bucharest (1983)

Watret, J.B. (Jim), Pilot 70 Squadron

Webb, F.W.J., Wireless Operator 37 Squadron

Weppler, Eileen Mrs, widow of WO A.C. Weppler RAAF, Navigator 70 Squadron

White, D.M. (Denys) DFC, Pilot 150 Squadron

Williams, Keith, Air Bomber 37 Squadron

Wolfe, David RAOC, Author's Assistant while Defence Attaché at Bucharest

Sources

Canadian Legion

Commonwealth War Graves Commission

Daily Express

Flight International

Imperial War Museum

Ministry of Defence
>   Air Historical Branch (RAF)
>   Copyright Section (CS(PS))
>   Historical Branch (Army)
>   JARIC, RAF Brampton

Ministry of National Defence Bucharest
>   The Centre of Studies and Historical Research and Military Theory (Centrul de Studii și Cercetări de Historie și Teorie Militară)
>   Foreign Liaison Section (Sectia Legaturi Externe)

Public Record Office, Kew

Returned Servicemen's Associations, Australia and New Zealand

Royal Air Forces Association

Royal Air Force News

Royal Air Force Museum, Hendon

Royal British Legion

BIBLIOGRAPHY

Bingham, Victor, *'Halifax Second to None'*, Air Life, Shrewsbury, 1986.

Bowyer, Chaz, *Wellington at War*, London, 1982.

Calvert, H.D., *A Rumanian Journal, May to September 1944*, published privately by the author.

Carter, Kit C. and Mueller Robert, *The Army Air Force in World War II, Combat Chronology 1941-45*. Compiled by The Albert F. Simpson Historical Research Center, Air University and Office of Air Force History, HQ USAF, 1973.

Cerchez, V., *Petrolul*, Romanian Oil Industry publication, Ploieşti, 1950.

Chappell, F.R., *Wellington Wings*, London, 1980.

Conyers Nesbit R., and Cooke, R.C. *Target: Hitler's Oil*, London, 1985.

Cubbins, William R., *War of the Cottontails*, Chapel Hill U.S.A., 1989.

Cucu, Vasile Professor, *Atlasul Judeţelor din R.S. România*, Bucureşti, 1978.

Dragomir, Vasile General-maior (and others), *România, Atlas Rutier*, Bucureşti, 1981.

Duggan, James and Stewart, Carroll, *Ploieşti*, London, 1962.

Frankland, Noble and Webster Sir Charles, *The Strategic Air Offensive Against Germany 1939-1945*, Volume III: Victory Part 5, HMSO, London, 1961.

Freeman, Roger, *B-24 Liberator at War*, London, 1983.

Giurescu, Dinu, *Illustrated History of the Romanian People*, Bucureşti, 1981.

Gunston, Bill, *Bombers of World War II*, London 1980.

Hart, Liddle, *History of the Second World War*, London, 1970.

Herington, John *'Air Power Over Europe 1944-45'*, (Series 3, Part IV of *Australia in The War of 1939-1945*), Australian War Memorial, Canberra, 1963.

Ives, G.R. Ex Warrant Officer DFM, *The Life of a RAF Rear Gunner*, published privately by the Author.

Jelavich, Barbara, *History of the Balkans*, Volume 2, Cambridge 1983.

Lee, Arthur S. Gould AVM MC Samson Low, *Special Duties*, Marston, London, 1946.

Lee, Arthur S. Gould, AVM, *Crown Against Sickle*, London, no date.

Markham, Reuben H. *Romania under the Russian Yoke*, Boston U.S.A., 1949.

Martin, H.J., Lieutenant General SM, CBE, DFC, and Orpen, Neil D. Colonel *Eagles Victorious*, Cape Town, 1977.

Morrison, Wilbur H., *Fortress without a Roof*, London, 1983.

Moyes, Philip, *Bomber Squadrons of the RAF and their Aircraft*, London, 1964.

Muirhead, John, *Those Who Fall*, London, 1988.

Newby, Leroy W., *Target Ploiesti*, London, 1983.

Pearton, Maurice, *Oil and the Romanian State*, Oxford, 1971.

Popa, Constantin General-locotenent (co-ordinated by) *The Romanian Armed Forces in the Anti-Hitlerist War*, Bucuresti, 1980.

Porter, Ivor, *Operation Autonomous*, London, 1989.

Rust, Kenn C., *Fifteenth Air Force Story*, Historical Aviation Album, Temple City, Ca, 1976.

Saunders, Hilary St G., *Royal Air Force 1939-45, Volume 3*, 'The Fight is Won', HMSO, London, 1975.

Seaton, Albert, *The Fall of Fortress Europe 1943-1945*, London, 1981.

Slessor, Sir John, MRAF, GCB, DSO, MC, *The Central Blue*, London, 1956.

Stone, Norman, *The Eastern Front 1914-1917*, London, 1975.

Summers, Eric W. Squadron Leader MM, *Blida's Bombers*, published privately in North Africa in 1943.

Wolff, Leon, *Low Level Mission*, London, 1958.

The Decline and Fall of the German Air Force 1933-45, Crown Copyright, London 1983.

Further Reading

Bowyer, Chaz and Shores, Christopher, *Desert Air Force at War*, London, 1981.

Bowyer, Chaz, *Bomber Barons*, London, 1983.

Brookes, Andrew, *Bomber Squadron at War*, London, 1983.

Freeman, Roger, *Airfields of the Eighth: Then and Now*, London, 1978.

Hastings, Max, *Bomber Command*, London, 1979.

Hoseason, James, *The Thousand Day Battle*, Lowestoft, 1979.

Peden, Murray, *A Thousand Shall Fall*, Ottawa, 1982.

Action Stations (series) published by Patrick Stephens Ltd, Cambridge.

205 GROUP

GERMANY

AUSTRI

FRANCE

YUG

CORSICA

SARDINIA

ITALY

ALBANIA
JUGOSLAVIA
BULGARIA
SYRIA
IRAQ
RHODES
CRETE
PIRAEUS
CORINTH
LEROS
DABA
CAPUZZO
FUKA
HALFAYA
EL ADEM
MARTUBA
TOBRUK
BENGHAZI
TRIPOLI
MARETH
GABES
CAPE BON
TUNIS

SICILY

ALGERIA   TUNISIA

MALTA

MED

TRIPOLITANIA

In the 1939
205 Group provided the only mobile force
the North African and Italian campaigns the
a tactical force, attacked communications and
during their advance to the Quattara Depressio
final capitulation in Tunisia. Without respite
Sicily, Italy and the South of France. As a str
refineries and factories-ranged over the Mediterr
and arms were dropped to Partizans in the Balka
Shining courage
We wi

JUNE 1940